Contested Mountains

For my grandparents and the generational pulses of family history:

Norman Curwen (Oct 1896 – Sept 1969)
Janet Curwen (April 1898 – Nov 1991)
Herbert Lambert (June 1904 – Dec 1996)
Catherine Lambert (born May 1904)

CONTESTED MOUNTAINS

Nature, Development and Environment
in the Cairngorms Region of Scotland,
1880–1980

Robert A. Lambert

The White Horse Press

British Library Cataloguing in Publication Data
A catalogue record for this book is available from the British Library

ISBN   1-874267-44-8 (HB); 978-1-912186-53-2 (PB)

Contents

viii

Abbreviations and Acronyms
used in Text and Notes

A.

AA	—	Automobile Association
Acc	—	Accessions
AF	—	Agriculture and Fisheries
AGM	—	Annual General Meeting
AMR	—	Aviemore Mountain Resort
APRS	—	Association for the Preservation (later Protection) of Rural Scotland
ASCC	—	Association of Scottish Climbing Clubs
ASH	—	ASH Consultancy
ATV	—	All Terrain Vehicle

B.

BBC	—	British Broadcasting Corporation
BES	—	British Ecological Society
BOU	—	British Ornithologists' Union
BP	—	British Petroleum
BSP	—	British Sessional Papers

C.

CC	—	Cairngorm Club
CCCL	—	Cairngorm Chairlift Company Limited
CCPR	—	Central Council of Physical Recreation
CCS	—	Countryside Commission for Scotland
CF	—	Caledonian Forest boxfile, NTS archives
CG	—	Cairngorm General boxfile, NTS archives
col.	—	Column
COSLA	—	Convention of Scottish Local Authorities
CPB	—	Cairngorms Partnership Board
CPRE	—	Council for the Preservation (later Protection) of Rural England
CPRW	—	Council for the Preservation (later Protection) of Rural Wales
CRTL	—	Cairngorm Recreation Trust Limited

CSDL	—	Cairngorm Sports Development Limited
CT	—	Cairngorm Trust
CTT	—	Capital Transfer Tax
CWLS	—	Cairngorm, White Lady Shieling boxfile, NTS archives
CWP	—	Cairngorms Working Party
CWSDA	—	Cairngorm Winter Sports Development Association
CWSDB	—	Cairngorm Winter Sports Development Board

D.

| DD | — | Development Department |

F.

| FC | — | Forestry Commission |
| FD | — | Forestry Department |

G.

| GAV | — | Gross Annual Value |
| GD | — | Gifts and Deposits |

H.

HFTC	—	Highland Fieldcraft Training Centre
HH	—	Home and Health
HIDB	—	Highlands and Islands Development Board
HM	—	His/Her Majesty's
HMSO	—	His/Her Majesty's Stationery Office
HPD	—	Hansard Parliamentary Debates
HQ	—	Headquarters
HRC	—	Highland Regional Council
HSC	—	Highland Ski Club

I.

| ITE | — | Institute of Terrestrial Ecology |
| IUCN | — | International Union for the Conservation of Nature and Natural Resources |

L.

| LNR | — | Local Nature Reserve |

J.

| JMCS | — | Junior Mountaineering Club of Scotland |

M.

| MCS | — | Mountaineering Council of Scotland |
| ms | — | Muniment/Manuscript |

N.

| NAS | — | National Archives of Scotland |

NB	—	North Britain
NC	—	Nature Conservancy
NCC	—	Nature Conservancy Council
NERC	—	Natural Environment Research Council
NFP	—	National Forest Park
NLS	—	National Library of Scotland
NNR	—	National Nature Reserve
NP	—	National Park
NRA	—	Nature Reserve Agreement
NRA(S)	—	National Register of Archives (Scotland)
NRIC	—	Nature Reserves Investigation Committee
NSA	—	National Scenic Area
NT	—	National Trust (England and Wales)
NTS	—	National Trust for Scotland
NY	—	New York
O.		
OS	—	Ordnance Survey
P.		
PSSSI	—	Proposed Site of Special Scientific Interest
R.		
RDC	—	Red Deer Commission
RHP	—	Register House Plans
RNVR	—	Royal Naval Volunteer Reserve
RSFS	—	Royal Scottish Forestry Society
RSPB	—	Royal Society for the Protection of Birds
RSPCA	—	Royal Society for the Prevention of Cruelty to Animals
S.		
SCC	—	Save the Cairngorms Campaign
SCNP	—	Scottish Council for National Parks
SCPR	—	Scottish Council of Physical Recreation
SDD	—	Scottish Development Department
SEFS	—	Scottish Estate Factors' Society
SFRC	—	Scottish Forest Reserve Committee
SLF	—	Scottish Landowners' Federation
SLPF	—	Scottish Land and Property Federation
SMC	—	Scottish Mountaineering Club
SMT	—	Scottish Motor Traction Company Limited

SNH	—	Scottish Natural Heritage
SNPC	—	Scottish National Parks Committee
SNPSC	—	Scottish National Parks Survey Committee
SNPWP	—	Scottish National Parks Working Party
SO	—	Scottish Office
SOA	—	Scottish Orienteering Association
SOC	—	Scottish Ornithologists' Club
SPNR	—	Society for the Promotion of Nature Reserves
SRO	—	Scottish Record Office
SRoWS	—	Scottish Rights of Way Society
SSC	—	Scottish Ski Club
SSSI	—	Site of Special Scientific Interest
STA	—	Scottish Travel Association
STB	—	Scottish Tourist Board
SWCL	—	Scottish Wildlife and Countryside Link
SWLCC	—	Scottish Wild Life Conservation Committee
SWLG	—	Scottish Wild Land Group
SWT	—	Scottish Wildlife Trust
SYHA	—	Scottish Youth Hostels Association
W.		
WRH	—	West Register House (Scottish Record Office)
WS	—	Writer to the Signet

Map 1. *The Cairngorms in Scottish context*

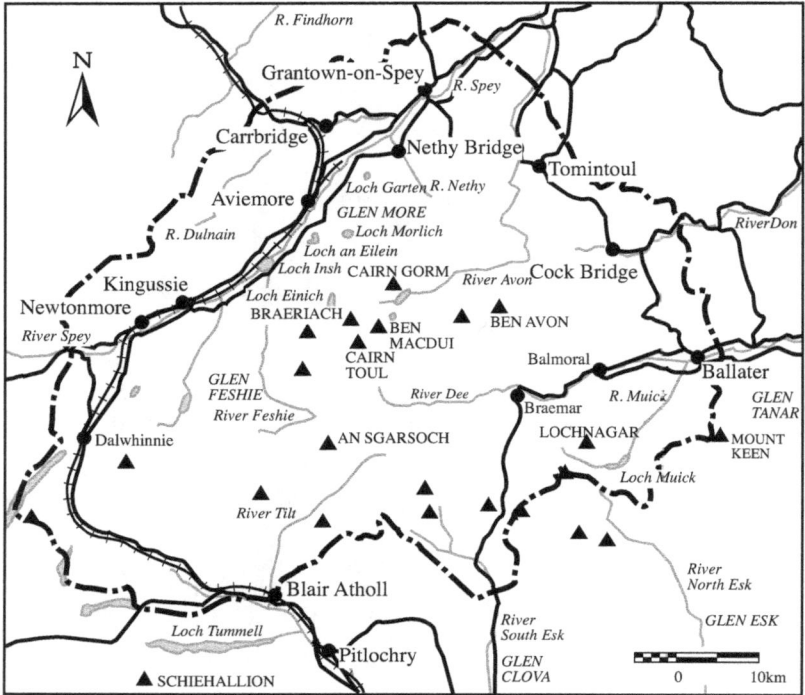

Map 2. The 'wider Cairngorms area'

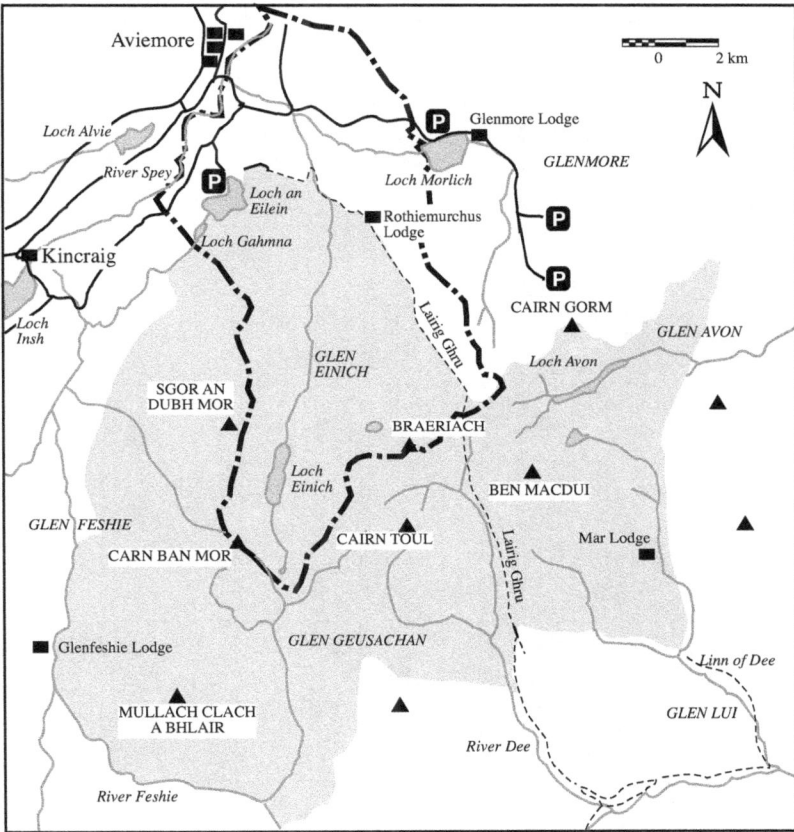

Map 3. The Cairngorms National Nature Reserve and the Rothiemurchus Estate

Foreword

It is a privilege – and a great personal pleasure – to be invited to contribute a Foreword to this important book. It is a book which will be welcomed by anyone and everyone with an interest in the Cairngorms, in the environment and in the long continuing tensions between the imperatives of nature conservation on the one hand and the demands of popular recreation and business development on the other.

All of us who are concerned about the environment in Scotland have our own views about the 'contested mountains' of the title, held with varying degrees of certainty and stubbornness and passion. We have our own attitudes, usually based on personal predilections or even political prejudices, where land ownership and the economics of the environment and the much-trumpeted 'right to roam' are concerned. What none of us could have claimed was an objective knowledge of the origins and development of the conflicts which generations have done their best to resolve.

Contested Mountains is an invaluable and timely contribution to the debate. Its sub-title says it all: 'Nature, Development and Environment in the Cairngorms Region of Scotland, 1880–1980'. It comes from a notable stable – the Institute for Environmental History which was established in St Andrews by that visionary historian, Professor Chris Smout, the Historiographer Royal in Scotland; and as is to be expected with such a pedigree, it is a strictly historical and disciplined recount of the way in which the still-unresolved issues of the environment versus competing economic requirements developed.

Robert Lambert adheres faithfully to the chronological constraints which he imposed on his study, although it must have been an almost irresistible temptation to allow it to spill over into the last two turbulent decades of the twentieth century as the tempo and the temperature of the debate escalated; but the story of the preceding century has immense relevance to the present situation. At the time of writing, the Scottish Executive is determined to have a National Park in the Cairngorms – but its boundaries are still under consultation and discussion, and all the old tensions between conservation, development and recreation are still very evident.

In my time as chairman of Scottish Natural Heritage (1992–1997), and especially as chairman of the Cairngorms Working Party (which produced its report, *Common Sense and Sustainability: a Partnership for the Cairngorms*, in 1993), I liked nothing better than listening to countless yarns and anecdotes from landowners, foresters, stalkers, ramblers, conservationists, SNH colleagues in the field and others. Robert Lambert has given these stories of the past a dimension of historically proven fact and an invaluable context for the discussions of the present and the future.

Individual chapters highlight individual themes – the 'discovery' and 'Balmorisation' of the Cairngorms in Victorian times, the Rights of Way debate, the Access campaign led by James Bryce, the return of the osprey and its promotion by RSPB, the development of hotels and tourism, the impact of forestry and the proliferation of designations intended to protect wildlife and habitats or to encourage responsible recreation – not just SSSIs but more broadly-based enterprises like the Glenmore National Forest Park and the Cairngorms National Nature Reserve (established after much acrimonious debate in 1954); that debate alone, so carefully documented here, was a wonderful microcosm of what the author calls in his Postscript 'the bitter contemporary environmental and developmental debates in the countryside'. Another profoundly significant chapter follows the long-running story of the agitation for National Park status for the Cairngorms.

Despite the copious use of archival material (much of it never studied before) there is nothing dusty or musty about this book. The protagonists in the many and varied debates are vividly delineated characters; and I was pleased to see the generations of Grants of Rothiemurchus being given well-deserved tribute for their role as conservationists and recreational entrepreneurs far ahead of their times.

Above all, the question of management has been paramount down the years, and never more so than now – especially proper visitor management. Good management is, and will continue to be, the key to the amicable resolution of what this book reveals as the entrenched, deep-seated and fiercely-held opinions of those with most to lose or with most to gain in this perennial confrontation. Its relevance is not just to the Cairngorms story, but to environmental issues everywhere.

MAGNUS MAGNUSSON

Introduction

This book is concerned with the origins and development of nature conservation and recreation in the Cairngorms (the eastern Scottish Highlands) during the century from 1880–1980. The bulk of the study is founded upon documentary-based environmental history as the work examines our changing attitudes to wildlife and to the use, appreciation and protection of upland and forest environments. Additionally, the study contains elements of social history, economic history and the history of our perceptions of the natural world as we struggle to seek an accommodation with it, or use it merely for our own enjoyment. Even though each chapter has its own intellectual logic and coherence as it deals with the development of a particular conservation or recreation ideal, the central problem which all the chapters examine is the extraordinary degree of change in attitudes to nature and the use of the land that has taken place in the Cairngorms from 1880. Although farming, forestry and the traditional sporting estates continue to play a valuable economic and social role in the Cairngorms area today, the twentieth century has seen the emergence, arguably even the dominance, of two powerful and competing landuses: nature conservation and popular recreation. However, although these landuses were not institutionalised until the twentieth century, they did not merely spring onto the Cairngorm scene in the modern era, as is too often assumed. Rather, they evolved as distinct ideals, and have a poorly understood history that goes back to the second half of the nineteenth century at least and, in the case of the earliest origins of the visitor tradition, back to the late eighteenth century.

It is important that we come to understand that nature conservation and recreation have a history; this will allow us to begin to understand the complex origins of the issues that lie behind the competing demands of access, nature conservation, recreation and traditional landuses in the modern era. Such landuse conflicts have become increasingly common in the UK over the past century and indeed, in Europe and North America. The Cairngorms now represent the most public and bitter manifestation of these conflicts in the UK.

The challenge to write this history came from a realisation that despite the enormous public interest in the Cairngorms over the last three decades, there had been no dispassionate study of the history of landuses in the Cairngorms prior to 1980. So much has been written about the period after 1980 that a well-known environmental campaigner has commented that a new Munro (a mountain over 3,000 feet) of material has been produced on the subject.[1] There was, however, no concrete understanding of why there was no National Park in the Cairngorms before, why a National Nature Reserve and National Forest Park were established there, how the area was developed as a year-round tourist resort and recreational playground, and how the early history of rambling, mountaineering and skiing hinged on the question of access into this admired mountainous region which challenged the rights of landed interest. This study, therefore, only seeks to set the scene up to 1980, but in no way examines the well known public conflicts in the Cairngorms during the 1980s (Lurchers Gully, the Northern Corries), which have been examined in great detail elsewhere and are now the chosen subject of numerous secondary school landuse projects across the UK.

The book is largely based on primary research conducted in 28 different manuscript, photographic and cartographic archives across the UK. Considerable use has been made of the archival holdings of the landowners, nature conservation/access/heritage organisations and official bodies that have played a key role in shaping the developmental direction that conservation and recreation took in the Cairngorms after 1880 [see Bibliography]. The majority of this archival material has never previously been studied, analysed or published; hence it is hoped that this work will be seen a contribution to an understanding of the modern environmental history of Great Britain. Too often the historical story presented through published sources, whilst valuable, is incomplete. I have sought (by principally using archive material, and by delving more deeply into formerly confidential files and personal communications of the time) to show how key decisions made about the Cairngorms from 1880–1980 appeared to those caught up in the actual decision-making processes. I have also sought to avoid merely telling institutional or organisational histories, but rather to tell 'the inside story'; to reveal the value of gaining greater understanding of how and why ideals were born, or policy initiatives were taken up, and how key personalities shaped the outcome of such developments. In writing up this archival material I have held the 1835 thoughts of Hugh Miller (the self-trained Cromarty stonemason and geologist) close to my heart:

> "I have seriously resolved not to be tedious, unless I cannot help it; and so, if I do not prove amusing, it will only be because I am unfortunate enough to be dull. I shall have the merit of doing my best, and what writer ever did more."[2]

We must, however, continue to ask fresh questions of the past. No published history can ever truly be definitive. Fresh archival material and personal recollections will often come to light. We must also endeavour always to give our environmental history a contemporary relevance, especially in the practical way that it can inform current policymaking. Some research problems were encountered. One landowner in Strathspey, despite several entreaties, refused access to private papers, but much of the material apparently held there proved to be duplicated elsewhere. Due to the present sensitive political and environmental debates concerning a funicular railway on Cairn Gorm, the Cairngorm Chairlift Company refused access to any material that they had relating to the development activities of their forerunner bodies in the 1950s, 1960s and 1970s, but again, some of this material was located in other archival deposits. Some official records held in the public domain were closed under the thirty-year rule, but advance permission ensured that I had access to minutes and papers into the late 1970s at least. In my dealings with those people who shaped government and agency policy in the Cairngorms during the inter-war years and after, I have sought to blend material derived from oral history interviews with archival material in order to present fact, and not to be overly judgmental and cause offence to those still living. I have sought to identify the key individuals in often pioneering situations; to show that personality can have a key role in shaping history. It has been necessary to place some incidental information in the endnotes to each chapter, especially that pertaining to the representation of agencies and organisations on investigative committees, or biographical details about individuals mentioned in the main text. I have sought to draw comprehensive conclusions at the end of all of the chapters, especially as some just address the origins and development of a single ideal or reserve. Many of the chapters are, however, inter-related and cross-references are provided in the text. At the end of the book I have consciously veered away from the repetition of conclusions already drawn in the text, and instead, have sought to provide a 'Postscript' which offers a brief opportunity to step back and place this history in context.

It has also been my wish to respond to the rallying cries for the production of good, accessible and thoroughly researched British environmental history. These calls can, I believe, be traced as far back as 1864 when the American diplomat George P. Marsh predicted the birth of the subject:

> "within a comparatively short space, there will be an accumulation of well established constant and historical facts, from which we can safely reason upon all the relations of action and reaction between man and external nature."[3]

Marsh spoke too soon; indeed, over a hundred years later (in 1972) John Stewart Collis called for the publication of a "monumental study linking the history of mankind and his civilisations with the reactions of Nature". He believed that the human species had only just "become aware that such history is the most important of all, and perhaps the kind of history that we can learn from".[4] In the mid-1970s when John Sheail wrote on the development of nature conservation in Great Britain, he also mused on the importance to the historian of a comprehensive archival record preserved by "individuals, societies and official departments" within the environmental movement. In a small way, back in 1976, he perhaps even envisaged the completion of a study such as this:

> "We do not know what questions the historian of the environment will be asking in ten, thirty, or fifty years' time, but his dependence on documentary evidence will be no less than it is today. As responsible members of the nature conservation movement, we have perhaps a moral duty to help him in his task."[5]

Acknowledgements

On reflection, I have decided not to list the names of a great swathe of people who have helped with the completion of this study, as it is so easy for a mass of surnames to give the overwhelming impression of a herd mentality, within which the author may seek solace and shelter. There is always that chance of the dreadful omission, which then haunts a guilty author for years to come. Rather, I have decided simply to offer grateful thanks to all the organisations, charities and agencies within the UK who have offered any specialist information or knowledge to me over the period 1994–1998. I have also sought the counsel of many retired or former employees of these organisations. From these individuals, I have gained valuable insights into events and personalities central to my work. At times, the advice and guidance I have received has merely confirmed my own impressions and theories as to how the history of nature conservation, tourism and recreation developed in the Cairngorms. However, the wealth and diversity of interest shown by others towards my study, has also shaped new avenues of thought and investigation, sometimes initially unseen by an author so immersed in his subject. I offer this historical work as an expression of gratitude to all those individuals (and characters) who answered my letters, volunteered valuable personal information, shared telephone conversations with me, passed critical documents into my hands, granted me privileged access to private archival holdings, and agreed to subject themselves to a formal oral history interview.

In October 1993, I joined the Institute for Environmental History at the University of St. Andrews, just a year after it had been founded on the visionary initiative of Professor T.C. Smout. His belief was that the UK desperately needed good, accessible and thoroughly researched environmental history to inform of our past relationships with the natural world. In a small way, the Institute for Environmental History has begun the task of closing the gap between the parsimonious state of documentary-based environmental history in Great Britain, compared with the intellectual health, popularity and vigour displayed for the subject over the past twenty years in North America, Southern Africa and Australasia. It is my belief that Chris Smout will come to be seen as the founding father of environmental history in North Britain in the modern era, inheriting the legacy of the earliest UK pioneers in many aspects of this subject area and building upon it. He has my eternal gratitude for all that he has done for me. So much of the success of the youthful Institute has been carried on the broad shoulders of Margaret Richards. She has willingly and selflessly offered her friendship, expertise and tireless support to the daily workings of the Institute; her commitment to its future, and her professionalism, have no equal.

My Australian wife, Kim Macpherson, has been a pillar of support, wisdom and affection throughout this entire Cairngorms project and I adore the influence that she has on my life. My mother and father, Joan and Stephen Lambert, first brought their son and daughter (Suzanne) to the Cairngorms area at a young age, ostensibly to visit the Ross family at Leault of Kincraig and now also Glen Feshie. From 1955–1957, my father and Donnie Ross Snr. served together during National Service in the Royal Army Veterinary Corps in North Africa, and from that serendipitous meeting of two young men overseas, a lifelong friendship was born between a shepherd from the Badenoch district of the eastern Scottish Highlands, and a Regional Controller of the Guide Dogs for the Blind Association from Bolton, Lancashire. Both families have grown older together, and it somehow seems a fitting tribute to this friendship that I was urged to undertake research on the Cairngorms area, 40 years after these two men met in the desert.

Many of my birding companions (especially my parents, James Walsh, Tim Elms, Jonathan Dean and Martin Dean, Amanda Martin, Rachael and Vicky Francis) have been forced to endure endless discourse about natural history and human history in the Scottish Highlands, as we looked for rare birds around Scotland, East Anglia and the Isles of Scilly. Birders are some of the best people; I thank them for sharing their knowledge, friendship and petrol allowances with me. Our birding adventures have been the perfect antidote to the sometimes cloistered lot of the fledgling environmental historian.

It is my sincere hope that this piece of research will contribute to the growing body of interest in the environmental history of Great Britain, and that it will be seen as a stepping stone in the emergence of the taught subject in British universities, served by a comprehensive body of published material. It is my fervent belief that the British environmental historian will not remain a rare and elusive species for much longer. My term as President of the European Society for Environmental History (ESEH) from 1999–2000, opened my eyes to the varied historical roots of the discipline across Europe, as well as allowing me to meet and share ideas with some of the energetic practitioners of environmental history in different languages and from different academic and cultural traditions. After all, the attractions of research in environmental history are many. The book has been the 'mud-on-your-boots' type of history:

> "My calling ties me to no office, makes me no man's slave, compels me to no action which my soul condemns. It sets me free from town life, which I loathe; and allows me to breathe clean air, to exercise limbs as well as brain, and to wake up each morning to that wide prospect which to my eyes is the dearest on earth."[6]

Dr ROBERT A. LAMBERT
University of St Andrews
Fife, Scotland, UK

Notes to Introduction

1 Michael M. Scott, Chairman SCC, *pers. comm.*

2 Hugh Miller, *Scenes and Legends of the North of Scotland, or the Traditional History of Cromarty* (Adam and Charles Black, Edinburgh, 1835), p. 11.

3 George P. Marsh, *Man and Nature: or Physical Geography as Modified by Human Action* (Sampson Low, Son and Marston, London, 1864), pp. 54-55.

4 John Stewart Collis, *The Vision of Glory* (Cardinal/Sphere Books, London, 1989), first published in 1972, p. 273.

5 John Sheail, *Nature in Trust: the History of Nature Conservation in Britain* (Blackie and Son, London, 1976), p. xiv.

6 J.H.B. Peel, *More Country Talk* (Robert Hale, London, 1973), p. 14.

1

'At last the full prospect of these glorious Cairngorms': The Discovery of the Mountains, Early Visitors and Victorian Tourists

This chapter aims to set the scene by tracing the history of recreation in the Cairngorms from the middle decades of the eighteenth century up to the last two decades of the nineteenth century. The primary focus will be on recreation and literary tours in Scotland, as only after 1870 were comprehensive investigations and surveys made of the natural history of the Cairngorms despite some pioneering work being done in the area by botanists as far back as the 1770s. In the last three decades of the eighteenth century, a clear taste developed within educated élite and middle class society in England and Lowland Scotland, for travel literature from the uplands of 'North Britain' (which in its widest definition included the English Lakes, Northumberland, the Border country and Highland Perthshire). The thrust of these early literary tours into Scotland was curious investigation into matters pertaining to geography, manners and customs, the state of local agriculture and estate management, little known antiquities and some aspects of natural history.[1] However, if Scotland as a whole witnessed the start of recreational tours in the period after 1770, the professional, leisured and literary men who made these journeys north did not venture past Highland Perthshire in numbers that could be claimed to have established a visitor trend until after the 1820s and 1830s. The Cairngorms were not truly 'discovered' as a recreational area for the traveller until the middle decades of the nineteenth century, although sporting visitors and some adventurous travellers had visited in the 1780s, 1790s and early nineteenth century. It is important that a distinction is also made between the visitor or traveller who came to the Cairngorms before 1830, and the tourists who came to the area in increasingly large numbers after the 1860s, who by the 1880s and 1890s can be seen to represent a Victorian manifestation of mass tourism.

Certain key changes in the overall development of recreation in the Cairngorms need to be stressed here. Much of the tourist discovery of the mountains came on the back of the rail service north to Aviemore in the mid-1860s; better roads and carriage services had earlier facilitated a widening in the ease of access after 1770. Sport (deer stalking, grouse shooting and fishing) had developed from being a visitor activity in the late eighteenth century, into a major industry in the second half of the nineteenth century, conducted with the full support of the estates. Tourism in the Cairngorms became an organised industry after 1860, becoming routine – even vulgar – by the late nineteenth century, whereas in the period 1770–1830 it had been, in its earliest phase, an adventurous experience for the individual traveller. This adventuring pioneering experience in the Cairngorms was, in part, recovered by the devotees of a new sport (mountaineering) after the 1880s, who retreated to the high ground to seek a sanctuary away from the growing popularity and ugliness of mass tourism on the low ground. Finally, the scientific exploration of the Cairngorms was a part of visitors' tours of investigation from the start, but from 1770 to 1870 (that is, from botanist James Robertson to naturalist John Harvie-Brown) the nature of that research had become more comprehensive, more expert and finer-grained. With these wider changes in mind, the discovery of the Cairngorms can now be examined in greater detail.

In the last decades of the eighteenth century and at the start of the nineteenth century, the visitor to the Cairngorms area was most likely to be a sportsman or traveller-adventurer, a pioneer upon whose subsequent observations and descriptions of landscape and plentiful game a fledgling Highland tourist industry would base itself. Colonel Thomas Thornton of Thornville Royal was perhaps the best known of these earliest visitors and led the English sporting invasion into the Highlands of Scotland, especially of Badenoch and Strathspey. Access north in the late eighteenth century was via the military road from Perth to Inverness that had been built in 1729 and joined up at Dalnaspidal; this road was maintained by the military until 1814, when that task was taken over by road commissioners. A coach service north from Perth did not become regular until 1806, with two services per week, the journey lasting two days; prior to this, the visitor to the Cairngorms would have had to either provide his/her own transport, or be willing to hire a coach in Edinburgh, Stirling or Perth to complete the journey north. By 1845 railway 'mania' had seized Scotland and in the ensuing decades the development of a rail network facilitated far easier access north past Perth and the Perthshire Highlands.[2] A direct rail line from London to Perth (through Edinburgh) was opened in 1848, and in 1850 the line was extended to Aberdeen. However, the visitor could not get to Aviemore by train until 1863/4. A direct line connecting Aviemore to Inverness was not completed until November 1898; prior to this the journey from Perth to Inverness was via Forres. The 'Highland Railway' company was established in June 1865. As late as the 1860s though, travel to the Cairngorms was still challenging, arduous and unpredictable.

The Sporting Visitor

The date of Thornton's 'Sporting Tour' has never been precisely known, although it is now commonly accepted as having taken place in 1786, with a brief reconnaissance trip to Inverness-shire in 1783 or 1784, where he perhaps first made the acquaintance of many of his future hosts, including the laird of Rothiemurchus. Thornton was a falconer of some repute, enjoyed running with the hounds, was a keen fisherman and a prodigious athlete who enjoyed a sporting bet.[3] The journal of his 'Sporting Tour' was not published until 1804 and was prone to wild exaggeration and lapses in factual detail. It received a vitriolic review from a young Edinburgh lawyer, Walter Scott, in *The Edinburgh Review*, who found the Colonel to be the natural enemy of good taste, scandalous in his behaviour towards women, wholly unsporting in his treatment of game (Scott was particularly concerned with the "childish" and "murderously bloody" pastime of falconry), and prone to describe topography using plagiarised phrases from Thomas Pennant and Thomas Gray. Scott found the book to be tedious:

> "because it contains a long, minute and prolific account of every grouse or blackcock which had the honour to fall by the gun of our literary sportsman – of every pike which gorged his bait – of every bird which was pounced by his hawks – of every blunder which was made by his servants – and of every bottle which was drunk by himself and his friends."[4]

Despite such criticism, Thornton does offer a unique if slightly eccentric view of the Cairngorms in the late eighteenth century, from a visitor's point of view. He certainly liked what he saw of the Scottish Highlands, concluding:

> "I cannot better repay my obligations to that romantic country, for the amusement it has afforded me, than by recommending its highly-varied charms to the notice of future travellers."

Thornton's prose extends to topographical descriptions of the Drumochter hills, Loch "Petulichge" [Pityoulish], Loch "Inch" [Insh], Loch "Neiland" [Loch an Eilein], "Rothemurcos" [Rothiemurchus], "Kingcraig" [Kincraig], Loch "Baugh" [Vaa], and of the "vale of Fische" [Glen Feshie] with its "extreme wild view". Speaking of the Forest of "Guiack" [Gaick], he offered his English readers a succinct explanation of a Highland deer forest:

> "A forest here differs from our idea of one in England; in general they mean large hills, having good grass; they are kept undisturbed, and of course, the red deer being quick, prefer these boundaries, but not a tree is to be seen."

Colonel Thornton was particularly taken with the scenic beauty of Rothiemurchus, and in particular Loch an Eilein, and thus stands as a direct forerunner of the many Victorian travellers who would gather at this part of the Cairngorms to find tranquillity and seclusion. Witness Thornton:

> "to the north is a forest composed of firs and junipers, and filled with roebucks and stags, whose foliage may well be said, by its thickness to be impenetrabile nullo astro as is the delightful Glenmore, where, I believe, the trees are still larger than Rothemurcos forest. So highly were we pleased with this heavenly scene, the very finest I think in Scotland, that we did not regard its growing late. In fact, it is such a charming spot, that I must strongly recommend it to all travellers into these parts; and to ladies as well as gentlemen."

He was similarly charmed with the view from "Avemore" [Aviemore] where, "the opposite hills are covered, almost to the very skies, with immense forests of fir, and Glenmore and Rothemurcos woods, about seven or eight miles broad and twelve or fourteen long, give a melancholy shade to the pearl-coloured mountains around them". He did venture up onto the high tops of the Cairngorms, up through Glen "Ennoch" [Einich], and noted "ptarmigant" [ptarmigan] ("but here they swarm"), although he was more concerned with the reaction of his travelling party to the immensity of the Cairngorm scene:

> "it is impossible to describe the astonishment of the whole party when they perceived themselves on the brink of that frightful precipice, which separated them from the lake below! They remained motionless a considerable time, equally struck with admiration and horror."

By the shores of Loch Insh, he mused on what was necessary for the full enjoyment of a glorious visual scene, and concluded that it depended upon who was with you, the nature of the weather, "and finally on the sensations of the admirer, who will perceive, more or less beauties, according as those sensations are, or are not, in unison with the scenery". Returning that day to Rothiemurchus, he felt that "no effect of art can possibly equal this terrestrial paradise ... we preceeded on, scarcely speaking ... to the right the murmuring Spey glides in curling eddies". He also spent a morning fishing on Loch "Alva" [Alvie] with some local lairds, observing "morning heavenly, Aurora peeping over the immense Cairngorms". Thornton's final recommendation to future travellers to the region was to undertake a horse ride along the Spey Valley:

> "I would, in this case, recommend the following route: from Pitmain take the road to Avemore, which is to be continued till you come opposite where the road turns off to the right; this leads to the ferry [over the Spey], from thence get a guide to Loch Neiland, which again turns off the road to the right, a mile on this side of Rothemurcos, and I pronounce this to be one of the very first rides in the world."[5]

Sir Herbert Maxwell, in his introduction to the 1896 Sportsman's Library edition of the 'Sporting Tour' believed that if the credit for opening up the Highlands to the ordinary tourist is given to Walter Scott, then Colonel Thornton "anticipated him in disclosing their unsuspected attractions for the sportsman ... the wealth of sport opened to the travellers, the freedom to angle, shoot and hawk where and when they pleased."[6]

From Colonel Thornton then we have some of the finest landscape descriptions of the Cairngorms in the 1780s, and often this aspect of his writing is ignored. He was obviously a great admirer of the Cairngorm mountains and, indeed, all the scenery he had passed through on his route north from Perthshire; in 1802, he toured France during the Peace of Amiens and often compared the forested landscape there to what he had seen in the Scottish Highlands, in particular, in the Grampians.[7] Thornton was a cavalier and brash individual, and the "arrival of the Colonel and his friends must have struck the natives as the descent of a little army, and the cavalcade, as it wound its way among the hills, must have created quite a sensation".[8] The Colonel journeyed into Badenoch carrying, in a kettle, a precious load of perch *Perca fluviatilis* with which he hoped to stock the local lochs, including those at Rothiemurchus. This introduction scheme met with certain logistical problems on the road north, and the Colonel sought local help:

> "The kettle having been found very inconvenient, on account of the water splashing out at every jolt ... I wished to hire a person to carry it on foot ... I proposed it to several peasants, but taking advantage of our necessity, they had the conscience to ask me eight days wages."[9]

He retired to France in 1815 after a series of public legal battles,[10] and died in Paris in March 1823; but his story was resurrected in the middle of the twentieth century by Michael Brander who set off 'On the Trail of Colonel Thornton' across Great Britain in 1959. Brander sought to identify the discrepancies as well as parallels and contrasts, between the scenes described by Thornton and those in 1959; he found the Cairngorms of the late 1950s to be a public playground for all types of recreational activity run by various organisations ("a cockpit of committees"); found the litter problem to be quite intolerable, and offered a witty description of the visitors' desire to see the ospreys *Pandion haliaetus* at Loch Garten:

> "Cars were lined up nose to tail on the roads leading to the site and the scene was more reminiscent of a Bank Holiday crowd on Hampstead Heath than bird-watching in the Highlands ... It was rather like queueing to see 'What the Butler Saw' on the pier at Brighton, and one of the watchers kept up a somewhat condescending patter of explanation."

Brander met with Lieutenant-Colonel J.P. Grant of Rothiemurchus, and both men agreed that Colonel Thornton was probably the biggest sporting liar unhung.[11] There were other pioneering sporting visitors to the Cairngorms in the late eighteenth century, although none have left such a full account of their exploits as Thornton has. Writing in 1931 for the *Highland Handbook* series, John Bulloch argued that Colonel Thornton had to fight with Colonel George Gordon of Invertromie and Charles Fyshe Palmer (MP for Reading) to gain a sporting foothold in Badenoch, and to curry favour with the local lairds. At the end of the eighteenth century, obtaining a suitable property in the area to rent during the sporting season was a pressing concern for a visiting sportsman in an expanding and competitive lease market. In September 1794, George Gordon wrote from Killiehuntly of his plans for the coming week; "we shall take a ride to-morrow … and fish Loch Guinach on Tuesday, and I hope to reach Kinrara on Wednesday, fish with Rothiemurchus on Friday, and start for Gordon Castle about Tuesday sen'night". Around 1794, Charles Palmer was renting a house at "Kennakyle" [Kinakyle] and was caught in a rent dispute with Grant of Rothiemurchus, whom he referred to in a letter to William Tod (the Duke of Gordon's factor in Lochaber and Badenoch) as a "damned rogue"; Palmer was later in trouble with the Duke himself for the illegal hunting of roe deer *Capreolus capreolus* in "Glenmoor" [Glenmore]. The dispute with the laird of Rothiemurchus seemed to rumble on for some years and centred on the sale of furnishings and the price of corn in transactions between the two protagonists.[12] These legal disputes between estate owners and sporting tenants were probably not unusual, especially in an era when a growing amount of profit could be made from the sporting visitor and his retinue, by the local provision of accommodation, the hire of horses and guides and the sale of foodstuffs from the estate. As the nineteenth century wore on, these sporting rents became highly inflated, as fishing, deer stalking and grouse shooting became both fashionable and a test of character and social standing.

Rothiemurchus became a deer forest in 1843 and shortly afterwards the laird introduced some red deer *Cervus elaphus* from Mar, releasing them into the woods near Loch an Eilein. Over the course of the nineteenth century Badenoch and Strathspey, and Deeside (to a lesser extent), became less isolated. By the 1880s and 1890s the estates were organised on a much greater commercial basis. The 1896 sporting season on Rothiemurchus Estate yielded 92 stags, 54 hinds, 14 roe deer, 108 brace of red grouse *Lagopus lagopus scoticus*, and eight brace of black grouse *Lyrurus tetrix*; the average weight of 70 stags being fourteen stone. The commercial advertisement, 'Particulars of Rothiemurchus Deer Forest, Inverness-shire, 1898' boasted of the comfort of Drumintoul Lodge, built in 1878 to accommodate the sporting visitor, and of the extent of the deer forest (over 19,000 acres with 3,000 acres of hill and wood). For the annual rent of £1,750 (payable in two instalments), the tenant could shoot a limit of 70 stags, "but the proprietor invariably allows the tenant to kill a few more"; could fish for Atlantic salmon *Salmo salar* and sea trout *Salmo trutta* along five miles of the Spey, "the right extends to the upper reach for three days a week, and the lower the other three days"; all game was to be taken "in a fair and sportsmanlike manner". Guests using Drumintoul Lodge in 1898 would find that it had four public rooms, twelve family bedrooms and eight servants' bedrooms, along with stables, kennels, a kitchen garden and even a tennis lawn; it was said to "command one of the finest views in the Highlands".[13]

Elizabeth Grant wrote a great deal about the many visitors who came to stay or dine at the Doune of Rothiemurchus, and of how it was accepted custom that neighbouring estates (in this case, Kinrara and Balavil) would accommodate some sporting guests during the busiest autumn weeks on Rothiemurchus when the Doune was full. One gets the impression that the authoress found these many visitors to be, on the one hand, an exciting influx of personalities and viewpoints, but also somewhat of a necessary curse to be endured. This, from 1812, about guests:

> "Visitors poured in as usual; no one then ever passed a friend's house in the highlands, nor was it ever thought necessary to send invitations on the one part, or to give information on the other; the doors were open literally, for ours had neither lock nor bolt, and people came in sure of a hearty welcome and good cheer."[14]

In the 1830s the Duchess of Bedford held a number of sporting rents in the Cairngorms. In April 1832 she started to construct a carriage road around Loch an Eilein, and asked permission to remove some trees that were in her way.[15] Her lover, Edwin Landseer made a number of visits to the Doune of Rothiemurchus, where he sketched at various locations on the estate.[16] Although always fond of the lands of Rothiemurchus, the Duchess is best known for her love of Glen Feshie, which she came to view as her own secret retreat, as she communicated to The Mackintosh of Mackintosh in November 1838:

> "I now enclose a draft for the shooting at Kincraig and Glen Feshie. I hope next year to see you there and show you what a little Paradise I have in that lovely Glen, as I flatter myself I improve it every year."[17]

Glen Feshie had been made a deer forest in 1833 by Edward Ellice MP; the nearby Glenmore was made a deer forest in 1856 by the Duke of Richmond and Gordon, who moved fifteen families off the land in the process.[18] William Collie described his first job working as a ghillie and stalker for the Duchess of Bedford in Glen Feshie from 1848 to 1854, and indirectly provided insights

into the lifestyles of some of the sporting tenants who rented shooting and
fishing rights in the Cairngorm area.[19] The sporting attraction of an estate
such as Glen Feshie (which in 1868 was said to extend to almost 5,600 acres)
remained strong throughout the second half of the nineteenth century and into
the early decades of the twentieth century; The Mackintosh received £1,175 for
a sporting rent of the deer forest over a year from 1915 to 1916.[20]

A.E. Knox spent some autumn seasons at Gordon Castle from 1865
to 1868, principally in pursuit of Atlantic salmon on the Spey. His 1872
collection of sporting stories *Autumns On The Spey*, provide descriptions of
landscape and geographical features, alongside a desire to convey the sporting
attractions of the Spey Valley to the reader. The train ride north from Kingussie
was especially admired:

> "… and the traveller, while sitting at his ease in a coupé of the Limited Mail
> train, may enjoy for many miles one of the finest panoramic views of romantic
> scenery that the British Islands can afford … an extensive valley advancing
> towards the north, through which the Spey meanders for many miles in the
> midst of most magnificent scenery."

There are echoes of Colonel Thornton's landscape prose in Knox's search for
the picturesque (which he found only at Kinrara) and his keen sporting eye for
aspects of natural history. The frontispiece contains a charming painting by J.
Wolf entitled 'Otherwise Engaged', depicting a sportsman with gun, leaning
against a Scots pine *Pinus sylvestris*, enthralled by a flock of nine Scottish crossbills
Loxia scotica nearby. He dedicated a poem to the glorious Spey.[21]

W.L. Calderwood of Edinburgh, in his monumental survey of fishing on
Scottish rivers published in 1909, paid tribute to the great sport to be had on
Deeside and Speyside throughout the Victorian era. He did, however, identify
some early environmental concerns about the health of the Speyside fishery in
particular, finding that sewage was being put into the river at Newtonmore "by
a long pipe carried in a mound across the local golf course"; that the waste "pot
ale" or "burnt ale" from the first distillation in the process of whisky making
was also being put into the Spey along its course. He also considered that the
practice of netting salmon on the Spey at the coast was having a deleterious
effect on the more gentlemanly sport to be had upstream on the Cairngorm
fishing beats.[22] Across all of the nineteenth century, the Spey was admired for its
scenic beauty as well as its sporting interest. Lionel Hinxman of HM Geological
Survey brought scientific investigation to the banks of the river in the last years
of the 1890s, believing his work to be unique, in that "the physiography and
geological history of the river Spey present several points of interest which, as
far as I am aware, have not been discussed by previous writers on the Physical
Geography of Scotland".[23]

The Late Eighteenth Century Visitors

Another type of visitor started to come to the Cairngorms area in the last decades of the eighteenth century, distinct from the sporting visitor, and keen to travel, observe and describe the people, scenery and customs that they encountered; these visitors often produced journals of travel which later no doubt fuelled Victorian visitors with a keen desire to visit the area. The factors that drove these pioneering individuals north past Perth and Stirling into the eastern Highlands at this time, are varied. Certainly, some came to visit family or friends in the north; others were imbued with a self-confessed wish to investigate; some were much taken with contemporary aesthetic theory as popularised in text by William Gilpin and other writers on the picturesque and sublime. Gilpin had journeyed north to Blair Atholl (and no further) in 1776, and found that the adorned grandeur of parks, woods, lakes and lawns of a typical southern English scene were not missed, or desired, in a sublime Highland landscape that blended the pleasurable sensations of terror, danger, mystery and wonder; the whole vista was awe-inspiring. He felt that the distant mountains formed the predominant picturesque component of the Highland view, especially in their immensity, colouring and the way in which they could frame a vista: "This whole vast distance, both of Strathern, and of the vale of Tay, is bounded by mountains; as the Scotch views in general are, which add both ornament, and dignity to them". Gilpin wished to visit the uplands north of Dunkeld (up into the Grampians) but was prevented from doing so, much to his dismay.

> "These wastes we wished much to visit; and should have found great amusement in traversing their extensive boundaries, and examining their various inhabitants ... but so wide are these domains, that we were informed we might have travelled twenty or thirty miles, before we could have gratified our curiosity."

In a sense, Gilpin's descriptions of lands he did not see, lying north of Killiecrankie, must have whetted the appetite and driven the curiosity of many future travellers who resolved to go on further north, although even up to 1830, few travellers in any numbers cared to venture past the romantic scenery of Highland Perthshire which was safely believed to represent the most magnificent and picturesque scenery in Scotland. Witness Gilpin again:

> "The pass of Killiecranky began now to open, which is the great entrance into the highlands in these parts; and may be called the Caledonian Thermopyle; tho indeed what are generally called the highlands, as I observed, begin at Dunkeld. This pass forms a very magnificent scene. The vallies, as we approach it, are beautiful." [24]

However, Deeside could claim to have hosted the first ever Cairngorm tourist, when John Taylor was invited to Braemar as a guest of the Earl of Mar, and later published an account of his experiences and observations in 1630. Taylor's journey in July 1618 'The Pennyless Pilgrimage', contained few actual descriptions of landscape, save this of the Braemar district, given before he headed off into "Bagenoch" [Badenoch] and "a strong house called Ruthven":

> "Thus with extreme travell, ascending and descending, mounting and alighting, I came at night to the place where I would be, in the Brea of Marr, which is a large country, all composed of such mountaines ... that ... Highgate hill, Hampsted hill ... or Malvernes hill ... are but mole-hills in comparison ... in respect of the altitude of their tops, or perpendicularitie of their bottomes. There I saw Mount Benawne, with a furr'd mist upon his snowie head instead of a night cap." [25]

This was a unique and isolated record of travel from the seventeenth century; it would not be until the 1760s and 1770s that the earliest batch of northern tours of scientific investigation were taken into the Cairngorm area, by the likes of Thomas Pennant,[26] the doctor Thomas Garnett[27] and James Robertson.[28] These first tours had a rigorous investigative purpose to them, whereas the tours taken from the middle of the nineteenth century were mainly founded on pleasure seeking and the romantic tradition, and it was these later tours that became an integral part of the late Victorian tourist discovery of regions such as Deeside and Strathspey from the 1860s and 1870s.

Yet perhaps the most remarkable traveller to have come to the Cairngorms was Mrs. Murray of Kensington, who first came in 1796 and later in 1801. She stands out as an exceptional and unique pioneering lady of travel, both admiring and critical of the landscape through which she passed, and a prodigious recorder of the detail of accommodation standards and the health of Highland estates. In the 1930s the popular travel writer H.V. Morton paid tribute to her enthusiasm and energy thus; "With the eye of a hawk and the campaigning spirit of Hannibal plus Caesar plus Napoleon, she drove her coach right into and over the Highlands; and nothing could frighten or deter her or blunt her stupendous curiosity ... What a woman!"[29] This is her first sight of Rothiemurchus and the Cairngorms on the 1796 tour:

> "On the opposite side of the river stands Rothamurchus, beautifully situated, bounded by crags, and near the river's edge. The crags around Rothamurchus are covered with wood, and the verdant meads are ornamented with fine trees; and the house is within sight of Cairngouram mountains, whose hollow cliffs are filled with never-melting snow. The cap of winter upon the crown of the luxuriant smiling summer below, was a contrast I had never before beheld, and I was delighted with it." [30]

She later mentioned that, "Cairngouram produces the finest Scotch pebbles"; this is a reference to Cairngorm Crystals, which over the course of the nineteenth century attracted many Victorian jewel hunters onto the high tops to seek them (and Scottish Topaz), for small personal profit.[31] On her 1796 visit, Sarah Murray stayed in the inn at Aviemore, and although charmed by the view from there of the distant Cairngorms, found the filth and smoke in the house to be quite unbearable; "It was impossible to breakfast at Aviemore Inn" she declared. By her second night there she could not sleep and confided that it was the worst inn (aside from the King's House on the Glen Coe road) that she had ever visited; "All out of doors, however, is beautiful".[32] Few visitors have ever been charmed by the town of Aviemore, even in the 1790s. Murray returned to Speyside in 1801 for two weeks and spent some time at the Doune of Rothiemurchus with Jane, Duchess of Gordon and Lady Georgina, "scrambling awhile in this bewitching sylvan scene". Murray noted the extremely fine echo off the Loch an Eilein castle walls; thrilled at a ride up Glen Einich where she tumbled from her horse ("it has the wildest rocks and mountains about it I ever saw"); thought Loch Gamhna to be "beautiful"; and urged the visitor to seek out "a cluster of small lakes in the midst of the firwoods". She rode up onto the Cairngorm plateau, and "through Glenmore and entered the firwoods of Rothiemurchus, which are in extent 16 square miles". Murray was one of the first writers ever to describe the high tops, believing the view from atop Cairn Gorm itself "very extensive, and the sublimity and terrific grandeur of the prospect, on the side towards Braemar, cannot be described". Even ptarmigan *Lagopus mutus* caught her eye on the summits:

"The top of Cairngorm, for the extent of three or four miles, is covered by an irregular bed of large loose stones, having not a grain of soil upon them. This rough bed is a favourite haunt for ptarmagen, which when flying, are the most beautiful birds I ever saw, and their feathers are elegantly marked."

Sarah Murray wrote much about the state of the Rothiemurchus woods, and became unexpectedly attached to them:

"The grandeur and sublimity of such venerable extensive woods cannot be conceived, when the eye has been accustomed only to plantations of firs; and till I saw the natural growth of pines in the Loch Leven Glen, Braemar, Rothiemurchus and Rannoch, I disliked a fir wood excessively, which from stiffness, is quite the reverse of picturesque. Mr. Grant annually cuts down, perhaps £1,500 worth of timber, and yet, when riding through his woods, not a tree to the eye is missing."[33]

Few readers of her first travelogue published in 1799, could disagree with her claim to have "seen Scotland, and its natural beauties, more completely than any other individual. I was alone, nor did I limit myself as to time. I took great pains to see every thing worth seeing … of exploring almost every famous glen, mountain pass and cataract."[34]

From the middle of the eighteenth century, some of the great Cairngorm estates began to commission the drawing of estate maps, as a direct result of the involvement of many of them in commercial woodland ventures, and spurred on by the earlier mapping work in the Highlands by William Roy from 1747–1755, and Daniel Paterson in 1746. These maps also in part symbolised the arrival of the 'outside world' in Badenoch and Strathspey. A small plan of Glenmore was produced in 1762 by the surveyor William Anderson, while the Duke of Gordon was resident in Geneva.[35] Two later maps of Glenmore and Kincardine were produced around 1766 and in the 1770s; these were more detailed, describing mountains, lochs, the age of woodland and the rate at which it was regenerating. One includes the notation: "A remarkable hill called Cairn Gorm".[36] By the middle of the nineteenth century, estate maps had been produced for Abernethy Forest.[37] Although the majority of those early maps (pre-1850) have more to do with estate management and government survey than with visitors and recreation, it should not be forgotten that the mere act of mapping constitutes a principal element in the human taming of a wilderness area. A first edition of the Ordnance Survey (OS) map of the Abernethy area was not produced until 1868; a second edition followed in 1900.

The Nineteenth Century Traveller and Tourist

Following in the footsteps of the very earliest travellers in the northern and eastern Highlands in the second half of the eighteenth century, came a new wave of adventurers, travellers and investigators, who did not simply focus on the sporting benefits of the Highlands, but sought to understand the manners and customs of the people they encountered, as well as to describe (in an increasingly romantic fashion as the century wore on) the landscapes through which they passed. They came north, in growing numbers after 1840, to search out "the simple magnificence of nature, exhibiting in sublime variety her stupendous monuments"; that visual balance and symmetry between the stark nakedness of the hills and the glorious beauty of the woods that clothed them. Some could also write in the words of a late twentieth century 'get away from it all' mentality:

> "They left without sorrow to its anxious inhabitants the ceaseless noise of carriages, the continual movement of busy feet and of feverish tongues, and those harassing tumults of the breast, which produce great wealth and splendour, but neither contentment or gratification."

J. Mawman caught his first glimpse of mountains in the summer of 1804 as he "advanced into a bold-featured, majestic, desolate country, where we first beheld the Highlands, sweeping along in that wild state of nature which produces an impression perfectly new to an untravelled Englishman. Here the tourist forcibly seizes their true character".[38] Writing about Strathspey in its entirety in 1848, Robert Somers picked up on the desolate theme, believing that "fertility and barrenness are here seen in closer contiguity than in other districts". His tour in the autumn of 1847, at the end of the two hardest Highland Famine years of 1846 and 1847, found that there was too much wasteland in the region, so "that a deep stratum of wretchedness lies under this fair exterior".[39] For the improving-minded Somers, and for William Cobbett (who toured Scotland in 1832), the Highlands were capable of producing nothing useful save scenery, what Cobbett called "sterling sterility, everywhere a heap of rocks".[40] This was a familiar theme, reproduced by many travel writers in the first four decades of the nineteenth century, but notably by those who cared not to venture past Killin or Callander, bravely if falsely claiming to their readers, that these two villages were at the very heart of the wild Highlands. Such Highland tours can best be labelled the accepted 'safe tours' that took in Perth, Dunkeld, Kenmore, Struan, Blair Atholl, Callander and Killin, and then a hasty retreat back to Perth. On such an excursion, Alexander Campbell gazed at the Highlands from "Down" [Doune]; "We now bid adieu to the fertile plains of the Lowlands. The Highlands present their awful bulwarks, in solemn grandeur, and sterile gloom … by degrees we get familiarized with nakedness and sterility".[41] Campbell, a musician, struggling Edinburgh socialite and miscellaneous writer, also penned an epic verse in six books *The Grampians Desolate* (1804) which is one of the first poems ever written in English about that mountain range (and hence, the Cairngorms), although its primary focus is a thorough denunciation of Highland sheep farming.[42] Other notable travellers in the Perthshire Highlands of the 1810s and 1820s included John Brown (the minister of Whitburn),[43] and J.D. Macculloch, who produced one of the first real guidebooks to the Dunkeld and Blair Atholl district in 1823.[44] On their tour of Scotland in 1803, William and Dorothy Wordsworth and Samuel Coleridge, took the customary 'safe tourist' route within the foothills of the Highlands, visiting Killin, Loch Tay, Aberfeldy, Crieff, Callander and the Pass of Killiecrankie.[45] It is a shame that writers such as the Wordsworths, so steeped in the romantic tradition of describing mountain scenery did not venture further north into Speyside or Deeside.

By 1824, John Macculloch had produced a four volume guidebook to the northern and western Highlands, that contained pages of description of the lands that lay beneath "the distant and blue ridge of Cairn Gorm", although he later described the views from the mountain as "very uninteresting … even less interesting than Ben Nevis". He found Kinrara to be more beautiful than neighbouring Rothiemurchus, although the pinewoods of the latter were of note when investigated in close detail. He made an interesting observation that to wander in Rothiemurchus or the "great and noble Glenmore" was like wandering in "an American forest" due to the amount of timber extraction work being undertaken. Macculloch conceded that the Cairngorms were "a country hitherto undescribed, and therefore unseen by the mass of travellers; though among the most engaging parts of the Highlands, as it is the most singular". Loch an Eilein came in for special praise: "a fir lake … this is the only very perfect example in the country". Two unusual scientific observations were recorded by Macculloch in the 1820s; that "to the botanist" Cairn Gorm "is almost a blank", and that to name a crystal after a mountain was just "making a profit out of a silly modification of patriotism".[46] Comprehensive scientific exploration of the Cairngorms would not come until the 1870s and, in particular, the last two decades of the nineteenth century. As late as 1850, George and Peter Anderson of Inverness, spoke of the Alpine qualities of the Cairngorm landscape but still maintained that "this district is little known, except from the report, and that only of late years, of a comparatively small number of adventurous tourists. The reason is, that these fastnesses cannot be explored, except by dint of a complete fagging day of resolute walking". The Anderson guidebook suggested that in the 1840s an inside coach seat from Inverness to Perth would cost in the region of 35s., an outside seat 25s. This publication attempted to compare Speyside with Deeside, believing the view from the Invercauld bridge to be "peculiarly imposing", but in general favouring the pinewoods of the western Cairngorms; the great Deeside pinewood having been "cleared off above the linn", and now being "only an imperfect semblance of its former self". They added, with some hope, "we trust a respectable remnant will yet be preserved of this fine forest". The botanist touring the mountains was urged to visit Loch Pulladern, "a small lake behind the Inn of Aviemore, at the base of Craigellachie", to find "quantities of Nuphar minima, the smallest and rarest of British water lilies". The Anderson guidebook also suggested that the tourist should visit some lesser known Cairngorm beauty spots, such as Ruthven Barracks ("as the mount commands a most magnificent view, especially of the course of the Spey"), Insh marshes ("a succession of most beautiful meadow haughs, along which there are numerous pools, abounding in water-fowl, and covered over by tall reeds and water lillies"), and the birch trees at Craigellachie ("their bright and lively green forming a strong contrast in the foreground to the sombre melancholy hue of the pine forests, which in the distance on the south, stretch up the sides of Glenmore and the Cairngorms"). Rothiemurchus, which was to become a particular favourite spot for late Victorian tourists, came in for special aesthetic praise: "proceeding now from the ferry at Rothiemurchus we must not omit to visit Loch-an-Eilein … but the lake, its castle, and its woods, recall to the imagination rather the things we read of in the novels of the Otranto school than a scene in real life".[47]

Perhaps the most interesting aspect of George and Peter Anderson's writing on the Cairngorms is that they had not travelled north to the area (as most of their readership would), rather they had visited the district from Inverness where they lived. Of the northern towns, perhaps Aberdeen can claim to have had the closest historic relationship to the Cairngorms, especially in the field of climbing and mountaineering. However, the founding of the Inverness Scientific Society and Field Club in 1875, acted as a local focus for amateur scientific investigation of the Cairngorm area, in particular its geology, natural history, archaeology and folklore; which in turn provided a forum for visiting geographers, historians and scientists to present their work over the late nineteenth century and on into the twentieth century.[48] Just prior to the founding of this Society, Arthur Mitchell had taken a holiday on Strathspey in 1873, and made some of the first notes and observations of local archaeological remains, writing incidentally that "Carr Bridge where I halted for some time, was a well known place in the old coaching days, though it is little heard of now".[49]

Lord Henry Cockburn appears to have been one of the most recurrent visitors to the Cairngorms in the nineteenth century, coming in April 1838, April 1839, September 1841, April 1844 and April 1848. His travel writing is notable for its comprehensive and exhaustive attention to geographical detail, and his prodigious and precise notes on dates and experiences. This on his first ever visit to Braemar, as part of his Aberdeen to Perth journey:

> "In their forms the hills are defective, scarcely a ravine; except about Invercauld, very little rock; and not one peak or pinnacle – all heavy monotonous masses. Their size and quantity, however, make them very respectable, and they fully perform their main duty of enclosing the valley."

Cockburn's first visit to Strathspey had been around 1797 or 1798, but he seemingly never tired of the vista:

> "Even the solitude and desolation of Dalwhinnie is sublime. The approach to Aviemore becomes interesting soon after the waters begin to flow Spey-ward, till at last the full prospect of these glorious Cairngorms, with their forests and peaks and valleys, exhibits one of the finest pieces of mountain scenery in Britain."

He also provides the historian with an insight into the history of the popular inn at Pitmain, which by 1844 had been converted into a farmhouse, but previously had served well the needs of the earliest travellers to the Cairngorms: "Old Pitmain! An abominable hostel, but it had served the public, I suppose, at least one hundred years, and all this time had received that type of welcome which is given by a vessel in distress to the only port it has to repair to".[50]

With such travel literature espousing the scenic grandeur of the Cairngorms by the 1850s, it is not unexpected that the very first book to be written entirely about these mountains came to be produced in 1864, by the hand of the Aberdeen-born historian, civil servant and climber, John Hill Burton. Pub-

lished in Edinburgh, *The Cairngorm Mountains*, can best be seen as the direct
forerunner of many popular twentieth century books written in praise of these
hills, beginning with Seton Gordon, Henry Alexander, then Adam Watson,
Desmond Nethersole-Thompson and Jim Crumley.[51] It carried an engraving
of the Shelter Stone on its cover, and contained some of the richest descriptive
prose ever written about the Cairngorms (still often quoted in the 1990s, by
those interests seeking to halt the destruction of the Cairngorm wilderness):

> "the depth and remoteness of the solitude, the huge mural precipices, the deep
> chasms between the rocks, the waterfalls of unknown height, the hoary remains
> of the primeval forest, the fields of eternal snow, and the deep black lakes at
> the foot of the precipices, are full of such associations of awe and grandeur and
> mystery, as no other scenery in Britain is capable of arousing."[52]

Burton's obituary in *Blackwood's Edinburgh Magazine* in September 1881 spoke of
how fitting it was that a man with such a refined interest in "books and outdoor
life ... an inveterate wanderer ... never happier than when tramping across the
country-side, or camping among the heather",[53] should have produced such a
literary paean to the mountains. In the 1860s, the commercial publication of
Burton's book was surely carefully judged to coincide with the arrival of the
new railway in the district.

Royal Deeside, Tourists, Naturalists and Mountaineers

In 'Hints for the Vacation Ramble' serialised in 1881, an 'Old Tramp' (the customary pseudonym for John Hill Burton) urged that visitors to the Cairngorms
should approach the mountains from the western side via Rothiemurchus, for
although it was possible to reach the high tops by "the valley of the Dee", this
could involve, "the risk of intrusion on the sorely beset privacy of Royalty – a
peril which every loyal and even humane subject ought dutifully to shun".[54]
Although a good deal of historical study has been done on the unique role that
Queen Victoria and Prince Albert played in the origins of a popular Deeside
tourist industry in the second half of the nineteenth century, it is not the remit
of this introductory chapter to revisit such well-covered ground. The Queen
was a prodigious journal writer, and her first sight of Deeside from Balmoral
in September 1848 was highly favourable:

> "To the left you look towards the beautiful hills surrounding Loch-na-Gar,
> and to the right, towards Ballater, to the glen (valley) along which the Dee
> winds, with beautiful wooded hills ... It was so calm, and so solitary, it did one
> good as one gazed around; and the pure mountain air was most refreshing. All
> seemed to breathe freedom and peace, and to make one forget the world and
> its sad turmoils. The scenery is wild, and yet not desolate ... The view of the
> hills towards Invercauld is exceedingly fine."[55]

In June 1852, Balmoral Estate passed into Royal possession for the sum of 30,000 guineas; the forest of Ballochbuie was not owned by the Royal family until 1878.[56] By the mid-1870s, and certainly by the 1880s, the Royal family's retreat to Balmoral Castle had become a part of British cultural heritage, and as Queen Victoria had made arrangements for the castle to become the established Scottish home of succeeding monarchs, the cult of 'Balmorality' was born. Innovations in transport services (the rail line reached Ballater in 1867) made sure that the Royal family at Balmoral became public property, and by the 1870s crowds of tourists gathered to watch the Queen attend Crathie kirk, or go out on her daily carriage drives. By 1860, Thomas Cook of Leicester claimed to have brought some 50,000 tourists to Scotland on organised excursions; Piers Brendon asserts that the businessman Cook "unblushingly declared" in his promotional literature for his 'Highland Tours' that "our good Queen leads the way in Excursion Trips and countenances them by her Royal example". Such was the demand in England to visit Scotland, and in particular the Highlands (Deeside) or places of literary association, that Cook himself claimed in 1872 that Scotland had "almost imperceptibly, transformed me from a cheap Excursion conductor to a tourist Organiser and Manager". As early as 1849, Cook brought 1,000 visitors to Scotland; in 1859, Cook took to disturbing the Royal family at Balmoral with his tours:

> "we pulled up opposite the Royal Castle at Balmoral, when the National Anthem was sung at about half past seven in the morning, a strong breeze wafting the sound direct to the Castle. One of our party, applying his opera glass, declared that he saw the Royal Prince Consort in his night cap(!) at a window; but for the accuracy of this vision we cannot vouch."[57]

By 1855 the Queen and Prince Albert had to appeal to tourists and the local people of Deeside to obtain privacy, in particular, from walkers using a right of way across the estate from Abergeldie to Brig of Dee. The Highway Act of 1835 was invoked, and in 1857 an iron bridge was erected which diverted pedestrian traffic and curious onlookers onto the north bank of the Dee at Crathie. Of course additional factors such as transport innovations and increased leisure time also contributed to the development of a holiday industry in the eastern Highlands after 1850. The main Highland rail line had opened in September 1863 running north from Perth; a West Highland line to Fort William only opened in August 1894, suggesting that the initial focus for the earliest mass tourist traffic was the eastern Highlands. Road tolls were halted in Scotland by 1883; the introduction of Dunlop's pneumatic tyre in 1888 acted as a considerable boost to the new pastime of holiday cycling which became popular in the Highlands; the Bank Holiday short break became more widespread after its first introduction in 1871.[58] Travel north of Edinburgh over the

River Forth was made easier in 1890 with the opening of the Forth Rail Bridge (construction had begun in 1882), which meant that Perth and the northern counties were even more accessible to holidaymakers. The proliferation of railway track in the Highlands did not please everybody. John Campbell Shairp, poet and Professor of Latin at the University of St. Andrews penned a critical verse (under a title stolen from the Clan Grant war-cry, 'Standfast, Craig-Ellachie') as he journeyed north by rail in 1864, "casting a mournful eye over the route". He was angered by the way that the "iron horses … that hideous roar … hear the shrieking whistle louder", would spoil the peace of the Cairngorms and its villages along the route, fearing that "Dark Glen More and cloven Glen Feshie, Over Spey, by Rothiemurchus … Is a wilderness no more".[59] By the time that Hugh Macmillan retired to his 'Forest Cabin' in the heart of Rothiemurchus in the last years of the 1890s, the railway had changed the nature of the Cairngorm holiday, and thus, the Cairngorms themselves.

> "Aviemore is now a busy junction where innumerable trains in the summer months pass north and south, and passengers from all parts of the world meet each other on the platforms. A row of new villas is built along the line and a modern hotel, with a noble background of hills and an incomparable view in front of the Cairngorm range … occupies the rising ground behind."

Loch an Eilein was no longer the peaceful mid-Victorian beauty spot that it had once been. In Macmillan's eyes, all was not well in this "most beautifully balanced" landscape picture, for during the summer months, tourists and pic-nickers cluttered the scene, and at the loch, "crowds of visitors who come from all parts of the country in carriages and on bicycles", brought an unwelcome human presence into this "special show-place of the district".[60] Perhaps here, then, is one of the earliest references to the Cairngorm landscape being 'loved to death'. By 1902, one of the first attempts was made to sell the Cairngorms to the American tourist market by Maria Lansdale's book published in Philadelphia, which talked of "the lovely position on an island in a loch" of Loch an Eilein castle.[61] Sometime in the 1880s, Gertrude Martineau (a regular summer visitor to the Polchar in Rothiemurchus from around 1876) noted that the crowds of visitors at Loch an Eilein had grown noticeably larger and more unruly; they began to do mischief she complained, and no longer appreciated the solitude and wildlife of the estate:

> "as the carriages passed under the trees the people laid hold of the boughs and tore them off and flung them on the road; they threw stones at the squirrels and screamed to each other across the loch; the men sang rude songs and the shouting to the 'old man in the castle' became so common and so noisy …"

It is hard to imagine "douce Victorian tourists", behaving in such a fashion, concludes Meta Scarlett.[62] In September 1848, visitors onto the lands of

Rothiemurchus caused some fire damage at Loch an Eilein, "near the foot of Corrybuie", sending the factor into "a sad consternation".[63]

A good number of both tourists and travellers who visited the eastern and western Cairngorms over the period 1770 to 1880 did venture onto the high tops (principally by pony). It appears that some of the local lairds, even early in this period, did take shooting and rambling parties up onto the Cairngorms; John Macpherson Grant of Ballindalloch recorded unusual shadows, an "atmospheric appearance" seen by himself and Thomas Dick Lauder on an ascent of Ben MacDhui in October 1830.[64] These were not mountaineering excursions in the purest definition of the sport, although D.B. Horn, in a misleading article, implies that anybody who merely reached the top of any Scottish hillside in the eighteenth and nineteenth century, should be classed as an accomplished mountaineer, a pioneer in the sport.[65] A more cautious approach suggests that in the thirty years prior to the First World War, Rothiemurchus and Braemar were used as gateways to the Cairngorms by the mountaineering clubs that had established themselves in the 1880s and 1890s in the north-east (Aberdeen) and Central Belt towns. This very first wave of climbing clubs, the radical Cairngorm Club officially founded in 1889 (but unofficially founded at the Shelter Stone in June 1887), and the Scottish Mountaineering Club born late in 1889, had a predominantly literate middle class and professional membership keen to record Cairngorm climbing experiences in the clubs' journals (a fashion that became more prevalent throughout the 1890s).[66] They marked the start of the development of the Cairngorms as a popular recreational playground; the mountains were, increasingly from the 1880s, being seen as an obstacle course.

One final group, whose most widespread interest in the Cairngorms dates from the second half of the nineteenth century, are the naturalists, who came to see the mountains as a unique scientific resource, the eventual culmination of this early research being the declaration of the Cairngorms National Nature Reserve in July 1954. Some of the first travel writers from the eighteenth century did make some limited observations of Cairngorm natural history, but the botanical notes of James Robertson who toured the Highlands from 1767 to 1771 were unusually thorough for that century. Geology also interested Robertson, and in 1771 on the summit of Ben Avon he noted that the mountain "is composed of white Granite. It's grain is coarse, and the stone is hard, tho' it easily moulders down when exposed to the air", later travelling into the "parish of Rothymurcus". Here he noted an "abundance of excellent Fir and Birch, together with some Hazle and Poplar". The island of Loch an Eilein castle, was said to abound with Toothwort *Lathraea squamaria*.[67] By the 1840s, Highland Perthshire, the Angus Glens and the Cairngorms were seen to be "the richest botanical district in Britain many parts of which had never been explored". This from James Backhouse as he explored Glen Muick, Braemar and down towards Glas Maol and Caenlochan in August 1848: "It was a delightful place for a botanist".[68] A year earlier, J.H. Balfour (of the 'Battle of Glen Tilt' fame), Professor of Botany at Edinburgh University, led a student botanical excursion to Braemar and the Angus Glens, with the crusading zeal of a progressive educationalist; the Professor argued that in the pursuit of scientific knowledge his pupils would, "combine that healthful and spirit-stirring recreation which tends materially to aid mental efforts. The companionship too of those who are prosecuting with zeal and enthusiasm the same path of science, is not the least delightful feature of such excursions". He hoped his field trips would have a lasting impact on youthful minds:

> "those who have lived and walked for weeks together in a Highland ramble, who have met in sunshine and in tempest, who have climbed together the misty summits, and have slept in the miserable sheiling – should have such scenes indelibly impressed on their memory. There is, moreover, something peculiarly attractive in the collecting of alpine plants." [69]

Botany played an early role in the development of the study of Cairngorm natural history, indeed, along with early geological and geographical observations, it predominated in the period from the 1770s to the 1850s. There were of course some exceptions to this trend, most notably William MacGillivray (Professor of Natural History at Marischal College, Aberdeen) who was perhaps the first 'all round' Cairngorm field naturalist in the half century up to 1850. The north-east of Scotland can claim the considerable distinction of having produced an unusually high number of both professional and amateur naturalists in the nineteenth century, many of whom worked on aspects of the natural history of the Cairngorms; the botanist George Dickie; the geologist James Nicol; the zoologist George Sim; the 'Banff naturalist' Thomas Edward; the botanist John Duncan. In an article celebrating their careers, published in *The Deeside Field* of 1931, they were all seen to be "pioneers of the past, whose work and example have helped to create and spread an interest in Nature for its own sake".[70] An interest in the invertebrate life of the Cairngorms was rather late in developing; indeed, when George Carpenter and William Evans visited Aviemore and Kincraig in 1889 and 1893, ostensibly to document "the richer spider fauna of the fine forests of Rothiemurchus, Glenmore and Abernethy", there was a pioneering edge to their work, for the district had not "received the attention it deserves".[71] In the mid-1890s, it would be two volumes of the comprehensive 'Vertebrate Fauna' series of John Harvie-Brown and T.E. Buckley, that first sought to understand the whole ecology of the area, providing in published form topographical notes, species history, species distribution information and extracts from communiqués with other distinguished naturalists on the topic of the fauna of the Cairngorms. The most southerly foothills of the Cairngorms were not written about for another ten years.[72]

In 1837, Thomas Dick Lauder offered some good advice to the traveller who found himself in the uplands of Scotland. He conceded that although, "a long stretch of dreary and uninteresting hill country is often found to extend between two rich or romantic valleys", the wilderness quality of a mountainous region made it a very special place, both mentally and physically for the visitor. Even as late as the 1830s, utilitarian commentators such as Lauder could still speak of the Cairngorm mountains being a "sterile desert", but this attitude was being rapidly diluted by a growing appreciation for the intrinsic value of romantic scenery, and even later by a desire to challenge the human body within the mountain environment:

> "these wildernesses are sometimes rather valuable to a solitary traveller – They afford him time for rumination whilst he is traversing them – They give him leisure to chew the cud of reflection, and he is thus enabled to digest the beauties of the valley which he last devoured."[73]

Notes to Chapter 1

1   Stana Nenadic, 'Land, the landed and relationships with England: literature and perception 1760–1830', in S.J. Connolly, R.A. Houston, R.J. Morris (eds.), *Conflict, Identity and Economic Development: Ireland and Scotland, 1600–1939* (Carnegie Publishing, Preston, 1996), pp. 148–160; T.C. Smout, 'Tours in the Scottish Highlands from the eighteenth to the twentieth centuries', *Northern Scotland*, Vol. 5, 1983, pp. 99–121; T.C. Smout, *The Highlands and the Roots of Green Consciousness, 1750–1990*, SNH Occasional Paper No. 1 (SNH, Battleby, 1993).

2   Michael Lynch, *Scotland – A New History* (Pimlico, London, 1993), p. 410.

3   Michael Brander, *The Hunting Instinct: the Development of Field Sports over the Ages* (Oliver and Boyd, Edinburgh, 1964), pp. 119–140.

4   Walter Scott, 'Article XI – Colonel Thornton's Sporting Tour', in *The Edinburgh Review (or Critical Journal)*, Vol. V, October–January 1804/5, pp. 398–405.

5   Colonel Thomas Thornton, *A Sporting Tour Through the Northern Parts of England, and Great Parts of the Highlands of Scotland ...* (James Swan, London, 1804).

6   Colonel Thomas Thornton, *A Sporting Tour Through the Northern Parts of England, and Great Parts of the Highlands of Scotland* (Edward Arnold, London, 1896). This edition edited by Sir Herbert Maxwell for the Sportsman's Library.

7   Colonel Thomas Thornton, *A Sporting Tour Through Various Parts of France in the Year 1802* (Longman, Hurst, Rees and Orme, London, 1806), p. 132.

8   J.M. Bulloch, *Sporting Visitors to Badenoch* (Highland Handbook V, Robert Carruthers, Inverness, 1931), p. 6.

9   Thornton, 1804, *op. cit.*, pp. 67–70.

10 Anon, 'Law Report', *London Times*, Monday 29 June, 1801, No. 5145, p. 3.

11 Michael Brander, *A Hunt Around the Highlands – On the Trail of Colonel Thornton* (The Standfast Press, Gloucs, 1973). First published in 1961.

12 Bulloch, *op. cit.*, pp. 13, 23.

13 The archives of the Grants of Rothiemurchus are privately held at the Doune of Rothiemurchus, by Aviemore, Inverness-shire, but they are catalogued in the Scottish Record Office (SRO), Edinburgh, at NRA(S) 102. See NRA(S) 102:483, 'Particulars of Rothiemurchus Deer Forest, Inverness-shire, 1898'.

14 Elizabeth Grant of Rothiemurchus, *Memoirs of a Highland Lady – Vols. I and II* (Canongate Press, Edinburgh, 1992), pp. 213–214. First published in 1898.

15 See the correspondence in NRA(S) 102:222.

16 J.P. and P. Grant, *pers. comm.*; see also David Black, 'Duty to the Duchus', *Country Living*, No. 121, January 1996, pp. 66–69.

17 The archive of Mackintosh of Mackintosh is held in the Scottish Record Office (SRO), Edinburgh, at GD 176. See SRO: GD 176-2226, Letter from Georgina, Duchess of Bedford, Brighton to The Mackintosh, dated 28 November 1838. See also SRO: GD 176-2230, Letter from Georgina, Duchess of Bedford, Doune of Rothiemurchus to The Mackintosh, dated 18 August 1839, in which she deplores the cutting down of trees in Glen Feshie to make a track: "I grieved over the track made amongst your beautiful trees – it is a sad pity, as it gives a look of desolation to a lovely spot".

18 Display boards, Glenmore National Forest Park Visitor Centre, *pers. obs.*

19 William Collie, *Memoirs of William Collie* (Sands and McDougall Ltd., Melbourne, Australia, 1908). A new limited edition was photographically reproduced by Highland Printers, Inverness in 1992.

20 SRO: GD 176-1493, 'Particulars of Glen Feshie Estate belonging to The Mackintosh of Mackintosh', dated 1919 and 1920.

21 A.E. Knox, *Autumns on the Spey* (John Van Voorst, London, 1872), pp. 2–3. The poem 'A Wish' is reproduced on pp. 170–171.

22 W.L. Calderwood, *The Salmon Rivers and Lochs of Scotland* (Edward Arnold, London, 1909).

23 Sir Thomas Dick Lauder, *Scottish Rivers* (Edmonston and Douglas, Edinburgh, 1874); Lionel W. Hinxman, 'The River Spey', *Scottish Geographical Magazine*, Vol. XVII, 1901, pp. 185–193.

24 William Gilpin, *Observtions on the Highlands of Scotland* (Richmond Publ. Co., Surrey, 1973). First published in 1789.

25 John Taylor (the Water Poet), *Early Prose and Poetical Works* (Thomas D. Morrison, Glasgow, 1888), pp. 17–60; P. Hume Brown (ed.), *Early Travellers in Scotland* (David Douglas, Edinburgh, 1891), pp. 104–131.

26 A.J. Youngson, *Beyond the Highland Line – Three Journals of Travel in Eighteenth Century Scotland* (Collins, London, 1974).

27 S.G.E. Lythe, 'Thomas Garnett: a Doctor on Tour in the Highlands', in Graeme Cruickshank (ed.), *A Sense of Place – Studies in Scottish Local History* (Scotland's Cultural Heritage Unit, University of Edinburgh, 1988), pp. 100–108.

28 J.H. Dickson and D.M. Henderson (eds.), *A Naturalist in the Highlands: James Robertson, His Life and Travels in Scotland, 1767–1771* (Scottish Academic Press, Edinburgh, 1994).

29 H.V. Morton, *In Scotland Again* (Methuen, London, 1933), p. 295.

30 Sarah Murray of Kensington, *A Companion and Useful Guide to the Beauties of Scotland ... to Which is added, A more Particular Description of Scotland, Especially That Part of it Called the Highlands* (George Nicol, London, 1799), p. 212.

31 Alfred W. Gibb, 'Cairngorms and Other Local Gemstones', *Deeside Field*, No. 2, 1925, pp. 11–14.

32 Murray of Kensington, 1799, *op. cit.*, pp. 67, 213.

33 Sarah Murray of Kensington, *A Companion and Useful Guide to the Beauties in the Western Highlands of Scotland, And In the Hebrides ... To Which is added, A Description of Part of the Main Land of Scotland* (W. Bulmer and Co., London, 1803), pp. 341–349.

34 Murray of Kensington, 1799, *op. cit.*, p. 42.

35 These maps are held at West Register House, the Scottish Record Office (SRO), Edinburgh, under the Register House Plans (RHP) section. See SRO: RHP 2504, 'Plan of Glen More, 1762', Surveyor, William Anderson.

36 SRO: RHP 2501, 'Plan of Lands of Kincardin with Glen More and Wood, 1766', Surveyor, William Anderson. This plan was presented to Alexander Duke of Gordon in 1766 and showed the foothills of the Cairngorms to be 'Hills and Pasture'. Places of interest marked on the map included 'The Glen More, Part of Rothimurcus, Cairn Gorum, forest of Avin, Loch Morlich and Blair More'. Heavily wooded areas were marked only to the south and east of Loch Morlich, with a small fringe of woodland in existence immediately on the northern shore of the loch.

      SRO: RHP 2502, 'Plan of Kincardine and Glen More, 18th century', No surveyor named. This map was formerly held by Records of Crown Estate Commissioners (CR) plans, and dates from the period when Fochabers Estate was the property of the Duke of Gordon. A footnote to RHP 2210 CR Plans, suggests that the majority of the unsigned and undated plans of this district date from the period 1770–1815, the greater part probably being the work of Thomas Milne between 1770 and 1780. Four other surveyors are listed in the vouchers and accounts at Gordon Castle, and they often worked in conjunction with one another: William Anderson, Peter May, George Brown, Alexander Taylor. This is a very detailed plan. Loch Pityoulish is marked as both 'Loch of Piteulish' and 'Loch Goulish'. Loch Morlich is said to 'Abound with Trout and Pyke'. Notations on the extent of the woodland cover are of interest to environmental historians. North of Loch Morlich runs the sentence 'Thin wood along here not recovered since it was burnt, most of the old trees are rotten but there are young ones rising'. To the north-east corner of the loch runs 'Good pasture along here. Thin young wood not thriving'. To the south and south-east of Loch Morlich runs 'Old Wood Along here', 'Good Full Grown Wood' and 'Young Wood Along here'. To the east runs 'Good Wood' and 'Shade – Wet Ground'. Across the entire map is the unfinished sentence 'These hills are very dry and stoney they afford little ...'. Some 'sheallings possessed by Rothymurchus' are also marked.

37 SRO: RHP 13995, 'Plan of Forest of Abernethy, 1858', Surveyor, William Brown. Within the enclosures marked on this map, there were 6684 acres of which about 2704 acres were 'Old Pine Timber', 649 acres were 'Young Pine Trees' and 1176 acres were described as 'Planted'. See also, Elspeth Grant, *Abernethy Forest: Its People and Its Past* (The Arkleton Trust, Nethybridge, 1994); Jean Munro, 'The Golden Groves of Abernethy: the cutting and extraction of timber before the Union', in Graeme Cruickshank (ed.), *A Sense of Place – Studies in Scottish Local History* (Scotland's Cultural Heritage Unit, University of Edinburgh, 1988), pp. 152–162.

38 J. Mawman, *An Excursion to the Highlands of Scotland, and the English Lakes, with Recollections, Descriptions and References to Historical Facts* (T. Gillet, London, 1805), pp. 6–7, 123–124.

39 Robert Somers, *Letters from the Highlands: the Famine of 1847* (Simpkin, Marshall and Co., Glasgow, 1848), pp. 28–38.

40 Daniel Green (ed.), *Cobbett's Tour in Scotland, By William Cobbett (1763-1835)* (Aberdeen University Press, Aberdeen, 1984), pp. 126–127.

41 Alexander Campbell, *A Journey from Edinburgh Through Parts of North Britain; Containing Remarks on Scottish Landscape* ... (John Stockdale, London, New edition in Two Volumes 1811), p. 101. First published in 1802.

42 Alexander Campbell, *The Grampians Desolate, A Poem* (Vernor and Hood, London, 1804). He writes of the Cairngorms:
  "Due east are seen. Still more remote discern
  Amid a hundred hills your azure cairn,
  Whence Dee and Don roll down their amber floods
  Thro' Mar's dark forest, and through Morvern's woods,
  Pours down in fury Spey's collected springs." (p. 108)
  Later he talks of Cairngorm Crystals on the eastern hills,
  "the principal of which are, Cairngorum and Coire-ghearich;
  the former remarkable for its rock-chrystal, called Cairn-gorums". (p. 245)

43 John Brown, *A Brief Account of a Tour of the Highlands of Perthshire, July 1818* (Ogle, Allardice and Thomson, Edinburgh, 1818).

44 J.D. Macculloch, *A Description of the Scenery of Dunkeld and Blair in Atholl* (Joseph Mallett, London, 1823).

45 J.C. Shairp (ed.), *Dorothy Wordsworth: Recollections of A Tour Made in Scotland AD 1803* (Edmonston and Douglas, Edinburgh, 1874).

46 John Macculloch, *The Highlands and Western Isles of Scotland, Containing Descriptions of their Scenery and Antiquities* ... (Longman *et al*, London, 1824), pp. 390–407.

47 George Anderson and Peter Anderson, *Guide to the Highlands and Islands of Scotland Including Orkney and Zetland, Descriptive of their Scenery, Statistics, Antiquities, and Natural History* ... (Adam and Charles Black, Edinburgh, 1850), pp. 62, 239–243, 276–280, 285–293; Peter Anderson, 'Memoranda of an Excursion to the Grampians and Strathspey in July 1863', *Cairngorm Club Journal*, Vol. 4, No. 21, July 1903, pp. 156–166. *Nuphar minima* is the old name for the Least Water-lily *Nuphar pumila*. Note: The Italian seaport of Otranto is famed for its association with the first of the true Gothic novels *The Castle of Otranto* (1764) written by Horace Walpole, the Fourth Earl of Orford. The Otranto novels were noted for their exuberance of invention, moments of sheer horror, and wild picturesque landscapes.

48 Anon, 'The Inverness Scientific Society and Field Club', *Transactions of the Inverness Scientific Society and Field Club*, Vol. I, 1875 to 1880, edited by James Barron (The Courier Office, Inverness), pp. 1–3, 373–374; William Forsyth, 'Place names of Abernethy' (lecture 10 April 1894), *Transactions of the Inverness Scientific Society and Field Club*, Vol. IV, 1888–1895, pp. 372–379; Marina Dennis, *A View from the Croft* (Colin Baxter Photography Ltd., Lanark, 1990); Alex Bremner, 'The Glaciation of the Cairngorms', *The Deeside Field*, No. 4, 1929, pp. 29–37. This article claims to be the first that deals with the glacial history of the entire Cairngorm range as one geographical unit.

49 Arthur Mitchell, *Vacation Notes in Cromar, Burghhead and Strathspey* (Neill and Co., Edinburgh, 1875), p. 69.

50 Lord Henry Cockburn, *Circuit Journeys* (David Douglas, Edinburgh, 1888), pp. 11, 141, 213.

51 Seton Gordon, *The Cairngorm Hills of Scotland* (Cassell and Co., London, 1925); Henry Alexander, *The Cairngorms* (Scottish Mountaineering Club, Edinburgh, 1950). First published in 1928; Adam Watson and Desmond Nethersole-Thompson, *The Cairngorms – their Natural History and Scenery* (Collins, London, 1974); Jim Crumley, *A High and Lonely Place: the Sanctuary and Plight of the Cairngorms* (Jonathan Cape, London, 1991); Adam Watson and Desmond Nethersole-Thompson, *The Cairngorms – their Natural History and Scenery* (The Melvern Press, Perth, 1981, II edition and enlarged); Jim Crumley, *The Heart of the Cairngorms* (Colin Baxter Photography, Grantown-on-Spey, 1997).

52 John Hill Burton, *The Cairngorm Mountains* (William Blackwood and Sons, Edinburgh, 1864), p. 15.

53 Anon, 'Obituary: The Late John Hill Burton', *Blackwood's Edinburgh Magazine*, No. DCCXCI, Vol. CXXX, September 1881, pp. 401–404.

54 An 'Old Tramp' (John Hill Burton) 'Hints for the Vacation Ramble', *Blackwood's Edinburgh Magazine*, No. DCCXC, Vol. CXXX, August 1881, pp. 173–174.

55 David Duff (ed.), *Queen Victoria's Highland Journals* (Lomond Books, London, 1994), p. 60.

56 Paul Harris, *By Appointment: The Story in Pictures of Royal Deeside and Balmoral* (The Press and Journal, Aberdeen, 1988).

57 Piers Brendon, *Thomas Cook: 150 Years of Popular Tourism* (Secker and Warburg, London, 1992), pp. 38–56. Exclamation is in the original.

58 Hartley Kemball Cook, *Over the Hills and Far Away: Three Centuries of Holidays* (George Allen and Unwin, London, 1949); Francis Thompson (ed.), *Victorian and Edwardian Highlands from Old Photographs* (Tantallon Books, Edinburgh, 1989); H.A. Vallance, *The Highland Railway* (David and Charles, Dawlish, 1963).

59 Alexander Macpherson, *Glimpses of Church and Social Life in the Highlands in Olden Times* (William Blackwood and Sons, Edinburgh, 1893), pp. 10–11; Robert Smith, *The Royal Glens* (John Donald, Edinburgh, 1990), pp. 53–54.

60 Hugh Macmillan, *Rothiemurchus* (J.M. Dent and Co., London, 1907), pp. 8, 27–53.

61 Maria Hornor Lansdale, *Scotland – Historic and Romantic, Vol. II* (Henry T. Coates and Co., Philadelphia PA, 1902), pp. 307–308.

62 Meta Humphrey Scarlett, *In the Glens Where I Was Young* (Siskin, Milton of Moy, 1988), p. 61.

63 NRA(S) 102:231, Letter from Alex M'Intosh (factor), Dell of Rothiemurchus, to John Caw, dated 7 September 1848:
   "We cannot say how this fire originated – a set of boys and girls was observed passing by the east of Lochan Eillan … and strong suspicions exist that some of them caused the accident by lighting fire for their tobacco pipes – it would be well to investigate the thing. The extent of ground burnt I consider to be from 12 to 15 acres."

64 John Macpherson Grant, 'Aërial Shadows Seen from the Cairngorm Mountains', *Edinburgh New Philosophical Journal*, Vol. 10, October 1830–April 1831, pp. 165–166.

65 D.B. Horn, 'The Origins of Mountaineering in Scotland', *Scottish Mountaineering Club Journal*, Vol. 28, No. 157, May 1966, pp. 157–173.

66 The archives of the Scottish Mountaineering Club (SMC) are held in the National Library of Scotland (NLS), Edinburgh at Acc 11538. Alex Inkson M'Connochie, 'The Cairngorms In Winter', *Scottish Mountaineering Club Journal*, No. 1, January 1890, pp. 12–19; Walter A. Smith, 'The Cairngorms In Summer', *Scottish Mountaineering Club Journal*, No. 3, September 1890, pp. 106–114.

67 Dickson and Henderson, *op. cit.*, pp. 155–169.

68 James Backhouse, 'A Few Days in Canlochen Glen and c.', *Phytologist*, Vol. 3, 1849, pp. 441–444.

69 J.M. Balfour, 'Notes of a Botanical Excursion, with Pupils, to the Mountains of Braemar, Glenisla, and Clova, and to Benlawers, in August 1847', *Edinburgh New Philosophical Journal*, Vol. XLV, April 1848–October 1848, pp. 122–128.

70 George Walker, 'Some Memorable Naturalists of the North-East', *The Deeside Field*, No. 5, 1931, pp. 2–4; George Sim, *The Vertebrate Fauna of Dee* (D. Wyllie and Son, Aberdeen, 1903); William MacGillivray, *The Natural History of Dee Side and Braemar* (Printed for private circulation by Bradbury and Evans, London, 1855); Samuel Smiles, *Life of a Scotch Naturalist: Thomas Edward* (John Murray, London,

1876); William Jolly, *The Life of John Duncan, Scotch Weaver and Botanist* (Kegan Paul, Trench and Co., London, 1883); James Nicol, *The Geology and Scenery of the North of Scotland: being two lectures given at the Philosophical Institution, Edinburgh* (Oliver and Boyd, Edinburgh, 1866); James Nicol, *Guide to the Geology of Scotland* (Oliver and Boyd, Edinburgh, 1844); William MacGillivray, *Descriptions of the Rapacious Birds of Great Britain* (Maclachlan and Stewart, Edinburgh, 1836); William MacGillivray, *A History of the Molluscous Animals of the Counties of Aberdeen, Kincardine and Banff* (Cunningham and Mortimer, London, 1843); David Elliston Allen, *The Naturalist in Britain – A Social History* (Allen Lane, London, 1976), pp. 77–78.

71 George Carpenter and William Evans, 'A List of Spiders Collected in the Neighbourhood of Aviemore, Inverness-shire', *Annals of Scottish Natural History*, No. 12, October 1894, pp. 227–235.

72 J.A. Harvie-Brown and T.E. Buckley, *A Vertebrate Fauna of the Moray Basin* – II Volumes (David Douglas, Edinburgh, 1895); J.A. Harvie-Brown, *A Vertebrate Fauna of the Tay Basin and Strathmore* (David Douglas, Edinburgh, 1906).

73 Sir Thomas Dick Lauder, *Highland Rambles, And Long Legends to Shorten The Way* (Adam and Charles Black, Edinburgh, 1837), pp. 1–2.

'By right and not by favour':
The Rights of Way Debate

Rights of way campaigns have played a crucial role in the development of a recreational open-air lobby in Scotland. From the formation of the earliest Footpath Preservation Societies, rights of way campaigns, the defence of open spaces and the rapid expansion of countryside recreational facilities and opportunities, have combined to ensure that localised squabbles over access in the Cairngorms developed into issues of national importance. In a recent study Harvey Taylor has shown that a national agenda to defend the traditional right to walk unhindered on public footpaths, was primarily shaped by events in Lancashire and Scotland in the nineteenth century.[1] There has been some appreciation of the importance of the role of the Scottish Rights of Way Society (SRoWS), although their archives remain under-used. Writers on the history of countryside recreation have concentrated too heavily on the most public successes and disputes of the SRoWS, falsely asserting that the issue of access in Scotland centred around the now much vaunted Battle of Glen Tilt in 1847, the Glen Doll case of 1883, the Battle of Braemar in 1891 and the 'Pet Lamb' case of 1884.[2] There has been one notable attempt to show the value of a localised study in a single geographical area, but the source material used was fragmentary, although it did focus in on the wider Cairngorms area.[3] What this chapter seeks to present is not an overview of the access debate and rights of way campaigns in Britain (or indeed, Scotland) in the period, but rather shows the value of studying localised disputes within a defined popular recreational area. It is thus the history of the SRoWS, of individual campaigners and their endeavours to keep paths open, of landlord opposition and of small triumphs and setbacks in the battle for Cairngorm rights of way. This battle in the Cairngorms area has been a continuous campaign of attrition against local landowners.

The Law of Trespass Myth and Rights of Way

Popular myth has it that there is no law of trespass in Scotland, and the written evidence would suggest that this myth was prevalent at the start of the twentieth century, suggesting nineteenth century roots. H.P. Macmillan wrote of it in October 1917: "The statement so often glibly made that there is no law of trespass in Scotland is a fallacy".[4] Trespass in Scotland is a civil offence, not a criminal offence (there can be no such thing as a prosecution for trespass), and as such civil law fully recognises the exclusive rights of private property in land. The ultimate sanction of the civil law of trespass requires that an interdict be taken out against each member of a group who wishes to walk on private land, and as this is time-consuming, it is seldom used. In reality, the trespass law in Scotland is a veritable morass of legal judgements and complications.

The definition of a right of way in Scotland is open to wide interpretation. Scottish law has always recognised the existence of public rights of way across private property, "by a more or less defined route leading from one public place to another public place". As George Cheyne went on to explain in 1948, "the constitution of such a right [of way] is founded on the use to which the public have put the way during the prescriptive period of forty years".[5] Thus proprietors have always had, at common law, to submit to the passage of walkers over their property along defined routes that have been established by continual use and widespread belief that such a route existed. As Macmillan concluded, this is a key issue in the history of recreation in Scotland.

> "The pedestrian in Scotland has a special interest in the law of right of way, for it bestows upon him an undeniable passport to some of the choicest spots among the Highland hills."[6]

The greatest controversy has arisen over what formally constitutes a public place. In 1917 Macmillan listed roads, churches, a harbour or market-place as a place where the public had a right to be, but he considered that "a mountain top or a spot of antiquarian or picturesque interest, no matter how constantly the public may have visited it", did not constitute a public place, nor did it thus, form a competent terminus for a right of way. By 1948 George Cheyne conceded that half a century ago the top of a mountain could not have been accepted as a public place in the eyes of the law, but the public's recreational and leisure tastes had now changed and so the laws of the land had surely to adapt. It is interesting that Cheyne does suggest that cyclists should be classed along with pedestrians in the use of footpaths, reflecting the popular boom in recreational cycling in the interwar years. What then was the right of a proprietor to defend his private land? The landowner could not use physical force to evict a walker but could ask for a name and address, though Macmillan argued that a proprietor was unable to ask a walker's destination if he was using a right of way. Individual interdicts against trespassers could be applied for, or the landowner could raise an action of declarator that the lands were free of any public right of way, which would often result in an investigation being made by a County Council (as a representative of the public interest) or the Scottish Rights of Way

Society. The proprietor, to avoid the declaration of a public right of way over his property, had to take active steps to defend his landholding rights, for if he gave in over public use of the path, then the public could assert that the right of way now existed as a matter of right, not merely permission. A gate could be erected on a right of way, but it could not be locked, although it was the duty of the users of the path to ensure that the gates were closed; similarly, the public could remove an obstruction that was blocking a right of way, and were responsible for the repair and maintenance of the path and any bridges or fords it may have. Finally, if a proprietor could offer a just reason for closing a right of way, this would be allowed, as long as an alternative route of "equal amenity and convenience to the public" was put in place.[7] Much of course, depended on the personality of the landowner in question and how far back he was willing to recognise full local use of a supposed right of way across his private property. Writing in 1921, George Sang feared the new wave of Highland landowners, such as the Grampian Electric Supply Company, might not be as flexible as the traditional family landowners had sometimes been, sensing "the day will come all too soon when no one will be able to go upon any hill without direct trespass, or the revolting procedure of writing to obtain permission from some all-powerful company. Let us be cranky for a spell, and at least keep our rights".[8]

The Scottish Rights of Way Society

An Association for the Protection of the Public Rights of Roadways and Footpaths was first formed in Edinburgh in 1847, with an initial membership of 67 including Adam Black, the publishers William and Robert Chambers and T.B. Macaulay MP. One of the Association's first reports was into the Glen Tilt case on the Atholl Estate in 1847/48, and the Association subsequently played a key role in the legal action taken against the Duke of Atholl and his ghillies in 1849, where the evidence presented for continual use of the road through Glen Tilt from Braemar to Blair Atholl was presented by an assortment of drovers, packmen and locals. From around 1861 to 1882 the Association seems to have slipped into obscurity, but at a meeting of the Board of Directors in 1883 it was decided that the Association should be reconstituted and incorporated under the Companies Acts as The Scottish Rights of Way and Recreation Society, which was born in March 1884, the last meeting of the old Association being held on 4 April 1884 under the Presidency of Adam Black (former Lord Provost of Edinburgh). A prospectus was sent out to 258 individuals encouraging them to subscribe to the SRoWS in early May.[9] The organisation of the new society must have taken some years, as a printed handbill of the objectives of the SRoWS was not circulated until around 1890, bearing the Wordsworth quote

'Therefore I am still a lover of the Meadows and the Woods and Mountains', showing the dominance of the aesthetic view of the Highlands at this time. Membership was priced at £1, as was the cost of and erection of a single Guide Post. The primary objects of the Society were listed as, "the preservation and recovery for the public of such legal Rights of Way as are in danger of being interrupted or permanently lost", and the subsequent guarding and upkeep of these established footpaths, with the erection of Guide Posts and the repair of bridges. The handbill was used as a membership recruitment flyer; "it is hoped that the general public will come forward and protect their own interests by giving to this society their countenance and support". In the first half of the twentieth century a membership recruitment poster was also circulated stating the society's aims.[10]

The old Association of 1847 had concerned itself only with the loss of public access to land around Edinburgh, notably Hawthornden and routes onto Corstorphine Hill, and as such had sought its early campaigning zeal from what Harvey Taylor has identified as, "the Scottish open-air culture of tramping". Many of the nineteenth century legal successes of the SRoWS were attributable to the presence in the ranks of the membership of the Edinburgh lawyer, Thomas Gillies, who had a remarkable ability to produce witnesses (be they drovers, local walkers, shepherds or packmen) willing to attest to a history of public use of a disputed right of way. This proved to be the most consistently successful tactic that the Society possessed, but it relied heavily on the financial health of the Society to enable it to challenge the closure of well known rights of way in the courts.[11]

Both Harvey Taylor and Robert Aitken have investigated the link between the SRoWS and the two most powerful mountaineering clubs in Scotland at the time, the Scottish Mountaineering Club (SMC) and the Cairngorm Club (CC). At its heart the core of the SMC was composed of Alpinists, who were often away in Europe when the Highland stalking season saw the closure of access to the hills. Additionally, the SMC membership was rooted in Edinburgh and Glasgow and much of the climbing was done to the west where deer forests did not prevail; almost without exception the most heated public rights of way battles occurred in the eastern Highlands, and often within the Cairngorms area. There were so-called 'stravagers and marauders' hiding within the SMC membership but they were never part of the mainstream development of the club, with its hotel holidays and black tie dinners. Taylor suggests that stravaging, or wandering at will, is perhaps indicative of the traditional (and Gaelic) custom to wander at will in all seasons on open moorland, and uncultivated land. Certainly the main associational and geographical focus of these "deer disturbers and signpost erectors who walked outwith the pale of SMC constitutional precept", was the rights of way campaign in the eastern Highlands, but many also came from the more radical Cairngorm Club based in Aberdeen.[12] The urban liberal tradition of the city of Aberdeen moulded the CC into a club favouring land reform and presenting a strong challenge to landed interests in the eastern Cairngorms. The editor of the *Cairngorm Club Journal* (which first appeared in 1893), Alex Inkson M'Connochie, was a well respected access campaigner who used the journal to disseminate and encourage the stravaging activities of fellow climbers in the Cairngorm range. Good quality maps became important to these climbers as new routes were explored and opened. The Ordnance Survey (OS) of the Cairngorms was conducted between 1858 and 1870, and individual map sheets were produced on the mountains between 1868 and 1877. A tourist edition of a Cairngorm and Deeside map appeared sometime from 1874 to 1877, "the map being a powerful stimulus to exploration" according to W.A. Ewen. In co-operation with the OS, the Cairngorm Club produced a revolutionary single sheet map of the Cairngorms in 1895, as previously four separate sheets had met irritatingly towards the summit of Ben MacDhui. This CC map was on a scale of one inch to the mile and measured 25 x 24 inches, and included the whole range, except for Lochnagar. This remained the only available single sheet map of the Cairngorms until April 1922 when J.A. Parker urged the OS to produce a layer-coloured edition with contours marked at intervals of 50 ft. (it retailed for 4s. and had an attractive sketch of Loch Morlich and Cairn Gorm on its cover). This map was eventually superseded by the popular 1936 Cairngorm 'Relief Edition' map. Under M'Connochie's tenure of the editorship of the *CC Journal* from 1889 to 1910, and armed with the new 1895 CC map of the area, the stravaging and marauding elements within the Aberdeen climbing fraternity were now well informed for the battle against ghillies and gamekeepers that came every stalking season.[13] Writing much later in 1935, Eric Linklater applauded these annual confrontations between landed interest in Scotland and the great popular mass of the people reinvading their own land. He sought to link this recreational movement in the straths and glens to wider events in Scotland's history, in particular, the Clearances:

> "But many of the hikers must be descendants of evicted Highlanders who sought refuge in the Lowland cities and in contrast to those who complain of their behaviour, I find it very pleasant to think of them worrying the deer that replaced the sheep that dispossessed their fathers. I should like to see hikers more numerous and brightly shirted than ever on every mountain in Scotland; for if they scatter the grouse and pursue the deer far enough, the Highlands may be available again for their rightful heritors of the earth, who are men."[14]

The Battle for Rothiemurchus 1880–1925

The interest that the SRoWS displayed in its access campaigns on the lands of Rothiemurchus, can be seen as a direct reflection of the growing level of popular recreational demand that was being placed on the Cairngorms area from around 1880. In the final two decades of the nineteenth century the SRoWS worked hard to convince the lairds of Rothiemurchus to recognise the existence of public footpaths and rights of way on the estate, through legal channels, threats of court action, subterfuge, the use of *agent provocateurs* on the estate and through a frank exchange of letters. To gain wider support for such a local campaign as this, the Society tried to appeal to respected political figures and prospective parliamentary candidates. In December 1885 it was reported in Society Minutes that W.A. Smith had pressed W.E. Gladstone on the rights of way debate in Scotland, during the politician's recent visit to Midlothian, and that Gladstone had declared himself "highly favourable" to entrusting the local authorities "with the guardianships of all Public Rights of Way"; also that he viewed "with regret and some jealousy the exclusion of the public from great tracts of wild country". Gladstone, rather like the SRoWS, did not see the need for liberal access to mountains legislation.[15] In July 1889, the SRoWS again urged Gladstone to make a firm commitment to condemn landowners who blocked rights of way.[16] On 22 June 1892, the SRoWS sent all parliamentary candidates for Scottish constituencies a statement of the aims of the Society, and notice of the "unwarrantable shutting up of old Footpaths and Drove Roads", as the subject would "doubtless be particularly referred to in localities during the period of the General Election". In a wide-ranging plea for support, the Society drew attention to the fact that there was no one in Scotland whose recognised duty it was to "act for the public interests in such matters of Rights of Way", and that a "great cost" had to be met in defence of a right of way, often funded by a public-spirited benefactor. The Society favoured some limited legislation on the protection and maintenance of existing rights of way, and hoped that when asked, "the present candidates for Parliament", will be "ready to give a pledge ... they will support such legislation".[17] Crucial to this battle for Rothiemurchus in the 1880s and later would be the Martineau family, whose monument now stands on the approach road to Loch an Eilein near the Polchar, the cottage that they leased from the laird of Rothiemurchus, after a brief family sojourn in Glen Feshie.[18] James Martineau, the Unitarian and Professor of Moral Philosophy, first came to Speyside around 1876 for health reasons; some time after that, he moved his family to the Polchar which, "for nearly fifty years was the Martineaus' summer home".[19] The family's love for the freedom of walking on the estate most probably led to their involvement in the rights of way campaigns on Rothiemurchus, in which they played a remarkable 'fifth-columnist' role on behalf of the SRoWS, this role being made all the more exceptional because they perpetrated minor acts of sabotage and bribed estate staff, whilst living no more than a half mile away from the laird's house (the Doune of Rothiemurchus), and because of the family's high standing in academic and professional circles. As the decades slipped by, it seems unusual that their presence at the Polchar was tolerated by the lairds of Rothiemurchus who, in an era of popular Highland tourism, would have been able to lease the Polchar to another, more conventional, holiday guest. It is a letter from James Martineau to Walter Smith of the SRoWS in September 1882, that signals the beginning of the public battle for rights of way on Rothiemurchus Estate. The "memorable exploits" of the laird are referred to, but never explained, and it must be conjectured that Grant of Rothiemurchus in the late summer of 1882 had shut or blocked a perceived public path from Coylumbridge to Aultdrue, as this remained a source of intense argument until 1885 and later. The September 1882 letter from Martineau is stinging in its criticism of the laird.

> "I wish we could believe that, in meeting with his deserts, he would be brought nearer to reformation. But he is full of fancied rights; he despises popular resistance; and will never be brought to reason but by the decision of a court."

James Martineau then went on to explain the difficulty of being a 'guest' on the estate, and also being embroiled in rights of way disputes when a traditional family holiday walking route is disrupted.

> "The worst of it is that we, who live upon the spot, cannot resort to defiant methods, including the application of force, without embittering all our neighbourly relations, and getting our dependents into scraps that may be ruinous to them when we are absent."

The second half of this important letter speaks of a case scenario where Hugh Smith (a summer Martineau family servant), if asked by his employers to use his key to bring the family carriage through the gate to Aultdrue, could thus be placed in a difficult situation; "he would lose his winter employment at the Doune, when I am gone, and is very likely to be turned out of his cottage and sent adrift". James Martineau concludes that only legal action can succeed for, "in any war outside the courts, short of a Wat Tyler insurrection, we must inevitably be beaten".[20] The matter seems to have lain dormant for three years, as the exchange of letters between the involved parties does not begin again until August 1885 – about the time that the SRoWS dispatched a group of its Directors to the Highlands to compile a report on 'Highland Roads and Rights of Way', and to supervise the controversial erection of guide posts on some

Cairngorm paths. The members of this group began their work on Deeside, then crossed *en masse*, "through the famous and well known Larig Ghru Pass between Ben Muich Dhui and Braeriach (so beautifully described by Dr. Hill Burton in his charming book on the Cairngorms) down to Aviemore, through some of the grandest scenery in Scotland". At the wooden bridge across the Dee they erected a guide post proclaiming 'To Aviemore by the Larig Ghru', and "afterwards crossed the Larig Ghru Pass to Rothiemurchus, where other guide posts, more important even perhaps as a protest against attempted obstruction, were to be erected next day".

They erected three guide posts within Rothiemurchus in August 1885:

1) "at Coylum Bridge".

2) "at the ruined cottage near the bridge over the Eunnach [Einich] about two and a half or three miles south of Coylum Bridge".

3) "at the gate into the forest at the north end of Loch an Eilan".

The Private Report stated that it was this final approach to the Cairngorm mountains (3) that was objected to by J.P. Grant of Rothiemurchus, "and his shooting tenants". Grave concern was expressed that, "the gate at Loch-an-Ellan is now kept locked during the summer and autumn; and the good woman at the cottage near at hand, faithfully refuses to produce the key". The Report also highlighted how the loss of this access route would have a detrimental effect on the recreational wishes of locals and visitors alike.

> "Great local irritation is felt at this iron-bound obstruction to an old-established road; and to regular visitors to Speyside it is a harsh and high-handed interference with their wonted quiet, and as they consider, perfectly legal, enjoyment of the beauties of this lovely country. The Larig Ghru Pass is as old – one may almost say – as the Cairngorm Mountains themselves; and yet, if locked gates are put on the roads leading to that pass, how is one to get up to it? The posts and direction boards erected by the Society are a first step at any rate towards answering that question."

Campaigning zeal concluded the Report, and laid down a challenge to both landowners and the rambling and hiking public in Scotland. All footpaths across the land should become as well known and used as the turnpike roads of the country, and they should be walked on by pedestrians "by right and not by favour".[21] As this was a private internal SRoWS document, the laird of Rothiemurchus would have been unaware of the strong line of action that the Society was now going to take from 1885, but letters from his Edinburgh legal counsel in the early days of August may have given some inkling of the gathering storm.

It appears that in late July 1885, John Harrison, Secretary of the SRoWS had informed the laird of Rothiemurchus that only two guide posts were to be erected on his land "on two paths through your property which they assumed to be public paths"; but had in essence also thrown down the gauntlet and challenged the laird to prevent this from occurring. Grant of Rothiemurchus instructed his legal representatives, John C. Brodie and Sons, that he was prepared to admit the existence of a right of way from Aviemore to Braemar across Rothiemurchus, but declined to admit any particular route for this path, and that he regarded the assertions of the SRoWS that a right of way ran from Lynwilg to join the road from Aviemore to Braemar, "to be utterly confounded".[22] The laird's objections were relayed to the SRoWS by his legal firm, stating in the strongest terms that, "Sir John entirely objects to the erection of guide posts upon the path mentioned in your circular and to the use of that path by any person without his express permission".[23] The landowner was clearly trying to reassert his claim to be able to decide who came onto his land, and by what route.

The SRoWS were enraged by this rebuttal, and immediately resorted to their most successful tactic, a threat of possible legal action:

> "I am further instructed to point out that the Society has in its hands so strong a body of evidence to prove the path from Lynwilg a Public Right of Way, that the directors feel bound to ask you to warn your Client against obstructing the public in the use of that road."[24]

A legal battle would prove expensive to both sides of the argument, and the laird knew that Rothiemurchus Estate could not mount an exhaustive financial challenge to the SRoWS, especially if public benefactors came forward to pay the Society's legal expenses, defending the individual against the perceived arrogance and bullying of landed interest. His legal counsel urged resistance only on the ground:

> "as regards the alleged right of way from Lynwilg, we think that on the whole, the best course will be not to pursue further correspondence with the Rights of Way Society, but to give your keepers and servants instructions to prevent as far as possible any unauthorized person passing along that route."[25]

It does appear that by late August 1885, both the laird and his legal counsel were well aware of the tactical manoeuvres of the SRoWS in this debate: "we have no doubt that the object of the Society is to endeavour to force you to vindicate your rights in Court, and we agree with you in thinking that this should if possible be avoided and that it should be left to them to take action".[26] Meanwhile, the Martineau ladies were expressing concern to the SRoWS about the blocked path from Coylumbridge to Aultdrue, and a fence that from 1882 had blocked their customary carriage rides around the shores of Loch an Eilein.

"Our man, James Cameron, says there used to be a cart track now superseded by the new (locked up) road, and also that the gates are too narrow
to admit a laden horse, which people have a right to take along there.

The way is certainly open, for a horse, all along the side of Lochaneilan
next the mountains, till you come to the stream flowing into it from Loch
Gam[hna] … this fence has now been there for 3 summers; before that time,
we used to drive around Lochaneilan."

This letter goes on to reveal that popular resistance to the laird of Rothiemurchus, in the form of minor sabotage, began in late August 1885, as a protest
against the closure of rights of way. Mary-Ellen Martineau reported that from
August 23 to 26, two locked gates were unlocked and taken off their hinges,
but the damage was immediately repaired. Rumour had it that the protest was
"done by people from Grantown", but the Martineau family believed that "it is
done by your Society's orders, but of course we do not <u>know</u> this".[27] It is likely
that the Martineaus' were themselves involved in the removal of these gates; so
keen an interest had they taken in the rights of way battles at Rothiemurchus,
they were by 1885 almost acting as local agents of the SRoWS.

The SRoWS chose to erect guide boards as both a visible assertion of the
existence of a right of way, and evidence of the activities of the Society at the
local level. The route-finding role of these guide posts was secondary, especially
as maps became more widespread in the 1890s. The SRoWS compiled a register
of their erected guide posts in 1885–1889, 1925 and 1946, and it is possible to
trace the game of cat and mouse that was played with certain landowners on this
issue. In a clever ploy, each board was 'issued' to the care of the named landowner.
Boards No. 71, 72 and 73 were issued to John Peter Grant of Rothiemurchus
in late July 1885 to stand along "the road from Aviemore to Braemar called the
Larig Ghru", and the hotly disputed "road from Lynwilg to join the above". In
a 'remarks' section it was noted that this Lynwilg board was taken down by the
laird shortly after it was deployed, and was then re-erected in September 1888,
"after mutual agreement with the proprietor and a narrow ticket placed below
the board stating 'Driving Road to Aultdruie'". In July 1888, Board 78 was
put up on this route also, 'to Lynwilg (facing N), to Braemar'. In September
1888, Board 80 was put up by Loch an Eilein as 'Public road to Kinrara'; all
these Boards were issued into the care of the laird of Rothiemurchus, forcing
him into a tricky situation as to how to react to them on his land, especially as
he was keen to avoid a legal wrangle with the Society. The register suggests that
the SRoWS campaign of saturating the lands of Rothiemurchus with signposts
halted in the late 1880s, as the next fresh erection came in July 1925 at the Saw
Mill on Rothiemurchus. On Deeside, similar tactics were employed. The Duke
of Fife was issued with board 68, to identify the route from Braemar to Insh and
Kingussie via Glen Geldie and Glen Feshie. Board 69 was issued to Sir George

Macpherson-Grant of Ballindalloch, to identify a public path to Braemar.[28]

There was obvious local support on Speyside for the public's continued use of popular rights of way, and for the work of the SRoWS. In August 1887, Emma Brooke wrote from Aviemore asking for leaflets to distribute amongst local farming families, no doubt to alert them to the perceived threat from landowners closing rights of way in the area. Brooke felt that she would like to take on this promotional and informative campaign for the Society and also to give leaflets, "to a family of influence and of liberal opinions living in the neighbourhood".[29] Perhaps she was referring here to the Martineau clan over at the Polchar, although, their various public endeavours to keep footpaths open must have been well known by 1887. The rights of way dispute on Rothiemurchus was destined to rumble on through the 1890s and into the first decade of the new century. The emphasis in this confrontation shifted slightly though, away from the mere recognition of the existence of a public right of way, into the muddy waters of who was to maintain such a plethora of footpaths. The laird of Rothiemurchus would have found it difficult to prevent public visitors from using the carriage road around the picturesque Loch an Eilein, as a previous laird had granted the Duchess of Bedford (then a tenant) full permission to construct such a road in April 1832 for her recreational carriage drives on the estate.[30] Many subsequent Victorian tourists had ensured that it had become a popular holiday walk, and it thus hosted continual use over that forty year period stipulated by the law.

Mary-Ellen Martineau wrote to the SRoWS in August 1891 about the upkeep of all Highland rights of way across private estates.

> "I wonder whether the Society can do anything to enforce the keeping up of the roads over which there is a public right of way; for certainly many of them are not kept up by public expense, and I don't see how the lairds, or their tenants, can be expected to keep them up, if they are for public use. Is it properly the business of the County Councils? I am afraid that the loss of right of way is often due to roads falling out of repair, and no one being responsible for the keeping of them."[31]

A further frenzy of dispute over Rothiemurchus rights of way came in 1903/4, when the new laird of Rothiemurchus attempted to interfere with "the old bridle path from Coylum Bridge to Auldruie" and the "driving road from the south end of Loch-an-Eilein to the same place". The laird, it appears, had also denied access along the Glen Einich road, for Walter Smith declared this route to be, "I fear, past praying (or fighting over) for now".[32] Fifteen years before this acceptance of temporary defeat, the SRoWS had sent Walter A. Smith to meet with a previous laird of Rothiemurchus in July 1888, at which a compromise was negotiated over recreational access to Loch an Eilein, W. Grant reporting that the gate at the loch was re-opened to visitors on 20 August 1888. In their 'agreement' of 1888, it was accepted that there should be "no interference with the public right to the roads from Rothiemurchus leading through the Cairngorms", however, the new laird would not be bound by the actions of his predecessor and the factor, Donald Grant. In July 1903, a dispute arose over the wording of a sign placed on the north side of Loch an Eilein along the driving road to Aultdrue, which the SRoWS felt implied that the road was private. The estate notice is quoted verbatim in the letter:

> " 'Rothiemurchus Forest. Permission is granted to Visitors to use the private roads and to explore the Mountains and Glens of the Forest throughout the year, except the Shooting Season from 12 August to 13 October. Fishing is not allowed and dogs should not be taken into the Forest'."

In the strongest terms, C.E.W. Macpherson of the Society, urged Grant of Rothiemurchus to either remove the notice or replace it with another; he even suggested some fresh wording:

> " 'This road is a permanent Public Driving Road to Auldruie at all times of the year connecting with the Public Road to Braemar by the Larig Ghru'." [33]

Almost immediately the laird and the SRoWS were plunged into an exchange of antagonistic letters over various rights of way and footpaths on the estate, although the laird did suggest that if the Society could prove that his late grandfather had once admitted the existence of a driving road on the north shore of Loch an Eilein, then he would consider giving a renewal of his family's "assurance with regard to it, if your Society so desires". [34] The seasoned rights of way campaigner James Martineau had died in 1900, but this cause was now being championed with fervent feminine vigour by his daughters, who continued to act as local spies and watchdogs of all that the lairds of Rothiemurchus did on this issue. Edith Martineau wrote to Walter Smith in June 1904, about the personality of the present laird, and the covert role that the Martineau ladies played on the estate. Little had changed.

> "It would be worse than useless for us to plead with the present laird, as he is hardened against us, and particularly obstinate when any of his Tenants ask for the smallest act of consideration, or even justice. So, should your society, or you personally, take any steps, we should beg you, for the cause's sake, as well as our own, not to hint that the information came through us."

Edith Martineau also complained bitterly about estate work that was detracting from the recreational enjoyment of the countryside. The removal of trees was "going on terribly fast in his woods", and Grant of Rothiemurchus had laid down a Tram Line in part of the forest to haul timber, which was now directly causing an obstruction on footpaths across the estate. Edith asked, "is not the laird allowing a perfectly illegal thing – and is not your Society's noticeboard reduced to a fiction and a delusion?" Her final complaint was that, "the timber carting and obstructions everywhere now render the roads most painful to drive".[35] The SRoWS had to tread carefully in their dealings with the Martineau daughters; they had to treat the information they received from them in the strictest confidence, for much of it was useful in planning a campaign against the laird of Rothiemurchus, but they also had to keep the Society from becoming embroiled in irrelevant skirmishes over quite legitimate estate work being done in the forest at Rothiemurchus, even if it did sometimes impinge on the recreational activities of the Martineaus. The Society continued to press the laird to recognise the existence of and, if possible, maintain rights of way on the estate. J.P. Grant wrote angrily to C.E.W. Macpherson in August 1904 about the driving road on the northern side of Loch an Eilein:

> "you call it a reply to mine ... but it contains no solution of my doubt whether your society contends that I am bound at my own expense to maintain this alleged driving right of way for the public."[36]

There was something different about the tone of this 1903/4 battle for rights of way at Rothiemurchus, as opposed to the earlier conflict of the mid-1880s. As resistance on both sides of the argument hardened, so personal insults and covert disclosures of private information increased, both sides seeking to out-manoeuvre each other to gain the upper hand; at the same time, the heavy cost of any legal battle probably guaranteed that this ultimate sanction was never used by either side. By far the most covert letter of the campaign was sent by a well-respected visitor to Rothiemurchus Estate, C.G. Cash, whose observations of the ospreys at the castle site on Loch an Eilein had begun in 1894. In August 1904, he sent a letter to the home of C.E.W. Macpherson in Edinburgh, not to the office of the SRoWS, containing remarkable information about the financial health of Rothiemurchus Estate, and the laird's delicate relationship with the solicitor, Donald Grant of the Royal Bank of Scotland in Grantown-on-Spey: "I am writing this separately sending it to your home instead of to your office, because I dont want it to go into any hands but your own." It carried on thus:

> "Popular rumour here, with which as a veteran visitor I am now some little acquainted, makes out that Donald Grant has JP Grant under his financial control, so that DG is de facto proprietor. I heard the remark made once that DG could put JPG out at his will. It may be as well for you to <u>know</u> this, but obviously it would not do for <u>me</u> to tell you! So burn this note.
> Weather glorious for three days. No osprey yet!"[37]

This note would have given the SRoWS some indication of the parlous state of Rothiemurchus Estate finances at that time, and a very good reason to launch a legal challenge to the laird, knowing that he did not have the cash to fight them for long. They did not take this line of action though, one senses because they had already achieved many satisfactory small victories in the twenty years or so that they had been involved in rights of way disputes on the estate.

Walter A. Smith visited Rothiemurchus in 1925 to inspect the state of the SRoWS guide posts and to ascertain if any new posts were required. His detailed report and notes on that visit suggested that four new iron posts were needed:

1) "at the wicket gate to the wood at Coylum Bridge" as 'Public Path to Braemar'.

2) "at the Cross Roads, half a mile south of Whitewell and put up, say about 2 yards or so, on the cart road to Auldrui beyond where it crosses the Glen Eunach Road" as 'Public Driving Road to Auldrui'.

3) "at about $^3/_4$ of a mile farther East along that road, a post where the path direct to Coylum Bridge goes North by west side of the Allt na Beinne Mohr with 2 tickets" as (a) pointing North 'To Coylum Bridge'. (b) pointing West 'To Aviemore by the Polchar'.

4) "at about a mile further on, E by S (after crossing the river) at the point where the path from the Larig comes out of the wood on to the cart road" as 'Public Path to Braemar by the pointing S, Larig Ghru'.[38]

This report certainly gives a flavour of how thorough the work of the SRoWS was on the lands of Rothiemurchus, and how complete their victory had been by the mid-1920s, without having to resort to a costly court battle with the laird during the previous forty-five years. A further indication of this SRoWS triumph, is evidence that suggests that by June 1962 there were as many as twelve Society guide posts on Rothiemurchus Estate, when the Warden at Glenmore Lodge volunteered the services of his visitors to paint and maintain the posts, and was duly sent green and white paint, paint brushes and a wire brush, and a hearty vote of thanks by the Honorary Secretary of the SRoWS.[39] This messy work was hardly the Cairngorm recreational adventure that the children at Glenmore Lodge had come to the area to enjoy.

Within the Cairngorms area, Rothiemurchus had become a focus for the campaigning efforts of the SRoWS from around 1880, but in a sense they relied heavily on information obtained from local activists (in particular, the Martineau family, but not exclusively) and on requests for action put to the Society by growing numbers of tourists, walkers and mountaineers who came to see Rothiemurchus Estate as a recreational gem, and a fundamental link in the access route to the high tops of the Cairngorms. Earlier successes for the predecessor body to the SRoWS were in brief and very public disputes, involving a courtroom battle in the public eye; in contrast, the campaign on Rothiemurchus was a 'war of attrition', in that it was made up of small gains and setbacks over a long period of time, and in that sense was unique in the nineteenth century. August proved to be the critical month in the dispute, and much of the correspondence from both sides fell during that month (the start of the Highland sporting season), when exclusion notices were put up in many glens and straths. A change of laird often saw little alteration in the tone of the defence of landed interest, as all lairds instructed their legal representatives to refer to a disputed route as just an 'alleged' right of way, for to admit the existence of a right of way in any official correspondence would have been tantamount to a complete surrender to the SRoWS demands. The campaign on Rothiemurchus did much to ensure the development and maturation of the SRoWS, and taught its members to be patient in long-running access disputes.

Other Cairngorm Rights of Way Disputes 1890–1930

Despite the attention of the SRoWS being focused on Rothiemurchus, they did open folders on other access and rights of way disputes within the wider Cairngorm area, but were often unable to involve themselves directly and wholeheartedly in the campaign. Over on Deeside, many routes around Braemar had been closed to recreational walkers in the 1850s, as the proprietors of deer forests sought to exclude walkers and tourists from their estates. In the second half of the nineteenth century, access restrictions were placed on the North Deeside Road west of the Invercauld Bridge of Dee, in Glen Ey and the Corienleireg route. The Duke of Leeds closed parts of the Mar Estate to walkers including Glen Lui Beg; by 1911, three lesser roads in Glen Ey had been closed including those leading to Glen Clunie, to Glen Shee by Alltanodhar and Glen Tatnich, and to Strathardle and Glen Fernate.[40] It was not until 1891 though, that Braemar became a centre for a public rights of way battle in which the SRoWS only kept an eye on the proceedings, preferring not to involve themselves directly in the confrontation. The laird of Invercauld had attempted to close a track (used frequently by local people) that led from the Glen Clunie road by the back of Craig Coinnich to a point on the present Braemar to Ballater road, near a distinctive local landmark, a rocky outcrop known as the 'Lion's Face'. The path was only $^3/_4$ mile long, but had been valued as both a school and church access road. The laird erected a fence across it four times in August 1891; four times the fence was broken down; summer visitors to the town were delighted with the local entertainment provided by this ongoing confrontation. It is even reported that in mid-August, as the estate factor Mr. Foggie rebuilt the fence at one end, it was being demolished by protestors at the other end. This dispute was reported as far away as Edinburgh, the *Evening*

Dispatch noting, "strong feeling in Braemar ... that the public right should be maintained", and that over £50 had been locally subscribed to fight the laird. The scenes on 13 August were described:

> "fence put over roadway was again attacked by a large party, the crossbars sawn through, and the wood broken so that everyone of the forty or fifty present might have a stick to put on the fire, which was quickly kindled, and the whole reduced to ashes. The party afterwards, walked in procession through the wood along the disputed path. Great excitement prevails."

A doggerel verse was sung:

> "Crush, crush, crush,
> Let's crush this Foggie man"

In response, the following verse was posted in Braemar on 14 August, showing support for the laird in this direct challenge to landed interest:

> "Shall we basely crouch to tourists?
> Shall we own a right of way?
> Shall our fence of pine be broken?
> Shall Southron strangers rule the day?
>
> Now the fence again is mended,
> Now triumphant is our cause.
> Auldowrie's knee has never bended,
> Nor shall it bend to Southron laws.
>
> Rouse, rouse, ye kilted ghillies!
> Rouse ye heroes of the North." [41]

The laird of Invercauld, sensing that some local people were not going to weaken in their resolve, and that the SRoWS might join the fray, decided to back down on this issue, after being informed by the Procurator Fiscal that the police could not become involved because it was a civil matter. A similar mass protest occurred in Newtonmore in late August 1904, reported in a letter sent to the SRoWS by a local supporter of the Society:

> "There was a great demonstration in Newtonmore on Saturday, starting on the Hill with a Piper, to open up all the old Right of Ways, against the Shooting Tenants challenge to prevent the people from going on the Hill." [42]

Throughout the 1920s, the SRoWS was deeply involved in the defence of numerous rights of way in Glen Tanar and its environs, including the Mounth over Mount Keen, the Fir Mounth road and the route from the Bridge of Muick via Glen Etnach to Mount Keen and south. Legal proceedings were undertaken on behalf of the Society by the Deeside Committee of Aberdeen County Council

and the County Council itself, and despite a protracted period of access negotiations following on from the court case in June 1930 before Lord Mackay,
many of the adjusted routes were declared rights of way – most importantly for
the Cairngorm Club, the road from Bridge of Ess towards Glentanar House.[43]

The most unusual file that the Society held for the Cairngorms area, is
one that focused on a dispute over access along the banks of the River Spey, and
subsequently raised the question of rights of way across Loch Insh in 1892/93.
The initial legal argument was between Mrs. M.A. Kinloch Grant who sought
to prevent John Henry (the Inland Revenue Officer at Craigellachie) "from
trespassing on the banks of the river and fishing for trout",[44] where the river
flowed through her property at Arndilly. By March 1893, she had broadened
her legal offensive to exclude J. Henry "from entering upon or passing along
the banks of the river Spey and from entering upon or passing along the alvens
or bed of the river".[45]

In autumn 1892, a Speyside Trout Fishers' Association was formed and
sought to raise money by subscription to defend John Henry: "with the view
of upholding and maintaining the public right of Trout Fishing and the Right
of Way along the banks of the River Spey and its Tributaries". They sought the
guidance and advice of the SRoWS in a circular letter urging that the issue was
"a very important one for Strathspey and the whole of Scotland". John Duncan,
the Secretary of this Association saw the SRoWS as a kindred organisation,
defending individual rights in the face of bully tactics by private landowners:

> "These rights have been exercised and enjoyed by the public from time imme-
> morial, but are at present threatened to be stopped by an action now pending
> in the Court of Session … The stoppage of Trout Fishing in rivers would be a
> serious loss, inasmuch that at the present time great numbers of people come
> from town annually, and take up summer lodgings along the banks of this
> and other rivers … the money received from this source by farmers, cottagers,
> tradesmen, is something very considerable … This newly formed Association
> have decided to advance funds for the defence of the case."[46]

There is no suggestion that the SRoWS offered financial help or legal advice
to the Association, but they were asked to investigate the whole question of
rights of way on river banks and over bodies of water, after all, "if the river is
navigable, which the pursuers admit, there must of necessity be a public right of
way along the Banks or alvens at least".[47] The question of recreational boating
on Loch Insh was answered thus in 1892:

> "The loch is practically an expanded portion of the River. The loch is let to a
> tenant for fishing. Of course he can refuse fishing on it, but can he refuse a
> boat on it <u>not</u> for fishing purposes …our impression is that as the loch is an

expanded part of the River, the rights regarding it are the laws of the River, and if the River (though not the fish in it) is a public right of way, then this particular loch is also."[48]

John Henry and the Association were defeated in court, but the existence of this file does show that the rights of way debate in northern Scotland had many difficult legal permutations, and addressed a wide range of geographical features in the landscape. In the Cairngorms area, it was never just a debate that focused on traditional local use of old cattle drove roads through the high passes, and the glens of the Feshie and the Geldie.[49]

Rights of Way Issues in the Cairngorms 1930–1980

During the middle years of the twentieth century, the tough battles of the period 1880–1920 were left behind, and the rights of way campaign in the Cairngorms noticeably slowed. After forty years of fervour, passion and hard won successes, this period can be seen historically as a time of consolidation, along with the maintenance and upkeep of guide posts and footpaths as a visible assertion of the Society's continued role in the area. In May 1939, the link between the SRoWS and the Cairngorm Club was evident when James A. Parker, Secretary of the CC, wrote to G.D. Cheyne, Honorary Secretary of the SRoWS, about the state of the Cairngorm Club Bridge in Rothiemurchus and some Society guide posts nearby; "and after a careful examination decided that the Cairngorm Club Bridge would require to be re-painted this year ... I have now received a Tender from Messrs. Dixon and Bain of Grantown-on-Spey ... they are quite good people and did the bridge very well in 1919 and 1929 ... I also examined your three posts". Parker suggested that the same painting firm should also spruce up the Society guide posts;[50] by 1948, the task of erecting, painting and aligning the SRoWS guide posts was being foisted off onto students at Glenmore Lodge.[51] The celebrated Cairngorm Club Footbridge across the Allt na Beinne Moire on Rothiemurchus was first opened to recreational hillwalkers and mountaineers on 3 August 1912 and, significantly, it was built in full co-operation with the laird, funded by financial donations from CC members under the direction of John Clarke and James Parker. As early as 1914, a suggestion was made in the CC to build a mountain indicator on Ben MacDui as a guide to hillwalkers, but it was not until August 1925, and in front of a crowd of 136, that the indicator on the mountain was unveiled. These two Cairngorm Club schemes blended well with the existing wider recreational and access provisions on Rothiemurchus and the high tops, as did another CC indicator placed on Lochnagar in July 1924, and unveiled before 142 people.[52]

There is humour in the suggested scheme whereby students taking courses at Glenmore Lodge would conduct SRoWS guide post work at Rothiemurchus. In July 1948, the Rev. R.J.B. Clark, who was supervising the students, expressed concern to W.D. Davidson of the SRoWS that the guide posts might be too heavy for the children to carry, especially as Glenmore was a good distance from Rothiemurchus, and "a tubular steel post could be very heavy". He also knew nothing of a rumour circulating, that his students were to erect a footbridge in Glen Feshie across the Eidart.[53] Davidson sought to calm the worries of the cleric by suggesting that the weight of a guide post, with a small name plate on the top was only 50 lbs., and that a direction plate only weighted 5 $1/_2$ lbs.[54] The Rev. Clarke resigned himself to the task: "they will be heavy to carry but we will do our best with them".[55] This fresh wave of guide post installation in the late 1940s came about because most of the former posts had been removed from the forests and mountains of the Cairngorms during the war years. The Society did encounter some problems during the re-erection of these posts as landowners and gamekeepers sought to prevent their redeployment on estates, claiming that some had not been present before 1939. In August 1948, the Rev. Clark was obstructed in his guide post work by the owner of Forest Lodge in Abernethy Forest who claimed that there never had been any posts at Ryvoan or Nethybridge, and that "the use of a right of way does not include the right to erect sign posts". This challenge to the activities of the Society angered Clark, who wrote that he would only continue to help the SRoWS if they were "only replacing posts removed during the war. I agreed to do this for you on the understanding that we were replacing posts, not erecting new posts. I do not like the countryside spoiled with posts".[56] In 1946, the Society had instigated one of their infrequent surveys of the guide posts that had been erected since 1925, the date of the last register.

Vandalism was also an issue that the Society had to confront as early as 1953, when an increasing number of youth clubs and organisations were venturing into the Cairngorms as part of a 'progressive education' doctrine which placed a good deal of emphasis on healthy open-air recreation. In July 1953, a party of Boy Scouts from Dumfries-shire contrived to break off the arm of a SRoWS direction sign, as they larked about at the entrance to the Larig Ghru. It was obviously seen as a serious disciplinary matter, as the Deputy Chief Constable of Inverness-shire wrote directly to the SRoWS,[57] and three weeks later an angry laird of Rothiemurchus voiced his frustration about the behaviour of such visitors to his property:

"[signs] have been apparently wilfully broken and destroyed. It would appear from an examination of some stones which have paint markings on them that the culprits must have caused the damage by throwing stones at the indicators."[58]

The significance of this letter from the laird, is that it now reveals some emerging landowner's pride for SRoWS guide posts and indicators placed into his care, in direct contrast to the bitter confrontations about rights of way and public access just 70 years earlier. However, in this new age of motor car recreation into the Cairngorms, guide posts originally erected to direct hillwalkers, began to cause confusion and irritation amongst the growing number of motorists using minor roads in the area. The Divisional Surveyor of Roads, based in Kingussie, voiced his concerns to the SRoWS in May 1956:

> "At the junction of the Drumguish Road with Route B970, Newtonmore/Nethy Bridge Road you have a sign 'To Glen Feshie and Glen Geldie' ... I have had numerous complaints from motorists mistaking this for the Glenfeshie Road which branches off the B970 about three and a half miles further North opposite Loch Insh ... I suggest it should be prefixed with 'Footpath'." [59]

A good indicator of how the conflict over rights of way had diminished greatly over the course of the twentieth century on a privately owned estate such as Rothiemurchus, is further shown by Colonel Grant's willingness to call a meeting in the Spring of 1973 (after his own discussions with the District Clerk of Badenoch) to discuss rights of way and to "work out a comprehensive sign-posting scheme for his estate".[60] Such a move by the lairds of Rothiemurchus would have been unthinkable prior to the 1950s. The designation of the Cairngorms National Nature Reserve in 1954 brought the likelihood of even more visitors coming into the area and walking through Rothiemurchus, and in a fashion dealt a fatal blow to any landowner opposition to the comprehensive sign-posting of all paths and rights of way on the estate. Elsewhere in the Cairngorms, some landowners still sought to try to take a confrontational stance well into the 1960s. The Society advised one of their local agents based in Rothiemurchus about events in Abernethy Forest in 1962:

> "to the best of my recollection, what happened about the sign 'Ryvoan' was that shortly after we put it up, the factor had it taken down and at that time we did not pursue the matter. Since then, ... we have had correspondence with the factor (somewhat one-sided as he does not usually reply)." [61]

Just as in the 1880s and 1890s, local agents and sympathisers of the Society continued to play an active role in the policing of the infrastructure of rights of way (guide post and footpath maintenance) in the Cairngorms in the 1960s and 1970s. These individuals were the eyes and ears of the Society in the district. An American SRoWS member, Robert Duncan, visiting the Cairngorms from New York in August 1963, wrote of his stay in Aviemore and his disappointment at not being able to go up Cairn Gorm on the chairlift, due to inclement weather. He also offered a suggestion about the sign-posting for the Larig Ghru, and at Loch an Eilein.

"I found the markings of the Lairig Ghru at both ends pretty vague for a first-time visitor … The metal sign at Loch-an-Eilean approach is badly rusted and somewhat hidden … there is a fork with no sign." [62]

Duncan wrote to the Society again in October, expressing his love for the Cairngorm mountains and enclosing a donation of £10, "to be of aid to the Society, especially if it were in any way connected with the Lairig Ghru". [63] Affleck Gray wrote to the SRoWS in May 1972 in search of part-time employment, having just retired from 20 years' with the Forestry Commission and having noticed on a recent walk through the Larig Ghru that "the signpost at the Rothiemurchus end had been broken, presumably by vandals". He asked if he could become a paid local agent of the Society, being a native of the Cairngorm district, and an active hillwalker and mountaineer, camping out "annually on the high plateaux … I know these mountains intimately. [64] Gray retired to Pitlochry and went on to write two popular books on the folklore and mythology of the Cairngorms. [65]

As the SRoWS aged, it became less radical and confrontational. While in the period 1847 to 1920 it had been in the vanguard of popular protest, as the 1970s wore on, and as an environmental awareness grew into a campaigning zeal within younger nature conservation and recreation organisations, the SRoWS became increasingly sidelined. One issue over which the Society showed little desire for a fight, was that of bulldozed estate tracks in remote and popular recreational glens in the Cairngorms. In September 1974, Ann Wakeling of the Strathspey Mountaineering Club, urged the SRoWS to take a stance against the proliferation of estate tracks in Glen Feshie, describing the scene thus:

"this ugly track has destroyed one of the pleasantest 'single file' footpaths I knew and is now most unpleasant to walk on … a new track was bulldozed on the steep and unstable hillside, this has now landslipped and is dangerous and impassable. A new track has been gouged out at the foot of this slope, and it appears that an attempt has been made to divert the river to the far side of its bed."

Wakeling sought action from the SRoWS on "the damage caused by haphazard bulldozing, or tracks for landrovers, where good footpaths have gone before". [66] The Society suggested that such disclosures about the landscape disfigurement in the glen would best be confined to an article in *The Scots Magazine*, as well as meekly accepting, "that there is not very much which either the Society, the local authorities or the public can do about the disfigurement". [67] One of the most positive acts of the Society during the 1970s was to publish a recreational map with accompanying route descriptions, titled *The Cairngorm Passes*; the tone was conciliatory in the attached 'Notes to Walkers'. Priced at 25p, and thus being published post-1971 and decimalisation, it urged hillwalkers and climbers in the Cairngorms to respect the countryside, keep dogs on a lead, to shut all gates and to take all litter home. Picnic fires were banned, unless "lit on rocks and gravel, and carefully extinguished afterwards with water", and all recreational visitors were to "avoid spoiling the sport of those who have the right to it ... you will help to assure for yourself and others a welcome when visiting the Highlands".[68] The production of maps was an important promotional activity undertaken by the SRoWS. The direct forerunner of this 'Cairngorm Passes' map was a collection of maps of Speyside and the Cairngorms from the first half of the twentieth century, marked to show alleged rights of way.[69] What is noticeable about the content of this map from the 1970s, is the wholly reasonable and conciliatory tone that it strikes, suggesting that over time the original confrontational stance taken by the Society and landowners such as the Grants of Rothiemurchus, had mellowed within the need to seek consensus in the modern era.

Notes to Chapter 2

1   Harvey Taylor, *A Claim On the Countryside – A History of the British Outdoor Movement* (Keele University Press, Edinburgh, 1997).

2   Tom Stephenson, *Forbidden Land – The Struggle For Access to Mountain and Moorland* (Manchester University Press, Manchester, 1989), pp. 118-130, 'The Highland Story'.

3   Sandy Anton, 'Battles for Cairngorm Rights of Way', *Cairngorm Club Journal*, Vol. 20, No. 102, 1991, pp. 23–29.

4   H.P. Macmillan, 'Rights of Way', *The Scottish Mountaineering Club Journal*, Vol. 14, No. 84, October 1917, pp. 288–291.

5   George D. Cheyne, 'Rights of Way', *The Scottish Moutaineering Club Journal*, Vol. 24, No. 139, May 1948, pp. 14–20.

6   Macmillan, *op. cit.*, p. 289.

7   Cheyne, *op. cit.*, pp. 15–16.

8   George Sang, 'The Menace to Rights-of-Way', *The Scottish Mountaineering Club Journal*, Vol. 16, No. 91, April 1921, pp. 18–22.

9   The archives of the Scottish Rights of Way Society are held in the Scottish Record Office (SRO), Edinburgh at GD 335. SRO: GD 335-1, 'Papers Relating to the Formation of the Scottish Rights of Way Society 1847-1885'.

10 SRO: GD 335-4, 'Printed Handbill Advertising the Objectives of the Scottish Rights of Way and Recreation Society c.1890'. Members could join the Society by paying instalments of five shillings per £1 share, with one share sufficing to constitute a membership. See also SRO: RHP 38090/4, 'Poster for Scottish Rights of Way Society', n.d., but probably from the first half of the twentieth century. Annual Membership Subscription was 10/-. The objects of the Society were listed as: (1)

The preservation, defence and acquisition of public rights of way in Scotland. (2) The erection and repair of bridges, guideposts, stiles etc. on public rights of way.

11 Taylor, *op. cit.*, pp. 16, 39.

12 Robert Aitken, 'Stravagers and Marauders', *The Scottish Mountaineering Club Journal*, Vol. 30, No. 166, 1975, pp. 351–357; Taylor, *op. cit.*, pp. 132, 139.

13 Robert Lippe, 'The Cairngorm Club', *Cairngorm Club Journal*, Vol. 1, No. 1, July 1893, pp. 7–14; J.A. Parker, *Reviews*: 'New Ordnance Survey Map of the Cairngorms', *The Scottish Mountaineering Club Journal*, Vol. 16, No. 94, October 1922, pp. 202–203; W.A. Ewen, 'Fifty Years of the Cairngorm Club', *Cairngorm Club Journal*, Vol. 15, No. 80, July 1939, pp. 1–14; see also SRO: GD 335-43, 'Cairngorm Club Map of Cairngorm Mountains 1895'.

14 Eric Linklater, *The Lion and the Unicorn* (George Routledge and Sons, London, 1935), pp. 90–91.

15 SRO: GD 335-49, 'Minute of meeting of Directors of Scottish Rights of Way Society, dated 15 December 1885, by C.E.W. Macpherson, Secretary'.

16 SRO: GD 335-49, Letter from C.E.W. Macpherson, Secretary, SRoWS to W.A. Smith, dated 16 July 1889:
   "Mr. Gladstone wishes me to acknowledge the receipt of your letter and to say that the matter referred to is receiving the careful attention of himself and friends."

17 SRO: GD 335-56, 'Statement by Scottish Rights of Way and Recreation Society to Parliamentary Candidates for Scottish Constituencies, from 20 George Street, Edinburgh, dated 22 June 1892, signed by Robert Cox, Chairman, and C.E.W. Macpherson, Secretary'.

18 Martineau Monument, junction of B970 and road to Loch an Eilein, Rothiemurchus, *pers. obs.*
   'This pillar commemorates James Martineau (1805–1900), Unitarian minister and philosopher, who loved this area, and on retirement made his home here, many years resident at the Polchar'. 'Mary-Ellen Martineau who established a library for the use of Rothiemurchus and District'. 'Gertrude Martineau who taught the art of wood carving to the people of this district over twenty five years, Edith who started summer drawing classes'.
      Restored by the Scottish Unitarian Association in 1974, the monument was designed by Hugh Mottram of Norwich as a triangular pillar with convex faces. The three-sided column bears the initials 'J.M.' on its cap.

19 Meta Humphrey Scarlett, *In the Glens Where I Was Young* (Siskin, Milton of Moy, 1988), pp. 59–62.

20 SRO: GD 335-22, Letter from James Martineau, The Polchar, Rothiemurchus, to Walter Smith, Scottish Rights of Way Society, dated 20 September 1882.

21 SRO: GD 335-22, 'Private Report on Highland Roads – Experiences of a Deputation of Directors in the North, dated 10 August 1885, Edinburgh'.

22 NRA(S) 102:532, Letter from John C. Brodie and Sons, Edinburgh, to Sir John Peter Grant of Rothiemurchus, dated 6 August 1885.

23 NRA(S) 102:532, Letter from John C. Brodie and Sons, Edinburgh to Scottish Rights of Way Society, Edinburgh, dated 6 August 1885.

24 NRA(S) 102:532, Letter from John Harrison, Secretary, Scottish Rights of Way Society, Edinburgh, to John C. Brodie and Sons, Edinburgh, dated 11 August 1885.

25 NRA(S) 102:532, Letter from John C. Brodie and Sons, Edinburgh, to J.P. Grant of Rothiemurchus, dated 25 August 1885.

26 NRA(S) 102:532, Letter from John C. Brodie and Sons, Edinburgh, to J.P. Grant of Rothiemurchus, dated 28 August 1885.

27 SRO: GD 335-22, Letter from Mary-Ellen Martineau, The Polchar, Rothiemurchus, to Walter Smith, Scottish Rights of Way Society, dated 26 August 1886. Underlining in the original.

28 SRO: GD 335-67, 'Register of Guide Boards Erected, 1885–1889, 1925, 1946'.

29 SRO: GD 335-22, Letter from Emma F. Brooke, Vulcan Cottage, Aviemore, to the Secretary, Scottish Rights of Way Society, Edinburgh, dated 29 August 1887.

30 NRA(S) 102:222, Letter from William Patrick Grant, Malshanger House, Basingstoke to Patrick Borthwick, Edinburgh, dated 10 April 1832; Letter from Patrick Borthwick, Edinburgh, to William Patrick Grant, dated 23 April 1832.

31 SRO: GD 335-22, Letter from M.E. Martineau, The Polchar, Rothiemurchus, to Walter Smith, Scottish Rights of Way Society, Edinburgh, dated 24 August 1891.

32 SRO: GD 335-22, Letter from Walter Smith, Scottish Rights of Way Society, to C.E.W. Macpherson, Scottish Rights of Way Society, dated 11 June 1903.

33 SRO: GD 335-22, Letter from C.E.W. Macpherson, Scottish Rights of Way Society to J.P. Grant of Rothiemurchus, dated 31 July 1903.

34 SRO: GD 335-22, Letter from J.P. Grant of Rothiemurchus, to C.E.W. Macpherson, dated 3 August 1903.

35 SRO: GD 335-22, Letter from Miss Edith Martineau, The Polchar, Rothiemurchus, to Walter A. Smith, Scottish Rights of Way Society, dated 26 June 1904.

36 SRO: GD 335-22, Letter from J.P. Grant of Rothiemurchus, to C.E.W. Macpherson, Scottish Rights of Way Society, Edinburgh, dated 8 August 1904.

37 SRO: GD 335-22, Letter from C.G. Cash, Fearn Bank, Aviemore, to C.E.W. Macpherson, Scottish Rights of Way Society, Edinburgh, dated 18 August 1904.

38 SRO: GD 335-22, Notes by Walter A. Smith on the Rothiemurchus Guide Posts, 1925.

39 SRO: GD 335-81, Letter from Honorary Secretary, Scottish Rights of Way Society, to The Warden, Glenmore Lodge, Glenmore, Cairngorms, dated 22 June 1962. This letter lists the locations of 12 SRoWS guide posts on Rothiemurchus Estate.

40 Anton, *op. cit.*, p. 23.

41 SRO: GD 335-22, Anon, 'A Braemar Right of Way Dispute', *Edinburgh Evening Dispatch,* 14 August 1891; see also, Anton, *op. cit.*, p. 27.

42 SRO: GD 335-22, Extract from a Letter from Newtonmore, dated 29 August 1904, a Monday.

43 Anton, *op. cit.*, pp. 27–28.

44 SRO: GD 335-28, Letter from John Duncan, Secretary, Speyside Trout Fishers' Association, Aberlour, to Secretary, Scottish Rights of Way Society, Edinburgh, dated 12 November 1892.

45 SRO: GD 335-28, Letter from John Duncan, Secretary, Speyside Trout Fishers' Association, Aberlour, to Secretary, Scottish Rights of Way Society, Edinburgh, dated 13 March 1893.

46 SRO: GD 335-28, Letter and Notice, 'Subscriptions invited towards the Protection of the Public Right of Trout Fishing by the Speyside Trout Fishers' Association'. The summons was served in the 'Spey Trout Fishing Case' on 14 October 1892.

47 See SRO:GD335-28, *loc. cit.*, Letter from John Duncan to Secretary, SRoWS Edinburgh, dated 13 March 1893.

48 SRO: GD 335-28, Notelet 'Loch Insh', dated 1892, Glasgow. Underlining is in original.

49 A.R.B. Haldane, *The Drove Roads of Scotland* (Thomas Nelson and Sons, London, 1953), pp. 110, 127–128; John Kerr, *Old Grampian Highways* (The Atholl Experience, Blair Atholl, 1984); see also SRO: RHP 38090/1-3, 'Plans of old Highland Roads traced from William Roy's (1747–1755) and Daniel Paterson's (1746) surveys', no surveyor, n.d. (probably from first half of twentieth century). Covers the counties of Argyll, Inverness and Ross and Cromarty. Formerly held in SRO: GD 335.

50 SRO: GD 335-80, 'Inverness-shire Guide Posts/Rights of Way File, 1931-1975', Letter from James A. Parker, Secretary, Cairngorm Club, Aberdeen, to G.D. Cheyne, Hon. Secretary, Scottish Rights of Way Society, Edinburgh, dated 18 May 1939.

51 SRO: GD 335-80, Letter from W.D. Davidson, Scottish Rights of Way Society, Edinburgh to Rev. R.J.B. Clark, Aviemore Hotel, Aviemore, dated 28 June 1948.

52 See Ewen, *op. cit.*, pp. 10–13; Plaque: Cairngorm Club Footbridge, Rothiemurchus, *pers. obs.* On the plate attached to the bridge, the word Beinne is mis-spelt as 'Bienne'. On modern OS maps the burn is now identified as Am Beanaidh.

53 SRO: GD 335-80, Letter from Rev. R.J.B. Clark, Aviemore Hotel, to W.D. Davidson, Scottish Rights of Way Society, dated 6 July 1948.

54 SRO: GD 335-80, Letter from W.D. Davidson, Scottish Rights of Way Society, to Rev. R.J.B. Clark, Aviemore Hotel, dated 14 July 1948.

55 SRO: GD 335-80, Letter from Rev. R.J.B. Clark, Aviemore Hotel, to W.D. Davidson, Scottish Rights of Way Society, dated 16 July 1948. The Rev. Clark (with his wife) was appointed the first Warden of Glenmore Lodge in September 1948, but they only stayed for eighteen months before departing to take up an Episcopal position in Edinburgh. The cleric had been a keen supporter of pioneering educational social work, and had led mountain rescue teams in Glencoe and Lochaber.

56 SRO: GD 335-80, Letter from Rev. R.J.B. Clark, Glenmore Lodge, Cairngorms, to W.D. Davidson, Scottish Rights of Way Society, Edinburgh, dated 30 August 1948.

57 SRO: GD 335-80, Letter from Deputy Chief Constable, Inverness-shire County Constabulary HQ, Inverness Castle, to Secretary, Scottish Rights of Way Society, Edinburgh, dated 17 August 1953.

58 SRO: GD 335-80, Letter from J.P. Grant of Rothiemurchus, Rothiemurchus Estate Office, Cairngorms, to Secretary, Scottish Rights of Way Society, Edinburgh, dated 7 September 1953.

59 SRO: GD 35-80, Letter from D.I. Junor, Divisional Surveyor, Kingussie, to Secretary, Scottish Rights of Way Society, Edinburgh, dated 29 May 1956.

60 SRO: GD 335-81. Letter from D.W. MacPherson, Secretary, Scottish Rights of Way Society, Edinburgh, to Richard Cameron, County Planning Officer, Inverness, dated 30 March 1973.

61 SRO: GD 335-81, Letter from Scottish Rights of Way Society, Edinburgh, to A.M. Leney, Rothiemurchus, dated 23 September 1962.

62 SRO: GD 335-81, Letter from Robert F. Duncan, Broad Street, NY, USA to W.D. Davidson, Honorary Secretary, Scottish Rights of Way Society, dated 18 September 1963.

63 SRO: GD 335-81, Letter from Robert F. Duncan, NY, USA, to Scottish Rights of Way Society, dated 22 October 1963.

64 SRO: GD 335-81. Letter from Affleck Gray, Pitlochry, to Secretary, Scottish Rights of Way Society, Edinburgh, dated 15 May 1972.

65 See Affleck Gray, *Legends of the Cairngorms* (Mainstream Pub. Co., Edinburgh, 1987), reprinted 1989; Affleck Gray, *The Big Grey Man of Ben MacDhui* (Birlinn Ltd., Edinburgh, 1994).

66 SRO: GD 335-81, Letter from Ann Wakeling, Secretary, Strathspey Mountaineering Club, Aviemore to the Scottish Rights of Way Society, Edinburgh, dated 13 September 1974.

67 SRO: GD 335-81, Letter from D.W. MacPherson, Secretary, Scottish Rights of Way Society, to Ann Wakeling, Secretary, Strathspey Mountaineering Club, dated 3 October 1974.

68 SRO: GD 335-109, Map: *The Cairngorm Passes*, published by Scottish Rights of Way Society Ltd., 1 Lutton Place, Edinburgh, n.d. (post-1971), price 25p. See section 'Notes to Walkers'.

69 See SRO: RHP 38093/1 and SRO: RHP 38093/2. 'Plan of Speyside and Cairngorms marked to show alleged rights of way', no surveyor, n.d., but probably first half of the twentieth century. Formerly held in SRO: GD 335. Both maps were drawn on the scale of 1 inch = 1 mile, and covered the counties of Aberdeen, Banff, Inverness, Perth and Moray and Nairn. The map showed First class roads, Second class roads, Third class roads, Unclassified roads, Scheduled Rights of Way, Rights of Way Claimed.

3

James Bryce:
His Access Campaign in Scotland,
his Legacy and his Critics

Running concurrently with the extra-parliamentary campaign for rights of way and access onto estates such as Rothiemurchus in the last two decades of the nineteenth century, there was an equally important parliamentary campaign for access to mountains in Scotland, led by the Liberal MP James Bryce (1838–1922). The contribution of Bryce to the history of countryside recreation, and the legacy of his campaign to the National Parks debate of the 1930s and 1940s has been well documented by historians, such as John Sheail, David Evans and Harvey Taylor,[1] and by an early champion of access to upland environments from the 1920s: E.A. Baker dedicated his book *The Highlands With Rope and Rucksack* to 'The Memory of Viscount Bryce – Vindicator of Access to Mountains'.[2] However, the focus of these studies of the Access to Mountains Bills dating from 1884 onwards, has been on placing the parliamentary campaign for access to the mountainous areas of Britain in the broadest national context; this short chapter comments only on the Parliamentary Bills that addressed solely the Scottish situation, that is the Bills from 1884 to 1908. The argument for this approach is that this parliamentary agitation for open access to the hills covers almost the same time period as the most confrontational exploits of the SRoWS in the Cairngorms, especially on Rothiemurchus and Deeside. James Bryce straddles both campaigns, for he was the first President (in 1889) of the radical Cairngorm Club born of the liberal political tradition of the city of Aberdeen, MP for South Aberdeen for 21 years from 1885, climber and amateur botanist. His father Dr James Bryce was an academic geologist. Harvey Taylor stresses Bryce's role at the local level in the eastern Highlands, alongside that at Westminster, believing that his "prominent role in the early parliamentary campaign for country access was augmented by his major contribution, in collaboration with colleagues in the Cairngorm Club, to the first real challenge to the practice of preventing walkers and others from roaming freely in the Scottish hills".[3] From February 1884 onwards, with the support of other parliamentarians, James Bryce introduced a dozen Private Member's Bills promoting access to the mountains and moorlands of Scotland, but they all failed due to a lack of time in the parliamentary session.[4]

The preamble to the first 'Bill to Secure To the Public Access to Mountains and Moorland in Scotland' spoke of the role of deer forests and associated concepts of exclusivity, that had recently (the 1870s and 1880s) deprived "Her Majesty's subjects of the rights which they have heretofore enjoyed of walking upon these and other tracts of uncultivated mountain and moorland for purposes of recreation and scientific or artistic study". Although it has been customary to view Bryce's Bill as one of the earliest attempts in the access campaign to bring 'new liberties' to the populace, it is apparent that Bryce himself drew much of his inspiration from the past, and sought the restoration of what he identified as ancient and traditional rights.[5] It was a short Bill, and in its second section it asked that "no owner or occupier of uncultivated mountain or moorlands in Scotland shall be entitled to exclude any person from walking on such lands for the purposes of recreation or scientific or artistic study, or to molest him in so walking". The Bill also stressed that any recreational activity of a scientific or artistic bent in an upland environment would be justifiable defence, against the threat of prosecution for 'alleged trespass' by an action of interdict taken out by a landowner. Of course, defining the boundaries of what Bryce saw as legitimate and respectful recreational activities was a central feature of the Bill. Bryce saw the need to tone down the radical elements of the Bill in the face of expected conservative opposition, and so included a list of activities that were to be excluded from the Bill, and for which exclusion from uncultivated land was to be permitted: the principal targets were poachers, egg collectors, dog walkers, vandals who wilfully destroyed fences or disturbed livestock – "where any person goes on land with any malicious intent or otherwise than for the purposes of recreation". Access to young plantations of trees, and parks and gardens adjacent to houses was also excluded from the Bill.[6]

Table 1 provides a quick reference to the parliamentary history of each of Bryce's Bills. Throughout its parliamentary history, Bryce's Bill remained little altered over the years. In 1887, a clause was added on scientific recreational activity, which sought to exclude collectors who destroyed or uprooted plants or shrubs. A clause to exclude visitors carrying firearms was added in 1888, along with other clauses that sought to curb illegal camping and the lighting of fires, and to prevent the defacement of trees (possibly with Victorian 'graffiti' initials). By 1897, the entire preamble to the Bill had been dramatically shortened, speaking simply of it being "desirable to secure to the public the right of free access to uncultivated mountains and moorlands, subject to proper provisions for preventing any abuse of such right".

Introducing his Bills in Parliament in the 1880s and 1890s, James Bryce expressed some very early concerns about the spiritual and physical needs of the populace to secure a wider and assured enjoyment of the countryside in

Year	Bill Number	(1) first reading (2) second reading
1884	122[7]	(1) 28 February 1884
1884/5	21[8]	(1) 29 October 1884
1886	90[9]	(1) 25 January 1886
1887	51[10]	(1) 28 January 1887 new clause added
1888	103[11]	(1) 13 February and (2) 17 April 1888 wording of Bill altered
1889	114[12]	(1) 25 February 1889
1890/1	20[13]	(1) 12 February 1890 and (1) 27 November 1890 [Bill 126]
1891	126[14]	resolution put forward 17 February 1891
1892	213[15]	(1) 9 March and (2) 16 June 1892 resolution put forward 4 March, questioned on 16 May
1897	44[16]	(1) 22 January 1897 preamble to Bill shortened
1898	71[17]	petitions in favour 21 April, 2 May, 5 May, 10 June 1898 petition against 7 June 1898
1900	39[18]	(1) 2 February and (2) 16 May 1900
1908	30[19]	(1) 3 February and (2) 29 May 1908

Table 1. Access to Mountains (Scotland) Bills 1884–1908
(Source: British Sessional Papers)

Scotland, "the need for the opportunity of enjoying nature and places where health may be regained by bracing air and exercise and where the jaded mind can rest in silence and in solitude". There was considerable anger in his speeches about private landowners and the rise of deer forests after 1840/50 in Scotland, and the subsequent exclusion of the people from the hills; "the scenery of our country has been filched away from us just when we have begun to desire it more than ever before", he argued in 1892. John Arnott has shown that Bryce was heavily influenced by what he had seen overseas in Switzerland and Italy, and in the concept of National Parks in the USA as a planned approach to the public recreational use of mountainous or uncultivated land. Indeed, there is a touch of John Muir in this passage from 1892, about a spiritual wilderness in Scotland.

> "The Creator speaks to his creatures through his works, and appointed the grandeur and the loveliness of the mountains and glens and the silence of the moorlands … to have their fitting influence on the thoughts of men, stirring their nature and touching their imagination, chasing away cares and the dull monotony of everyday life and opening up new and inexhaustible sources of enjoyment and delight.
>
> It is on behalf of these enjoyments and those who need them most and in the hope of preserving for the people one of the most precious parts of their national inheritance that I ask the House to agree to this Resolution."[20]

The Bill first passed to a second reading in April 1888. In 1892, in a Conservative Parliament, a statement was passed approving the general principle of the Bill, which passed to a second reading that year. When the Bill was eventually withdrawn on 16 June, Bryce argued that the government, "having taken heart of grace, and recognised the right of the people to enjoy their own scenery", failed to build on that momentum due to the insidious influence of "their friends the landlords and sporting tenants". The First Lord of the Treasury, A.J. Balfour retorted that the entire access issue had, "nothing to do with the rights of the public, who have no rights in this matter; it is a question of privileges to be granted".[21] In the debate over the Bill in 1900, Bryce spoke of his desire to welcome in a "spirit of compromise" (at the dawn of a new century) over the question of access to the countryside in Scotland, although he still described the situation thus: "a grievance exists in the exclusion of the public from large tracts of country containing the finest scenery". In this debate, the MP for West Renfrewshire, believed that there was no cause for such a Bill in Scotland, where only in truly exceptional circumstances were the public excluded from the Scottish hills – "I would not hesitate to say we have as great freedom in 999 cases out of 1,000 in Scotland as is enjoyed in any other part of the United Kingdom"– Scotland he believed had no cause for grievance.[22]

Criticism of the Bryce Bill was not confined to Parliament. In August 1891, J. Parker Smith MP for Partick (and a member of the SMC and SRoWS) penned an article strongly opposing the need for legislation in the access debate in Scotland, believing that the line taken by the Edinburgh-based Scottish Mountaineering Club, that of informed collaboration between groups of mountaineers and private landowners on the issue, should be retained as it had proved its worth. Parker Smith believed that the constant agitation by Bryce, with the support of the more radical Cairngorm Club, was destined to "set the heather on fire, cause an amount of irritation entirely disproportionate to any advantage to be derived from it". The fear was that landowners would be put on the defensive, and react by erecting walls and fences, closing inns and prohibiting their estate gamekeepers and shepherds from offering hospitality. Common sense, he felt, kept most climbers off the hills in the August grouse season. He did urge Parliament to act not on the access question *per se*, but on the need to protect and maintain rights of way in Scotland, which he saw as the "first consequence for the public enjoyment of the Highlands ... They open much of the finest scenery in Scotland, and would go far to satisfy the wants of the active-bodied tourist". He felt the Bill was purely for climbers, English tourists and pleasure-seekers, and that Bryce should be considering crofters, who need to traverse the hills "in pursuance of the needs of daily life", ahead of visitors. Parker Smith was also concerned that any Bill seeking access for scientists could also open up the hills to "scientific marauders" like oologists, plant collectors, poachers and smugglers. In his investigations, he also canvassed the thoughts of sportsmen (Prof. Veitch), and other climbers (Prof. G.G. Ramsay, then President of the SMC; SMC Treasurer Gilbert Thomson; Mr Munro of Lindertis). They all felt that legislation was uncalled for, indeed, would be objectionable and mischievous. [23] Such a prominent anti-legislation stance no doubt gave considerable succour to those opposing Bryce's Bills, and further reinforced the different political and cultural roots of the Cairngorm Club and the Scottish Mountaineering Club. Mountaineers in Scotland in the last two decades of the nineteenth century were not speaking with one voice. Indeed, a Bill against widespread open access was put forward in 1892 (first read 26 May) by Sir C.J. Pearson (The Lord Advocate) 'To Regulate the Access of the Public to Mountains in Scotland', which sought to allow only limited recreational use of the hills, whilst excluding visitors at all times from enclosed woods or plantations, from lands registered as deer forest during the stalking season (August 12 – October 15), and from certain designated types of agricultural land. It stood for everything that Bryce despised about landed interest in Scotland.[24] In 1907 Bryce was appointed British Ambassador in Washington, having previously held a junior Foreign Office post, been Chancellor of the Duchy of Lancaster in 1882, President of the Board of Trade in 1894, and Secretary for Ireland in 1905. He was created Viscount Bryce of Dechmont in 1914.

The Access to Mountains Bill, introduced in 1908 by Sir Charles Trevelyan owed much to Bryce's earlier Bills but applied to England and Wales, as well as to Scotland. This Bill went on to a second reading and had the support of Winston Churchill MP and hillwalker Ramsay MacDonald MP.[25] A separate Scottish Bill was also attempted in 1908.[26] In a long and wide-ranging debate in the House in May 1908, it was obvious that conservative landed interest, both in England and Scotland, would prevent the Bill from passing into law, despite a growing body of parliamentary support. The rights of the sporting tenant were keenly defended. J.F. Mason (MP for Windsor) spoke of the curse of walkers on the hills during the stalking season, as the glens were thus cleared of deer; he even asked if a clause could be included whereby "the tourist should become invisible and divest himself of this [tourist] odour". A Yorkshire MP spoke of the well known "failings of tourists", as they invaded the countryside, "forest burning, names cut in trees, plants taken up and destroyed, horns blowing and cornets playing". Lord Willoughby de Eresby (MP for Horncastle in Lincolnshire) expressed concern about the effect that unrestricted access might have on Highland golf courses, many of which had been built in the 1880s and 1890s on what could be identified as uncultivated land. He could not tolerate his legitimate recreational sport disturbed by "anybody who wished to make himself a nuisance sitting down with a sandwich on the eighteenth green and refusing to move. He could say he was sitting there for recreation." He went on to express his frustration that the champions of access legislation constantly referred to Switzerland as a role model for open access to the hills. He then made a quite remarkable statement that holds immense relevance to the future of Cairn Gorm in the twenty-first century, begging that Scotland, "would never be reduced to such a state as Switzerland, with funicular railways climbing up the mountains".[27] Remember, this prophetic statement was made in May 1908.

The perceived threat from legislation regarding access to estates in Scotland in the first decades of the twentieth century, brought an organised and co-ordinated response from Scottish landowners in the face of such a recreational challenge to their property rights. They had created a national organisation, the Scottish Land and Property Federation in 1906 (which became the Scottish Landowners' Federation in 1950), holding a preliminary meeting on 10 November in the Balmoral Hotel in Edinburgh, with the Earl of Dalkeith in the chair. The call was for an organisation that would promote united action on the part of "Landowners, their Tenants, and others interested in landed property and the welfare of agriculture", though the main stimulus to the foundation of the SLF was the general anti-landlord, pro-land tax, pro-death duty liberal government of the time. Lord Polwarth and Sir Kenneth Mackenzie anticipated a fierce battle ahead with those who would seek to disturb the rural *status quo*, urging; "That this meeting resolve to form a Central Association or Union for all Scotland for the Defence of Property in Land and the Promotion of Agricultural and other rural interests".[28] The impetus to create a national body had come from the creation of a regional organisation, the North East of Scotland Land Defence Association, which held its first meeting in Aberdeen in August 1906, and concerned itself in particular with the defence of Highland estates (including those in the Cairngorms area) against "unjust and injurious legislation" (a reference to the Access to Mountains Bills), and urged the "interchange of information and co-operation between landowners of the district". The Duke of Richmond and Gordon was elected President.[29] This north-east of Scotland body of landowners should be seen as a direct forerunner of the way that Strathspey and Deeside landowners came together during 1930 to offer concerted opposition to the earliest proposals to create a National Park in the Cairngorms [see Chapter 8]. However, the initial landowners' call to arms was not widely heeded and the archives record that in September 1919 there was grave concern that the Scottish Land and Property Federation (SLPF) would fold due to proprietor lack of interest and support, and low finances. The organisation was saved by a rallying cry from the Earl of Moray, after a crisis meeting.[30]

By 1924, it was clear that the SLPF were well enough organised to oppose stridently that year's Access to Mountains Bill for Scotland. The Duke of Atholl wrote to G. Erskine Jackson, Secretary of the SLPF, delighted that the conservative Scottish Mountaineering Club had once again come out against the need for access legislation, and that all sheep farmers in Scotland were also opposed to any such damaging legislation. He then launched into a vitriolic personal attack on the countryside writer and access campaigner, Ernest Baker:

> "It is a Club called the Rucksack in Birmingham, of which Dr. Baker is a shining light, that supports it … This Dr. Baker has written a lot of poisonous stuff on the subject and presumably will continue to do so, and I fancy literature on the subject at the next election will be prepared by him."[31]

Additional succour to the SLPF campaign of opposition, came from the Scottish Estate Factors' Society (SEFS), also based in Edinburgh, who wrote in August 1924 of the widespread damage to agricultural interests in Scotland, should recreational provision win the day in Parliament. The list included damage to dykes, fences and gates; disturbance of livestock; an increased risk of fire; the loss of grazing by the repeated tramping down of grass; a walkers' habit of not closing gates would lead to stock straying and spreading disease; as a consequence there "would be a reduction in value of land and consequently of rents, and diminution of stock and of employment".[32] Two years later, in the face of another Access to Mountains Bill in 1926/27, the SLPF produced a document entitled 'Arguments against the Bill' which they circulated amongst members and other allied organisations. They fell prey to the trespass myth, boldly stating, "There is no law of trespass in Scotland. People can go where they choose … There is no necessity for such Bill". The SLPF, in its wisdom, felt that the tourist in Scotland had few expectations or demands: "Tourists seldom want to go off the high road except for a picnic up a burn near the road". The document reiterated many of the points made by the SEFS in 1924, fearful of a decline in sporting rentals in the Highlands from the deleterious effects of any increased recreational pressure on mountain or moorland. It was felt that some visitors to the Highlands were just not responsible enough to be there; "such persons may damage fences and leave gates open". The word 'recreation' was felt to be too vague a term, as concern was expressed that 'unworthy' tourists and visitors might bring "football, cricket, anything" to the glens.[33] It is fascinating that the Scottish Branch of the RSPB took a similar line in May 1926, when their Honorary Secretary, John Crosthwaite, corresponded with James Hunter Blair of Ayr. Crosthwaite stressed that a love of nature and beautiful scenery was often sadly, "accompanied by other ill regulated desires and still more objectionable unregulated action". There was a danger in presenting legislation that would offer greater recreational freedom in the Highlands of Scotland, not just to "rarer nesting Scottish birds", but also "bearing in mind the inherent destructiveness of undisciplined man". Crosthwaite did believe that all people should have access to "the treasures of nature", but that such access had to be strictly regulated.[34] Once again then, we have a call for access to be granted to those who were considered morally and professionally 'fit' enough to be on mountain and moorland, which still in the mid-1920s meant scientists and responsible and respectable mountaineers. Others, had no cause to be there.

The SLPF was urged to act over calls for existing estate roads and paths to be opened up for wider recreational use. T.M. Murray, while admitting that such things were created "to help lazy people get about", urged all landowners to take a strong stance against the public being allowed to make use of any private routes across estates: "There should be no right granted to the public to use such private roads and paths which take some keeping", he explained.[35] All these canvassed opinions from landowners and other organisations and bodies allied against the Access to Mountains Bills in the 1920s, bolstered the stance that the SLPF took in Scotland as a whole and in a region such as the Cairngorms. On the parliamentary front, certain MPs known to be friendly to the landlords' cause were targeted to receive SLPF propaganda, in particular George Balfour, who was seen as a willing crusader "in preventing contentious bills from slipping through".[36]

Access to Mountains Bills were attempted in 1924, 1927, 1930 and 1938. An Access to Mountains Act was finally passed in 1939, but it was "emasculated by the landowning interests" during its passage through the House of Lords, so that few champions of the cause of unrestricted access to the hills celebrated its arrival on the statute book.[37] It is now widely accepted that the real culmination of the campaign for access started by James Bryce and the Cairngorm Club in the 1880s, both in the hills and at Westminster, was the passing into law of the National Parks and Access to the Countryside Act of 1949, although the distinctive Scottish origins of the campaign were subsumed and then lost within a wider British campaigning lobby in the middle of the twentieth century. One angle of this campaign that has not yet been investigated, and would be very hard to prove, is that the right of access to mountains might be a nineteenth-century invention of tradition. Could Bryce have elaborated on the uncertainties and ambiguity of the right to roam tradition, in order to present a situation in the 1880s that appeared to be more cut and dried than was the reality?

On 8 June 1897, James Bryce delivered a fascinating speech to the Cairngorm Club in Aberdeen. In this address entitled 'The Preservation of Natural Scenery', which was subsequently published verbatim in the *CC Journal* of July 1897, Bryce sought to identify the "worth of natural scenery and what steps can be taken to preserve it", and revealed the visionary nature of his own thinking on the role of mankind within the natural world. Much of what he said that summer evening in 1897, albeit to a home audience not far from his beloved Cairngorms, holds a degree of late twentieth century environmental thought over 75 years ahead of its time. He identified three enemies to our scenic appreciation of the Highlands namely, advertisers, commercial companies and the railways; he also spoke of the need for regulation in countryside planning lest "scenery was injured by the putting up of buildings in unsuitable sites and places". Bryce sought the creation of a Department of State that could protect "buildings and sites of great historical interest, ancient buildings of exceptional beauty and architectural interest, and striking and remarkable pieces of natural scenery", which to the modern ear would be akin to calling for the creation of an all-encompassing agency blending Scottish Natural Heritage, with Historic Scotland and the National Trust for Scotland. Indeed, the text of Bryce's address rather reads like a proposal for the creation of National Scenic Areas (NSA) rather than a call for National Parks in Scotland, although he does talk of his access campaign seeking provisions for all people to enjoy Scotland's scenery, and of his battles to prevent "the destruction of unique and wonderfully beautiful pieces of scenery ... There ought to be some means of preserving for the nation as a whole a thing in which the nation as a whole had an interest, and which was part of the inheritance the nation had received and wished to hand on". There was much in the speech about generative influences, with Bryce even urging the CC members to be aware that they were just trustees of this "priceless source of the purest pleasures";[38] there was loud applause after this remark, as the climbers and mountaineers of Aberdeen warmly accepted their role as 'searchers after the beautiful'. Even the rival SMC, just a year later, seemed to have warmed to Bryce's message about mountaineers being aesthetes.[39]

James Bryce conducted his parliamentary and extra-parliamentary campaigns for the public recreational access to the mountains and moorlands of Scotland, at a time when the power of the private landowners in the Highlands, and the attached concept of exclusivity via sporting interests and deer forests, was at its greatest. The expansion of the deer forest as a geographical and financial landuse unit was particularly evident in the eastern Highlands, in an area such as the Cairngorms, during the last decades of the nineteenth century. Prior to 1750, some high and poor ground had long been called 'deer forest' in places such as Mar, Atholl and Invercauld where the deer were hunted in deer drives.[40] It would be during the second half of the nineteenth century that so many estates in the Highlands converted to deer forest, especially after the mid-1870s when the value of wool fell, and the mid-1880s when the value of sheep declined. A Departmental Committee reported the following growth figures for land used as deer forest in Scotland by 1922:

Year	Total Acreage
1883	1,975,209
1892	2,472,133
1906	3,327,086
1912	3,584,966
1920	3,432,385

Table 2: Land used as Deer Forest in Scotland 1883–1920
(Source: *Lands in Scotland Used as Deer Forests*, Cmd. 1636)[41]

It did not become customary to let Highland shootings to sporting tenants until the 1860s and 1870s, but this form of recreational sporting income remained a mainstay of many estates past 1912 when the deer forest area reached its zenith, and into the modern era.[42] It is interesting that the Departmental Committee of 1919 thought it wise to tackle the issue of widespread recreational activity on land used as deer forest, although James Bryce would have gained no heart from their belief that "the value of certain forests adjacent to tourist centres is considerably depreciated by the frequency of disturbance during the stalking season". There was a whiff of the SMC in their conclusion, that in general good relations existed between estate owners and tourists and climbers, and that those visitors who take "the trouble to ask for leave are usually given every facility, and often, when necessary, offered accommodation".[43] This was conciliatory to landed interest, to the extreme. Indeed in May 1901, the SMC allowed the landowner Duncan Darroch of Torridon to express warm sentiments towards scientific visitors on Highland estates (although he did concede that "deer disliked the odour of a scientist") in an *SMC Journal* article that reeked of those good relations the Edinburgh mountaineering élite sought to maintain with west Highland landowners.[44] It was all very different in the eastern Highlands, especially when the Cairngorm Club was involved.

From around 1990, both the CCS and later SNH have sought to provide some clarification on the law, practice and procedure of the public's access to the countryside and rights of way in Scotland. A practical guide was produced, but concluded that the only definitive statements on the law would come from the courtroom. Despite the campaigning vigour of James Bryce, the Cairngorm Club and the Scottish Rights of Way Society from the 1880s onwards, even now "public rights of way are viewed somewhat negatively as an interference with the primary rights of landowners, rather than positively as rights which members of the public are entitled to exercise and enjoy ..." A day's stalking can, indeed, be wrecked by walkers at the wrong point, and cattle can be lost, and sheep worried as a result of recreational activity. It remains an extremely controversial and confusing issue for both landowners and recreationalists.[45]

Notes to Chapter 3

1   John Sheail, *Nature in Trust – The History of Nature Conservation in Britain* (Blackie and Son Ltd., London, 1976), pp. 69, 87–88; David Evans, *A History of Nature Conservation in Britain* (Routledge, London, 1997), p. 39; Harvey Taylor, *A Claim on the Countryside – A History of the British Outdoor Movement* (Keele University Press, Edinburgh, 1997), pp. 126–148.

2   Ernest A. Baker, *The Highlands With Rope and Rucksack* (H.F. and G. Witherby, London, 1923), Frontispiece.

3   Taylor, *op. cit.*, p. 148.

4   Hansard Parliamentary Debates (HPD), HPD, Vol. 285, III Series, 1884, col. 187.

5   *National Parks and Access to the Countryside* (HMSO, London, n.d., c.1950).

6   British Sessional Papers (BSP), BSP – House of Commons Bills – Public, 1884, Vol. I, pp. 1–2, Bill 122.

7   BSP and HPD, 1884, *Ibid.*

8   BSP, 1884–1885, Vol. I, pp. 1–2. HPD, Vol. 293, III Series, 1884, col. 514.

9   BSP, 1886, Vol. I, pp. 1–2. HPD, Vol. 302, III Series, 1886, col. 405.

10 BSP, 1887, Vol. I, pp. 1–2. HPD, Vol. 310, III Series, 1887, col. 234.

11 BSP, 1888, Vol. I, pp. 1–2. HPD, Vol. 322, III Series, 1888, col. 364; Vol. 324, 1888, col. 1463.

12 BSP, 1889, Vol. I, pp. 1–2. HPD, Vol. 333, III Series, 1889, col. 368.

13 BSP, 1890, Vol. I, pp. 1–2. HPD, Vol. 341, III Series, 1890, col. 168; Vol. 349, 1890/1, col. 156.

14 BSP, 1890–1891, Vol. I, pp. 1–2. HPD, Vol. 350, III Series, 1891, col. 846.

15 BSP, 1892, Vol. I, pp. 1–2. HPD, Vol. 2, IV Series, 1892, col. 442; Vol. 5, 1892, cols. 1382–1383.

16 BSP, 1897, Vol. I, pp. 1–2. HPD, Vol. 45, IV Series, 1897, col. 299.

17 BSP, 1898, Vol. I, pp. 1–2. HPD, Vol. LVI, IV Series, 1898, col. 621; Vol. LVII, 1898, cols. 8b, 352a; Vol. LVIII, 1898, cols. 847, 1290.

18 BSP, 1900, Vol. I, pp. 1–2. HPD, IV Series, Vol. LXXVIII, 1900, col. 420; Vol. LXXXIII, 1900, cols. 375–376.

19 BSP, 1908, Vol. I, pp. 29–30. HPD, Vol. 183, IV Series, 1908, col. 546; Vol. 189, 1908, col. 1439.

20 John M.S. Arnott, 'James Bryce 1838–1922', Internal SNH memo, n.d., c. mid-1990s, Ref: SERB/95/2/10.

21 HPD, Vol. 5, IV Series, 1892, cols. 215, 1002–1003.

22 HPD, Vol. LXXXIII, IV Series, 1900, cols. 375–376.

23 J. Parker Smith, 'Access to Mountains', *Blackwood's Edinburgh Magazine*, Vol. CL, No. DCCCCX, August 1891, pp. 259–272.

24 BSP, 1892, Vol. I, pp. 5–6, as Bill 379. First read 26 May 1892.

25 BSP, 1908, Vol. I, pp. 25–26, 'Access to Mountains Bill', Bill 21. First read 3 February 1908, second reading 15 May 1908, report from Standing Committee 13 July 1908.

26 BSP, 1908, Vol. I, pp. 29–30, 'Access to Mountains (Scotland) Bill', Bill 30. First read 3 February 1908, second reading 29 May 1908; HPD, Vol. 189, Fourth Series, 1908, col. 1439.

27 HPD, Vol. 188, Fourth Series, 1908, cols. 1439–1524.

28 The archive of the Scottish Landowners' Federation is held in West Register House, Scottish Record Office, Edinburgh, at GD 325. SRO: GD 325-1/370, Report of the First Meeting of the Scottish Land and Property Federation, 10 December 1906. The minimum subscription per annum was £1. 1s. The following appointments were made:

Duke of Buccleuch	–	President
Marquis of Tullibardine	–	President
Sir Ralph Anstruther	–	Vice President
The Mackintosh	–	Vice President
Colonel Robert Dundas	–	Honorary Secretary.

29 SRO: GD 325-1/252. Newspaper cutting from *Aberdeen Daily Journal* from 25 August 1906, to report on the formation of an association to be called the Aberdeen, Banff and Kincardine Land Defence Association.

30 SRO: GD 325-1/212. Minutes of meeting of Scottish Land and Property Federation, dated 17 September 1919.

31 SRO: GD 325-1/198. Letter from Duke of Atholl to G. Erskine Jackson, Secretary, Scottish Land and Property Federation, dated 1 July 1924.

32 SRO: GD 325-1/198. Letter from Robert Galloway, Scottish Estate Factors' Society, Edinburgh, to G. Erskine Jackson, Scottish Land and Property Federation, Edinburgh, dated 5 August 1924.

33 SRO: GD 325-1/201. Access to Mountains Bill – Arguments Against the Bill, n.d., c.1926.

34 SRO: GD 325-1/201. Letter from John Crosthwaite, Honorary Secretary, RSPB Scottish Branch, Glasgow, to James Hunter Blair, Ayr, dated 18 May 1926.

35 SRO: GD 325-1/201. Letter from T.M. Murray, Albyn Place, Edinburgh, to G. Erskine Jackson, Scottsh Land and Property Federation, Edinburgh, dated 19 May 1926.

36 SRO: GD 325-1/201. Letter from Francis Marchant, Secretary, Freeholders Society, London, to G. Erskine Jackson, Scottish Land and Property Federation, Edinburgh, dated 24 April 1926.

37 Donald Mackay, *Scotland's Rural Land Use Agencies* (Scottish Cultural Press, Aberdeen, 1995), p. 143.

38 James Bryce, 'The Preservation of Natural Scenery – An Address', *Cairngorm Club Journal*, Vol. II, No. 9, July 1897, pp. 125–139.

39 See especially, W. Inglis Clark, 'The Mountaineer as a Searcher after the Beautiful', *Scottish Mountaineering Club Journal*, Vol. V, No. 26, May 1898, pp. 121–125; Euan B. Robertson, 'Mountains and Art', *Scottish Mountaineering Club Journal*, Vol. XIII, No. 77, June 1915, pp. 259–267; H. Welsh, 'Beauty in High Places', *The Deeside Field*, Second Series, No. 6, 1970, pp. 73–77; John Haldane, 'Admiring the High Mountains: The Aesthetics of Environment', *Environmental Values*, Vol. 3, No. 2, Summer 1994, pp. 97–106; Ronald Macdonald Douglas, *The Scots Book* (E.P. Dutton and Co., New York, 1935), pp. 336–337 for section 'The Cairngorms'.

40 A.D. Chessell, 'The Great Estates in the Cairngorm and Grampian Mountains', *Cairngorm Club Journal*, Vol. 19, No. 98, 1980, pp. 28–31; Adam Watson and Elizabeth Allan, 'Depopulation by Clearances and Non-enforced Emigration in the North East Highlands', *Northern Scotland*, Vol. 10, 1990, pp. 31–46; Adam Watson and Elizabeth Allan, 'Papers Relating to Game Poaching on Deeside 1766–1832', *Northern Scotland*, Vol. 7, No. 1, 1986, pp. 39–45.

41 *Report of the Departmental Committee To Enquire and Report with regard to Lands in Scotland Used as Deer Forests*, Cmd. 1636 (HMSO, Edinburgh, 1922), p. 1. The Committee, chaired by Sir John Stirling Maxwell, was appointed in November 1919. Willie Orr, 'The Economic Impact of Deer Forests in the Scottish Highlands', *Scottish Economic and Social History*, Vol. 2, 1982, pp. 44-59.

42 John Lumsden, 'Deerstalking Experiences of an Urban Sportsman', *The Deeside Field*, No. 3, 1927, pp. 5–9; David Hudson, *Highland Deer Stalking* (The Crowood Press, Marlborough, 1989); Sir Hugh Fraser, *Amid the High Hills* (A. and C. Black, London, 1923); Charles St. John, *Short Sketches of the Wild Sports and Natural History of the Highlands* (Ashford Press Publ., Southampton, 1986). First published in 1893; Duff Hart-Davis, *Monarchs of the Glen – A History of Deer Stalking in the Scottish Highlands* (Jonathan Cape, London, 1978); Lea MacNally, *Highland Deer Forest* (Pan Books, London, 1973).

43 *Lands in Scotland Used as Deer Forest*, Cmd. 1636, *op. cit.*, p. 28.

44 Duncan Darroch of Torridon, 'Deer and Deer Forests' *Scottish Mountaineering Club Journal*, Vol. VI, No. 35, May 1901, pp. 139–145.

45 Jeremy Rowan-Robinson, W.M. Gordon, Colin T. Reid, *Public Access to the Countryside – A Guide to the Law, Practice and Procedure in Scotland* (SNH/COSLA, Battleby, n.d., c.1992).

4

The Osprey on Speyside:
An Environmental History

The Nineteenth Century

The most public success story in the history of nature conservation in the Cairngorms has been the return of the osprey *Pandion haliaetus* to breed in Strathspey during the 1950s. Prior to that decade the last known breeding attempt in Britain had occurred at Loch Loyne in 1916,[1] although the osprey was already a rare breeding bird by the last three decades of the nineteenth century. The osprey stands now as a symbol of the benefit of organised nature conservation (in this instance by the RSPB at Loch Garten) and what Jim Crumley has described as the "miracle of forgiving ornithological regeneration in the Highlands ... an unprecedented public relations exercise on behalf of birds".[2] This is an historical story though, that can be traced back to the nineteenth century, most probably to the 1870s, and represents a notable change in human attitudes to the natural world. Central to the development of our admiration for the osprey was Rothiemurchus Estate and the Grants of Rothiemurchus, for it was here at Loch an Eilein castle that the first recreational and aesthetic observations of ospreys were recorded by a diverse range of visitors. When the tenor of the nineteenth century was the ruthless persecution of birds of prey across Scotland, Rothiemurchus is a rare example from that century of the site of a nesting bird of prey being admired and preserved, and represents the very beginning of human attempts to protect the osprey.

Roy Dennis has traced historical references to the osprey in Badenoch and Strathspey back to 1804;[3] in her celebrated memoirs, Elizabeth Grant of Rothiemurchus ('the Highland Lady') wrote of the birds' residency on the estate in 1808 although she called them 'eagles', perhaps as a shortened version of 'fish eagle':

> "Often the birds rose majestically as we were watching their eyrie, and wheeled skimming over the lake in search of food required by the young eaglets, who could be seen peeping over the pile of sticks that formed their home."[4]

Unfortunately, Elizabeth left the estate for India and then married life in Ireland, before the decades that saw the most extended persecution of the Loch an Eilein osprey nest (primarily the 1840s and 1850s), for it would be valuable to have her observations of such pilfering, and the men who carried it out. In the second half of the nineteenth century, the Victorian tourist saw Loch an Eilein as the most attractive and interesting part of Rothiemurchus, and this was in part due to the osprey nest on the ruins of the castle in the loch. The presence of the birds and their fishing expeditions in the loch, seemed to add an ornithological charm to the whole vista. There was, however, nothing unusual about the castle nest site at Loch an Eilein as ospreys also nested in the nineteenth century on Ardvreck Castle on Loch Assynt, at Kilchurn Castle on Loch Awe, on a ruined building on an island in Loch Lomond and on an old shooting lodge at Loch Morlich.[5] What was different, though, at Loch an Eilein was that the nest was easily observed from the lochside. It became so well known to visitors that its history was compiled by C.G. Cash and later published in popular natural history and hill-walking journals with a wide readership.[6]

Around 1880 the laird of Rothiemurchus decreed that visitors were not allowed to use a boat on Loch an Eilein, in case they forced the ospreys to desert the nest on the castle. Much of the damage done to the species in Scotland by egg collectors had been perpetrated in the 1840s and 1850s by visitors to the estate who came under the cover of darkness to raid the nest. The concentrated and successful persecution of this individual nest makes for sinister reading. Sometime before 1843 and his departure for southern Africa, Roualeyn Gordon-Cumming robbed the nest. Lewis Dunbar visited the estate in 1848 and took three eggs from the nest; in 1849 he took another three eggs which he sent to Charles St. John in Sutherland, and also spent some hours skulking around Loch Gamhna looking for another nest to rob. Dunbar returned in 1850 to take a further three eggs which he sent to John Hancock in Newcastle. In 1851, in a celebrated and often-quoted raid, Dunbar walked through the night to Loch an Eilein, and at 3 a.m. on the 3 May, swam across to the castle, stole two eggs, swam back to the shore holding an egg in each hand; he blew the eggs in the boat-house and washed the insides out with whisky, later sending the eggs to John Wolley for his collection. In 1852, he took a further three eggs.[7] This annual raiding of the nest, often to supply English-based egg collectors who would pay good money to obtain the eggs of a scarce breeding bird, would have continued unabated had Dunbar not emigrated to Australia in 1853, thus allowing the ospreys a chance to recover at this site.

Successive lairds of Rothiemurchus did seek various ways to protect the ospreys at Loch an Eilein in the second half of the nineteenth century, a nascent nature preservation practice no doubt stimulated by their own emotional attachment to the estate, their 'beloved duchus' as Elizabeth Grant had called it. In April of 1893, the Zoological Society of London awarded silver medals designed by Edwin Landseer, to both Donald Cameron of Lochiel and John Peter Grant of Rothiemurchus, "in recognition of the efforts made to protect the ospreys in their respective districts".[8] Successful breeding though was only sporadically achieved. By 1908, the nest on the island in Loch Arkaig had police protection and barbed wire defences; this stands as a direct forerunner to the heavy security employed by the RSPB at Loch Garten from 1959 onwards, in the battle against malicious vandals or egg collectors. In a fascinating study of the psychology and ethics of egg collecting, the Cheshire ornithologist Thomas Alfred Coward, writing in 1926, noted that all common birds had to endure the attentions of the egg collector, although he did warn that egg collecting by young boys might seem trivial enough, "but it may be the first step towards degradation, a carelessness which may degenerate into deliberate, ruthless cruelty". His tolerance of oology had a resonance and justification that harks back to the mid-nineteenth century. He believed that sympathetic people who opposed egg collecting were mistakenly acting out of "aesthetic impulses". However, they should be fuelled with anger because the oologist, "the miserly accumulator", was robbing Britain of a precious inheritance. It is interesting to note that Coward believed this to be a battle that the birds should fight un-aided against the egg collector, although he did concede that oological science now had enough eggs in private and public collections to facilitate continued scientific study. He observed that, "the white-tailed eagle and the osprey have given up the contest, and gone under". In the final analysis, Coward believed that to take an egg from a bird such as an osprey was in effect to take a life, although in moral terms it could be reasoned that the pain or disappointment of the parent birds "lasts for less than an hour".[9] Of course, a number of Britain's most eminent post WWII professional and amateur ornithologists came to the study of birds from the pastimes of egg collecting or wildfowling in the first half of the century.

T.A. Coward later wrote more about the osprey and its status in Britain; "whether it may still be classed as a resident in Britain is an annual question, for one after another its historical eyries have been deserted". Writing in 1930, Coward showed considerable pessimism regarding the return of the osprey to breed in Britain, or the projected success of any measures employed to preserve the birds. The lessons of history could not be ignored, he believed: after all, "careful efforts to preserve the few remaining sites in the Scottish Highlands have usually ended in failure". He also sought to identify the most impor-tant reasons for the osprey's extinction as a breeding bird in Britain; blind game-preservation; the greed of collectors; human objection to avian rivals on trout and salmon streams; the insane habit of shooting any unfamiliar bird. These capture not only how birds of prey were seen in the nineteenth century and early twentieth century, but also continue to have topical resonance in the modern debate between estate owners and nature conservationists over the role of birds of prey in upland ecosystems.[10]

Written visitor observations of the Loch an Eilein ospreys became common after 1870, and the tone of these notes and letters reflects the rising tide of interest within educated society for making careful observations of all facets of British flora and fauna. By the 1880s the laird of Rothiemurchus could boast that his ospreys added to the attractiveness of the vista, which is certainly now the case at the RSPB reserve in Boat of Garten. This is surely a unique example of a link between nature preservation and recreation that runs across two different centuries, with a gap of fifty-five years from 1899 to 1954 when the species was extinct as a breeder in Badenoch and Strathspey.

William Jolly (HM Inspector of Schools) visited Loch an Eilein in 1879 and 1880 and was much taken with Rothiemurchus Estate and the ospreys:

> "And it certainly was a romantic and impressive scene not easily forgotten, to be seated there by the shores of one of the most alpine and solitary of lakes, amidst the venerable remains of the Caledonian forest of yore … Go to Rothiemurchus if you want to feel the dignity and power of what vegetable life may become, even under our northern skies."[11]

Jolly had hoped to be fortunate enough to see the osprey "stoop to catch a fish", but missed out on this, and so turned his pen to lambasting those who would shoot such birds or steal the eggs for a collection:

> "Nothing too severe can be said in reprobation of such wanton slaughter of the wilder inhabitants of our hills and moors, and especially of the insensate and heartless destruction of our rarer animals … the arm of the law should be invoked to declare it criminal so to indulge their savage propensities in thoughtless itch for notoriety, or for the possession of a rarity."[12]

William Jolly had a great deal to say about the state of the trees in the surrounding woods, but sought also to identify irresponsible sporting visitors to the estate (in this case Lord Stamford who mistakenly killed an osprey at Loch an Eilein in 1872) and egg collectors who continually put the future of the nest in jeopardy. Lord Stamford, it was said, was consumed with guilt, and was haunted by his foolhardy actions for many years to come. He was pilloried thus: "when a noble Lord, it seems, inspired by the noble British tendency 'to kill something', amidst even the grandest scenes of nature, shot one of the birds".[13]

Although Jolly's 1879 article is in praise of the osprey, a week after its publication in *The Scotsman*, an irate letter from an early nature preservationist living in Edinburgh, drew attention to Jolly's own foolhardiness in broadcasting his observations and ornithological memories in the national press.

"Sir, I write to remonstrate with the author of the communication for giving the name of the locality of the breeding-place of any rare bird. The writer seems interested in the preservation of the osprey, a bird equally innocent and interesting, yet he has taken the surest means for its destruction by publishing to the world the definite information he has given." [14]

The anonymous correspondent, signing only an 'S', felt that the protection of these birds should be the responsibility of the estate owners, a commitment which rang true with the Grants of Rothiemurchus, if no other landowners in Scotland.

"The eyrie of an eagle or an osprey should now be regarded by the owners of estates as one of the heirlooms they have to be proud of." [15]

C.G. Cash was another visitor who remained suspicious of sporting visitors, and being "a man of wide good-will" and yet "of a few close intimacies, at his best on the heather or the ptarmigan ground above it", [16] found in the ospreys at Loch an Eilein a sense of the spirit and serenity of the natural world in the face of such human indifference to the suffering of wild creatures. He was aware too of why the ospreys were so popular with visitors, and these words penned in 1903 still have some relevance to the holidaymaker who joins the thousands of visitors who flock to the Loch Garten Osprey Centre every summer.

"There is, perhaps, no other of our raptores at once so interesting and so easy to observe. The dark, stern golden eagle will not brook observation, but sails off indignant on majestic wing; the smaller falcons and hawks dart in arrowy flight from the presence of man. But the Osprey allows of moderately near approach, and permits itself to be inspected as it stands or sits on its nest, or as it soars in wide curves above the loch." [17]

Cash made observations of the Rothiemurchus ospreys from 1894 to 1903, believing the birds "add such a charm to that most beautiful of Highland beauty-spots, Loch an Eilein". [18] He was present at the loch in the summer of 1895 when O.A.J. Lee took some of the first photographs of ospreys in Britain there. In April 1900 Cash wrote to the laird of Rothiemurchus from his home in Edinburgh, explaining his concern for the safety of an osprey nest he had observed at Loch Gamhna, and urging the laird and his estate staff to keep a careful watch over the site. The letter is evidence of the pro-active protectionist stance taken by the landowner at Rothiemurchus and by visitors to the estate, as it is also evidence of the threat posed by egg collectors at the very dawn of the twentieth century. Cash's concern is clearly explained to the laird:

"The tree is easily approached, and would be quite easily climbed and I think it well to let you know of this, that the birds may be protected if possible. I at once went to keeper Cox and told him, but I have told no one else at Rothiemurchus following on that my own feeling of what was best and Cox's advice. But I fear the new nest is too obvious and too easily accessible to remain unmolested."

The nest at Loch Gamhna was "in a fir tree that overhangs the fence between the low ground shootings and the 'forest' ... and when I approached, both birds flew over with loud cries".[19] Cash, though, was probably already aware that the new laird of Rothiemurchus, who had taken over the running of the estate in 1893 and had accepted his late father's Zoological Society silver medal, thus directly inheriting the Grant family's traditional commitment to protecting these ospreys, had put in place his own 'osprey-watch' scheme involving the estate gamekeepers. Throughout the summer of 1898, the keeper F.R. Cox who resided at the Doune Cottage was in regular correspondence with his employer on the subject of ospreys. Cox wrote with bad news in May:

> "I am sorry to have to report that on Saturday 7 May a third osprey arrived at Lock en Elan and fought near all day ... two have left and only one remains at present."[20]

Cox was obviously urged by the laird to continue with his observations of the ospreys, and to make an assessment of the damage done to the established breeding pair by the aggressive behaviour of the intruding osprey. In early July, Cox checked his notes, noting that "Ospreys arrived as usual on 9th of April. On 7th May the third one arrived ... one remained on the 2nd of June – one came back and as I thought, commenced to rebuild the nest – but he only stayed five days". These precisely dated recordings reveal that this was a sincere and structured attempt by the laird and his staff to make detailed observations of osprey behaviour and to look after the species as a breeding bird at Rothiemurchus. Later on in the same letter Cox offered a bleak outlook for the 1898 breeding season at the loch:

> "Since that there has only been one seen in the neighbourhood but, he never stayed on the castle, but in the trees at the back of the Lock. It is fully a fortnight now since I have seen him, so I fear he must have left altogether."[21]

Some excitement came in the second half of July when Cox was fishing at Loch Gamhna and saw two ospreys "hovering over the lock and about the trees for over an hour". "They seemed to be quite at home, so that I think they must be living somewhere near", he confided to the laird. Word was immediately sent over to A. McBain the keeper at South Kinrara to keep a look out for these birds,[22] should they stray onto neighbouring estates.

It is obvious from letters to the laird of Rothiemurchus in the late 1890s that there were some people, both residents of Strathspey and English visitors to the estate, who were becoming increasingly concerned over that decade as each summer went by about the low numbers of ospreys returning to breed in the region. As concern developed for the welfare of each individual bird, some anti-English sentiment arose over reports that ospreys were being shot in English counties on their migration route north to the Cairngorms. The first hint of this came in April 1897 when E. Baddeley wrote to the laird of Rothiemurchus from Higher Broughton in Manchester, concerned that an osprey recently shot in Lancashire might have been a Rothiemurchus bird. Baddeley was "greatly relieved to hear that both the Ospreys have returned to Rothiemurchus", and went on to explain that a local Manchester-based Natural History Society had asked "to find out for themselves that we have not after all murdered one of your ospreys in Lancashire. The bird killed here may be from one of the very few other nests in Scotland". This is an important letter because it reflects a growing concern outside of the Scottish Highlands for the welfare of ospreys migrating across Britain, and in a sense it is a barometer of changing public opinion towards the preservation of birds. It is also ample evidence that tourists and holidaymakers who saw ospreys at Rothiemurchus in the 1880s and 1890s carried that memory with them for many years, and were prepared to condemn those that wished to harm birds that had given them so much pleasure. Baddeley continued thus:

> "it is extremely probable that the young birds killed last year in Lincolnshire and Sussex and elsewhere, were from your and other nests, and would if unmolested, return to breed in Scotland. Although these matters move very slowly, I have no doubt that we shall before long get protection during the whole year for the osprey and several other species in Lancashire and other counties."

Baddeley now believed that "public opinion is moving in this direction".[23] However, it would be the 1960s before the British public started to obtain real pleasure from watching ospreys.

A letter from July 1898 from W.G. Stewart Menzies at Aikenway, Craigellachie to the laird of Rothiemurchus similarly exposed the problems facing migrating ospreys both in England and Scotland.

> "My dear Grant – many thanks for your sad letter about the Osprey. There was a hen coming north full of eggs, but she met a brute in Yorkshire who shot her. If another was shot in Perthshire it must be the other hen."

Menzies then recounts just how easy it would be to shoot an osprey on his land; a statement which the laird of Rothiemurchus surely would have preferred not to have known.

> "I could have shot mine $^1/_2$ a dozen times but he luckily kept on our ground and never went off it, as far as I saw, except when he came and departed."

The letter shows that there was some communication between neighbouring landowners and sporting tenants over the osprey issue, and Grant of Rothiemurchus learned of the fate of his male bird from Loch an Eilein in this way.

F.R. Cox was also blamed for not shooting the rogue osprey that disturbed the breeding pair in the summer of 1898:

> "He was here twice and looked ragged and unhappy and I expect he was your cock bird right through. What a pity your keeper didn't shoot one of the cocks, when they were fighting. I should like to hear anything more about the bird." [24]

The 1899 breeding season was partially disrupted by the arrival of a third bird at Loch an Eilein, and a forest fire at Rothiemurchus. Ospreys were seen at Rothiemurchus in 1902 although no breeding was recorded at the Loch an Eilein castle site after 1899. Writing in 1903, C.G. Cash predicted that the osprey would return as a breeding bird to Rothiemurchus and the traditional Loch an Eilein nest-site, and that they then should "be protected even more carefully than in the past" and "that a systematic record should be kept of such points as dates of arrival, of hatching, and of departure. This could probably be done by arrangement between the keeper and the tenant of the Loch Cottage". [25] The RSPB at the Loch Garten Osprey Centre, with the help of energetic volunteer staff, have been following Cash's proposed scheme almost exactly.

Re-Colonisation by the Osprey

There were recorded sightings of ospreys in Badenoch and Strathspey during the 1930s and 1940s; these observations were becoming more frequent by the earliest years of the 1950s, and there was considerable hope amongst the region's naturalists that the osprey would return to breed. Seton Gordon, in 1925, noted that gamekeepers and stalkers were also seeing single ospreys migrating through Deeside glens. [26] In 1954, a pair of ospreys nested near Loch Garten and reared two young; the species had now returned to breed in the Cairngorms. Sporadic nesting attempts were made by a single pair of ospreys from 1955 to 1958, all in the Loch Garten area, although 'frustration' eyries were built elsewhere in Rothiemurchus and at Loch Morlich. RSPB staff based in Scotland were now aware that the osprey was trying to re-establish itself on Speyside, and so in the summer of 1958 a team of volunteers, members of the society and staff of the Nature Conservancy manned an observation post on the southern side of Loch Garten, principally in an effort to protect the nest from egg collectors. The nest was robbed in a now famous night raid in early June 1958, but the decision by the RSPB to publicise this disaster, was to have a dramatic impact on the protection and viewing of ospreys in Scotland. Under the direction of George Waterston (he retired in 1972), the RSPB in Scotland were determined that the osprey would not be harried by egg collectors in the second half of the twentieth century, as it had been in the Victorian era. To this end, the RSPB negotiated with the landowner at Loch Garten (the Countess of Seafield) and, with her collaboration, saw the Secretary of State for Scotland make an Order under Section III of the Protection of Birds Act (1954), which declared an area of 667 acres surrounding the eyrie tree a statutory bird sanctuary. This order was made in 1959, and made it an offence for any person to enter this designated sanctuary between 1 April and 31 July each year, without the prior permission of the RSPB staff.[27] Only part of what we now know as 'Operation Osprey' was born from this collaboration between government, a nature conservation charity and a landowner. In 1959, a bold decision was taken by George Waterston to allow visitors controlled access to the site under the strict guidance of RSPB staff. Roy Dennis saw this particular intervention as "a brave and, in retrospect, very far-sighted decision to open the observation post to allow the general public to see the ospreys and their young".[28] In the remaining six weeks of the 1959 breeding season around 14,000 visitors came to Loch Garten to see the ospreys. Lord Hurcomb reported visitor numbers to the NC Scottish Committee in July 1959, and all agreed that although expensive, the protection of ospreys to enable them to re-colonise Scotland was well worth while.[29]

Much of this interest from visitors stems from the popularity and impact of radio, as earlier in 1959 Bob Wade of BBC Radio had broadcast sounds of ospreys from the nest to the whole nation. Indeed, the clever use of television and radio by the RSPB at Loch Garten to further the cause of nature conservation has been one of the most telling historical lessons of 'Operation Osprey', and

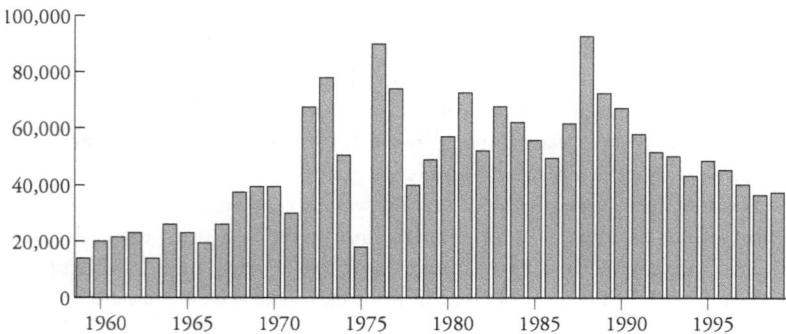

Chart 1. Annual visitor numbers, RSPB Loch Garten Osprey Centre, 1959–1999 [30]
(Source: RSPB Archives)

has been successfully copied in Scotland by the Scottish Wildlife Trust (SWT) at the public osprey-breeding site in Perthshire at the Loch of Lowes. George Waterston's vision was to blend successful nature conservation practice, with visitor management and recreational provision and, in the long-run, to divert the attention of birdwatchers from other nesting pairs of ospreys in Scotland, especially after 1963 when a second pair did breed. The annual visitor totals given in Chart 1 are an indication of how well the balancing act between nature conservation and recreation, inherent in Waterston's vision, has appealed to the British public.

In the 1960s, George Waterston wrote annual progress reports on the successes and failures of 'Operation Osprey' at Loch Garten, and these appeared in *Bird Notes*, keeping RSPB members and keen ornithologists fully informed of events at the nest.[31] Increasingly in the 1970s, television took over the role of disseminator of nature conservation news from Speyside, and this was no doubt encouraged by the influence of the newsreader Robert Dougall under his tenure as President of the RSPB from 1970 to 1975. In his autobiography, Dougall records his pleasure at attending an RSPB Council 'Grand Tour' of Scotland in June 1972 which took in a visit to the new reserve at Insh Marshes, as well as a visit to Loch Garten to see "the most observed birds in history".[32] National membership of the RSPB hit 100,000 in October 1972. In 1978, Dougall explained how his involvement with BBC Television News projected the annual story of 'Operation Osprey' into a regular Nine o'Clock News slot during the summer months, and directly brought the cause of nature conservation into living rooms across Britain, no doubt encouraging many to visit the site. It was, as Dougall concluded, "one of the most uplifting wildlife stories of our generation, a classic case of how controlled access can safely be allowed to shy and rare breeding birds".[33] Yet to some naturalists, the invasion of visitors at Loch Garten detracted from the necessary solitary experience of watching British wildlife, as Henry Tegner observed: "Every year thousands of people in cars, on bicycles, in buses and on foot began to arrive at Loch Garten to see the ospreys." It was little more than an "avian exhibition, an annual show" he moaned.[34]

A wider link between RSPB publicity, television and nature conservation can actually be traced back to October 1960, when the President of the RSPB, Lord Forester, presented the Society's Silver Medal to Desmond Hawkins of the BBC Natural History Unit.[35] It had been minuted at an RSPB Education and General Purposes Committee meeting on 20 April 1960 that Hawkins had been "responsible for putting the RSPB on the television map, dating from the days when he was producer of the natural history programme".[36] The Society's AGM in October 1960 in London also saw a commemoration of the continued involvement of the Grants of Rothiemurchus in efforts to protect the osprey in the region. Chairman of the RSPB Council, Lord Hurcomb, paid tribute to the "help and co-operation" given by Colonel J.P. Grant of Rothiemurchus (the great-grandson of the recipient of the silver medal in 1893), "without whose commitment the operation could hardly have succeeded". Later that evening, Lord Forester presented the RSPB's Silver Medal to Grant of Rothiemurchus, who throughout 1959 had assisted the osprey wardens with night-watches at the Loch Garten eyrie, and provided many useful household objects for the nearby warden's camp.[37]

In 1975, as a result of the campaign 'Save a Place for Birds' launched by Lord Home and Robert Dougall, the RSPB was able to buy about 15,000 acres of Caledonian pine forest around Loch Garten to create a larger nature reserve. In 1988, the Abernethy Forest RSPB Reserve was born out of an appeal to RSPB members and the additional provision of NCC funding, to create a reserve of about 30,000 acres. In a sense, the financial aid given by the NCC to this project in the late 1980s, mirrors the little-known manpower aid that the NC gave to the RSPB in 1958 towards the wardening of the osprey eyrie, and stands as an example of an historic and symbolic level of co-operation between two nature conservation organisations on Speyside. In 1958, despite then being under considerable financial restraints themselves, the NC in Scotland responded to a direct appeal for help from George Waterston, and subsequently provided two full-time 'watchers' from March until August (bringing in E.L. Roberts from Caerlaverock NNR) and urging Archie MacDonald, Warden of the Cairngorms NNR, to lend a hand when he could. The NC help was given again in 1959, but by 1960 the RSPB were able to man the osprey-watch centre alone.[38] Philip Brown (who was Secretary of the RSPB from 1952) has looked back on that decision taken by Waterston to publicise the location of the Loch Garten eyrie and open it up to visitors, and admitted that he was at first "quite horrified" by the proposals and "advised against such a course"; now he believes that "it was a decision which has been fully justified by the results".[39]

In the public debate in Scotland during the 1980s over the competing demands of nature conservation and development, it was commonly argued that nature conservation was of little direct economic benefit to local communities, even that nature conservation had cost jobs. In 1988, the RSPB instigated a research programme to investigate the economic benefits of nature conservation, and focused on Loch Garten as an ideal nature reserve in which to conduct a pilot study. The survey work and sampling took place from July to August in 1988 (peak visitor period at Loch Garten) and the conclusion was that the existence of the Osprey Centre at Loch Garten generated accommodation spending of £280,000 in the local districts of Badenoch and Strathspey, plus an additional attributable spending figure of £322,000 on other items such as food, petrol and gifts. The survey also found that the overwhelming majority of visitors to

Loch Garten are holidaymakers, not day trippers, and that many were from beyond the Highlands and, indeed, Scotland.[40] Although national membership of the RSPB rose dramatically after 1970 (from 87,448 in 1971 to 306,000 in 1980), its support in Scotland has remained lower than would be expected. By 1987, the RSPB had a national membership of 427,000, of whom 31,000 (or 7.25% of the total) were Scottish. Many more Scots (160,000 in 1987) preferred to be members of the National Trust for Scotland, which was seen to have a more distinctive Scottish identity and a broader remit, taking in landscape and historic building conservation. On that evidence, Scots have historically been slow to rally to the single cause of nature conservation.[41] However, the majority of visitors to Loch Garten are from the financial power-base of the RSPB in England, and the site is valued as one of the most accessible, informative and popular nature reserves in the UK; 'AA' road signs now direct visitors to Loch Garten, and Boat of Garten proclaims itself to be the 'Osprey Village'. Valerie Thom was right to call Loch Garten and its ospreys, "the best-known conservation success story in Scotland".[42] From 1959–1999, 74 ospreys have fledged from the RSPB Loch Garten site. By 2000, there were some 130 pairs of osprey breeding in Scotland, and since 1997 a long-term re-introduction scheme is underway at Rutland Water in England using young birds from Scottish nests.

Just as Victorian visitors watched the osprey fishing in Loch an Eilein at Rothiemurchus, so the modern birdwatcher or tourist can again watch these birds fishing in that loch, or sit in the specially-built hide at the fish farm at Inverdruie where some of the Speyside osprey population regularly fishes in the summer months. Ospreys remain an integral part of the 'visitor experience' both at Rothiemurchus and in the wider Cairngorms area.

Conclusion

It is important that the Osprey preservation efforts of the Grants of Rothiemurchus in the mid- to late-nineteenth century are placed in context. The lairds of Rothiemurchus stand out as pioneers in the field of species preservation, particularly when that species was a bird of prey. Garth Christian has shown that the persecution of ospreys in England in the nineteenth century was a widespread phenomenon, most often linked to sporting estates: "We are shocked at the Tamworth landowner who complained, when a visiting osprey appeared in the district, that 'a gamekeeper who should have known better let it go' ".[43] However, in the UK a burgeoning bird protection movement did begin in the late nineteenth century.

John Sheail has shown that one of the favoured ways of protecting wildlife from wanton slaughter and the craze of collecting in the second half of the nineteenth century, was to lobby for protective legislation, and to rely on the publicity and educational benefits generated from high profile campaigns. From around the 1860s, probably as a direct result of the earliest campaigning efforts of the Royal Society for the Prevention of Cruelty to Animals (RSPCA) which had been founded in 1824, mounting opposition grew to the cruel and often indiscriminate slaughter of wild birds in Britain. Brian Harrison has revealed that the thrust of the RSPCA's work in the 1860s and 1870s was actually in the defence of wild birds which involved, in his view, not only defending the rural environment against urban desecration, but also "subordinating the country-side's food-getting role to its role as provider of recreation for an increasingly urban population". Amateur naturalists and the British Association contributed enormously to the fostering of widespread support in relation to wild birds' legislation, although all the organisations involved knew that it would prove fatal to run too far ahead of public opinion in this matter.[44]

Most of the early nineteenth century Wildlife Acts related to the pres-ervation of game for sporting interests (for example, the Game Act of 1831), the combating of poaching, the issue of game licences and the spreading of poisoned grain. The first purely 'preservation' Act came in 1869 with the Sea Birds Preservation Act brought in by pressure groups to prevent the shooting of seabirds from battues on Flamborough Head.[45] A rush of Wild Bird Pro-tection Acts then came from 1872 to 1925, with specific Acts targeting fragile endemic island subspecies such as the St. Kilda wren *Troglodytes troglodytes hirtensis*. Birds of prey were absent from the majority of these Acts, although certain species of owl were offered protection. Indeed, it would not be until the Protection of Birds Act of 1954 simplified the protection laws pertaining to British birds by repealing all previous Acts, that most species were afforded full legislative protection; a scientific egg-collecting clause still remained tied to this Act and it was not removed until the Protection of Birds Act of 1967.[46] Much of this era of legislation from 1869 was born from a little humanitarian sentiment, but principally from the perceived economic benefits that each bird species might have to humankind. Walter Collinge wrote a great deal about the national importance of wild birds at the very start of the twentieth century and, indeed, went as far as to propose the creation of a Department of Eco-nomic Ornithology that could operate from within a reorganised Department of Agriculture, and would decide the fate of injurious species.[47] Most birds of prey (apart from the kestrel *Falco tinnunculus* which was seen to eat farmyard vermin) received little legislative protection because they were seen to compete directly with humans, whether it be for grouse on the moor, or for salmon and trout in rivers and lochs. There were, though, notable voices in the wilderness, even in Scotland. In 1867, Canon H.B. Tristram spoke at the British Association in Dundee of the benefit of birds of prey on Scottish uplands in the removal of sick and disabled grouse, thus ensuring healthy stock for August shoots.

Similarly, Ogilvie Grant addressed the Inverness Scientific Society and Field Club in January 1888 on the subject of 'Highland Ornithology', and made an impassioned plea for the study of avian biology in Scotland, believing that the "prosperity of the Highlands depends almost entirely on the welfare of the zoological kingdom". Whilst there was an element of conservation urged in the polemic, the dominant tone of the lecture was the economic benefit of nature to mankind; "the rent of grouse moors in Inverness-shire alone is very many thousands, and even on the mountain top, where the grouse cannot live, the beautiful ptarmigan is found".[48]

We now have evidence that successive lairds of Rothiemurchus offered protection to the breeding ospreys at Loch an Eilein throughout the nineteenth century, although no date can be found for the actual start of this practice. In the long run, what made the various preservation schemes in operation at Rothiemurchus so unique was the fact that the ospreys were not seen in an economic light, but rather were offered protection because of their beauty, their site faithfulness and the joy that they gave to the lairds and visitors to the estate. Protection was given because of human sentiment and the intrinsic value of the birds at Rothiemurchus. Walter Collinge did not come to see the inherent value of conservation based on these principles until 1921 when he quoted an anonymous writer, and also drew attention to the mental and physical benefits to humankind in the watching of birds:

> "The study of the living bird afield is rejuvenating to both mind and body. The outdoor use of eye, ear, and limb necessitated by field work tends to fit both the body and mind of the student for the practical work of life. It brings one into contact with nature – out into the sunlight, where balmy airs stir the whispering pines or fresh breezes ripple the blue water."[49]

In the middle of the nineteenth century the osprey on Speyside faced two threats; one was from egg-collecting, the other from indiscriminate shooting by sportsmen keen to acquire a trophy bird and to demonstrate their shooting prowess. Apart from the Grants of Rothiemurchus, few in the Scottish countryside took a stand against this slaughter; when a Society for the Protection of Birds was formed in 1889 (becoming the RSPB with a Royal Charter in 1904) it was an urban-based English organisation focused on a single issue – the killing of birds for plumes for the millinery trade. The lot of British birds of prey in the uplands has not improved greatly over the last century and a half.[50] Even in the 1990s the pilfering of egg-collectors and mindless vandalism still persecutes ospreys breeding in Scotland, and such activities have not declined from a peak in the 1960s and 1970s. In the years just before the war, Leslie Brown visited the Cairngorms to watch and photograph raptors and found to his dismay that, as in the nineteenth century, well-known individuals were responsible for much of the stealing of birds of prey eggs. He visited an unnamed glen near Aviemore only to encounter, "the most bitter disappointment I had had". He continues:

> "The stalker mentioned the name of a wretched man, who he said, robbed most of the Cairngorm eyries yearly; he said he had seen the eggs in the nest a day or two before I first found it. Anyway it was shameful that they should have been taken at all."

In these ornithological memoirs of 1947, Brown urged that any enlightened landowners should no longer continue to turn a blind eye to the ravages of the egg-collectors, but conceded that in the case of the golden eagle *Aquila chrysaetos*, "most persons have no interest in the protection of the eagle, while some, such as proprietors of grouse moors, are definitely antagonistic".[51] Brown sadly admitted that there were very few such enlightened landowners in the Scottish Highlands.

Notes to Chapter 4

1   Simon Holloway, *The Historical Atlas of Breeding Birds in Britain and Ireland, 1875–1900* (T. and A.D. Poyser, London, 1996), pp. 122–123.

2   Jim Crumley, *A High and Lonely Place – The Sanctuary and Plight of the Cairngorms* (Jonathan Cape, London, 1991), pp. 89–101.

3   Roy Dennis, *The Birds of Badenoch and Strathspey* Colin Baxter Photography, Grantown-on-Spey, 1995), pp. 58–60.

4   Elizabeth Grant of Rothiemurchus, *Memoirs of a Highland Lady* – Vols. I and II (Canongate Classics, Edinburgh, 1992) p. 99.

5   Philip Brown and George Waterston, *The Return of the Osprey* (Collins, London, 1962), pp. 80–115.

6   C.G. Cash, 'The Loch-an-Eilein Ospreys', *Cairngorm Club Journal*, Vol. IV, No. 21, July 1903, pp. 125–131; C.G. Cash, 'History of the Loch An Eilein Ospreys', *Scottish Naturalist*, No. 31, July 1914, pp. 149–158.

7   Roy Dennis, *Ospreys* (Colin Baxter Photography, Grantown-on-Spey, 1992), pp. 7–9.

8   George Waterston, *Ospreys in Speyside* (RSPB, Edinburgh, 1966) p. 19.

9   T.A. Coward, 'Ethics of Egg-Collecting', *The Nineteenth Century and After*, Vol. 100, July 1926, pp. 101–109.

10 T.A. Coward, *The Birds of the British Isles and their Eggs* (Frederick Warne and Co., London, 1930), pp.346–348. I would like to thank Joy Nelson, a former tennis opponent of mine from my youth in Bolton, who kindly allowed me to look through her private collection of T.A. Coward texts in 1997.

11 William Jolly, 'Loch-an-Eilein and its Ospreys', *The Scotsman*, 9 June 1879, p. 5.

12 Jolly, *Ibid.*, p. 5.

13 Jolly, *Ibid.*, p. 5. The attic of the Doune of Rothiemurchus holds a stuffed osprey in a glass case, which is perhaps the bird shot by Lord Stamford in 1872.

14 Anon ('S'), 'The Osprey', *The Scotsman*, 12 June 1879, p. 3. Letter to the Editor.

15 Anon., *Ibid.*, p. 3.

16 Anon., 'Obituary – C.G. Cash', *Scottish Geographical Magazine*, Vol. 33, October 1917, pp. 465–466.

17 Cash, 1903, *op. cit.*, p. 125.

18 Cash, 1914, *op. cit.*, p. 158.

19 The archives of the Grants of Rothiemurchus NRA (S) 102 are privately held in the attic at the Doune of Rothiemurchus. See NRA (S) 102:337, Letter from C.G. Cash at 49, Comely Bank Road, Edinburgh to J.P. Grant of Rothiemurchus, dated 28 April 1900.

20 NRA (S) 102:337, Letter from F.R. Cox, Doune Cottage to J.P. Grant of Rothiemurchus, dated 10 May 1898.

21 NRA (S) 102:337, Letter from F.R. Cox to J.P. Grant of Rothiemurchus, dated 6 July 1898.

22 NRA (S) 102:337, Letter from F.R. Cox to J.P. Grant of Rothiemurchus, dated 18 July 1898.

23 NRA (S) 102:337, Letter from E. Baddeley, Bank House, Higher Broughton, Manchester to J.P. Grant of Rothiemurchus, dated 10 April 1897.

24 NRA (S) 102:337, Letter from W.G. Stewart Menzies, Aikenway, Craig Ellachie, N.B. to J.P. Grant of Rothiemurchus, dated 7 July 1898. The underlining is in the original letter.

25 Cash, 1903, *op. cit.*, p. 131.

26 Seton Gordon, *The Cairngorm Hills of Scotland* (Cassell and Co. Ltd., London, 1925), pp. 195–196.

27 Anon. (RSPB), *Ospreys and Speyside Wildlife* (RSPB, Sandy, 1973), p. 18.

28 Dennis, 1991, *op. cit.*, p. 10. Roy Dennis was the RSPB Warden at Loch Garten from 1960 to 1963.

29 SRO: SNH 1-2, Minutes of the meeting of the NC Scottish Committee, Edinburgh, 24 July 1959.

30 RSPB internal reports, RSPB Archives and Library, Sandy, Bedfordshire. I am grateful to Ian Dawson (RSPB Librarian) for helping me with my historical searches over the autumn of 1994. A useful resource was: Philippa Bassett. 'A List of the Historical Records of the Royal Society for the Protection of Birds', August 1980, compiled as part of a research project funded by the Social Science Research Council in conjunction with the Centre for Urban and Regional Studies at the University of Birmingham, and the Institute of Agricultural History at the University of Reading.

        See especially: RSPB   File 01.05.71   'Operation Osprey'

                                RSPB   File 01.08.02   'Birds Eggs'

                                RSPB   File 01.13.01   'Spey Valley'

31 For example: George Waterston, 'Operation Osprey, 1961', *Bird Notes*, Vol. 30, No. 1, Winter 1963, p. 13; George Waterston, 'Operation Osprey, 1964', *Bird Notes*, Vol. 31, No. 4, July–August 1964, pp. 126–129.

32 Robert Dougall, *In and Out of the Box* (Fontana, Glasgow, 1975), p. 297.

33 Robert Dougall, *A Celebration of Birds* (Collins and Harvill Press, London, 1978): see Chap. 13, 'The Osprey', pp. 175–182.

34 Henry Tegner, *A Naturalist on Speyside* (Geoffrey Bles, London, 1971), Chap. 9, 'The Ospreys of Strathspey', pp. 45–50.

35 Anon., 'Miscellany', *Bird Notes*, Vol. 29 (5), Winter 1960–1961, pp. 126-127. Report of the 69th AGM of the RSPB held on 4 October 1960 at Hoare Memorial Hall, Church House, Westminster.

36 RSPB Archives, IV – 7, Minute Book, Publicity Committee, February 1949 to September 1964.

37 RSPB Archives, I – 21, Council Minute Books, May 1960 to March 1967, Minutes of Council, dated 11 May 1960, 'RSPB Medals'; V – 1, Minute Book, Annual General Meeting, March 1955 to October 1977, Minutes of AGM, October 1960.

38 Brown and Waterston, 1962, *op. cit.*, pp. 28, 39–40, 54. The initial RSPB plea for help seems to have been sent to Max Nicholson, Director-General of the NC.

39 Tony Samstag, *For Love of Birds – The Story of the RSPB* (RSPB, Sandy, 1988), p. 83.

40 D.C. Harley and N.D. Hanley, *Economic Benefit Estimates for Nature Reserves: Methods and Results* (Discussion Paper in Economics 89/6, Department of Economics, University of Stirling, July 1989).

41 T.C. Smout, *The Highlands and the Roots of Green Consciousness, 1750-1990* (Occasional Paper No. 1, SNH, Battleby, 1993), p. 26.

42 Valerie M. Thom, *Birds in Scotland* (T. and A.D. Poyser, Calton, 1986), p. 146.

43 Gareth Christian, *While Some Trees Stand – Wild Life in Our Vanishing Countryside* (Newnes, London, 1963), p. 99.

44 Brian Harrison, 'Animals and the State in Nineteenth-century England', *English Historical Review*, No. CCCXLIX, Vol. LXXXVIII, October 1973, pp. 786–820.

45 Walter E. Collinge, 'Wild Birds and Legislation', *Journal of the Land Agents Society*, Vol. 17, July 1918, pp. 278–285.

46 John Sheail, *Nature in Trust – The History of Nature Conservation in Britain* (Blackie and Son, London, 1976); see pp. 22–36.

47 Walter E. Collinge, *The National Importance of Wild Birds* (RSPB pamphlet, London, 1927).

48 Dr. Ogilvie Grant (lecture) on 'Highland Ornithology' delivered on 10 January 1888 in Inverness and reproduced in *Transactions of the Inverness Scientific Society and Field Club*, Vol. III, 1883–1888 (Courier Office, Inverness, 1888), pp. 310–311.

49 Walter E. Collinge, 'The Necessity of State Action for the Protection of Wild Birds', in *The Smithsonian Report for 1919* (Government Printing Office, Washington, USA, 1921), pp. 349–353.

50 For the Cairngorm area see especially the published results of the Speyside Preda-
    tor Survey undertaken from March 1964 to February 1969 and presented to the
    Conservation Committee of the RSPB; D.N. Weir, 'Mortality of Hawks and Owls
    in Speyside', *Bird Study*, Vol. 18, No. 3, September 1971, pp. 147–154.

51 Leslie Brown, *Birds and I* (Michael Joseph Ltd., London, 1947), pp. 66–76.

5

Hotels, Hoteliers and Cairngorms Tourism
1900–1955

Little academic work has been done in Scotland on the history of tourism and recreation, and within that field of inquiry, no work has been done on the history of individual hotel companies that were, after all, one of the most visible manifestations of the development of a rising tide of public recreational provision across the nineteenth and twentieth centuries.[1] Aspects of hotel history are presented here for two Speyside hotels, in order to illustrate the interface between recreation and economic activity, and to show how recreation has created a new industry in the Cairngorms area, and in particular in Badenoch and Strathspey. It is the study of recreation as a part of economic history, but also shows how hotel companies, hoteliers and developers have often been at the forefront of the creation of a wide range of recreational and leisure activities and facilities in the area, which have sprung directly from the successful establishment of a Speyside holiday industry in the late nineteenth century, built in turn upon a tradition of visiting the Cairngorms area that can be traced back to the 1780s at least [see Chapter 1].

The earliest pioneering visitors to Badenoch and Strathspey at the end of the eighteenth century, stayed in many of the Highland inns that were strategically placed along carriage routes or ancient drove roads; the inn at Aviemore, the inn at Raitts and the Pitmain inn, featured prominently in journals of these Highland tours. By the second half of the nineteenth century, Badenoch and Strathspey began to host a greater number of sporting visitors (and their retinues) along with other holidaymakers, some on organised tours, some travelling alone. Easier access to the region had been facilitated by improvements to the district roads from 1813 to 1820 and the construction of the railway line (the 'Highland Railway') from Perth to Inverness, which had been mooted as early as 1845 by Joseph Mitchell (Senior Inspector of Roads under the Commissioners). It was not until 1861 that an Act was passed to allow rail construction from Dunkeld north over the Drumochter Pass and down the Spey Valley to Forres, which was already an existing station on the Aberdeen to Keith railway. In 1863, the 'Inverness and Perth Junction Railway' opened.[2] The 'Highland Railway' had been founded by local enterprise and lobbying, and was fundamental to the creation of a new tourist industry on Speyside. In the 1880s and 1890s, railway hotels began to open next to the town stations on the line north, showing how the presence of the rail link acted as a commercial catalyst for a burgeoning holiday industry. One such hotel was the Aviemore Station Hotel.

The Aviemore Station Hotel Company

The Aviemore Station Hotel Company was set up on 21 August 1899. The starting capital of the Company was £25,000 divided into 500 preference shares of £10 each and 2,000 ordinary shares of £10 each. Those wishing to form a hotel company in Aviemore came from across Scotland and from a variety of occupational backgrounds, including the hotel industry on Royal Deeside; they were Donald Grant, a solicitor from Grantown-on-Spey; Livingstone Macdonald, the proprietor of the Fife Arms Hotel in Braemar; William Purves, a solicitor from Edinburgh; James Bontein of Oban; Robert Macbeth, an architect; William Aikman, a manufacturer; Augustus Baillie of Edinburgh. The declared aims of the hotel company in 1899, included not only the erection of a hotel building, but also to "provide a golf course and recreation ground at or near Aviemore". A legal and financial document drawn up under the direction of the Companies Acts 1862–1890 also mentioned, in its wide-ranging objectives, the construction at Aviemore of, "a restaurant, café, tavern, beer house, refreshment room, boarding and lodging-house"; those in the Company could also let furnished or unfurnished flats and apartments, and were later described as "caterers for public amusements".[3]

The hotel was opened to paying guests in June 1901, but was not entirely out of the tradesman's hands until August of that year. Initial trade was good, and it was anticipated that the first costs of building the hotel, at £10,765. 5s. 6d., would be recovered by the issuing of further shares and commercial success in the tourist market. By 31 December 1902 the expenditure on the hotel buildings, grounds and the golf course totalled £25,993. 17s. 10d., with the furnishings costing an additional £9,601. Profit for 1901 was £2,298 and for 1902 was £2,675; by 1906, profits had risen to £3,814. In 1904, the hotel had purchased the tenancy of the farm of Aviemore from the Countess of Seafield to expand the property and golf course on a nineteen year lease.[4]

Both European Wars dealt harsh blows to the holiday industry across the UK, and the Aviemore Station Hotel suffered badly. At the Ordinary General Meeting of the Company in Edinburgh in March 1915, the Directors reported a severe loss of trade due to holiday cancellations and the curtailment of holidays in August and September of 1914; this had been especially hard to bear as up to 31 July the annual income of the hotel had been in excess of all previous years. Solace was sought in the fact that, "no part of the British Isles is in a safer or more attractive situation than is Aviemore", and that holidaymakers would return *en masse*. The early part of 1914 had seen considerable expenditure in the hotel on improved accommodation and additional furniture, in preparation for what was widely anticipated as a coming summer of a record tourist numbers.[5] In 1926, the Company purchased another hotel which they named the Cairngorm Hotel. By July 1937, the Aviemore Station Hotel had 100 rooms and charged a weekly tariff in season of £7. 7s. 0d., whilst the newer Cairngorm Hotel had only 30 rooms.

Table 3 shows that even in the 1930s it was considerably more expensive to stay in Aviemore, as opposed to a holiday based in one of the other towns in the district, which perhaps indicates the development of core and periphery tourism areas in the Cairngorms, long before the dramatic tourism development boom in Aviemore during the 1960s. The attraction of Aviemore in the 1930s is best explained by the size of its hotels and by its close proximity to the Cairngorm mountains allowing easier pedestrian access to the straths and glens and the high tops.

Town/Village	Hotel Name	Number of Rooms	Weekly Tariff in Season
Kingussie	The Star	27	£4. 14s. 6d. (by 1939)
Kingussie	The Duke of Gordon	50 (80 by 1939)	No data available
Aviemore	The Cairngorm Hotel	30	£5. 5s. 0d. (but not licensed in 1937)
Aviemore	Aviemore Hotel	100	£7. 7s. 0d.
Newtonmore	The Main's	40	£4. 4s. 0d.
Newtonmore	The Temperance Hotel	17	£3. 10s. 0d.
Newtonmore	The Balavil Arms	38	£4. 4s. 0d.
Rothiemurchus	The Dell of Rothiemurchus	18	from $3^{1}/_{2}$ guineas
Rothiemurchus	The Doune of Rothiemurchus	23	from 4 guineas

Table 3. The Hotels on Speyside in the 1930s: a comparison[6]
(Source: *SMT Magazines*)

The Aviemore Station Hotel was requisitioned on 1 October 1942, after Air Ministry officials had measured all rooms at both the Aviemore and Cairngorm Hotels in December 1940. The War Department paid an annual rental of £175 to the Company for some detached buildings which they had requisitioned from 21 April 1941. A small commercial concession was made by the War Department in that they allowed the hotel bar to be kept open while the hotel was under requisition, and that one room on the ground floor was to be kept aside for any chance customers.[7] De-requisitioning of the hotel came on 3 March 1945. The Directors immediately put in a compensation claim for £2,000 *per annum* to the War Department to cover the cost of reconditioning the hotel and to take in the Grid Supply of electricity. The estimated cost of the work was £11,477 and the hotel claimed a total wartime loss of £12,102. They were forced to negotiate an £8,000 overdraft with the Bank of Scotland in Edinburgh, as well as applying to the Ministry of Works for a building licence to make good the damage caused during "the occupation of the hotel by the War Department".[8] The hotel operators were obviously keen to get the venture up and running again, confident that a post-war boom in tourism would occur in the Highlands. Indeed, it is noticeable that by 1953, a much wider range of local hotel accommodation was available in Speyside, the number of Automobile Association (AA) listed hotels being as follows:

Aviemore 3	Boat of Garten 2	Carrbridge 2	Grantown-on-Spey 6
Kincraig 1	Kingussie 3	Nethybridge 1	Newtonmore 5

The average weekly tariff in 1953 was in the range of six guineas to twelve guineas, with the majority around eight to nine guineas.[9] In the 1950s and 1960s the Aviemore Station Hotel Company enjoyed considerable financial success (although the hotel did suffer catastrophic fire damage in September 1950), as Aviemore itself developed into Scotland's only all-year-round tourist resort, catering now for a winter sports industry based on Cairn Gorm. The hotel archive runs out in 1968, when the newly opened Aviemore Centre and its wide-ranging cheaper tourist facilities swallowed up some of the local holiday traffic, although Aviemore still has a good mix of older hotels and guest houses, and new holiday centres.

The Doune of Rothiemurchus Hotel

The ancestral home of the Grants of Rothiemurchus, the Doune of Rothiemurchus, first became a commercial hotel sometime in the 1880s, although the archival evidence for this venture is based on just one letter.[10] When the Doune next became a commercial hotel in 1935 it was only able to survive for seven years before the holiday trade on which it depended was eradicated by the

Second World War. It was begun though as a venture with enormous potential, in that the Doune of Rothiemurchus Hotel was located within an area of natural beauty, scenic splendour and history – with the added literary association of the estate with Elizabeth Grant of Rothiemurchus, the 'Highland Lady', whose memoirs had first been published in 1898.[11] A lease was negotiated for the use of the property as a hotel, probably directly between the major provider of the initial monies for the venture, John Johnson, and the owner, Colonel Grant of Rothiemurchus. Under the terms of the lease various adjustments to the trading profit/loss account were permitted, and Grant of Rothiemurchus was entitled to 25% of the adjusted profits of the enterprise, in addition to an annual rent of £200. A hotel manager, R.T. Bowyer, was employed from January 1935 at an annual salary of £78, and he put an initial £22 capital into the venture; over the life of the hotel, Johnson contributed a total of £2,400 and had to forego many interest payments on that capital.[12]

The hotel opened on 15 April 1935, with the first paying guests arriving on 19 April by car, as garage space was provided. The last guests left in late October, with chance teas still being provided until 27 October, indicating that the number of visitors who might come in the winter months to mountaineer or ski in the Cairngorms were not seen to be great enough to warrant keeping the hotel open all year. Indeed, this hotel continued to close each year in early October until around 1938 or 1939 when a half-hearted attempt was made to entice winter visitors; it seems to have had no visible financial success. Across the late 1930s, the hotel saw visitor numbers at a peak in August each year (notably August 1938), with numbers building up noticeably from late May. Throughout, the hotel venture seemed to make little profit, and barely kept its head above water due to wage payments, advertising costs, the annual rent payment and property maintenance costs. In 1936 a profit of just £295 was made. In all other years a loss ranging from £273 to £490 had to be endured.[13] Over the first three years of the hotel enterprise there must have been general optimism that the venture would be successful, although the fact that in 1937 John Johnson declined his interest payment for 1936, could be seen as an anticipation of future problems. As a European War began to look more imminent, people began to change the way in which they took their holidays. By 1941, the hotel was essentially running on a care and maintenance basis; release from the continued drain on capital came with the auction of the furniture from the hotel in September 1942.[14]

Outside of the history of the financial health of this commercial hotel, additional information more widely relevant to the history of recreation in the Cairngorms area can be found in the manner in which the Doune of Rothiemurchus advertised itself and sought to entice visitors to stay. The hotel management made use of two distinct advertising strategies.

The first concerned the ancestral link between the Doune and Eliza-beth Grant of Rothiemurchus, indeed, the tariff brochure itself contained an attractive photograph of the Doune on its front cover, accompanying a direct quotation from *Memoirs of a Highland Lady*, which spoke of Elizabeth Grant's visual impressions of her "beloved duchus" in the summer of 1812, as she returned there from England. It was as if the tourist in the 1930s was making that journey of 1812 with the authoress.[15]

The second marketing style makes much more of the hotel's facilities, but also plays upon the 1930s fashion for healthy recreation in a scenic area. Around this time, many of the Speyside hotels were vying for custom in an expanding tourist market and this competition is reflected in the assertions made in their respective newspaper adverts. The earliest newspaper adverts for the Doune of Rothiemurchus Hotel from February 1936, merely announce that the hotel will open at Easter.[16] By March 1936, the Cairngorm Hotel in Aviemore had inserted a large block of advertisements in *The Scotsman* to make room for its claims to provide, "magnificent scenery and health-giving air … electric light, central heating and running hot and cold water in all bedrooms".[17] By April 1936 the Doune's advert had matured to describe the hotel as, "a Mansion House beautifully situated in 17 acres of Parkland on the banks of the River Spey". Additional attractions were listed as, "Home Farm produce, free fishing, near golf course and tennis courts, mountaineering". The car-borne tourist is obviously the target, with the hotel describing itself as an, "excellent centre for motoring".[18] As the summer of 1936 progressed, the advert changed again, this time to make more of the beauty of the pine forest on the estate at Roth-iemurchus. The terms were described as moderate, with the hotel "beautifully situated near Rothiemurchus forest in the Cairngorms".[19]

Perhaps the most interesting aspect of this catalogue of advertisements, is the way in which the natural landscape of the hotel's surrounds were carefully deployed as a lure to bring visitors to the Doune. The Doune of Rothiemurchus Hotel did not have a monopoly on this type of commercial tourism linking traditional field sports with a clean environment, for the nearby Dell of Roth-iemurchus Hotel was advertising itself as equally, "beautifully situated in own ground at the edge of the Forest facing Cairngorms … own farm and garden produce … Fishing and personal supervision … very comfortable".[20] Advertising was obviously a key factor in the success of a hotel company in a congested local marketplace. The Doune of Rothiemurchus Hotel spent as little as £29 (1936) or as much as £109 (1938) a year on advertising costs, in a variety of sources. Early adverts in April 1935 were placed locally in just the *Inverness Courier* and the *Strathspey Herald*. In 1936, the hotel was also advertising with painted boards, updated in 1938, at Aviemore Rail Station (six months' rent £1. 11s. 6d.), realising that most of the Cairngorm area's visitors passed through this developing tourist and recreational centre. They also advertised as far afield as the *Yorkshire Post*, the *Glasgow Herald* and the *Dundee Courier*. In the 1930s the recreation and tourism industry in Scotland was beginning to organise itself better on a countrywide basis in order to offer structured holiday and travel advice and facilities, and as a direct result of that, the Doune of Rothiemurchus Hotel paid an annual subscription from 1937 to be a member of the Scottish Travel Association (STA), and in 1938 gave money to publicise Cairngorm holidays at the Empire Exhibition via the STA. The hotel also began to keep the boards up at Aviemore Rail Station on a yearly basis, rather than for just the summer months. In 1936 the hotel management placed an advert in the *Scottish Ski Club Journal*, ostensibly it seems to attract only summer hillwalkers. In 1938 as the volume of traffic grew on Highland roads, the hotel commissioned the painting of a hotel road sign and indicator arrows.[21] However, perhaps the most damaging blow to the success of the hotel came because of its failure to be listed in the Scottish Motor Traction Co. Ltd. Magazine (SMT) 'Directory of Recommended British Hotels' which began in April 1934. This must surely have been a serious disadvantage, especially in an age of holidays by motor car and omnibus, with those hotels on the list seeing a rise in the level of passing tourist traffic, in which the Doune was unable to participate.

This detailed and localised study of hotels in Aviemore, at Rothiemurchus and in other towns, gives a flavour of the importance of factors such as geographical location, financial backing, management strategy and the facilities on offer when considering the history of commercial recreation on Speyside. The contrast between an hotel at the railhead of Aviemore, or within the pine forest of Rothiemurchus, is not just built upon scenic differences; rather it lies at the heart of a geographical and economic contrast between core and periphery in the provision of tourist facilities, and an overall responsiveness to the development and vagaries of a fluctuating tourism industry in the middle of the twentieth century.

Early Entrepreneurs

Of course, hotels were not just places of accommodation, they often played out a role as the focus of other recreational activities, and the establishment of a large hotel in a Speyside town often directly led to the construction and provision of other local recreational facilities. There is ample evidence in Badenoch and Strathspey, that hoteliers were often the driving force behind the expansion of the leisure industry. As early as 1890, the Scottish Rights of Way Society targeted hotels across Scotland in an attempt to increase their membership and gain valuable publicity for their campaigns to prevent the closure of rights of way in rural areas by landed interests. The Secretary and Acting Treasurer of the

Society, E.W. Macpherson, wrote to hotel proprietors in August 1890, asking if hotel management would place leaflets and subscription forms in the hotel Smoking and Reading Room to promote, "the useful and important public work which the Society endeavours to perform". The Cairngorms area, along with parts of Deeside, Perthshire and the Oban district was especially targeted by the Society; in Strathspey, leaflets were sent to the Hotel in Boat of Garten; Lynwilg Hotel, Aviemore; the Royal Hotel, Grantown-on-Spey.[22] The fact that the Cairngorms area was seen to be worthy of a concentrated campaign by the Society reflects not only the continued battles held there for access and the freedom to roam, but also indirectly presents the district as a very popular area for tourists by 1890.

 Kingussie Golf Course opened in 1891 as a direct result of the growth of the town as a recreational holiday centre. A new club house was erected in 1911;[23] a Bowling Club in Kingussie was born in 1877. Indeed, across the Highlands in the last two decades of the nineteenth century, a number of golf courses were built to cater for holidaymakers and hotel clients. The Aviemore Station Hotel chose to erect a warning notice on its golf course in May 1913, that the playing of golf was not to be undertaken by any chauffeurs and valets and other employees of hotel visitors, following numerous complaints from the paying visitors.[24] In its promotional brochure from 1935, the Doune of Rothiemurchus Hotel stressed its proximity to the beautiful Cairngorm mountains and the pine forest of Rothiemurchus, alongside its claims to be adjacent to Rothiemurchus Golf Course and tennis courts, and to allow recreational boating on Loch an Eilein now that ospreys no longer nested on the castle there. Residents of the hotel also had exclusive fishing rights on a stretch of one-and-a-half miles on the banks of the River Spey; additional permits could be obtained to fish the Rivers Druie and Bennie, another beat on the Spey and Loch Gamhna.[25] Almost twenty years later, Ewan Ormiston started pony trekking as a commercial recreational activity available to hotel guests in the town of Newtonmore, staying at the Balavil Arms Hotel. In conjunction with the Scottish Council of Physical Recreation (SCPR), he opened for business in 1952, having devised this activity as a useful form of employment for hill ponies outside of the stalking season. In the late 1940s, it had been Ormiston who had encouraged guests at his Newtonmore hotel to enjoy a day's stalking on the hill, allowing visitors to shoot a stag for £10, if Ormiston could then sell on the venison. By the late 1950s, other hotel owners had followed Ormiston's lead in linking their hotel to a diverse range of regional recreational activity.

 Hoteliers in the Cairngorms area took the lead again in the late 1940s by providing skiing holidays, and in 1948 a ski school was started by Bill Bracken on the Drumochter hills.[26] However, the fate of the sport in the Cairngorms was decided by an Austrian, Karl Fuchs, who established the Austrian Ski School in Carrbridge in 1954/55, and linked it to the hotel and leisure industry, in particular the Struan House Hotel. Other hotels in the area were quick to offer cheap skiing holidays with instruction.[27]

It is apparent that the laird of Rothiemurchus was first asked to let the Doune of Rothiemurchus to a skiing party during the winter of 1931/2. He refused, not yet convinced that the Cairngorm area offered any decent skiing save for a few isolated days, and aware that the Aviemore Hotel had agreed to open for that winter season on condition that they could attract 100 guests, which was proving difficult. There was a concern that commercial skiing would "disturb the ground" especially on Braeriach and at Inshriach. Mrs. Grainger Stewart wrote to the laird from London expressing her worry over a proposed Scottish Travel Association skiing permit scheme for the area, which she hoped Grant would oppose, as "they will press for permits for mountaineering, and certainly Hotel Proprietors and others are all out to exploit that part of the country for their own ends". Those first groups of skiers in the early 1930s sought solitude and low-key development for their sport in the area.[28] By 1935, the Scottish Ski Club membership in Glasgow wanted their club to negotiate special vehicular access for them up the Glen Einich road to the lower bothy on Rothiemurchus. W.R. Higginbotham, Honorary Secretary of the Club volunteered that members would pay a reasonable charge to the laird for this privilege (as was done on the Glen Derry Lodge road) for "it is a pretty strenuous undertaking to carry one's skis five miles before one even starts to climb". At this time, Cairn Gorm was not recognised as the best run for skiers in the district; Higginbotham voted "the best slope ... the finest skiing run in Scotland" to be from the western top of Braeriach down the north-west gully to the lower bothy.[29] Grant of Rothiemurchus gave his permission for vehicular access during the 1936/37 winter season, or if the Club held any meets in Aviemore, although the laird was angered by damage done to estate property by skiers in the Spring of 1936. The SSC were put on probation,[30] as was the SYHA after some of its members camped rough and lit fires up Glen Einich in the summer of 1934.[31] Although skiers had been visiting the north-facing corries on Cairn Gorm since the early 1930s, it was not until the last years of the 1940s that numbers were felt to be sufficient to contemplate a permanent ski development on the mountain. The idea lay dormant, until a group of local hoteliers once again seized the initiative and, linking up with ski clubs and recreational organisations, founded the Cairngorm Winter Sports Development Association (CWSDA) at Nethybridge in March 1956. The sole concern of this new organisation was to build a road from Glenmore to the ski grounds in Coire Cas, as Bob Clyde, the Clydeside engineer who has built and managed the ski facilities on Cairn Gorm since 1961, has explained.[32]

Other Types of Accommodation

In the summer of 1861, Queen Victoria and Prince Albert passed through Kingussie from Glen Feshie, at a time when the majority of the tourists in the district would have been sporting visitors. Colonel Thomas Thornton visited the Cairngorms in 1874 and rented the house of Raitts from Mrs. Mackintosh of Borlum, three miles to the north of Kingussie and, as J.A. MacDonald explained, "the gallant Colonel may be regarded a forerunner of the shooting parties that arrived by special train at Kingussie prior to 1914".[33] Although hotels were built in the town in the second half of the nineteenth century, Kingussie became more famous for its villa accommodation; from 1880 to 1900, over £200,000 of private capital was spent on summer villas in Kingussie, and owners often constructed a wooden summer house nearby to which they retired when the main house was let to sporting visitors or tourists. Robert Louis Stevenson and the academic Sidney Colvin stayed in the Royal Hotel in Kingussie in 1882, later renting out a cottage in Spey Street. The author enjoyed sailing paper boats down the Gynack burn during that summer, and walking in the district. Visiting in 1916, the American author Clayton Hamilton, recorded his displeasure at how Kingussie had changed since Stevenson's visit:

> "Kingussie is now overgrown with many monstrous villas of recent erection, and Sir Sidney Colvin has assured me that the place has been spoiled since that summer of 1882, but the pilgrim who will wander ... may still catch some echo of that far-off music that made melody in the ear of RLS when he lolled and dreamed by Speyside over thirty years ago."[34]

From 1903, the local Kingussie newspaper began to print summer and autumn visitor lists, as the town population was seen to double in the months of July and August from 1909 to 1914. A common holiday lease for a house in the town was a month, sometimes two months. Such summer letting in Kingussie continued until the outbreak of the Second World War, although the flood level of sporting visitors came from 1880 to 1914: "the continual movement of such shooting parties as made Kingussie their postal and shopping centre and their railhead".

From the mid-1930s onwards, Kingussie came to rely on the transient voyager – bus parties, caravanners, campers, cyclists and walkers, and this trend continued after the war; only from the early 1950s did visitors and tourists come to the town in significant numbers during the winter and early spring. Indeed, writing in 1966, J.A. MacDonald expressed the early concern of burgh officials that the town was left on the fringe of the winter sports development area, and would thus receive few economic benefits derived from passing tourist traffic. There was, he reported, "a hint of desperation" in the town that "Aviemore is a hive of activity engaged in the provision of the extra accommodation and all other facilities expected by the skier and the mountaineer".[35] Of course, not all the mountaineers sought to sleep every night in the comfort of an Aviemore hotel; many generations of hill walkers and climbers going back to the second half of the nineteenth century had slept at the Shelter Stone at Loch Avon in the heart of the Cairngorms. In August 1924, members of the Cairngorm Club finally placed a Visitors' Book there, "to furnish a record of those who visit that rather outlandish region".[36] The book recorded that from August 1924 to August 1925, there had been over 150 visitors including two dogs. The majority of the visitors were from NE Scotland, and students of Scottish universities were well represented. An American visitor was noted. As is also reflected in the available hotel records, the bulk of the visitors to the Shelter Stone in the late 1920s came in June, July or August to enjoy, "the sweetness of the mountain air".[37] The former Prime Minister, J. Ramsay MacDonald slept two nights there with a party from Lossiemouth in August 1926. As the early volumes of this Visitors' Book were consigned to the Cairngorm Club Library in Aberdeen, James Duncan mused on the value of recording visitors' observations in such a fashion:

> "The Visitors' Book has, I think, served its purpose well. It has shown the lovers of these mountains to be by no means a small band. Adventuring in the Cairngorms is the pleasantest escape imaginable from a world of streets and houses, and, for those whose blood demands such an escape, may the Shelter Stone long have an open door!"[38]

A Junior Mountaineering Club of Scotland was formed in 1925 having an Edinburgh and Glasgow branch[39]. After the birth of the Scottish Youth Hostels Association (SYHA) in 1931, as a distinct geographical entity separate from an English association founded in 1930, alternative accommodation became available in the Cairngorms area for those visitors who did not wish to pay rising hotel prices. By 1933, the SYHA had four hostels on the northern and eastern fringes of the Cairngorm mountains at Aviemore, Tomintoul, Invernan and Ballater, with a total of 124 beds available for just a shilling per night. The hostels at Ballater (48 beds) and at Aviemore (32 beds) were the largest, in what was advertised as the 'Cairngorm Chain' of hostels, which "does give the walker a chance of seeing some of the finest scenery". The Aviemore hostel was the first wooden hostel built by the Aberdeen Committee of the SYHA, who had initially struggled to find suitable buildings near to the Cairngorms in 1933. This hostel was described as being, "magnificently situated beside the main road and opposite the Spey bridge, a gap in the trees allowing a grand view of the Lairig Ghru from the hostel doorstep". As early as 1933, the SYHA had plans to expand the 'Cairngorm Chain' of hostels, showing that they were very aware of the popularity of the area with walkers, and thus the potential membership subscriptions they could generate from having hostels in or near to the district.[40] Alastair Borthwick, writing at the end of the 1930s, already saw the enormous potential of youth hostelling in Scotland:

> "I cannot rid myself of the conviction that the youth hostel movement is one of the more important social innovations of this century. It has opened up thousands of Scotland's deserted square miles … the Association numbers its members by the tens of thousands. What was once not even within reach of a summer holiday has become a week-end playground."[41]

Youth hostelling had an immediate appeal in Scotland to the young, the unemployed and the adventurous. In 1931, the SYHA nationally had only nine hostels and saw only 3,120 bed-nights in its properties; in 1932, nineteen hostels existed which had seen 22,366 bed-nights; in 1933, there were 33 hostels built with a further two pending. This was a dramatic surge in popularity, as much a product of home-grown enthusiasm, as it was from the international nature of hostelling. By 1991/92 the SYHA had 86 hostels and catered for 633,817 bed-nights, which represented a "substantial contribution to the Scottish tourist economy".[42]

Motorised Transport and Recreation 1920–1950

> "Here I did not stay long. Aviemore is merely a one-horse hamlet where motorists pull up to fill up, and is noted chiefly, if it is noted at all, for the number and excellence of its chocolate machines."

Matt Marshall's view of Aviemore in the early 1930s is not too far from that held by visitors in the 1980s and 1990s.[43] He was not alone in his scathing views of a town that even then, seemed on the surface only to cater for the car tourist. Charles Plumb, writing in 1935, found Aviemore to be, "a wretched place, a mere line of petrol-pumps and tin shops planted at the side of the Great North Road". Plumb urged the outdoor enthusiast to seek spiritual refreshment by staying overnight at Coylumbridge, a "pretty village …air rich with the pines", as close as one could to Rothiemurchus. A stay in Aviemore, he felt, drained the "self-sufficiency of health and strength which comes of having given yourself to the wilds and allowed yourself to forget the dismalities of organised society".[44] The world of the Speyside holiday was changing in the 1920s and 1930s, and romantics like Marshall and Plumb found themselves ill at ease with the new era of popular Highland tourism, fuelled by better roads, improved rail access and services, and increased leisure time. Visitors had come to the area by rail during the second half of the nineteenth century, and the scenic view from Aviemore station gained much fame with holidaymakers, although that transport innovation met with some adverse comment about noise and dirt even in the 1860s.[45] However, the car, the motor coach and the omnibus offered a different prospect.

Motoring enthusiasts subscribed to the *SMT Magazine*, which offered both advice on car purchase and gave numerous suggestions for motoring holidays in Scotland. The summer of 1934 saw unprecedented numbers of holidaymakers using Scotland's roads, and they were celebrated as very ordinary folk, reclaiming their right to look at Scotland's landscape heritage; "the liberation of the week-end crowd has come to stay", wrote Moray Maclaren that year.[46] Some of the most popular articles in the *SMT Magazine* were those that detailed accessible and beautiful drives in the Highlands, and there were no doubt many Speyside holidays planned from the comfort of armchairs. May Lawrence and her family recorded how they had come north from London in 1935, "to breathe the air among these wonderful old Scots pines of Rothiemurchus and Glenmore".[47] Articles that fondly recalled a visit to Rothiemurchus, especially Loch an Eilein, were commonplace, and it made no difference to the enthusiasm of the prose if the writer had journeyed by car or motor coach.[48]

There was undoubtedly a keen sense in the motoring literature of the early 1930s that the volume of traffic using Scottish roads was destined to increase greatly year by year, and enthusiasts felt that they were in at the start of a motoring revolution; after all "Scotland is the natural motoring paradise of Great Britain, alike in respect of scenic grandeur, sporting roads for the driver, and freedom for picnic meals", wrote the editors of the *Glasgow Herald* in their 1935 *Motoring in Scotland – a Touring Guide*, as they praised the visionary modernisation of the main north road to Inverness, via Pitlochry and Aviemore.[49] It was this rapid increase in tourist motor traffic that led to the improvements in the road north in the late 1920s, as part of the comprehensive scheme for Highland roads proposed by Inverness County Council. The north road was widened and resurfaced, an awkward bend on the Slochd was rectified and some blind corners were removed.[50]

In 1949, Alexander's Bus Services were advertising a service from Glasgow to Aviemore that took $6\frac{1}{2}$ hours and cost 14/3d. (single) and 26/– (return). The service also ran from Stirling, lasting 5 hours 33 minutes. The buses stopped at Newtonmore and Kingussie on the way north. This was only a seasonal service in the late 1940s, with one trip per day.[51] Matt Marshall found this motorised transport revolution a curse, for as cars fell in price and became more widely available:

> "These motorists are rapidly making the roads impossible for trampers. One can't walk a hundred yards but a motor pulls up, a head sticks out, and a voice says 'Jump in'."[52]

Contemporary observations of hotel life are rare, although some travel writers in the 1930s did record their observations of Speyside hotels. In the summer of 1934, Edwin Muir found a Kingussie hotel to be full of middle-aged ladies from Glasgow taking afternoon tea, "who sailed into the room like miniature battleships and bore down on their chosen tables as if they were enemies to be ruthlessly breached". Muir returned to his 1921 Standard car feeling that he "had seen a representative example of Scottish hotel life".[53] Hugh Quigley, in his 1936 collection of travel suggestions, *The Highlands of Scotland*, admitted that the book contained, "fireside adventures, armchair expeditions with the hint of vast spaces and infinite stretches of colour-filled air", but his readers were told that if they ventured anywhere, it should be to the Cairngorms, and to a certain unnamed hotel in Aviemore, from the terrace of which "one can watch sunsets so tumultuous and so extravagant in colour that no painter could reproduce them without being accused of crudeness or sensationalism".[54]

In 1937, the author Neil Gunn penned a stinging attack on those who felt that tourism (and its accompanying financial rewards and development potential) was the sole solution to the economic ills of the Scottish Highlands, individuals he called "half-sycophant depending on the whims of a passing tourist". This was part of a wider debate in the late 1930s about the somewhat inappropriate nature of earning a living through tourism in the remoter rural areas, which continues to the present day. It is interesting that Gunn singles out Badenoch, as a district where tourist money in the late 1930s did find its way into the pockets of the local communities, citing the "regular house-letting business, run for the most part by women who otherwise have only slender means of support". Gunn did have a frightening vision; that of "a complete and swarming tourism" in the Scottish Highlands, and of the landscape turned into a national lung, "so that folk from south of the Highland line could clamber into its emptiness to breathe".[55] Much of that vision seems to have become fact, fifty years or so later, in a region such as the Cairngorms.

This chapter has provided more evidence to suggest an expanding tradition of coming to the Cairngorms to enjoy recreational activity and holidays in the first half of the twentieth century, and earlier evidence has revealed that this tradition of visiting has its origins in the last decades of the eighteenth century. In the twentieth century, the motor car, improved access and the hotel industry have been central to the development of recreation and tourism in the district. Local hoteliers and businesses have taken the lead in promoting new and varied forms of commercial recreational activity in the first half of the twentieth century, leading to a wider development remit since the establishment of the Highlands and Islands Development Board (HIDB) in 1965. It is of note, that Donald Getz identified many of these factors listed above in his own statistical study of tourism in Badenoch and Strathspey, first published in 1986. He concludes; "There appears to be great resiliency in tourism as an economic mainstay for Badenoch and Strathspey. Part of this resiliency is tourism's propensity for encouraging individual entrepreneurship. There are many owners, and many small businesses, in addition to the few large operations".[56]

The years of the Second World War and the decade after 1945 saw little recreational or tourism development in the Cairngorms, principally due to the privations of the war years and the era of food and petrol rationing that followed. Much needed road improvements had been made in the inter-war years and the Spey Valley had come to be seen as an important and popular holiday centre on the main Highland tourist route north. The autobiography of Lord Rowallan presents military training in the Cairngorms during the war years as a contributory factor towards the development of outdoor sports in the Cairngorms range, as the presence of troops in the glens demonstrated the potential of the area for both commercial mountaineering and skiing, and stimulated thought on future recreational development initiatives. From May 1943 to November 1944, the Highland Fieldcraft Training Centre (HFTC) was based in Glen Feshie, as a direct replacement of the Mountain and Snow Warfare School which had previously peppered this glen with Nissen huts. A strong legacy of this military presence in the Cairngorms was the blending of a fervent social mission, preaching health and fitness, with an almost evangelical (and yet military) doctrine of disciplined recreation in an unspoilt wilderness area close to one's God, suggesting an early progenitor of the modern Outward Bound schools; witness Lord Rowallan's first view of the glen in late April 1943:

> "Here was ample silence in which the human spirit could expand and develop, where the sense of awareness could become keen and subtle. I followed the winding river, a natural obstacle in this varied assault-course. I halted at Glen-feshie Lodge, which would be the officer's quarters."[57]

Certainly much of the remit of the HFTC, including woodcraft, rock climbing, skiing, map reading and compass work, astronomy, observation training, survival courses and basic natural history lessons, seems to later have become an integral part of the social mission and recreational creed preached at Glenmore Lodge, which officially opened in September 1948. Initially, during the Easter holidays of 1947 and 1948, the Central Council of Physical Recreation (CCPR) and the Scottish Tourist Board (STB) had successfully liaised with Hugh Ross (Manager of the Aviemore Hotel) for Outdoor Holiday Training Courses to be based at the hotel. The Glenmore Lodge project in 1948 was a direct descendant of pilot ventures in Scotland run by David Douglas-Hamilton in 1938/39 at Guisachan in Glen Affric, and at Gordon Castle in Morayshire. The Glenmore scheme grew alongside the similar Outward Bound Sea School at Aberdyfi in mid-Wales.

The war seemed a long way away, when RAF wireless mechanic and Devon-born ornithologist E.H. Ware visited the Cairngorms in June 1942, although he did encounter squads of soldiers training along the narrow paths of Rothiemurchus on the route to the Lairig Ghru. This was a trip of a lifetime for this southern English birdwatcher, and his recollections of the parlous state for cycling of the road that ran from Coylumbridge towards Glenmore offers an insight into how little tourist infrastructure had been put in place in some localities. Making use of cheap RAF service rail travel from Braintree to Aviemore via Glasgow, E.H. Ware saw almost all of the Speyside bird specialities that he longed to add to his British list, but failed to see a capercaillie *Tetrao urogallus* in his week-long holiday,[58] a failure that many visiting birdwatchers must now endure.

The popular appeal of walking, climbing and rambling in the Cairngorms over the 1910s, 1920s, 1930s and on into the 1950s is apparent from even the most cursory glance at past editions of climbing club journals, where personal recollections of days out on the hills are reproduced for public consumption; this is especially true for the *Scottish Mountaineering Club Journal*.[59] Of course, not all came to the Spey Valley willing to be uncritical and simply admire and enjoy the scenery. Wilfred Taylor found that the Cairngorms did not please the aesthete in him: the hills held "big, lumpish, clumsy summits", and he agreed with Lord Gough that the Lairig Ghru was little more than "the Wee Nick" amidst uninspiring hills. Witness his most scathing comments:

> "as it happens I am not an impassioned lover of the upper Spey Valley. Much though I like the secret little lochans tucked away in the forest, I find the atmosphere peculiarly neutral and at times gloomy and oppressive. The Monadh Ruadh [the Cairngorms] are not very theatrical mountains and they are too far from the sea."[60]

Notes to Chapter 5

1   For recent historical writing on aspects of the history of tourism in Scotland see especially: Alastair J. Durie, 'Tourism in Victorian Scotland: the Case of Abbotsford', *Scottish Economic and Social History*, Vol. 12, 1992, pp. 42–54; R.W. Butler, 'Evolution of Tourism in the Scottish Highlands', *Annals of Tourism Research*, Vol. 12, 1985, pp. 371–395; T.C. Smout, 'Tours in the Scottish Highlands from the Eighteenth to the Twentieth Centuries', *Northern Scotland*, Vol. 5, 1983, pp. 99–121; Piers Brendon, *Thomas Cook – 150 Years of Popular Tourism* (Secker and Warburg, London, 1992); Alastair J. Durie, 'Tourism and Commercial Photography in Victorian Scotland: the Rise and Fall of G.W. Wilson and Co., 1853–1908', *Northern*

Scotland, Vol. 12, 1992, pp. 89–104; Eric Simpson, 'Aberdour: the Evolution of a Seaside Resort', in Graeme Cruickshank (ed.), *A Sense of Place – Studies in Scottish Local History* (Scotland's Cultural Heritage Unit, Edinburgh, 1988).

2   I.F. Grant, *Along a Highland Road* (Shepheard-Walwyn Publ. Ltd., London, 1980), pp. 11–14.

3   The archives of the Aviemore Station Hotel Company are held in the Scottish Record Office, West Register House, Edinburgh at SRO: GD 387/9, which was formerly NRA (S) 3017. SRO: GD 387/9-1, 'The Aviemore Station Hotel Company Limited, Memorandum and Articles of Association, 21 August 1899'.

4   SRO: GD 387/9-2, 'Directors Report and Accounts 1899–1912'.

Shares issued by December 1900

500 Preference Shares at	£6. 7. 6.	£ 3,187. 10. 0.
Ordinary Shares at	£6. 7. 6.	£ 5,756. 12. 6.
	Cash Creditor	£ 2,107. 0. 0.
	Total	**£11,051. 2. 6.**

5   SRO: GD 387/9-4, 'Ordinary General Meeting, Edinburgh, 2 March 1915'.

6   Anon., 'Our Directory of Recommended British Hotels', *SMT Magazine*, April 1934, and subsequent issues. The information for this table was taken from the *SMT Magazine* of July 1937. Hotels on the list in 1934 on Speyside were The Aviemore Station Hotel, Aviemore; The Star and the Duke of Gordon, Kingussie; The Balavil Arms, Newtonmore; The Grant Arms and the Palace Hotel, Grantown-on-Spey. Similar prices were still advertised in May 1939, although by May 1940, both the Aviemore-based hotels had disappeared from the list, probably due to the imminence of wartime requisitioning. Anon, 'The Doune of Rothiemurchus – Promotional Brochure', including Terms and Paragraphs on the Hotel. Phone: Aviemore 31. No date, perhaps 1935 or later.

7   SRO: GD 387/9-4, 'Directors Meetings Minutes, 1908–1945'. Meetings dated 10 April 1941, 27 September 1941, 28 September 1942.

8   SRO: GD 387/9-4, 'Report of Meeting of Directors, 12 April 1945'.

9   AA, *AA Hotels: England, Wales and Scotland* (AA, London, 1953).

10 See NRA (S) 102:483, Letter from John Peter Grant to a relative, James, dated 28 June 1887: "The Doune has been a hotel for some years past and I expected my father was at least living up to his income but I did not know what his income was."

11 Elizabeth Grant of Rothiemurchus, *Memoirs of a Highland Lady* (John Murray, London, 1898).

12 The archives of the Doune of Rothiemurchus Hotel are held in the Scottish Record Office, West Register House, Edinburgh, at SRO: GD 387/11. SRO: GD 387/11-1. 'Loan Account: Ledger, 1935–1940'; SRO: GD 387/11-1, 'Capital Account'.

13 SRO: GD 387/11-2, 'Day Book, 1935'; SRO: GD 387/11-3, 'Day Book, 1936–1939'; SRO: GD 387/11-4, 'Trading Accounts, 1936–1942'.

14 I would like to thank David Calvert of St. Andrews who has shared my enthusiasm for researching hotel history, and has helped with some incidental statistical analysis of hotel finances.

15 Anon., 'The Doune of Rothiemurchus – Promotional Brochure', *loc. cit.* The quotation used can be found at Elizabeth Grant of Rothiemurchus, *Memoirs of a Highland Lady – Volume One* (Canongate Classics, Edinburgh, 1992), pp. 208–209, beginning, "Tor Alvie on the right … ". I would like to thank Philippa Grant of Rothiemurchus who kindly gave me a copy of this brochure.

16 *The Scotsman*, Saturday 29 February 1936, p. 7. This advert was repeated weekly, until 21 March.

17 *The Scotsman*, Saturday 21 March 1936, p. 7.

18 *The Scotsman*, Saturday 18 April 1936, p. 6. R.T. Bowyer had his name under this advert. This particular style of advert remained the same until 23 May.

19 *The Scotsman*, Saturday 23 May 1936, p. 5. This advert was kept until 20 June.

20 *The Scotsman*, Saturday 27 June 1936, p. 5. Aviemore – Rothiemurchus – The Dell Private Hotel.

21 SRO: GD 387/11-1, 'Ledger, 1935–1940'. Road Sign, 'The Doune of Rothiemurchus Hotel – Sharp Turn at Fork, Half Mile On'. Philippa Grant showed me a paper copy of the design of this sign, with an attractive view of the Doune on it, dated 1938.

22 SRO: GD 335-15, 'List of Scottish Hotels where Society leaflets might be placed'. Including a letter from E.W. Macpherson, dated 6 August 1890, Scottish Rights of Way Society, George Street, Edinburgh to Hotel Owners.

23 Cairn: Kingussie Golf Club, *pers. obs.* Incidentally, there is a good and viewable black grouse *Tetrao tetrix* lek on the greens of this golf course, revealing a serendipitous link between nature conservation and recreation.

24 SRO: GD 387/9-41. 'Notice', dated 20 May 1913.

25 Anon., 'The Doune of Rothiemurchus – Promotional Brochure', *loc. cit.*

26 Hilary Parke, *Scottish Skiing Handbook* (Luath Press, Barr, 1989), p. 29.

27 Cairn: Carrbridge, Struan House Hotel, *pers. obs.*, 'In memory of Karl Fuchs 1924–1990, founder of the Austrian Ski School in Carrbridge. Erected by this community to honour his vision in establishing skiing in Scotland. A special thanks from the youngsters of the village'.

28 NRA(S) 102:399, Letter from Mrs. Grainger Stewart, London to Lt. Col. J.P. Grant of Rothiemurchus, Rothiemurchus Estate, dated 19 November 1931.

29 NRA(S) 102:398, Letter from W.R. Higginbotham, Honorary Secretary, Scottish Ski Club, Glasgow to Lt. Col. J.P. Grant of Rothiemurchus, Rothiemurchus Estate, dated 29 January 1935.

30 NRA(S) 102:398, Letters from W.R. Higginbotham, Honorary Secretary, Scottish Ski Club, Glasgow to Lt. Col. J.P. Grant of Rothiemurchus, dated 18 April 1936 and 22 May 1936.

31 NRA(S) 102:398, Letter from G.W. Cheyne, Honorary Secretary, Scottish Youth Hostels Association, Edinburgh to Lt. Col. J.P. Grant of Rothiemurchus, Rothiemurchus Estate, dated 18 July 1934.

32 Anon., 'Scottish Skiing Comes of Age', *The Highlands and Islands Today*, Issue No. 6, November–December 1982, p. 3.

33 J.A. MacDonald, *The Burgh of Kingussie 1867–1967* (Kingussie Town Council, Badenoch, 1966), p. 30. I would like to thank Margaret Ross of Leault of Kincraig who gave me a sight of this rare and much sought after book. This book is also part of the privately held archive of Badenoch Printers, Kingussie, catalogued in the SRO at NRA(S) 2081. See SRO: NRA(S) 2081-3/8. Guide books, local history and folklore texts about Kingussie from the period 1911 to 1946 are held at SRO: NRA 2081-2.

34 Louis Stott, *Robert Louis Stevenson and the Highlands and Islands of Scotland* (Creag Darach Publications, Milton-of-Aberfoyle, 1992), pp. 97-100, 113.

35 J.A. MacDonald, *op. cit.*, pp. 31–33.

36 James L. Duncan, 'Visitors' Book at the Shelter Stone', *Cairngorm Club Journal*, Vol. 12, No. 69, January 1930, pp. 117–121.

37 James L. Duncan, 'The Shelter Stone Visitors' Book', *Cairngorm Club Journal*, Vol. 11, No. 64, July 1926, pp. 212–213.

38 J.L. Duncan (1930), *op. cit.*, p. 121.

39 See archives of the Scottish Mountaineering Club (SMC) held at NLS: Acc 11538-273/274.

40 D.G. Moir, 'Scottish Youth Hostels', *Cairngorm Club Journal*, Vol. 13, No. 74, July 1933, pp. 132–138.

41 Alastair Borthwick, *Always a Little Further* (Eneas Mackay, Stirling, 1947), pp. 132–133. First published in 1939 by Faber and Faber Ltd.

42 Magnus Fladmark and Philip Lawson, 'Access Through Hostelling – The Role and Policies of the SYHA', in J.M. Fladmark (ed.), *Heritage – Conservation, Interpretation and Enterprise* (Donhead Publ. Ltd., London, 1993), p. 163.

43 Matt Marshall, *The Travels of Tramp-Royal* (W.M. Blackwood and Sons Ltd., Edinburgh, 1933), p. 172.

44 Charles Plumb, *Walking in the Grampians* (Alexander Maclehose and Co., London, 1935), pp. 70–71.

45 See Principal Shairp of St. Andrews' angry poem 'A Cry from Craigellachie' written as he journeyed north to Inverness on the newly opened Highland Line in 1864. It is reproduced in Alexander Macpherson, *Glimpses of Church and Social Life in the Highlands in Olden Times* (William Blackwood and Sons, Edinburgh, 1893), pp. 10–11.

46 Moray Maclaren, 'The Freedom of the Countryside – Scotland and the Motor Age', *SMT Magazine*, Vol. 13, No. 6, December 1934, pp. 54–56.

47 May Lawrence, 'Aviemore amid the Pines', *SMT Magazine*, Vol. 16, No. 4, April 1936, pp. 40–43.

48 See especially Margaret L. Murdoch, 'In the Heart of the Cairngorms – through Glen Einich with a Camera', *SMT Magazine*, Vol. 17, No. 2, August 1936, pp. 45–48; Anon, 'A Day's Run – to the Majestic Cairngorms', *SMT Magazine*, Vol. 19, No. 3, September 1937, no page numbers; William Newton Macartney, 'The Central Highlands and the Coasts of Lorne', *SMT Magazine*, Vol. 12, No. 6, June 1934, pp. 106–115; Anonymous Photograph, 'Loch-an-Eilein, Rothiemurchus', in *Take Note* (The Magazine of the Scottish Tourist Board), October 1947, p. 9.

49 Glasgow Herald, *Motoring in Scotland – A Touring Guide* (George Outram and Co. Ltd., Glasgow, 1935), p. 5. The tours described in this popular book, which sold for 2/–, had appeared serially in the *Glasgow Herald* in 1927, 1928 and 1929. A total of 45 individual motoring tours were included, with maps and historical notes. For the most complete stock of Motoring Maps outside of London, readers were directed to William Porteous and Co. of Glasgow.

50 I.F. Grant, *op. cit.*, p. 17.

51 *Scottish Omnibus Annual – 1949* (Travel Press and Publicity Co., Edinburgh, 1949), p. 132.

52 Marshall, *op. cit.*, p. 173.

53 Edwin Muir, *Scottish Journey* (Mainstream Publishing, Edinburgh, 1996), pp. 188–189. First published in 1935.

54 Hugh Quigley, *The Highlands of Scotland* (B.T. Batsford Ltd., London, 1949), p. 19. First published in 1936.

55 Neil M. Gunn, ' "Gentlemen – the Tourist!" the New Highland Toast', *Scots Magazine*, New Series, Vol. 26, No. 6, March 1937, pp. 410–415.

56 Donald Getz, 'Tourism and Population Change: Long-term Impacts of Tourism in the Badenoch and Strathspey District of the Scottish Highlands', *Scottish Geographical Magazine*, Vol. 102, No. 2, September 1986, pp. 113–126.

57 Lord Rowallan (compiled by Lorn Macintyre), *The Autobiography of Lord Rowallan* (Paul Harris Publishing, Edinburgh, 1976), pp. 121–132; Cairn: Carnachuin, Glen Feshie, *pers. obs.*, 'Highland Fieldcraft Training Centre 1943–44. In memory of those who gave their lives for their country. Erected by their friends who trained with them in the glen and at Poolewe, Wester Ross'. See also 'The Glenfeshie Prayer', reproduced on p. 131 of Rowallan's autobiography.

58 E.H. Ware, *Wing to Wing – Bird Watching Adventures at Home and Abroad with the RAF* (The Paternoster Press, London, 1946), pp. 30–38, 'Highland Highlights'.

59 See especially: E.P. Buchanan, 'Through Rothiemurchus to Rebhoan', *Scottish Mountaineering Club Journal*, Vol. 13, No. 77, June 1915, pp. 251–258; G. Murray Lawson, 'The Cairngorms – An Appreciation', *Scottish Mountaineering Club Journal*, Vol. 15, No. 89, April 1920, pp 233–240; David W. Robinson, 'Ghosts' High Noon on the Cairngorms', *Scottish Mountaineering Club Journal*, Vol. 19, No. 112, November 1931, pp. 261–265; A.W. Russell, 'Some Memories of Braeriach', *Scottish Mountaineering Club Journal*, Vol. 18, No. 106, November 1928, pp. 214-219; W. Inglis Clark, 'Reminiscences of the Cairngorms', *Scottish Mountaineering Club Journal*, Vol. 16, No. 93, April 1922, pp. 109–116; Alexander B. Beattie, 'A Day on

Braeriach' *Scottish Mountaineering Club Journal*, Vol. 16, No. 94, October 1922, pp. 174–181; William Smithard, 'First Impressions of the Cairngorms' *Cairngorm Club Journal*, Vol. 4, No. 21, July 1903, pp. 143–148; Edward Backhouse, 'Midnight Wanderings in the Lairig', *Scottish Mountaineering Club Journal*, Vol. 12, No. 71, June 1913, pp. 286–290; Walter A. Smith, 'A Visit to the Cairngorms in 1875', *Scottish Mountaineering Club Journal*, Vol. 14, No. 83, June 1917, pp. 224–234; James Maclay, 'The Cairngorms from Deeside', *Scottish Mountaineering Club Journal*, Vol. 8, No. 46, January 1905, pp. 192–196; Richard B. Frere, 'A Cairngorm Odyssey', *Scottish Mountaineering Club Journal*, Vol. 25, No. 144, April 1953, pp. 124–131; John Eaton, 'In a Pine Wood', *The Deeside Field*, No. 7, 1935, pp. 21–25.

60 Wilfred Taylor, *Scot Easy – Travels of a Roads Scholar* (Max Reinhardt, London, 1955), pp. 11–12.

6

The Post-war Recreation Boom

The twenty years from 1955 saw a dramatic boom in recreational provision and tourist accommodation and facilities in the Cairngorms area. The town of Aviemore was irrevocably altered, and the central corridor from Aviemore to Glenmore and up onto Cairn Gorm itself, became dominant in terms of economic, commercial and recreational activity. As Donald Getz explained, "the centralisation of growth at Aviemore will remain the dominant feature of tourism in the area".[1] These unprecedented changes were principally brought about by two factors; the winter sports developments on Cairn Gorm, and the construction of large multi-purpose Holiday Centres to cater for mass popular tourism in the 1960s. The 1960s and 1970s saw the birth of what Ernest Cross had discerningly described as the "fleshpots of Aviemore".[2]

Skiing and the Cairngorms

Skiing can trace its recreational pedigree back to November 1907, and the foundation of the Scottish Ski Club (SSC). The club lay dormant from 1914 to 1929, when it was revived and, under energetic leadership, its membership began to rise. In 1932 the SSC built a mountain hut on Ben Lawers in the Alpine fashion; by 1936, C.N. Fraser reported that it was possible to encounter fifty or sixty skiers in the vicinity of this hut. Unfortunately, the misguided optimism of the winter of 1931/2, when hundreds of people travelled north to Braemar and Ben Nevis to ski, did much damage to the prospects of the sport in Scotland; "skiable snow is *never* absolutely certain in Scotland";[3] that winter was one of the mildest on record. Writing in the *The Scots Magazine* in February 1937, Fraser made a concerted effort to keep the sport alive, boldly citing the Cairngorms area as providing, "the finest and most certain skiing in Scotland". There were some disadvantages which he identified, primarily that access to the high tops was long and arduous and the weather unpredictable. He also noted that the hills were becoming known only as a late spring skiing area (May), but at the worst, "one has had a lot of healthy exercise, and a long day in the open air and magnificent scenery". Dalwhinnie was also proposed as a possible alternative ski development area in this article of 1937.[4] Fraser would not have recognised Cairn Gorm just thirty years later.

After the Second World War, the growth of leisure time, and increasing affluence and mobility, laid the foundations for the recreational utilisation and exploitation of the natural resources of snow and scenery in the Cairngorms. With the impetus of Karl Fuchs' Austrian Ski School in Carrbridge, and the formation in Nethybridge of the Cairngorm Winter Sports Development Association (CWSDA) in March 1956, informal plans to develop the recreational potential of the mountains were made more focused and structured. Thus in April 1957 the CWSDA, was turned into the Cairngorm Winter Sports Development Board (CWSDB), which was registered under the Companies Act as a charity. This and all subsequent developments on Cairn Gorm took place within what the geographer Allen Perry has described as, "the context of generally lower winter temperatures and later springs than were experienced in the earlier part of the century". Climatic influences had an important role to play in the development of the Scottish skiing industry at this time.[5] It is also noteworthy, that much of the earliest skiing in the Cairngorms in the first half of the twentieth century was ski-touring (*langlauf*) and cross-country skiing; the SCC only organised their first slalom race in 1934, on Beinn Ghlas above Loch Tay, but by 1953 there were rope-tows running at this site and at Cairnwell. Commercial downhill skiing would, however, be developed elsewhere.[6] There appears to have been some fear in the mountaineering and hill-walking fraternity that the development of Scotland's hills for skiing could lead to a clash of interests, "and may provoke wrathful comment on all plank-straddlers from members-who-do-not-ski". Writing in May 1957, the mountaineer Geoffrey J.F. Dutton urged members of the Scottish Mountaineering Club (SMC) to seek a compromise with the growing band of skiers in an area such as the Cairngorms, and take up what he called "ski-mountaineering". There was a hint of club snobbery here, for the thrust of Dutton's plea was that skiers, whose pursuit he labelled as "pointless and frustrating", would clutter the most scenically majestic mountain areas of Scotland with "a successful ski lift … its attendant flags, loudspeakers, race-cards and sleigh bells".[7] In 1984, Raymond Simpson was similarly confrontational, attacking all "climbers who showed a healthy disdain for stray skiers".[8]

The CWSDA had been the driving force behind the campaign to construct a surfaced road from Glenmore to the ski grounds at Coire Cas after 1956; however, with the creation of the CWSDB in 1957 (whose sole purpose was to provide uplift and other appropriate facilities for skiers) the search for money took on a more organised approach. Fund raising by the CWSDB brought a total of £14,000 for this venture, but in the late 1950s Inverness County Council decided to build the road themselves, interested in the tangible returns to be gained from the development of skiing infrastructure on Cairn Gorm. This road was built in 1960. At this stage the CWSDB had declared their three objectives to be:

1. To establish and develop as a National Winter Sports Area the Cairngorms and adjoining districts of Strathspey and Badenoch.

2. To provide, maintain and develop in the area particularly on the north side of the Cairngorms, winter sports facilities of all kinds, including roads and means of access to the location of such facilities.

3. To foster and encourage in Great Britain and in particular in the youth of the nation an active interest in winter sports.[9]

These are quite wide-ranging objectives taking in development and education, and the promotion of the sport of skiing in the nation. They also reveal how strong the organisation's desire was to develop the winter sports recreational potential of just the Cairngorms range. The £14,000 saved was pooled together with an anonymous donation of £20,000 to construct a first chairlift on Cairn Gorm, which opened on 29 December 1961 as the White Lady Chairlift.[10] The uplift facilities on the mountain were an immediate success and over the winter seasons of 1962/63 to 1964/65 there was a tenfold increase in the number of skiers on Cairn Gorm.[11] By 1966, the CWSDB had broadened their objectives to cover all types of recreation on the high tops, in this clause:

A. To provide, maintain and develop sports facilities of all kinds, including roads and means of access to the location of such facilities.[12]

This had been done to bring the CWSDB into the framework for the wider recreational and tourist developments proposed for Aviemore, which reached a high point in the middle years of the 1960s. To reflect these wider objectives, the CWSDB saw another name change around 1966, becoming the Cairngorm Recreation Trust Limited (CRTL), and at the same time the building and operational activities of the CWSDB were transferred to a subsidiary company, the Cairngorm Sports Development Limited (CSDL), who principally held a developmental remit which would start to bring them into direct conflict with nature conservation interests in the late 1970s, as environmental awareness led to vocal public outcry about the despoilation of the Cairngorm range. A further name change came in 1978, when the CSDL became the Cairngorm Chairlift Company Limited (CCCL) with directors being drawn from the old board.[13]

Throughout the 1960s the private sector led the way in the development of downhill skiing facilities on Cairn Gorm, and although the local authorities played an important supporting role, their approach can best be described as just reactive and promotional. Inverness County Council did provide the nec-

essary infrastructure support in the construction of roads and services crucial
to the success of a private sector ski facility, and sought to include recreational
development programmes at Aviemore in the 1960s within their own statutory
development plans for the region. However, this was done principally because
the growth of Aviemore as a winter tourist resort would see the extension of the
Strathspey tourist season and produce considerable financial returns. Inverness
County Council appeared confident that its own guardianship of the Cairngorm
range was adequate and would best serve the interests of the local people, in a
decade that saw developmental benefits triumph over fledgling environmental
and nature conservation concerns.[14]

In the first months of 1963 it became obvious to the CWSDB that
demand was exceeding supply at the Cairn Gorm chairlift, due not only to the
exciting recreational possibilities offered there, but also to outside publicity. On
14 March 1963, *The Scotsman* displayed on page 1 a large photograph of skiers
on Cairngorm, under a banner caption entitled:

> "Youth – High in the heart of the Cairngorms skiers head towards the skilift
> through deep snow. This has been a boom year for Speyside, and the Cairngorms
> are now recognised as the winter playground of Britain." [15]

An Early Development Plan 1963

The National Trust for Scotland holds a copy of the CWSDB application to the
Board of Trade in January 1963 for loan facilities to support more development
in the Cairngorms area, and it shows how popular the ski facility on Cairn Gorm
had become since the opening of the first chairlift just 14 months earlier. The
loan was refused in March 1963, but the application offers a valuable insight
into the mindset of the CWSDB. From December 1961 to 24 August 1962,
the chairlift made £10,928 from paying customers, which the CWSDB stressed
was an indication of how valuable their role was on the mountain, "and the great
benefit the Board's activities have conferred on the Youth of Scotland and on the
tourist industry in the area, which now has a Winter Sports Season in addition
to a Summer Holiday Season". Later the CWSDB named hotels that could
now stay open all year round since the chairlift opened, and cited which hotels
had built accommodation extensions to cater for the influx of visiting skiers;
they predicted that upwards of 100 local hotel jobs would be created during
the winter season and that over 200 jobs could be generated by the successful
installation of proposed development initiatives. Other tangible benefits listed
by the CWSDB were to the construction industry in the modernisation of
hotels, to 30 ski instructors who worked in the district, to two sports shops in
Aviemore, to a local bus operator who ran eight buses a day to transport skiers

up onto the skiing grounds, to petrol filling stations in the area and at towns on the road north, and to the passenger traffic at local railway stations (which may have helped to prevent station closures in coming government cutbacks in rail services).

Some mention was also made of the financial structure of the CWSDB, as the geographical site for the chairlift was in Glenmore National Forest Park, and the Forestry Commission (FC) had refused to allow any overtly commercial development there. A public appeal for funds was made and a Cairngorm Trust was formed in September 1960 (mainly from funds given by the benefactor George Boyd Anderson; the NTS eventually donated £1,000) to provide shelter for skiers on the mountain. The land on which the chairlift was built was held on a 99-year lease from the FC. The loan application was made to the Board of Trade in 1963 because the directors of the CWSDB felt that no further public appeal for money could legitimately be made; a proposed development plan with finances was submitted and totalled £142,000, with the work envisaged being completed over the coming four years.[16] It was broken down as follows:

A. Primary Requirements:

T-Bar Tow in Corrie Cas	£10,000
Extension of present chairlift from Shieling down to Car Park	£30,000
Shelter at Top Station with Toilets and Coffee Bar	£10,000
Small T-Bar Tow on White Lady	£5,000
Large T-Bar Tow on Corrie Na Ciste	£15,000
Small T-Bar Tow on Corrie Cas	£5,000
Toilets at Car Park with Small Kiosk	£5,000
Essential Equipment	£14,700
Working Capital	£2,300
Total	**£97,000**

(Source: NTS Archives)

B. Secondary Requirements:

Chairlift at Corrie Na Ciste	£30,000
Housing for Staff	£ 9,000
Snow Making Machine	£ 5,000
Plastic Mats	£ 1,000
Total	**£45,000** [17]

(Source: NTS Archives)

In the concluding section of the original loan application, the CWSDB asked that they be judged not just on their own business enterprise, but also on the enormous contribution they made to the Speyside economy: "as a service to the community and as the Board hopes, a pilot scheme to be adopted for other areas in the Highlands".[18] Although the loan application was refused and the CWSDB had its earliest development plans thwarted, there is much in this document that shows the CWSDB to be keenly aware that the widest possible development remit (that is the Cairngorm area, and not just Cairn Gorm itself), could prove the most attractive proposal for donors or lenders. Although much of the document stresses the need for ski infrastructure improvements on the mountain, there are a sufficient number of paragraphs covering tourism and recreation in the district to show that the scheme was regional and not localised in its scope. Construction of a shieling building, funded by the Cairngorm Trust, had begun in May 1961 and cost around £25,000.

Indeed, this issue which first surfaced in 1963, would predominate in the mid-1960s. The NTS, who owned the White Lady Shieling on Cairn Gorm from May 1964 to May 1967 were similarly seeking a structured development plan for recreational facilities in the area, under the guidance of one individual or leading organisation. J.C. Stormonth Darling, Secretary of the NTS wrote to George Boyd Anderson[19] of the Cairngorm Trust in July 1963, about his uneasiness over the White Lady Shieling's position on the ground and in the eyes of the CWSDB. He then vocalised his concerns about the wider picture:

> "It is so clear to me that this whole enterprise from the road and railway station at Aviemore right to the top of Cairngorm requires a 'managing director' who could enthuse everyone, mould the various interests and co-ordinate into one big endeavour. I feel the present lack of co-ordination and confidence and what appears to be the absence of development plans and improvements for this winter can be disastrous. The excellent name won for Cairngorm can so easily be lost by the reputation that things were disorganised, that the road once again failed, and that there was not sufficient diversification for 'uplift' on Cairngorm."[20]

This letter would suggest that the NTS did not then know about the proposed development plans submitted by the CWSDB earlier in the year, but this is not surprising as poor relations existed between the NTS, the Cairngorm Trust and the CWSDB in the mid-1960s. These internal disputes were not made public until the late 1960s, and in the years prior to that an outsider's view of developments on Cairn Gorm was of numerous organisations working together, not of too many cooks spoiling the broth (which was closer to reality). In a NTS press release of April 1964 the White Lady Shieling and Cairn Gorm was to be developed by joint consultation between the NTS, the CWSDB, the NC, the Scottish Council of Physical Recreation (SCPR), the FC, the mountaineering clubs and other 'open air' societies, although the NTS did claim that only they had the necessary experience and knowledge to run such a venture because of their "numerous experiments in multiple use of mountainous properties" at Goatfell on Arran, Ben Lawers in Perthshire and Glencoe and Kintail in Wester Ross. It is noteworthy that the local authorities were excluded from this list, for what the NTS was now calling "the Cairngorm enterprise",[21] showing how a mountain range was now clearly being seen as a marketable commodity, as well as a recreational obstacle course. A year later in April 1965, an internal NTS document sought to clarify the nature of the Trust's ownership of the White Lady Shieling and the relationship between the FC and the CWSDB on Cairn Gorm itself. Confusion still reigned, although some flavour of the original agreement is given; the CWSDB were granted exclusive rights to carry out the development of winter sports amenities by the FC, in an area which lay within the Glenmore National Forest Park and which included the White Lady Corrie, Coire Cas and Coire na Ciste. However, the FC remained as landlords, and as such had already refused approaches from the Scottish Ski Club and the Highland Ski Club to erect club huts on the mountain, urging that the NTS cater for these demands by extending the White Lady Shieling. The NTS announced that such an extension, including club quarters, an information centre and additional shelter would cost £23,000 in April 1965 and that they had already spent £10,000 on improvements since taking over the property in May 1964. More importantly, the Treasurer of the NTS, A.C. Laing, was aware that this proposed development and extension of the White Lady Shieling came at a time when major capital investment was being made in hotels, motels and ancillary facilities in Aviemore, and that this expansion in the tourism and recreation markets should be rigorously co-ordinated to offer the greatest mutual benefit to all involved. By the middle of 1965 there was a wait-and-see approach in evidence on Cairn Gorm, as the CWSDB and the NTS looked down into the Spey Valley to see how developments there might pan out; as Laing conceded:

> "At this stage it is difficult to judge what may be the future pressures on the use of the Shieling. There has been much discussion about the opening up of further ski slopes and new access routes to the mountains. Whatever new developments may come – as they must come – it is not difficult to envisage a situation where the White Lady Shieling would not remain as a base point on a primary and popular route."[22]

Little progress had been made by June 1966.[23] In May 1967, the NTS sold the White Lady Shieling to CWSDB for £13,807 after their ownership of it proved a financial and administrative headache. They had hoped to use it as a new place to recruit NTS members, but this did not materialise as expected, and instead they become embroiled in legal disputes and debates over the further development of Cairn Gorm.

Further ski developments on Cairn Gorm were given a kickstart in 1967 with the publication of the Scottish Development Department's *Cairngorm Area* report which almost went as far as to state that new ski development on the mountain would be serving the national interest, both in terms of tourism, recreation and local economies. The report urged the development of Coire na Ciste, Lurcher's Gully, Corrie an t-Sneachda and Corrie an Lochain, with the building of a new ski road (envisaged as costing £55,000) and new car parks, chairlifts and ski tows. The report was the work of local authority planning officers, under the chairmanship of F.J. Evans (Regional Planning Officer of the SDD); it anticipated a huge increase in the popularity of skiing in Scotland and set out to devise a planned response and development framework to accommodate that coming demand. Road construction was central to the structure of the report with the primary consideration being a road through Glen Feshie to connect Braemar with Kingussie (at £2m), a road link to Beinn a' Bhuird, and a road through the Pass of Ryvoan linking Nethybridge to Glenmore. The report failed to offer policies and counter measures to stem any identifiable environmental damage being done on the Cairn Gorm ski grounds, nor did it ever approach offering a strategic policy framework for the regulation and management of proposed ski developments.[24] National planning guidelines for ski developments in Scotland were not produced until as late as February 1984, by the SDD in response to the Lurcher's Gully Public Inquiry in 1981/82. The Evans report, "effectively legitimized the continuing development of the Cairngorms".[25] Evans and his fellow planners also sought agreement with the Scottish Branch of the National Playing Fields Association, and urged an immediate increase in the provision of football pitches, tennis courts, bowling greens and playgrounds in the Aviemore area.

However, the SDD report of 1967 did at least end the post-war un-planned, *ad hoc* development of skiing in the Cairngorms, and offered some sense of planning direction and guidelines. Development of Cairn Gorm continued apace. In 1968 a new road was built up into Coire na Ciste, and in that same year the Ptarmigan Restaurant was built just beneath the summit of the mountain. Allan Campbell McLean later labelled it an "impertinent pimple on the majestic brow of Cairngorm".[26] Only in 1979 was a definitive report on landscape appraisal and building in the countryside produced for the Highland Regional Council (HRC) by Betty L.C. Moira, and this particular restaurant was shown to offer different visual impressions across the seasons:

> "It should be remembered that recreational buildings at ski slopes have a different appearance in winter when they are partially snow-covered and rounded, whereas in summer they are completely revealed, with any paths or eroded areas around them."

In a series of line drawings of the restaurant, Moira conceded that at least skyline siting of the building had been avoided.[27]

Throughout the early 1970s there was continual ski development on Cairn Gorm, with an almost annual provision of new ski tows; the peak in visiting skiers came in the winter of 1973/74. Previously, during 1973, Coire na Ciste had been developed with the construction of a new car park and chairlifts, from funding sought in 1970 from the HIDB. This was the second major expansion of the available skiing area, into a corrie that had long been recognised as suitable for ski development. However, it was in 1971 that the HIDB took on a leading role in recreational provision in the Cairngorms, by securing an area of around 6,000 acres on Cairn Gorm from the FC, including all the present and potential ski development areas, and then leasing 1,600 acres of it to the Cairngorm Sports Development Ltd. (which they now in fact jointly owned along with the Cairngorm Recreation Trust). HIDB renamed this land as the Cairngorm Estate. Despite the immense popularity of the ski slopes on Cairn Gorm in the first years of the 1960s, it was not until 1968 that formal recognition of this came from within the sport, when the National Ski Federation of Great Britain held the British Alpine Ski Championships on Cairn Gorm for the first time.

The Aviemore Centre and Coylumbridge Hotel

The first public announcement that the village of Coylumbridge had been targeted by a group of wealthy businessmen as the ideal place to construct a new type of holiday and leisure park, came in April 1963, when the Chairman of Scottish and Newcastle Breweries Ltd. reported on his company's "participation in the proposed Holiday Centre at Coylumbridge, Inverness-shire",[28] although it must be assumed that private negotiations between the interested parties had been ongoing for some months prior to this public disclosure of a radical new tourism development plan for the Cairngorms. The original idea was that the Aviemore area in the 1960s could have room for one good quality hotel complex, and Coylumbridge was always the first choice by businessmen and industrialists keen to invest in the new leisure industry boom, but also motivated by mildly philanthropic ideals to help the economy of the remoter Highlands of Scotland: tourism seemed to fit the bill well. The story of how two separate holiday centres were built, at Coylumbridge and Aviemore is an interesting and politically-charged reflection on how seductive the development craze in the tourism industry became in the Highlands in the mid-1960s, and sits well alongside parallel developments that were occurring on Cairn Gorm at the same time. It is noteworthy that these big tourist developments in the Cairngorms came just before the long overdue inception of the Scottish Tourist Board as a statutory body under the Development of Tourism Act 1969, when a more structured organisational promotion of tourism facilities in the Highlands became the norm.

Even a key player in the area, such as the NTS, was caught off-guard by the announcement of April 1963. In August 1963, J.C. Stormonth Darling wrote to W. McEwan Younger in Edinburgh urging restraint and a greater consideration of the wider recreational picture:

> "... but I do honestly think that the proposed holiday centre at Coylumbridge needs a good deal more thought. There seems to have been a conspiracy of silence about all this, and your statement at your AGM is the first time this proposition seems to have surfaced publicly ... I sincerely hope that large sums (some say £ $^3/_4$/1m) will not be injected into one scheme."

The NTS letter sought clarity on what was the proposed overall plan for the area, and urged full co-operation with the various landowners. Above all, the NTS took a stance against greedy developers too focused on one isolated project. Stormonth Darling continued:

> "I think that private enterprise would develop at Aviemore quite rapidly if there was confirmation of the arrangements for the chairlift (i.e.) a guaranteed road, giving access to the chairlift, and further diversification on Cairngorm for different types of skiers, with the linking up of Deeside, thus opening the door to trekking over the plateau, stopping overnight and coming back again."

Darling told Younger that the NTS was now irrevocably bound to the tourist industry, and sought "better facilities by everyone along the road ... they must all be organised at the highest standards".[29] Sadly, such high standards did not prevail in the subsequent completion of architectural designs, negotiations over planning permission, the world of business etiquette or the financial dealings between the interested parties. The NTS, who by late 1963 were seemingly destined to take over the running of the White Lady Shieling on Cairn Gorm, were a little detached from these negotiations on the valley floor below, but did maintain a healthy interest in the coming shenanigans. As with all controversial financial and developmental projects, hearsay played a key role, as Stormonth Darling reported to J.F.A. Gibson, Vice-President of the NTS, in August 1963:

> "The controversy <u>contra</u> Coylumbridge is now getting hot. Alice Maconochie, staying with the Youngers, reports that she retired to bed at 1 a.m. this morning having failed to convince Bill that his ideas of a millions of pounds development of six hotels at Coylumbridge is wrong. He is inferring that everyone is behind it – Government, petrol companies, Fraser and the lot – and that, therefore, it is almost a <u>fait accompli</u>. I think it will receive the most almighty smack both in the national press and locally ..."[30]

This is a key letter, for much of what Gibson predicted in late August 1963, did in fact come true. By September 1963, the Scottish Office had put their full weight behind the scheme and W.G. Pottinger had been given the task of taking the Coylumbridge development to its fruition. Douglas Cochrane of the Cairngorm Trust continued to put pressure on the NTS to take over the White Lady Shieling on Cairn Gorm warning that, "due to a little madness over development in Rothiemurchus, on the part of St. Andrews House aided and abetted by Hugh Fraser, I think it important that items like the Shieling are in safe hands, and I rather like the look of yours".[31] It was in the autumn of 1963 that matters came to a head, when Pottinger brought in the architect J.G.L. Poulson and also linked up with Hugh Fraser and other businessmen to form a consortium whose aim it was to create a self-contained holiday village. It was the most ambitious tourism and recreational project of its kind undertaken in the UK in the 1960s, and was cited by those involved as a massive investment in the leisure industry. The success of the Coylumbridge venture depended upon a foundation of goodwill being generated with the landowner, Colonel Grant of Rothiemurchus, and his acceptance of the Poulson architectural plan for the site. A letter from Stormonth Darling of the NTS to W.G. Pottinger in St. Andrews House gives a flavour of that original Poulson design. Stormonth Darling protests that a complex with 1,750 beds "seems to be a disproportionate increase until the slopes on Cairngorm are able to absorb so many". He also pointed out that the road up the mountain was still vulnerable, that summer facilities on Speyside could not measure up to such an influx, and in addition, "it is not clear how the landowners in the area are prepared to open up their land for walking, pony trekking, motoring, birdwatching etc." Poulson's plan was to cut down many old trees to clear a site for the hotel, and then plant some small spruce trees. The development area totalled 60 acres, and included a "skyscraper hotel" which the NTS felt "might well appear very offensive". The NTS letter sent to Pottinger and A.C. Sheldrake in the Scottish Development Department is full of healthy criticism, and a warning that the Scottish Office had not fully thought the proposal out; they were rushing ahead with the scheme, caught up in the rush of a development craze. For instance, Stormonth Darling asked if Pottinger had yet canvassed the opinion of the Nature Conservancy (NC) on the project, for "without advice as to where visitors should go there might well be chaos and certainly friction, and, of course, we have to bear in mind that so much of the area is close to the Nature Reserve, to which access should presumably be guided and attracted along certain paths".

The point was also again made that such a proposed development should take place closer to Aviemore, "since this seemed the only hope of putting fresh life into the village with a move towards some degree of co-ordination of a community which has developed in a very haphazard way". The geographical financial implications of the project also provoked comment, in that the proposed cost (now £1.25m) was too much to be spent on just one scheme; "Tourist money needs spreading round the country and Speyside is already doing pretty well", argued Stormonth Darling. Most importantly, the NTS drew Pottinger's attention to the key role of Grant of Rothiemurchus as the landowner at Coylumbridge. Were Pottinger and Poulson confident that the laird of Rothiemurchus would accept the consortium's plan for the area; did they have his full co-operation in this exercise? As Stormonth Darling concluded; "in other words the co-operation of neighbouring landowners seems to be essential as part of an overall tourist development plan in order to absorb this large invasion concentrated at Coylumbridge, where more will be accommodated than in the whole of Speyside on present figures".[32] There was much for Pottinger and Poulson to think about in this letter. It should have acted as a clear warning.

Much then hinged on the response of Colonel Grant of Rothiemurchus. It is believed that the laird was initially impressed with George Pottinger, and had long held the view that some recreational development at a site such as Coylumbridge on the Rothiemurchus Estate, would be of benefit to visitors who wished to stay closer to the Caledonian pine forest and soak up its atmosphere and antiquity.[33] Before eventually going on to reject the Pottinger-Poulson plan for Coylumbridge and asking them to redraw it, the laird of Rothiemurchus first communicated his thoughts on the plan to J.C. Stormonth Darling in early October 1963, probably because he already knew that the NTS considered the plan to be ill-conceived. Indeed, Rothiemurchus Estate Office gained strength from acting in unison against the plan with the NTS, in the face of concerted pressure from government sources for them to support Pottinger's scheme. Grant of Rothiemurchus was angry that Pottinger had been making incorrect claims of support for the plan in political circles: "he has no justification for claiming, as indeed he did, that the National Trust was wholly supporting the Fraser Development Plan for Coylum Bridge", wrote the laird. Grant called the architectural plan that he had been given by Poulson, "a monstrosity of a scheme ... which is obviously far too large to be absorbed within this area". It is equally interesting that, despite being on the same side in this argument, Grant of Rothiemurchus actually disagreed with the line that the NTS had adopted in wanting to concentrate all new tourist development at Aviemore. He told Stormonth Darling that Aviemore was not a popular holiday centre and spoke as if the town now lay beyond the salvation offered by a new leisure industry.

> "A great many people do not relish staying in Aviemore, chiefly because of the noise of the diesel trains (much louder than the old steam engines) and partly the traffic on the Great North Road. I do not consider it at all reasonable to suggest that these people should not be catered for in a quieter and more peace-

ful area in Rothiemurchus, which would be the choice of very many visitors of all types. I have always thought this could be done by judicious use of the Coylum Bridge site." [34]

In Grant of Rothiemurchus' eyes the Pottinger-Poulson-Fraser plan submitted for Coylumbridge in the last months of 1963 was not a judicious use of the land, but in opposing it the laird brought himself into direct conflict with the development consortium. Pottinger had clearly assured the architect J.G.L. Poulson that his plan would not meet with any local opposition or planning difficulties, and when Grant refused to countenance such a proposed development on his land, Poulson flatly refused to redraw the plans to the laird's liking. Grant of Rothiemurchus then chose to ditch the consortium and open up the Coylumbridge site to an architectural competition in 1964 to find another architect and design. A Rank Organisation plan was later accepted by the laird and in November 1965 the Coylumbridge Hotel was opened.

In a misuse of political power George Pottinger telephoned Grant of Rothiemurchus in early 1964 and threatened the laird, saying that if he did not go ahead with the original Poulson design, then Pottinger would use his considerable influence in the SDD and the Scottish Office to see that no planning permission would ever be given for another hotel on the Coylumbridge site. [35] Colonel Grant complained bitterly to the Scottish Office about Pottinger's behaviour. In the face of a developing political argument and local opposition to the Coylumbridge plan, the consortium reluctantly turned its attention towards a development in Aviemore itself, and in 1964 Hugh Fraser founded Highland Tourist (Cairngorm Development) Limited, and appointed Capt. John G. Wells as General Manager. Meanwhile, the Coylumbridge Hotel proved to be a public success and brought even greater numbers of visitors into the heart of Rothiemurchus; as did the free publicity that *The Scotsman* gave the estate in October 1965, by running a series of photographs by R.W. Munro from the newly opened Loch an Eilein Nature Trail. The laird expressed his thanks to Alastair Dunnett, Editor of *The Scotsman*, for showing "this small example of the active co-operation of private landownership with the Nature Conservancy". [36] It was in 1965 that proposals were first made for the upgrading of the Coylumbridge to Glenmore road, for which the laird of Rothiemurchus had long campaigned.

The Aviemore Centre is Built

In 1964, the Board of Directors of Highland Tourist (Cairngorm Development) Limited under the Chairmanship of Lord Fraser of Allander, comprised a strong contingent of magnates from the Scottish brewing industry, such as Sir William McEwan Younger (Chairman of Scottish and Newcastle Breweries) and W.R.C. Elliott (Managing Director of Tennent Caledonian Breweries), sitting alongside A.W. Hardie (Managing Director of Shell and BP Scotland). As this industrial and entrepreneurial might pushed for the rejuvenation of the Highland economy through tourism, the architect J.G.L. Poulson worked on a new holiday centre development for Aviemore, which he submitted in April 1964. This second plan offers an insight into the enormous scale of the proposed construction. The Aviemore Centre was to have a Hostel Complex (with 250 beds), a Scottish Breweries Ltd. Hotel (with 100 beds), a British Railways Hotel (with 90 beds), plus eight more smaller hotels sleeping from 50 to 75 visitors. A total of five large car parks were included on the plan, with one huge general car park in the centre. Other recreational facilities outlined on the draft plan were a cinema (to seat 700), a swimming pool and changing area, shops, a Conference and Exhibition Hall, a seven-lane international-size curling and skating rink, a plethora of bars, cafés and restaurants and tourist offices and kiosks deployed around the complex. Poulson offered a suggested route for a proposed by-pass of Aviemore town centre, and his vision held the space for parking over 1,200 cars.[37] The total project covered about 30 acres and sat beneath the Craigellachie National Nature Reserve; it is believed that Poulson based his design for the Aviemore Centre on a previously discarded design he had made for a holiday centre on a Mediterranean island,[38] evidence perhaps of the rushed nature of the architectural job, as the consortium sought to keep their Highland Holiday Centre dream alive in the months after the Coylumbridge development setback.

The Aviemore Centre was completed in the autumn of 1966, and was officially opened by Lady Fraser of Allander on 14 December 1966. An invitation to attend this ceremony was sent to J.C. Stormonth Darling by the Directors of Highland Tourist (Cairngorm Development) Ltd., but this was curtly refused in late November, perhaps indicating lingering resentment over the Coylumbridge Hotel *débâcle*.[39] In a promotional brochure for the summer of 1967, a wide range of sports and holiday activities were on offer for the domestic holidaymaker who could not yet afford to travel to the Mediterranean on the cheaper package holidays overseas that were becoming more available in the second half of the 1960s. A six-day fishing course was available at the Centre's own Fishing School on Loch Pulladern for £5. 5s. 0d.; pony trekking for six days would cost a visitor £10. 10s. 0d; holiday package deals were available to introduce holidaymakers to canoeing, sailing, skiing and hill walking, a five day course costing £6. 0s. 0d. Accommodation in one of the Aviemore Chalets cost £1. 1s. 0d. per night, with concessions available for larger parties and longer stays. The brochure boasted that "Scotland's newest all year round all weather sports centre offers facilities for individual and family holidays from early May through to October".[40] Under the management of John Wells (former submarine officer) the holiday centre became known locally as 'HMS Aviemore'.[41] The Aviemore Centre was a bold and ambitious project, and its success in the leisure market was immediate, offering an enormous range of recreational opportunities and providing a cheaper base than a conventional hotel, from which to explore the wider Cairngorms area. Indeed, hotels based in the more traditional holiday centres on Speyside, say Newtonmore or Grantown-on-Spey, struggled to compete with the considerable allure of Aviemore for mass popular Highland tourism across the 1970s.

Praised in the brash development era of the 1960s, the siting and design of the Aviemore Centre came in for an increasing amount of criticism for its impact on the landscape (its visual pollution) from the mid-1970s onwards. In 1976, Allan McLean questioned the "mediocrity of the architecture" of the Aviemore Centre, sensing that "this assortment of geometric concrete blocks constitutes an offence against nature in the shape of the Monadhliath mountains and the mighty Cairngorms". Few would now dispute his conclusion that in neighbouring Rothiemurchus "the Scandinavian-style Rank complex at Coylumbridge merges much more happily with its surroundings".[42]

A fascinating link between nature conservation and recreation surfaced from research into the history of the Aviemore Centre. It appears that as early as February 1966, Lord Fraser of Allander and the consortium expressed a desire to incorporate an educational 'Highland Wildlife Exhibition' within the grounds of the holiday centre, occupying one third of the Exhibition Hall. The consortium had acted in such a fashion, keenly aware of the growing popularity of the RSPB Loch Garten osprey hide, and aware that "the opportunity to observe wildlife is a feature of the summer hill walking expeditions and nature trails".[43] The evidence suggests that, in Edinburgh in November 1965, George Waterston (of the RSPB in Scotland) convened a meeting to discuss the link between tourism, recreation and nature conservation on Speyside. No minutes were taken at that meeting, but a meeting to be held on 7 June 1966 was seen as a direct successor to that first informal gathering. From the agenda for this second meeting, it is apparent that John Wells proposed the establishment of a joint wild life information centre on Speyside to be run on behalf of the participating organisations, which by August 1966 were the RSPB, the Scottish Wildlife Trust (SWT), NC and the FC. Wells also proposed that display cases should be incorporated into the scheme to promote the local work of these organisations. Douglas Weir and K.M. Wallace (of the NC) urged that the discussion should include reports on local conservation work in relation to tourism in the area, stressing a greater degree of co-operation and efficiency in the disseminating of a nature conservation message on Speyside. John Wells stressed that nature conservation was a message that had to be 'sold' to the general public arriving *en masse* in Aviemore, and that an area master plan to balance recreation and nature conservation had to be the long-term goal of the partnership.[44] These are all now prominent themes in the work of the Cairngorms Partnership (founded in 1994), based in Grantown-on-Spey, as they seek to plan for the future of the wider Cairngorms area into the twenty-first century.[45] There are no further records of any later meetings of this early partnership in the late 1960s. By the early 1970s HIDB had funded the publication of a number of books on wildlife in the Scottish Highlands, written by naturalists such as Desmond Nethersole-Thompson and David Stephen.[46] Sponsorship for this Highland Wild Life Exhibition was obtained from Shell-Mex and BP Limited, who held a presence on the Board of Directors of Highland Tourist (Cairngorm Development) Ltd. anyway. However, it does seem that from the outset of the consortium's involvement at Aviemore, it was a declared policy of the company to inform the public of the wildlife potential of the area and "to promote a better understanding of the countryside". Lord Fraser of Allander, in a press release from April 1966, argued that the exhibition was "not just another tourist gimmick", rather it represented his own "sincere desire to preserve one of the last remaining natural environment areas in Britain by offering a focal point of interest allied to a measure of control and direction". Ironic words, when his development consortium had just provided the accommodation and recreational facilities to bring visitors to the Cairngorms in historically unprecedented numbers. Indeed, Fraser of Allander did quietly admit that the Aviemore Centre could bring "thoughtless and ill-informed individuals" into the Cairngorms, and that there was local concern that the "effect of an influx of tourists on the Cairngorm Nature Reserve" might be "unwarranted damage to its wealth of wild plants and animals". There was, however, a driving campaigning zeal to the fore here, and Lord Fraser was not going to let a few worries stifle his vision of tourism as saviour of the Speyside economy, with due deference given to existing nature conservation interests. He concluded:

> "If promoting the desire to retain a priceless national asset also brings pleasure to a large number of people then something worthwhile will have been achieved."[47]

The Wider Recreational Picture

A leading article from the *Glasgow Herald* on 25 January 1963, addressed the issue of new 'Holiday Towns' in the Highlands of Scotland. The writer drew attention to the visit of Colin Campbell and his colleagues of the Sutherland Tourist and Holiday Development Association to Glasgow, to promote tourism as a growth point for the Highland economy, and to show how the proper organisation of winter sports, and improved access to quality fishing could make Sutherland a key player in the Highland leisure industry. Interesting parallels were drawn between the Cairngorms and Sutherland, and although in early 1963 the massive injection of industrial, commercial and government capital was still to come, Lord Fraser assured the writer that it was just on the horizon, and that the Highland Tourist Development Company had already financed £160,000 worth of work on the extension and improvement of hotels across northern Scotland. The article went on to say that, as new factory towns were born in southern Scotland, surely new holiday towns should be created in the north to revive the Highland economy and to provide a playground for industrial workers in the Central Belt. Strong criticism was meted out to the non-commercial CWSDB:

> "the question must be raised whether a rate-aided, non-profit making organisation can give the operating efficiency or all the expansion that is now needed. There would at least be a stronger incentive to satisfy the customers if the facilities were on a commercial basis."[48]

George Pottinger wrote in September 1959 to Michael Lorimer, the Secretary of the Scottish Landowners' Federation (SLF), envisaging the coming years of expanding tourism in the Highlands, and urging estate owners to sign up for the considerable financial benefits to come. Pottinger assured Lorimer that the unrivalled sporting attractions of the Highlands would not be overshadowed by any grand tourism plans or publicity from the STB, and indeed, went on to suggest that the SLF became involved in the promotion of a contest for top sportsmen throughout the world, to be held in the Highlands, and to be called the 'John MacNab trophy' (after the John Buchan novel of 1925).[49] This was an attractive proposition to some SLF members, including James Hunter Blair of Maybole who asked (in an internal SLF memo) that estate owners might signpost their estates and plantations in the Highlands, a scheme which the STB also supported.[50] It does appear that landowners in the Cairngorms were encouraged to become fully involved in the development of tourism plans from the outset, and it is recorded that Hugh Fraser sought the counsel of the SLF and the British Field Sports Society as part of his initial review for the expansion of tourism in the Highlands. By the mid-1960s it seems that Cairngorm landowners, rather than just accepting an advisory role, now took the initiative and formed themselves into an SLF-sponsored action group that they called the 'Cairngorm Working Party', under the chairmanship of the Earl of Haddo. Incidentally, this evidence reveals that Magnus Magnusson's later Cairngorm Working Party of 1991/92 did not have an original name. Much of the stimulus for the creation of such an informal association came from a desire amongst Cairngorm SLF members to scrutinise the proposals contained in the Interim Report of the Technical Group of the Scottish Development Department, issued for consultation in January 1964.

The SLF Cairngorm Working Party was formed on 7 August 1964 at an Inverness meeting of Cairngorm landowners (which was well attended, with 44 estates represented, Lord MacDonald acted as Chairman) convened to discuss a Cairngorm Tourist Development Plan. This Working Party submitted a four page report to the SLF on 22 September that year, urging that the Cairngorm tourist development area proposed by the government should be governed by a Development Commission with statutory powers based in Grantown-on-Spey, on which all interests should be represented. The Working Party also recommended the appointment of local gamekeepers/foresters/shepherds as Special Constables for the area, and the creation of a Tourist Warden Service. More picnic places, shelter huts, information lay-bys and caravan sites were called for. The Commission should receive a 100% government grant they believed, and it should be given powers to formulate and enforce bye-laws dealing with the control of public access.[51] At the Inverness gathering of Cairngorm landowners in August 1964, J.P. Grant of Rothiemurchus encouraged all the estate owners present to inform the SLF just how much tourist infrastructure they did allow on their land and, "what further facilities they were prepared to provide, and subject to whatever condition they might feel was reasonable to accept in return for allowing tourists on their land". By far the longest return in this informal survey (completed on 18 January 1965) was that by the laird of Rothiemurchus, who certainly seemed to have embraced tourism warmly, as he explained at Inverness:

> "I would be prepared to do more provided there was, on a quid pro quo basis, a warden service and controlled access. The state would be getting a very good bargain if some of the landowners were to provide such facilities in return for a measure of control."

There was some humour at the Inverness meeting. Major W.G. Gordon of Lude said that he was personally more interested in tourism in the Caribbean than in the Cairngorms, going on to state his actual dislike for the word 'tourism' which implied that people had to move about all the time. He concluded; "What was wanted was for people to come and stay in the area, not to move from place to place". He also pushed for the strengthening of the Litter Act and the Caravan Act, to curb the behaviour of irresponsible visitors.[52] Looking at the way in which the Cairngorm landowners came together in 1930 to fight a National Park designation for the area [see Chapter 8], and in this formation of a Cairngorm Working Party in 1964 to assess tourism development in the area, not forgetting the early formation of a North-East Scotland Land Defence Association in 1906 [see Chapter 3], there is ample evidence that estate owners in the Cairngorms from the start of the twentieth century have proved themselves perfectly willing and able to come together and fight their corner. They have shown great determination and resiliency in these confrontations with outside interests or government. In 1964, the Working Party urged the SLF to begin a comprehensive landownership survey for just the Cairngorms area, and the resulting map and paperwork (with 70 estates and owners listed) is an overwhelming geographical confirmation of how, at times, the landowners have seen themselves as an independent single regional unit.[53]

Tourism development became a dominant landuse in the Cairngorms during the 1960s, and from 1961 to 1981 tourism rapidly became the leading employer in Badenoch and Strathspey, to a point where the area is clearly heavily dependent on tourism as its economic mainstay. Although ski developments on Cairn Gorm provided a considerable impetus, the most dramatic change came with the completion of the Aviemore Centre in 1966 and its subsequent demand for labour. Aviemore, as a Highland town, has been profoundly altered since the early 1960s, as Donald Getz has shown: "since 1961 the Spey Valley has experienced a pronounced process of urbanisation, its character changing from that of a rural Highland community to a population much more resembling the British norm". Factors such as transport, television, and increased personal mobility are important to this change, but Aviemore has hosted a large-scale in-migration of young professional and entrepreneurial workers who favour tourism as a force for creating employment and making money in the area.[54] National trends in holiday-making for the 1960s, 'suggest that the inception of Aviemore as the focus for Cairngorms tourism and recreation, came at an appropriate time. In 1962, around 60% of the British population was taking a holiday, compared with 50% during the period from 1949 to 1956. In 1962, about 4.5 million people took two or more holidays, and in 1960 a social survey estimated that British people made at least 7.5 million day trips, "so that secondary holidays and day trips now contribute substantially to the total volume of holiday movement particularly at weekends and at Bank Holidays". A Speyside and Deeside local accommodation survey took place in August 1964 and concluded that there was little slack in Speyside hotel and bed and breakfast capacity, whereas on Deeside there were beds available all the year round.[55] Tourism and recreational development continued apace in the Cairngorms throughout the 1960s, with accelerated development in the last four years of that decade and the first half of the 1970s.

It is rather difficult to place the recreational and tourist development of the Cairngorms in the 1960s in a wider context, as there is little statistical evidence in existence for this decade or indeed, for much of the 1970s. The comprehensive Cairngorms area visitor survey is a product of the 1980s.[56] Only by 1972 was the *Scottish Abstract of Statistics* providing detailed information on a wide range of leisure and recreational activities, although the earlier *Digest of Scottish Statistics* had started to provide a small assortment of leisure and social statistics as early as 1965, focusing principally on the purchase of television licences, visits to Ancient Monuments in Scotland and visits to NTS properties.

Small gleanings can be taken from a variety of reports and other published sources. The Scottish Development Department (SDD) report of 1967 *Cairngorm Area*, uses statistical evidence to show an increasing tourist traffic for the wider Cairngorms area from 1960 to 1964. The number of visitors to Blair Castle was recorded by the Scottish Tourist Board in 1960 as 43,285; by 1964, this figure was 54,905. The number of visitors at Am Fasgadh ('The Shelter': the folk museum), Kingussie, increased from 8,590 in 1960, to 11,000 in 1964. An estimate of the number of holiday beds available on Speyside and Deeside in 1964 was made at around 5,100, with 511 beds available in the SYHA network of hostels, which now included a new hostel at Aviemore (with capacity doubled to 64 beds) and additional hostels at Corgarff (28 beds), Loch Morlich (144 beds), Kingussie (80 beds) and Braemar (95 beds).[57] The Cairngorms Working Party (CWP) calculated that in 1977/78 around 1.5m 'bed nights' were spent in Badenoch and Strathspey; by 1989 this figure had risen to 1.9m 'bed nights', with Pitlochry in the south hosting an additional 1.2m 'bed nights' alone in 1990. The report concluded that from the early 1970s, visitor numbers in the eastern Cairngorms (Deeside) stood at just a tenth of those for Badenoch and Strathspey, and the scale of tourist provision was thus similarly smaller.[58] These findings of the Working Party are in stark contrast to the euphoria displayed by the editors of *The Scotsman* in March 1967 when they predicted the massive development of Deeside as a winter sports centre, just a day after the publication of the SDD report with its £35m plan for the development of the wider Cairngorms area. In an editorial, the Coylumbridge Hotel and the Aviemore Centre were seen as just stepping stones in the "check list for action", given the overriding need to promote tourism as the universal cure-all for the regeneration of the Highlands. The editors suggested, "There is no other area so suitable for development – rugged, provenly attractive to skiers, and yet comparatively accessible from the South. The bulk of the initial investment on the vital infrastructure, must come from the Government. Roads are a priority". The writers had first asked if such an "extensive area of relatively undisturbed beauty" should even be developed at all – answering their own question later with a resounding 'yes' and a plea for immediate action.[59] Inverness County Council did finance major road improvements up onto Cairn Gorm from 1967 to 1969; in 1978/79 the A9 was re-routed and a number of towns and villages were by-passed (Dalwhinnie being the first on a list that included Newtonmore, Kingussie, Kincraig and Aviemore), facilitating speedier access on the route north, but signalling a decline in passing tourist traffic through the centre of the holiday towns. In a photographic essay to accompany the writing of James Grassie on the modern Highlands and Islands from 1962 to 1984, the Italian-born Oscar Marzaroli included a photograph of the Cairngorm Ski Slopes taken in the winter of 1970, showing hundreds of visiting skiers enjoying their sport beneath lines of ski tows: an important reflection of how the outsider's view of the Cairngorms and the wider Highland region had broadened to include the sense of the mountains being a playground or adventure course for those who sought to master Nature.[60]

One visitor survey of note in the 1970s was that undertaken in-house by the Nature Conservancy Council (NCC) in July 1973, which provides a useful comparison with the better-known investigations of Mackay Consultants in 1985/6 and from July to September 1987. The findings of the NCC survey were published alongside those of a Summer Visitor Survey undertaken by ASH during August 1980 as part of the environmental impact analysis commissioned by the CCCL. The 1985/6 winter survey calculated that Cairn Gorm, with 350,000 skier days that season (next came Glenshee with 120,000), generated £9.8m for the local economy, giving 280 full-time jobs on an annual basis (or 673 full-time jobs in the season) plus upwards of 2,000 part-time jobs in season. The average daily spend of a skier on Cairn Gorm was £28.22, compared with £15.61 over at Glencoe; campers in the wider Cairngorms area spent on average £23.21 a day; hotel guests spent £39.46 a day[61]. The 1987 report warned that, "in the absence of historical data, it is very difficult to draw conclusions about how the total number of visitors to the area has changed over time"; and this has proved a difficult hurdle to negotiate in this book. However, by making use of the NCC survey of 1973, it is conjectured that visitor numbers to the Cairngorms had increased by c.40% by 1987. At the seven common interview sites around the mountains the average daily numbers in July 1987 were 40% higher than in July 1973. However, Coire Cas and Loch an Eilein, where there has been a substantial increase in visitor numbers, are excluded from the statistical comparison made above. The Summer 1987 Survey concluded that from July to September about 150/175,000 'person visits' were made to the Cairngorms NNR and the adjacent HIDB estate; on the nineteen survey days alone, over 23,923 people were counted, and 3,727 people were interviewed. On the basis of the complete summer survey of 1987, group size increased from an average of 3.2 in 1973, to 3.9 in 1987; there was a notable increase in the period 1973 to 1987 in certain recreational activities; climbing up from 2% to 14%, botany up from 7% to 11% and ornithology up from 12% to 17%. Interestingly, around 44% of questionnaire respondents in 1973 were on their first visit to the Cairngorms; this figure had fallen to 25% by 1987. A useful aspect of the 1980 survey by ASH was that it focused on patterns of recreational use of the Cairngorm plateau and the Northern Corries in August of that year, recording that on fine days over 809 people reached the summit of Cairn Gorm and 31 reached Ben MacDhui; on poor weather days only 90 reached the summit of Cairn Gorm and 12 forged on to Ben MacDhui.[62] Using chairlift ticket sales, it does appear as if summer use (June to October) of the uplift facilities at Coire Cas has been in decline from 1972/73 to 1980, with the results indicting a 4% per year decrease, strikingly similar to the results from 1980 to 1987. The peak summer use of the chairlift was recorded in 1972 with 104,913 visits, followed by 1973 with 100,994 visits. By 1978 this figure had fallen to 74,642 and in 1987 it stood at just 52,372 visits.[63] In commissioning the 1987 Summer Visitor Survey the Countryside Commission for Scotland hoped that it would be the first comprehensive recreational survey in the area to "lay the foundation for more systematic monitoring and surveying of the Cairngorms in future years".[64] This emphasises the unique and pioneering nature of this visitor survey, and provides ample evidence of how the lot of the historian of countryside recreation in Britain can be so frustratingly lacking in good statistical source material prior to the 1980s.

The years from 1960 to the present day can be categorised as an era of mass leisure and car ownership, and it has seen an area such as the Cairngorms being valued by outsiders as an invigorating obstacle course for recreational pursuits, a haven of unique flora and fauna, and perhaps a last haven of wilderness (certainly of 'wild land') in Britain, where the landscape both inspires and uplifts the human spirit and allows brief moments of tranquil contemplation and a momentary withdrawal from an increasingly urban society. The tourist industry in the Cairngorms, whether it services the needs of a nature lover, a week-end driver and scenery admirer or a passionate devotee of winter sports, or indeed, the mass charabanc or coach-borne tourist who only desires to be led from a scenic viewpoint to a café to a hotel, has flourished enormously since the 1960s. A plethora of tourist attractions opened in the Cairngorms in the 1970s as a response to the growing tourist trade and the accompanying post-romantic user interests in the Cairngorms range. A Highland Wildlife Park opened at Kincraig in 1972; a water sports centre was built on Loch Morlich in 1978 revealing how full recreational use of the Cairngorms now incorporated leisure pursuits on loch and river; the Landmark Visitor Centre was built in Carrbridge in 1970, bringing a major commercial recreational development to the area, incorporating tourism with environmental education. The Aviemore Centre continued to provide for on-site family-based entertainment by opening the garish Santa Claus Land and a Craft Centre in 1975. The district of Badenoch and Strathspey alone could offer around 12,000 beds to visitors in 1978, over double the 5,100 on offer in the SDD calculation for both the eastern and western Cairngorms in 1964.[65] It is worth noting that the Aviemore Centre was initially the jewel in the crown in the marketing strategy of the Aviemore and Spey Valley Tourist Board during the 1970s and 1980s. In the mid-1970s winter sports holidays in the Spey Valley were aggressively marketed: a 'Spey Pack' costing £14 in 1973 gave the skier an all inclusive holiday with equipment hire, tuition and local transport[66]. In 1975, 'SnoRail' and 'SnoAir' travel deals were available from London and other cities, along with learn-to-ski holidays costing £50 per week[67]. By 1992 the Aviemore Centre was not even photographed for the local tourist brochure. Its decline came about due to two recessions in the 1980s and 1990s and several poor ski seasons, along with competition from cheap package holidays overseas. In 1986, the original owners of the Centre sold it to an hotel company, sensing that tourism and recreational development had actually peaked during the mid-1980s,[68] and that growing national environmental concerns could now thwart any proposed development projects, especially any projected expansion of ski facilities on the high tops.

Emerging Environmental Concerns

The 1970s were also the decade that saw an emerging environmental concern for mountainous areas, in particular, how recreational development was running unchecked in fragile mountain ecosystems. Few objections were ever raised about the initial development of Cairn Gorm in the early 1960s, and the CWSDB began a reseeding programme on the mountain as early as 1962, but the situation changed as an annual build-up of access roads, ski tows and car parks occurred. J.B. Nimlin (NTS Principal Field Officer) visited Cairn Gorm just prior to NTS acquisition of the White Lady Shieling on the mountain. His report of August 1963 offered a first-hand account of the level of environmental degradation already occurring at the site, and should have stood as a warning to the NTS that their role as custodians of the shieling building needed to be well thought out. Nimlin spoke of a crying need for environmental education on Cairn Gorm for the visiting public, skiers and chairlift staff, observing a good deal of litter, and people collecting moss campion *Silene acaulis*. The bulk of his report drew attention to visual amenity issues; the Coire Cas road would "add to the scars which mar the view from Rothiemurchus" he observed. Nimlin felt that chairlift company staff were aware of the problem, but were "at present busy adding to the scars". Finally, Nimlin sought reassurance from his employers that they would "watch this expansion, with its inherent threats to flora, fauna and scenery".[69] NTS ownership of the White Lady Shieling would fall very short of Nimlin's expectations. It was becoming increasingly obvious by 1975 that ski development could have a harmful effect on the mountain fauna and flora, and could impinge on other user interests. The growth in popular voluntary charitable nature conservation bodies and the developing role of the NCC allowed scientific research to be pursued on this issue, and kept the debate in the public arena.[70] As the power of the emerging environmental lobby grew in the 1970s, so the blind *ad hoc* recreational developmental era of the1960s came to a halt, running up against first, the Lurcher's Gully public inquiry of 1981/82, and later the conflict between developers and nature conservationists in the Northern Corries in 1989/90. A new ski access road was built in August 1981,[71] and the Cairngorm ski centre continues to bring visitors to the area who see the mountains as little more than an obstacle course, what Hilary Parke in her *Scottish Skiing Handbook* has recently called:

> "a truly heady dose of the powerful and totally addictive drug to which thousands of us fall prey every year … those few precious moments when suddenly, magically, it all comes together and your skis do just what you want them to."[72]

Equally, other visitors come to admire the aesthetic beauty of the landscape, often armed with Ernest Cross's guide to *Walks in the Cairngorms* or his wide-ranging *Speyside Holiday Guide*.[73]

One of the most eclectic bodies concerned with nature conservation issues in the Cairngorms was formed as early as autumn 1974, as a group within the Aberdeen Branch of the Conservation Society, reflecting a long-standing interest in the mountains uniquely shown by that north-east city, that dates back into the late nineteenth century and the formation of the Cairngorm Club. Over fifty people joined the Group in 1974, ranging from climbers, hillwalkers and naturalists to research scientists, and "also some people who simply value fine country and scenery"; amongst the earliest recruits were broadcaster, writer and rambler Tom Weir and ornithologist Desmond Nethersole-Thompson. The Cairngorms Group (as they named themselves) sent out a long letter to other organisations in November 1974, in this instance the Scottish Rights of Way Society (SRoWS), in an attempt to publicise their formation and to state their own intention "to become an action group, an internal information service, so that advance warning of new developments is sent to members". The Group sought to forge links with climbing clubs, voluntary conservation agencies and organisations, government bodies, planning departments and private estates, in an effort to avoid unnecessary confrontation over any proposed developments in the Cairngorms that were "likely to go against good planning and to damage the outstanding features of the area". Avoiding conflict by preparatory consultation and constructive co-operation was the key here; after all, the Group explained, they were a "body of people who would far rather enjoy being out on the Cairngorms than get involved in unnecessary conflict". The SRoWS were urged to involve themselves fully in constructive contact with the Group, "so as to lessen the likelihood of future conflict and to conserve the finest features of the area for the benefit of this and future generations".[74] Historically, this local group should be seen as a direct forerunner of another north-east group, the North East Mountain Trust, formed in 1980, which sought to preserve the natural heritage of the Cairngorms, both for recreation and nature conservation interests.[75] Both these Aberdeen-based bodies stand as regional groups passionately concerned about the future of the Cairngorms in the late 1970s and 1980s, and determined to find a balance between competing landuse interests in the years of conflict with recreationalists, nature conservationists, developers and private landowners. Such concerted action, taken at a local geographical level, directly influenced the formation of more widely-based 'Scottish' groups in the 1980s that drew in support from all over the UK, and decided to take a more radical, confrontational, proactive stance against the intrusion of ski developments into the Cairngorms area: for example, the Scottish Wild Land Group, formed in 1982,[76] and the Save the Cairngorms Campaign (SCC) launched in 1988 with its *Manifesto for the Cairngorms*.[77]

Mountaineering and climbing clubs in Scotland after 1970 began to evolve into more than just organisations for the promotion of recreation in upland areas. The Association of Scottish Climbing Clubs (ASCC), which had formed in the mid-1950s, had come under increasing pressure during the late 1960s for its failure to recognise that many of its members, as well as being devotees of mountaineering, had a keen interest in natural history and thus, nature conservation. The ASCC was also criticised for its administrative structure which could not react or function effectively in the face of growing recreational pressures on mountainous areas in Scotland, and it was felt that the loosely associated body would have to form itself into a "properly constituted Council, with an Executive Committee meeting regularly", in order to speak with any authority on the need for a balance between landuse interests in an area such as the Cairngorms. At an informal ASCC meeting in July 1969 at Strathclyde University, a decision was taken to rename the organisation the Mountaineering Council of Scotland (MCS), which was duly formed in January 1970. As well as promoting the interests of mountaineers and mountaineering in Scotland, and providing technical advice, the new constitution sought to "educate mountaineers and the public about the conservation of the environment and mountaineering ethics",[78] which in itself reflected a sea change of opinion within the mountaineering fraternity in Scotland. At a meeting in November 1970, the President of the MCS recorded an income of £150 and 31 member clubs, including the Cairngorm Club of Aberdeen, the Aberdeen University Lairig Club, the Glasgow Glenmore Club from Paisley, the Grampian Club from Dundee, the Moray Mountaineering Club from Elgin, the Ladies Scottish Climbing Club from Glasgow, along with other clubs and Holiday Fellowship bodies from Stirling, Glasgow, St. Andrews, Edinburgh and Inverness. The Honorary Secretary, T. Muir Wright of Dunblane, also recorded having attended the 1970 Mountain Rescue Course at Glenmore Lodge in the Cairngorms, praising both the training, the technical guidance and the hospitality he received. It was felt that "members of various Scottish climbing clubs should attend such courses".[79]

In the first two years of its existence, the MCS was urged by its members to make two notable interventions on issues affecting the Cairngorms. First, in September 1970, it voiced the concerns of many climbing clubs in Scotland over the 'occupation' of Cairngorm bothies by large Army parties for extensive periods of time, feeling that it was "reasonable to assume that bothies were really for small parties on short one/two night stops".[80] Later, in January 1972, the MCS were called upon to explain how the balancing act between the recreational demands of skiers and climbers was actually worked out on Cairn Gorm, after clarification was sought by a group of visiting climbers from North Wales who, much to their irritation, had been caught up in some altercation on the mountain about future ski developments:

> "The Committee regard Coire Cas as the skiers and summer tourists domain, and therefore if they want these things, the climbers stand aside. We do not feel this is any thin ended wedge; we feel that the north corries Cas and Ciste could be made to let the skiers enjoy themselves on chairlifts, on the piste and in the coffee bars. I wonder why the North Wales people are concerned. Maybe they are not aware of the restricted area all this affects and look at it as some further degeneration of the wild area of the Cairngorms in general."[81]

Notes to Chapter 6

1   Donald Getz, 'Tourism and Population Change: Long-term Impacts of Tourism in the Badenoch and Strathspey District of the Scottish Highlands', *Scottish Geographical Magazine*, Vol. 102, No. 2, September 1986, pp. 113–126.

2   Ernest Cross, *Short Walks in the Cairngorms* (Luath Press, Barr, 1994), p. 10.

3   C.N. Fraser, 'Scotland and Skiing', *The Scots Magazine*, New Series, Vol. 26, No. 5, February 1937, pp. 344–349 (italics in original).

4   C.N. Fraser, *Ibid.*, pp. 346, 347, 348.

5   Allen H. Perry, 'Climatic Influences on the Development of the Scottish Skiing Industry', *Scottish Geographical Magazine*, Vol. 87, No. 3, December 1971, pp. 196–201.

6   Roger Smith, 'The Playground of the Future', in Magnus Magnusson and Graham White (eds.), *The Nature of Scotland – Landscape, Wildlife and People* (Canongate/ Scottish Post Office Board, Edinburgh, 1991), pp. 196–210. As late as April 1962, Adam Watson still preferred *langlauf* skiing in the Cairngorms over the newer sport of downhill racing, as he recorded in 'Cairngorm Langlauf', *The Scottish Mountaineering Club Journal*, Vol. 27, 1960–1963, pp. 348–352.

7   Geoffrey J.F. Dutton, 'Skis in Scottish Mountaineering', *The Scottish Mountaineering Club Journal*, Vol. 26, No. 148, May 1957, pp. 121–125.

8   Raymond Simpson, 'Cairngorm Crossing', *The Scottish Mountaineering Club Journal*, Vol. 33, No. 175, 1984, pp. 39–42.

9   No access was allowed to whatever private archives the Cairngorm Chairlift Company may hold, although they did claim on a number of occasions by telephone, that all records from before 1970 had been destroyed. An Administrative Officer in the company who had worked there from the 1960s, said that at its outset, the CWSDB was just "a group of eight men whose job it was to build a chairlift".

I am grateful to Tanya Adams of the Cairngorm Chairlift Company who did send me a number of outline historical sheets of paper in 1995, from which this more detailed information is taken. They were titled: Cairngorm Chairlift Company: A Short History; Cairngorm Recreation Trust; Economic and Social Impact.

10 Cairngorm Chairlift Company information.

11 R.G. Elliott, M.G. Lloyd and J. Rowan-Robinson, 'Land Use Policy for Skiing in Scotland', *Land Use Policy*, Vol. 5, No. 2, April 1988, pp. 232-244.

12 Cairngorm Chairlift Company information.

13 Cairngorm Chairlift Company information.

14 Elliott, Lloyd and Rowan-Robinson, *op. cit.*, p.234.

15 Anon., Photograph: 'Skiers on Cairngorm – Youth', *The Scotsman*, 14 March 1963, p. 1. Page 2 held a piece entitled 'The Haunting Melodies of Speyside'. Also held in NTS; CWLS 1, C43.

16 The archives of the National Trust for Scotland are held at 28 Charlotte Square, Edinburgh. NTS; CWLS 1, C43, 'General background concerning the Cairngorm Winter Sports Development Board Limited and its Application to the Board of Trade for loan facilities to further Development in the Cairngorms area', drafted January 1963.

17 NTS; CWLS 1, C43, 'Cairngorm Winter Sports Development Board Limited, details of additional capital expenditure, cost and reasons for the proposed extension of the facilities in the Cairngorm area', drafted January 1963.

18 NTS; CWLS 1, C43, *loc. cit.*, 'Loan application by CWSDB', drafted January 1963; see ftn. 16. The CWSDB probably sent the NTS a copy of this document because of the NTS role on Cairn Gorm at the White Lady Shieling in the mid-1960s.

19 George Boyd Anderson was born in Elgin, and made his fortune in the rubber trade in Malaya as a planter. His interest in skiing came late in life, from a winter holiday to Switzerland in the early 1960s. He became determined that those in Scotland who could not afford to travel to the Alps to ski, especially the young, should have access to the sport. His enthusiasm and fortune established the Hillend Ski Centre, and artificial ski slope in the Pentland Hills near Edinburgh, in 1966. The first experimental slope there was a mere 50 metres long. The trust deed for the Cairngorm Trust was drafted on 13 July 1960, and signed on 9 September. It spoke

of the need "to provide shelter especially during blizzards for the large numbers of people likely to be attracted by the Cairngorm chairlift to this remote and exposed mountain area". Anderson wanted his building at the foot of the White Lady Corrie to be used by skiers, hillwalkers and the general public.

20 NTS; CWLS 1, C43, Letter from J.C. Stormonth Darling, NTS, to G. Boyd Anderson, 26 July 1963.

21 NTS; CWLS 2, C41, Press Release: Cairngorm – White Lady Shieling, issued 16 April 1964.

22 NTS; CWLS 2, C41, 'The White Lady Shieling, Cairngorm. Plans for Extension', drafted by A.C. Laing, Treasurer NTS, 6 April 1965.

23 NTS; CWLS 2, C41, Agenda and Minutes of NTS Executive Committee meeting held on 8 June 1966.

24 Scottish Development Department, *Cairngorm Area – Report of the Technical Group on the Cairngorm Area of the Eastern Highlands of Scotland* (HMSO, Edinburgh, 1967), pp. 27–30, 52–56.

25 Elliott, Lloyd and Rowan-Robinson, *op. cit.*, p. 234.

26 Allan Campbell McLean, *The Highlands and Islands of Scotland* (Crescent Books, New York, 1976), p. 56.

27 Betty L.C. Moira, *Highland Landscape – A Report on Landscape Appraisal and Building in the Countryside*, prepared for the Highland Regional Council by Moira, Moira and Wann, Architects and Landscape Consultants (Inverness, 1979), p. 21.

28 NTS; CWLS 1, C43, 'Coylumbridge Development, Scottish and Newcastle Breweries Ltd. – Statement by Chairman for year ending 30 April 1963', p. 1.

29 NTS; CWLS 1, C43, Letter from J.C. Stormonth Darling, NTS, to W. McEwan Younger, Edinburgh, 21 August 1963.

30 NTS; CWLS 1, C43, Letter from J.C. Stormonth Darling, NTS, to J.F.A. Gibson, NTS, 21 August 1963 (underlining in original).

31 NTS; CWLS 1, C43, Letter from Douglas Cochrane, Cairngorm Trust to J.C. Stormonth Darling, NTS, 19 September 1963.

32 NTS; CWLS 1, C43, Letter from J.C. Stormonth Darling, NTS, to W.G. Pottinger, Scottish Development Department, St. Andrews House, Edinburgh, 4 October 1963 (underlining in original).

33 Interview: J.P. Grant of Rothiemurchus, 22 July 1994 and *pers. comm.*

34 NTS; CWLS 1, C43, Letter from J.P. Grant of Rothiemurchus, Rothiemurchus Estate Office, By Aviemore, to J.C. Stormonth Darling, NTS, Edinburgh, 7 October 1963.

35 This incident came to light through Colonel Grant's diligent recording of all the telephone conversations he had with George Pottinger over this winter of 1963/64. See also a recent newspaper article: Alastair Robertson, 'Never Never Land', *Sunday Times*, Ecosse, Section 12, 21 September 1997, pp. 1–2. George Pottinger was ultimately imprisoned after it was revealed that he had accepted over £30,000 worth of bribes from the architect John Poulson in the 1960s. W.G. Pottinger sat on the NC Scottish Committee as Scottish Office Assessor, from January 1965 to early 1968

at least. By 1984, the House of Fraser were losing £10,000 a week on the Aviemore Mountain Resort (AMR), and the centre was sold to Reo Stakis for £800,000 in 1986, having originally cost £3m to build, a good deal of which was taxpayer's money. Billy Connolly's comedic touch is cited, when he famously described the Aviemore of the late 1980s as "an air-raid shelter wi' windaes".

36 NTS; CWLS 2, C41A, Letter from Colonel J.P. Grant of Rothiemurchus, Rothiemurchus Estate, By Aviemore, to Alastair M. Dunnett, Editor *The Scotsman*, Edinburgh, 14 October 1965.

37 SRO: RHP 49696, 'Architectural Site Plan of Proposed Re-development at Aviemore', by J.G.L. Poulson, Architects and Town Planning Consultants, Pontefract/London/ Middlesborough/Edinburgh, Drawing No. 1614/15A (scale 64 feet to 1 inch), April 1964.

38 J.P. Grant of Rothiemurchus, *pers. comm.*

39 NTS; Cairngorm – General, C42, Invitation to J.C. Stormonth Darling and his wife, from the Board of Directors, Highland Tourist (Cairngorm Development) Ltd. (declined 30 November 1966).

40 NTS; Cairngorm – General, C42, Temporary File, 'Aviemore Centre, Inverness-shire, Scotland presenting Sports and Holiday Activities – summer 1967'.

41 J.P. Grant of Rothiemurchus, *pers. comm.*

42 Allan Campbell McLean, *The Highlands and Islands of Scotland, op. cit.*, pp. 52–53.

43 NTS; Cairngorm – General, C42, Press Release: 'Aviemore Highland Wild Life Exhibition', February 1966.

44 NTS; Cairngorm – General, C42, 'Agenda for the Meeting to discuss conservation in Speyside', 7 June 1966.

45 Cairngorms Working Party, *Common Sense and Sustainability: a Partnership for the Cairngorms* (HMSO Scottish Office, Edinburgh, December 1992); Cairngorms Partnership, *The Cairngorms Assets – a Cairngorms Partnership Working Paper* (CPB, Grantown-on-Spey, 1996).

46 See SRO: HDB21-11 Desmond Nethersole-Thompson, *Highland Birds* (HIDB, Inverness, 1971) reprinted 1977; SRO: HDB21-12 David Stephen, *Highland Animals* (HIDB, Inverness, 1974). Both were part of the popular 'Highland Life' series.

47 NTS; Cairngorm – General, C42, Information Document: 'Highland Wild Life Exhibition, Aviemore, Inverness-shire', from the Aviemore Holiday Centre, April 1966.

48 NTS; CWLS 1, C42, Offprint: 'Leading Article from the *Glasgow Herald*', 25 January 1963.

49 See SRO: GD 325-2/174, Letter from George Pottinger, Scottish Tourist Board to Michael Lorimer WS, Secretary, Scottish Landowners' Federation, dated 19 September 1959.

50 SRO: GD 325-2/174, Memo, SLF, dated 17 September 1959.

51 See correspondence in SRO: GD 325-2/174, including a list of members of the Cairngorm Working Party of the SLF, namely the Earl of Haddo, Col. J. South, Major Sir Ewan Macpherson-Grant of Ballindalloch, Lt. Col. J.P. Grant of Rothiemurchus,

Lt. Col. W. Sandison of Killiehuntly, Capt. A.A.C. Farquharson of Invercauld, the Duke of Atholl, T.P. Stewart, A.J.P. Falconer Wallace of Candacraig. See the Press Release by SLF compiled by G. Hunter, dated 17 March 1965.

52 SRO: GD 325-2/191, Minutes of meeting of Cairngorm Area Landowners – SLF Cairngorm Tourist Development Plan, held in Inverness, 7 August 1964.

53 SRO: GD 325-2/191, *Map*, Cairngorm Area – Major Land Ownership 1964-1967.

54 Donald Getz, *op. cit.*, pp. 115, 123.

55 Scottish Development Department, *Cairngorm Area, op. cit.*, pp. 33–34.

56 See especially, Mackay Consultants, *Cairngorm Visitor Survey – Summer 1987*, a Report for the Countryside Commission for Scotland, Highlands and Islands Development Board, Highland Regional Council, Nature Conservancy Council, published September 1988.

57 Scottish Development Department, *Cairngorm Area, op. cit.*, pp. 33–35.

58 Cairngorms Working Party, *Common Sense and Sustainability: a Partnership for the Cairngorms*, Report of the Cairngorms Working Party to the Secretary of State for Scotland, December 1992 (HMSO, Edinburgh, 1992), p. 56.

59 Anon, 'Upper Deeside Area Seen as Winter Sports Centre', *The Scotsman*, Friday, 3 March 1967.

60 Oscar Marzaroli, *One Man's World: Photographs 1955–1984* (Third Eye Centre and Glasgow District Libraries Publications Board, Glasgow, 1984), p. 70. Oscar Marzaroli spent some months in 1954 and 1955 in the Grampian Sanatorium in Kingussie recovering from tuberculosis, where he first came to love the Spey Valley and the Cairngorm mountains.

61 See SRO: HDB21-204 Report by Mackay Consultants of Inverness, *Expenditure of Skiers at Cairngorm and Glencoe* (published August 1986).The report also concluded that skier spending in the Cairngorms was first concentrated on ski passes and accommodation, then came meals, clothing and entertainment. It identified an inbalance between weekend and weekday numbers on Cairn Gorm, and called for the greater manufacture of ski equipment in Scotland. Cairn Gorm led the way with 350,000 skier days in the 1985/6 season, followed by Glenshee with 120,000; The Lecht with 55,000 and Glencoe with 24,000.

62 Mackay Consultants, *Cairngorm Visitor Survey, op. cit.*, pp. 56–65.

63 Mackay Consultants, *Ibid.*, Appendix 6.

64 Mackay Consultants, *Ibid.*, Countryside Commission for Scotland: Cairngorm Recreation Survey – A Brief for Prospective Consultants, 1 June 1987.

65 Donald Getz, *The Impact of Tourism in Badenoch and Strathspey* (Highlands and Islands Development Board, May 1982), pp. 9, 17–23. This report is also held in the archives of the Highlands and Islands Development Board, in the Scottish Record Office, Edinburgh at HDB21-106.

66 See SRO: HDB21-4 Leaflet 'Winter Sports in Spey Valley 1973 – Scotland's Top Winter Holiday Resort'. A £14 'Spey Pack' gave the visitor hire of skis, sticks, boots, tuition, the use of chairlifts and the ski area bus. Learn-to-ski holidays were available (a week) priced by rail from London at £44 to £63, by car at £29 to £48.

Inclusive holidays in regional hotels spread from Carrbridge to Newtonmore were priced from £13 to £28 per week.

67 See SRO: HDB21-21 Booklet with maps 'Winter Sports Holidays in Spey Valley 1975', designed for HIDB by McCallum Advertising of Edinburgh. Also SRO: HDB21-30 Booklet 'Winter Holidays in Spey Valley 1976', advertising ski holidays from £35 a week depending on accommodation and location in the region.

68 Donald Getz, 'Residents' Attitudes Towards Tourism – A Longitudinal Study in Spey Valley, Scotland', *Tourism Management*, Vol. 15, Pt. 4, 1994, pp, 247–258; ASH Consulting Group, Institute of Terrestrial Ecology, Ruth Tillyard, *Cairn Gorm Summit Tourism Management Programme* (ASH, Edinburgh, April 1994); Scottish Tourist Board, *Tourism and the Scottish Environment* (STB/Tourism and Environment Taskforce, June 1993); Centre for Leisure Research, *Aviemore and Spey Valley Visitor Survey – A Report to HIDB* (Centre for Leisure Research, Edinburgh, March 1989). See also the area profiles and information sheets published by the Aviemore and Spey Valley Tourist Board; the Highlands and Islands Enterprise Economic Updates; HIDB area profiles of the Moray, Badenoch and Strathspey Local Enterprise Area.

69 NTS; CWLS 1, C43. 'Report- White Lady Shieling', by J.B. Nimlin, Field Officer, NTS, dated 19 August 1963.

70 One of the first studies to investigate the impact of mankind and footpaths in upland areas was, G.H. Bates, 'Track Making by Man and Domestic Animals', *Journal of Animal Ecology*, Vol. 19, No. 1, May 1950, pp. 21–28. Scientific research into the impact of some recreational activities on the erosion of vegetation and the width of footpaths in the landscape of the Cairngorms, can be traced back to the early 1970s. See especially, R. Bruce King, 'Vegetation Destruction in the Sub-Alpine and Alpine Zones of the Cairngorm Mountains', *Scottish Geographical Magazine*, Vol. 87, No. 2, September 1971, pp. 103–115; Neil G. Bayfield, 'Some Effects of Walking and Skiing on Vegetation at Cairngorm', in A.S. Watt and E. Duffey (eds.), *The Scientific Management of Animal and Plant Communities for Conservation* (Blackwell Scientific Publ., Oxford, 1971), pp. 469–485; R.F. Burden and P.F. Randerson, 'Quantitative Studies of the Effects of Human Trampling on Vegetation as an Aid to the Management of Semi-Natural Areas', *Journal of Applied Ecology*, Vol. 9, 1972, pp. 439–457; Neil G. Bayfield, 'Use and Deterioration of some Scottish Hill Paths', *Journal of Applied Ecology*, Vol. 10, 1973, pp. 635–644; Neil G. Bayfield, 'Burial of Vegetation by Erosion Debris near Ski Lifts on Cairngorm, Scotland', *Biological Conservation*, Vol. 6, No. 4, October 1974, pp. 246-251; Neil G. Bayfield, 'Recovery of Four Montane Heath Communities on Cairngorm, Scotland, from Disturbance by Trampling', *Biological Conservation*, Vol. 15, No. 3, April 1979, pp. 165–179; N.G. Bayfield, U.H. Urquhart, S.M. Cooper, 'Susceptibility of Four Species of Cladonia to Disturbance by Trampling in the Cairngorm Mountains, Scotland', *Journal of Applied Ecology*, Vol. 18, 1981, pp. 303–310; Adam Watson, 'Increase of People on Cairn Gorm Plateau following Easier Access', *Scottish Geographical Magazine*, Vol. 207, No. 2, 1991, pp. 99–105; Art Lance, Richard Thaxton, Adam Watson, 'Recent Changes in Footpath Width in the Cairngorms', *Scottish Geographical Magazine*, Vol. 107, No. 2, 1991, pp. 106–109. See also, Ed Blamey, 'The Consequences of Skiing on Scottish Mountain Vegetation and a Review of Current Monitoring and Manage-

ment Techniques', unpublished B.Sc. dissertation, Departments of Environmental Biology and Geography, University of St. Andrews, 1994; Richard Hebbletwaite, 'Land Use Conflicts in the Cairngorms – a Review', unpublished B.Sc. dissertation, Department of Geography, University of St. Andrews, 1991.

71 Cairn: Road up to Cairngorm Ski Area, *pers. obs.*, 'White Horse road earthworks completed by 61 Field Support Squadron – Royal Engineers, June/August 1981'.

72 Hilary Parke, *Scottish Skiing Handbook* (Luath Press, Barr, 1989), p. 3.

73 Ernest Cross, *Walks in the Cairngorms – Near Aviemore* (Luath Press, Barr, 1992), first published in 1984; Ernest Cross, *The Speyside Holiday Guide* (Luath Press, Barr, 1993).

74 SRO: GD 335-68, Letter from A.G. Payne, Cairngorms Group – Aberdeen Conservation Society, Aberdeen to Scottish Rights of Way Society, Edinburgh, 27 November 1974.

75 Kai Curry-Lindahl, Adam Watson, R. Drennan Watson, *The Future of the Cairngorms* (The North East Mountain Trust, Aberdeen, 1982).

76 Scottish Wild Land Group, *Cairngorms at the Crossroads* (SWLG, Edinburgh, 1987).

77 Save the Cairngorms Campaign, *Manifesto for the Cairngorms* (SCC, Inverness, 1992); Save the Cairngorms Campaign, Scottish Wildlife and Countryside Link, *The Northern Corries: an Alternative Approach* (SCC/SWCL, Inverness and Perth, 1996); Michael M. Scott, Chairman, Save the Cairngorms Campaign, *pers. comm.*

78 The archives of the Mountaineering Council of Scotland are held in the Scottish Record Office (SRO) Edinburgh, at GD 429. SRO: GD 429-1, Minutes of the Association of Scottish Climbing Clubs meeting held at Strathclyde University, 2 July 1969; SRO: GD 429-1, Mountaineering Council of Scotland – Adoption of New Constitution, 17 January 1970. In 1970, the annual subscription to the new organisation was 2/– per member, or 15/– per associate club membership. The first MCS Newsletter was produced in Autumn 1970.

79 SRO: GD 429-1, Minutes of the Mountaineering Council of Scotland meeting, 25 November 1970. The elected officials were:

President:	W.M. Mackenzie, Glasgow
Vice-President:	A.G. Cousins, Glasgow
Hon. Treasurer:	S. Drysdale, Glasgow
Hon. Secretary:	T. Muir Wright, Dunblane.

80 SRO: GD 429-1, Minutes of the Mountaineering Council of Scotland meeting, 16 September 1970.

81 SRO: GD 429-1, Letter from Sandy Cousins, Honorary Secretary of the Mountaineering Council of Scotland to J.P. Ledeboer, London, 24 January 1972.

Plate I. The Cairngorm Hills. One of the earliest photographs we have.
Photograph by J.E.A. Steggall, September 1893. [Chapter 1]

Plate II. The Lairig Ghru. Photograph by J.E.A. Steggall, September 1893. [Chapter 1]

Plate III. Dalnaspidal, entrance to Drumochter Pass. Boar of Badenoch and Sow of Atholl snow-tipped. Photograph by R.M. Adam, 6 April, 1935. [Chapter 2]

Plate IV. Rothiemurchus Forest and Cairngorm range (in cloud). Trees on slopes of Ord Ban with glimpse of Loch an Eilein. Photograph by R.M. Adam, 24 August 1924. [Chapter2]

Plate V. Victorian tourists looking out over Loch an Eilein, perhaps hoping to see an osprey. Photograph by J.E.A. Steggall, July 1901. [Chapters 2 and 4]

Plate VI. Access through Rothiemurchus and Glenmore on to the high tops. Cairn Gorm on the way up. Photograph by J.E.A. Steggall, August 1901. [Chapter 3]

Plate VII. Osprey with fish.
[Chapter 4]

Plate VIII.
The public osprey nest at RSPB
Loch Garten Osprey Centre.
[Chapter 4]

Plate IX. The Doune of Rothiemurchus Hotel sign, late 1930s. [Chapter 5]

Plate X. Strathspey and Loch Insh at Kincraig, viewed from An Suidhe.
Photograph by R.M. Adam, April 1946. [Chapter 5]

Plate XI. Hanoverian Ruthven Barracks, built in 1718, overlooking the Insh Marshes near Kingussie. Photograph registered in 1939 in the Valentine Collection. [Chapter 5]

Plate XII. Loch Pityoulish with three birch trees. Photograph by R.M. Adam, 27 July 1936. [Chapter 5]

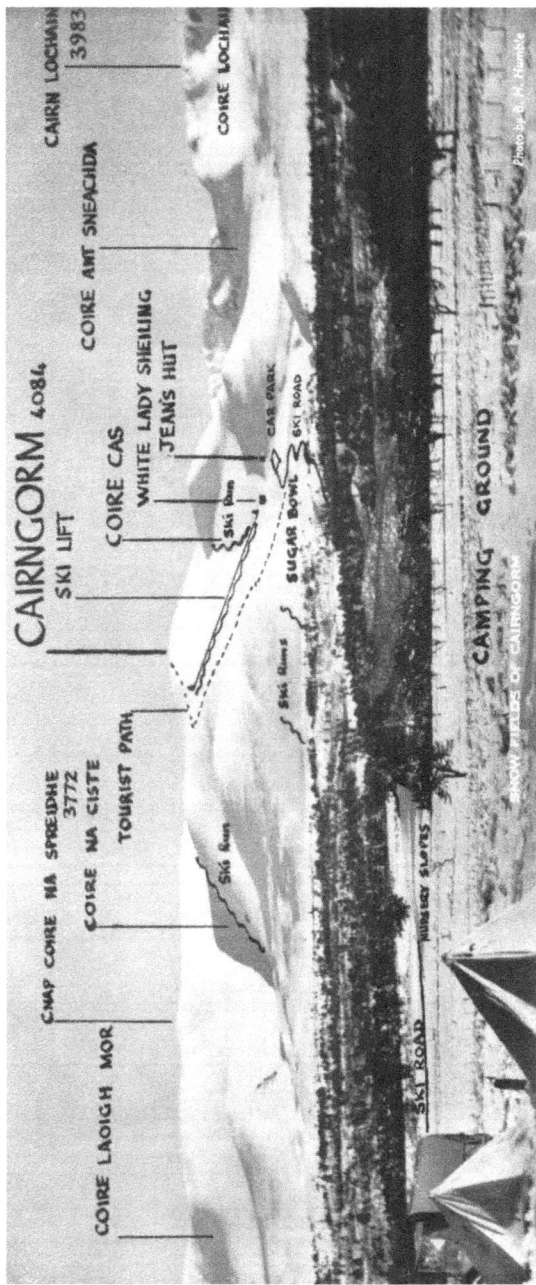

Plate XIII. The snow fields and ski access of the Cairngorms. Photograph by B.H. Humble, made into a postcard, probably early 1960s. [Chapter 6]

Plate XIV. The Cairngorms from the Great North Road, Aviemore (1939).
From the Valentine Collection. [Chapters 5 and 9]

Plate XV. The weir at Loch Morlich, Glenmore.
Photograph by J.E.A. Steggall, September 1893. [Chapter 7]

By kind permission of the University of St Andrews Photographic Collection

Plate XVI. Loch Morlich, Glenmore and the Cairngorms. Photograph registered in 1939 in the Valentine Collection. [Chapter 7]

By kind permission of the University of St Andrews Photographic Collection

Plate XVII. The River Spey near Aviemore. Cairngorms snow-capped in the distance. Photograph by R.M. Adam, 6 April 1935. [Chapter 8]

By kind permission of Paul Ramsay of Bamff
Photograph of portrait taken by Roger Crofts, April 2000

Plate XVIII. Sir James Douglas Ramsay, Bt, M.V.O., F.R.I.C.S. (Born 19 April 1878, died 14 March 1959). Former HM Commissioner to Balmoral Estate, Chairman of Scottish Forest Reserve Committee, Chairman of Scottish National Parks Survey Committee, Chairman of Scottish National Parks Committee, Member of Scottish Wild Life Conservation Committee. Douglas Ramsay was also a qualified engineer, keen piper and good Highland dancer. [Chapter 8]

Plate XIX. The Lairig Ghru in cloud. Photograph by R.M. Adam, July 1925.
[Chapters 8 and 9]

Plate XX. Loch an Eilein and Rothiemurchus Forest, from Ord Ban.
Photograph by R.M. Adam, August 1924. [Chapters 8 and 9]

Plate XXI. The Nature Conservancy Scots pine seedling beds at Achnagoichan, Rothie-murchus. Photograph by J. Grant Roger, April 1958. [Chapter 10]

Plate XXII. Cairngorm hills, the section above Feshie, pinewoods of Balavil in foreground. Photograph by R.M. Adam, 29 March 1955. [Chapter 10]

7

Enjoying the Pinewoods:
The Glenmore National Forest Park Ideal

There has been just one previous attempt to trace the history of Glenmore National Forest Park (NFP), in the form of a critique commissioned by the Save the Cairngorms Campaign as part of its political lobbying in the 1990s. The author did not consult the archives of the Forestry Commission nor analyse many of the events prior to 1980; indeed, the establishment of the NFP, and events in the 1950s and 1960s were covered in three pages.[1] This chapter presents a more comprehensively researched history of Glenmore NFP to 1980, and examines the role that the Forestry Commission (FC) and other organisations played in the creation of structured commercial recreational facilities in a state forest in Scotland. Others, notably John Sheail and Donald Mackay, whilst writing on the history of the FC on a national scale, have placed the establishment of NFPs within the wider history of countryside recreation and the development of rural landuse agencies. This history uses and builds upon their work.[2]

Glenmore National Forest Park, born over 1947/48, was an early experiment in the multiple use of land in the Cairngorms. However, from the outset the national FC had great difficulty in defining the role and function of a NFP. Indeed, they left this task to their local Advisory Committees. The FC also failed adequately to monitor recreational activities in the NFP, and were consistently unable to create a management strategy that paid heed to the chief functions of the Park's existence. Nevertheless, Glenmore NFP was a visionary step by the FC into the arena of rural recreation at a time when the provision of recreational facilities in the countryside was urgently sought by various campaigning pressure groups. More importantly, the FC concentrated their efforts in Scotland, especially in the 1930s and 1940s; this tradition of providing free access to forests and tourist facilities has endured, and is seen by the public to be a successful aspect of FC policy.

'Dark Glenmore'

The Forestry Commission had every reason to expect the area to be popular. Visitors had been coming to Glenmore since before 1780 [see Chapter 1] and the woods held a special fascination to many. John Lightfoot toured Scotland with Thomas Pennant in the summer of 1772, and wrote much on the 'Wild Pine or Scotch Fir' which was to be found at Abernethy, "Rothy murcha [Rothiemurchus] ... Glen-more ... and Glen Taner [Tanar]", although his focus tended to be on the useful qualities of the wood.[3] In the middle of the nineteenth century Donald Shaw, who styled himself 'Glenmore', wrote in aesthetic praise of the district, describing "scenes of sylvan solitude of very great beauty" and of Loch Morlich; "in a calm summer evening, when the bordering wooded steeps reflect their shadows in the bosom of the lake, the effect produced is really indescribable". Shaw also composed a plethora of simple verse about 'dark Glenmore' and Cairn Gorm.[4] The main period of commercial exploitation of the woods came after 1783, when the Duke of Gordon sold some trees to a Hull timber company for £10,000. These operations continued until 1805;[5] in 1856, Glenmore was converted into a deer forest. Articles that fondly recall pinewood walks in the forests of Strathspey litter editions of the *Cairngorm Club Journal* and the *Scottish Mountaineering Club Journal* after 1890, in an age when Glenmore was seen as an attractive approach to the high tops. These articles represent the first popular manifestation of the recreational woodland walk in the Cairngorms; by the mid-1930s, such walks were increasingly popular,[6] and have remained so across the twentieth century, a theme that naturalist Eric Simms explored in his prose on walking amidst the 'Bottle-Green Pines' around Loch Morlich.[7]

We may draw a comparison between Scotland and Scandinavia. Lars Kardell notes that, in Sweden, most of the rural recreational habits popular in the 1980s were already established a hundred years ago. Much the same can be said of Scotland, although the Swedish concept of *allemansrätt* and the Norwegian tradition of *friluftsliv* which guarantee rights (with responsibility) to all to wander over uncultivated land has no parallel in Scotland, despite some nineteenth century campaigners for rights of way and access to the countryside seeking to invent such a tradition, spurred on by romantic attachments to the wandering Gael. Both *allemansrätt* and *friluftsliv* have an educational content as well as a wider spiritual and physical element. The average Swede visited a recreational forest 18 times in 1963, 28 times in 1976 and 76–92 times in the mid-1980s, which "shows the status value that urban Swedes place on outdoor recreation", and which is far above the normal trend in Scotland.[8] These were almost exclusively day trips, but Glenmore NFP tended to attract the holidaymaker rather than the daytripper, principally due to its location away from sizeable urban centres.[9] However, only by 1979 was the Swedish forest conservation law modified to include a general statement on the blending of open-air recreation with all forestry operations, whereas in the UK, the Forestry Act of 1927 sought (albeit in vague terms) to control the public access to state woodlands, but acknowledged a need "for regulating the reasonable use of the land by the public for the purposes of exercise and recreation".[10] The gap of over fifty years can, in part, be explained by an enduring public and governmental attachment to the inherited customs of *allemansrätt* and *friluftsliv*, a more generous and widespread acknowledgement of public rights in Scandinavia, and a far more deeply developed 'cult of the Great Outdoors' within society.

When the Duke of Richmond and Gordon sold Glenmore to the FC in 1923, an excited editorial in the *Cairngorm Club Journal* saw it as an "augury of the future when the nation will acquire the whole of the Cairngorms", which itself is perhaps an early declaration of recreational interest in National Park status for the area. Speaking of the unique blend of loch, forest and mountain in Glenmore, the writer sensed that "the whole experiment will be watched with intense interest and sympathy by mountain lovers", believing that although sylviculture would predominate, Glenmore could become in the future "a reserve like the noble national parks which have been established in the United States and Canada and South Africa".[11] This was 1924; little was to happen for another twenty four years. Glenmore had been purchased, though, in the years of urgency over the strategic timber reserve that came after the creation of the Forestry Commission in 1919, and as part of the rapid acquisition of large properties in the 1920s and 1930s when land values were low and plantation forestry management, not integrated estate management, was to the fore.[12]

The National Forest Park Ideal and the Argyll Advisory Committee 1925–1945

If we accept the wording of the Forestry Act of 1927 at face value, then a NFP ideal can be traced back into the second half of the 1920s; John Sheail has shown that the very first positive response of the FC to the trend in outdoor recreation came in an internal FC memo by Sir John Stirling-Maxwell (one of the earliest Forestry Commissioners) in 1925, although he spoke only of northern England. In 1929, as a direct result of the involvement of Stirling-Maxwell on the National Parks Committee, the FC proposed Glenmore as a suitable tract of land for National Park (NP) status, especially if £5,000 could be obtained for capital expenditure on roads, camp sites and rest houses and a further £900 for tourist infrastructure. The ideal was resuscitated again in 1933 with the support of the Prime Minister, Ramsay MacDonald, himself a keen walker and climber (often in the Cairngorms), although the Treasury remained to be convinced. MacDonald wrote of the Cairngorms in a letter to the Treasury, which had urged that the Ministry of Health should hold all responsibility for public recreation: "sooner or later, especially when the flood spreads over desirable country like, for instance, the Cairngorms, something must be done, otherwise by fires and less disastrous incidents the countryside will be devastated except in very remote parts".[13] Aside from this need to control the growing number of people who were enjoying the new state forests, and the important issue of fire damage (which cost the FC £46,000 in 1929 from over 400 incidents) the FC sought a way to earn public goodwill, as they had come in for considerable criticism over their utilitarian planting in the Lake District in the 1920s, and had again sought to muscle in on the area from 1934 to 1938, under the auspices of the Special Areas Act of 1934. As J.P.D. Dunbabin has concluded, there was a necessary and obvious public image angle to the NFP ideal.[14]

The Scottish aspect of the NFP scheme was taken forward by J.D. Sutherland (a Forestry Commissioner for Scotland), and it was his knowledge of the western Highlands as an agriculturist that directed the attention of Roy Robinson (Chairman of the FC) to Argyll in late 1935. Robinson wrote on 17 January 1936 to G. Erskine Jackson of the Scottish Land and Property Federation (SLPF), informing him that a meeting of the FC on 6 January had decided to set up a working Committee under J.D. Sutherland, "to advise the Commissioners on the constitution and management of the National Forest Park in Argyll".[15] The first ever meeting of an Advisory Committee for a Scottish National Forest Park was scheduled for 14 February 1936, but it was pre-empted by an article in *The Scotsman* two days earlier which thrilled at the possible "public use of surplus and unplantable land in the forests of Ardgartan, Glenfinart, Benmore and Glenbranter in Argyll", especially as the "whole area under review was particularly suitable for rambling", warning that the "sound policy would be to encourage the use of the area by members of responsible organisations".[16] At the February meeting of the Committee, discussion ranged widely on what the NFP should provide, the FC wishing to supply "a really up to date public camping ground and car park to be quite independent of the various Associations"; there were calls for an improved water supply, cooking facilities, a drying room, latrines, but no football field. Professor J. Walton, a botanist at the University of Glasgow, asked that the FC would construct all the buildings with an eye on the visual amenity of the area, and that part of the NFP function would be to preserve some of the existing local birchwoods *Betula spp* in their natural state. Argyll NFP was born in 1936 as a purely recreational venture, and Professor Walton was to remain a lone voice for many years championing the cause of amenity, nature conservation and environmental education. The Treasury gave £5,000 to the FC scheme, which included the City of Glasgow Corporation, the Scottish Youth Hostels Association (SYHA) and the King George V Jubilee Trust Fund, to create a NFP of 35,000 acres, along with 19,000 acres at Ardgoil of Glasgow Corporation land. Some of these earliest decisions were taken blind: only in February 1936 was a Sub-Committee appointed to actually visit and view the area; this included the celebrated Cairngorm author and mountaineer Sir Henry Alexander, who expressed his appreciation "of serving in connection with such an interesting National project".[17] At a meeting of the Committee in November 1936, J. Walton again spoke about certain beauty spots in the NFP and the need to draw the visitors' attention to them, whilst Professor Baily of the Association for the Preservation of Rural Scotland urged that, should an Ordnance Survey map of the area be produced soon, careful consideration must be given to its size, as the existing Cairngorm map was "too big for outdoor use".[18] The establishment of the Argyll NFP is central to an understanding of later events at Glenmore in the years after World War II. The Argyll NFP as the first in the UK had to be seen by the FC and other participating organisations to be a success, for other NFPs to be considered at all. Similarly, the tactic of appointing an Advisory Committee had to be seen to have worked on both the regional and national scale, as a way of encouraging all interests to work together. The Argyll Committee continued to meet regularly throughout 1937 and 1938, up to April 1939; they next met in May 1942, with a noticeably broader remit. Visitor numbers were key to the continuation of the scheme outside of Argyll, and the following figures are displayed in the minutes of the Advisory Committee meetings:[19]

Year	'Person Nights'
1936	13,312
1937	20,419
1938	29,525
1939*	30,870
1940*	24,495
1941*	32,080

Table 4. Argyll NFP Visitor Numbers 1936–1941
* mainly in youth hostels, as the public camping grounds at Ardgartan and Succoth were closed under Defence of the Realm Regulations. (Source: GD 325)

In March 1938, the Argyll Advisory Committee passed an important resolution that "they wished to urge the extension in Scotland of the National Forest Park scheme", and suggested that the FC start looking for suitable areas. An interesting debate at this meeting concerned the sporting lets which the FC

and City of Glasgow Corporation were still advertising for the NFP, principally
to raise additional revenue. It was felt by some Committee members that this
was a wholly inappropriate use of a NFP and that visitors and guns did not
mix. The Committee concluded (and thus, in part, tried to define the function
of a NFP) that it "would be desirable for a Forest Park area to be reserved as a
sanctuary for birds and animals, as far as this was compatible with the Commission's work", never mind "the fear of injury to members of the public who
were being encouraged to visit the area". The FC agreed to allow the shooting
lets to lapse gradually as the opportunity occurred.[20] Despite this laudable
statement about the protection of forest wildlife, few members of the Advisory
Committee came to meetings to encourage this role for the NFP, although the
task of editing an "interesting guide" for the NFP fell in early 1938 to Professor J. Walton, the most vocal nature conservationist on the Committee.[21] By
December 1938 the NFP guide had been produced and was celebrated as a
best-seller at the Stationery Office stall at the British Empire Exhibition and
"favourably received by press and public", in 1939.[22]

Further evidence that nature conservation actually had a low profile
in the NFP ideal in Scotland came when John Walton wrote to F.C. Handford, Secretary of the Argyll NFP Committee, to urge the future creation of
a Voluntary Forest Warden scheme. He was forced reluctantly to accept that
the candidates would only be given training in the fields of arboriculture and
forestry, and have a good grounding in the leisure industry, for they were all to
be drawn from the Guides and Scouts, the SYHA, and other recreational and
youth organisations.[23] In April 1939, John Sutherland called for the formation
of a NFP Association, to raise funds for improvements to tourist facilities.[24]
Over in the Cairngorms, in 1935 the FC had given the title of 'Queen's Forest'
to Glenmore, in commemoration of the Jubilee of King George V and Queen
Mary that year.[25] In 1937, the FC acquired nearby Inshriach Forest of 2,297
acres, planting 1,332 acres of that from 1938 to 1951;[26] a commercial purchase
that came about when the Treasury was willing to support the FC NFP scheme,
preferring this to the greater evil of having to support "a grandiose National
Parks Authority". Roy Robinson assured the Treasury that the FC could pick
up 'unplantable' land cheaply: "earlier in the year [1937] the Commission could
have bought a couple of thousand acres of the Cairngorms at 10 to 20 shillings
per acre in connection with the purchase of our new Inshriach Forest", but had
"refrained because most of it was unplantable".[27]

The war years halted the further development of NFPs in Scotland, but
it is known that active consideration was given to the designation of a NFP at
Glenmore, by the FC and by the local Argyll NFP Advisory Committee which
was now acting as the leading forum for the wider extension of the NFP scheme.
F.C. Handford reconvened this Advisory Committee, with a memo in March

1942, stating that "in view of the general interest in National Parks at present being expressed and the attention that is being afforded to post war problems, it is suggested that we might hold a meeting in May".[28] However, the May 1942 meeting concentrated its discussions on creating a NFP at Glentrool, although an Advisory Committee was not constituted to investigate this property until 22 October 1943.[29] This May 1942 meeting, called due to members' wishes "to help the movements" of NPs and NFPs, issued a bold statement to the government and the FC: "in view of the work already carried out by the FC in connection with National Forest Parks, the FC should be entrusted with the development and management of National Park areas in Scotland".[30] This shows the extent to which the Argyll Advisory Committee was now broadening its own remit and seeking to speak out on regional and national issues of landuse in Scotland. Against the backdrop of the growing independence and audacity of this Committee, Glenmore was seized upon some time during the war years, as suitable for NFP status. By October 1946, the Argyll Advisory Committee's freedom of action was complete, as F.C. Handford explained to Michael Lorimer WS of the SLPF; it was being slowly reconstituted under the chairmanship of J.M. Bannerman to deal with all National Forest Park Areas in Scotland.[31]

In April 1941, the FC met in London to try to outline subjects that were suitable for departmental enquiries in such a time of national emergency. NFPs were rather surprisingly listed as high as No. 5, which again suggests that the NFP ideal remained alive over the war years[32]; the Forest of Dean NFP was declared in 1939, after Viscount Bledisloe, as Senior Verderer of the Forest, gave his endorsement, alongside that of the Forest Freeminers' and Commoners' Associations, and Local Authorities[33]. Snowdonia NFP was declared in 1940. However, the most strident declaration of the future of NFPs across the UK, came in *Post-War Forest Policy* published by the FC in February 1943. The FC outlined their future spending on NFPs over ten years as follows:

The Desirable Programme	£150,000
The Intermediate Programme	£100,000
Pre-War Basis	£ 50,000

This report sought further to define the role of a NFP, in that it made good use of unplantable land "to the public for recreation and, at the same time, to provide cheap camping facilities at convenient places. Access to plantations will be allowed when there is no risk of damage from fire". Glentrool and Glenmore (both in Scotland) were described as "eminently suited for National Forest Parks". The FC boldly asserted that their goal was to create a new NFP every year for the next decade, "at a capital outlay not exceeding £50,000". They did, however, remain open to making 'a special feature' out of the NFP scheme, and could even offer an additional £100,000 to establish around twenty NFPs by 1955.[34] Glenmore NFP would be born out of such hyperbole.

Clearly the creation and development of the Argyll NFP Advisory Committee has to be understood before any attempt can be made to trace the history of other NFPs in Scotland, indeed, across the UK. The key role that the Argyll NFP Advisory Committee played in the 1930s and 1940s has not previously been fully understood, and it is now apparent that it laid many of the ground rules for what was to come after World War II.

Glenmore 1945–1950

Glenmore was discussed at the first post-war meeting of the Scottish National Committee of the FC in October 1945 in Edinburgh, a body chaired by Thomas Johnston MP, and including in its members, J.M. Bannerman, the Duke of Buccleuch, Col. Stirling of Keir, Sir Samuel Strang Steel, with F.C. Handford and A.H. Gosling of the FC staff. Apparently the FC had been approached by Lord Malcolm Douglas Hamilton who wished to 'rent or purchase' Glenmore Lodge for use as a 'Youth Movement Training Centre'. A.H. Gosling informed the Committee that the Lodge had already been refused to the SYHA, as the FC deemed it would be required for adaption into Forest Workers' dwelling-houses.[35] Lord Hamilton would only have to wait three years before the FC would acquiesce to his request. More importantly, this Committee in April 1946 formally reconstituted the Argyll NFP Advisory Committee and charged them with overall responsibility for NFPs in Scotland, suggesting that the Scottish Tourist Board be invited to join the committee; J.M. Bannerman was designated as Chairman.[36] The first meeting of the post-war Advisory Committee was scheduled for mid-November, but prior to that J.M. Bannerman and the Director of the FC visited the Cairngorms in October 1946 to investigate the Glenmore site and to formulate recommendations to put before the Advisory Committee, to press for an "early establishment of a Forest Park in that area". At the same time, the FC Scottish Committee urged that Tom Johnston inform the Secretary of State for Scotland, "to prevent the possibility of any subsequent criticism on the ground of premature Forest Park development to the detriment of National Park interests in this locality".[37] A resurgent National Park debate was running alongside the NFP ideal in the second half of the 1940s, and although the FC always stressed the uniqueness of their NFP scheme, John Sheail has exposed evidence to show that they had staked a claim (with the connivance of the Treasury) to become the UK National Parks Authority in the late 1930s.[38] Johnston himself (when Scottish Secretary) had been angered by having been omitted from the earliest discussions for the Glentrool NFP in 1943.[39]

The Scottish NFP Advisory Committee that first met in November 1946 looked like a grander version of the Argyll Committee, with its impressive recruitment of representatives from youth and recreational organisations from across Scotland. It urged the development of Argyll, Glentrool and Glenmore so that they could take visitors during the summer of 1947. Tom Johnston reported that he had discussed Glenmore with the Secretary of State for Scotland, who had suggested that an inter-departmental conference might be held of all interested groups. There was still no firm decision yet about the future of Glenmore; the FC described the NFP idea, as just "tentative proposals" at this meeting and seemed reluctant to appoint a full committee of enquiry as they had done at Glentrool; indeed, no such committee was ever constituted. J.M. Bannerman explained to the meeting that the problem at Glenmore lay in a lack of suitable sites for camping, "keeping in mind that the Commissioners must also provide housing accommodation for their own workmen". He also drew attention to the popularity with motorists of the Sluggan Pass road conceding that "upkeep of this long stretch would become a serious matter", but that "a toll charge for vehicular traffic would not be unreasonable", as each NFP had to raise some of its own revenue. This was a long and important meeting to decide the future of Glenmore. John Walton fought his lone battle over environmental education at the site, believing the area to be unique in its natural history educational attractions, but accepting that "the great general appeal of Glenmore and the Cairngorms made it impossible to reserve the area for educational purposes only". He would, though, hold on to his 'living classroom' vision for Glenmore. The STB urged that they be allowed to play a leading role in all tourist development at Glenmore; the Boy's Brigade called for commercial postcards to be produced; the Camping Club begged that any appointed warden would hold a stock of midge repellent for sale! It was agreed that youth organisations would only have to pay a small charge per head as cost "did affect the extent to which advantage could be taken of the facilities offered".[40]

The FC moved discussions forward in November 1946 by contacting the Department of Health in Scotland to table their plans for a NFP, but seeking only to develop a camping ground in front of Glenmore Lodge of 2 $1/_2$ acres, and to maintain the existing wooden huts that were already used by Elgin Academy and Nairn County Boys' Organisations. The FC called these 'initial developments',[41] but in reality no firm decisions had yet been taken. Indeed, the NP/NFP debate was still not resolved, and F.C. Handford was called before the Scottish National Parks Committee to help explain the FC role at Glenmore and to explain, "with the aid of a map, full details of the proposals": these seemed to impress the Chairman (J. Douglas Ramsay) who "regarded them with approval".[42] By December 1946, the inter-departmental conference proposed by the Scottish Secretary had debated the Glenmore issue, and the

FC could submit formal proposals to the County Councils and local planning authorities;[43] the relevant County Councils agreed to NFPs at Glentrool and Glenmore in February 1947.[44] Just four months later, the first reports of unruly guests at a NFP came through, with complaints that the Ardgartan camping ground (Argyll NFP), "was being rendered untenable at weekends by rowdy and ill-conducted day parties travelling by privately hired buses from Glasgow and Greenock". The post-war boom in recreation was bringing city dwellers into their local NFP in growing numbers, and the FC freely admitted that they had no clue how to "eliminate the undesirable element",[45] in their effort to advertise 'recreation with responsibility'.

There was no grand opening ceremony for Glenmore NFP in 1948. The public camping ground and a reserved area for Juvenile Organisations was opened in June, with only limited publicity in newspapers and tourist magazines, and Glentrool NFP opened in July.[46] In 1947 the STB had praised the Argyll NFP as being, "one of Scotland's greatest recreation lungs".[47] It appears that Glenmore NFP was put together and opened in a rush, as in mid-March 1948 shelters, toilets and washing blocks were under construction, and the FC were seeking to calm the SYHA (who were desperate not to be sidelined by a NFP designation) by promising a site for a hostel. A visitor tariff was still under review: the former charge for the Norwegian Huts at Glenmore had been £4 per month, but this was now doubled by the FC, with £2 per weekend period, £2/10/– per week, or £5 per fortnight.[48] Professor John Walton still sought to make Glenmore something more than a mere place of fun, asking in March if "a hall could be used for lectures, country dancing and recreation in very bad weather". F.C. Handford didn't care for this lecture idea: "Lectures could hardly proceed under conditions likely to prevail in the general recreational shelter".[49] Walton refused to give in and, having failed in his attempt to have natural history lectures put on, sought in April 1949 to meet his committee colleagues halfway, proposing that visitors might "welcome a talk or conducted tour of the plantations and nursery" – "a fortnightly tour during the summer months would prove very popular", he enthused. His fellow committee members now seemed more interested in investigating the possibility of establishing a NFP "within easier reach of Edinburgh".[50]

In light of the Advisory Committee considering more NFPs, and nearer to urban areas, and with the visitor management problems that had surfaced at Argyll NFP in June 1947 fresh in representatives' minds, the FC decided to forestall trouble in the years to come. The Scottish NFP Advisory Committee working with the Scottish National Committee of the FC in June 1948, sought to invoke the Forestry Act of 1927 and introduce Forest Byelaws, under the direction of the FC London headquarters.[51] Glenmore NFP Byelaws were introduced on 11 August 1948, and a £5 fine limit was agreed for acts of trespass onto land being prepared for planting, the lighting of fires, the smoking of cigarettes in wooded areas, dropping litter, damming watercourses, removing FC fencing, committing acts of wilful vandalism to trees, egg-collecting or rough camping.[52] The FC had introduced NFP Byelaws as early as July 1936, but the spate of NFP Byelaws from August 1948 to 1954 shows that they felt that prohibitive regulation was now necessary for visitor management on their land.

National Forest Parks	Byelaws introduced
Argyll	15 July 1936
Glenmore	11 August 1948
Glentrool	4 January 1949
Snowdonia	4 January 1949
Queen Elizabeth	6 August 1954
Border	1962

Table 5. National Forest Park Byelaws
Source: Note; all these local Byelaws were made obsolete in July 1971 with the introduction of national *FC Byelaws 1971*, No. 997, under statutory instruments (HMSO, London, 1971).[53]

In 1948, the FC *Annual Report* looked back with some satisfaction on the establishment of Glenmore NFP, "a Park of 12,500 acres", that extends "from the shores of Loch Morlich to the summit of the Cairngorm". A new comprehensive working definition of a NFP was offered:

> "At all these Forest Parks, attention is given to the conservation of natural resources of all kinds. Good land utilisation as between forestry and agriculture is practised, and throughout the area wild life is protected. Careful regard is paid to amenities and scenic effects both in the arrangement of plantations and the design and siting of buildings."[54]

This was good public relations fodder, but was quite blatantly untrue. Only perhaps from the mid-1960s did the FC pay some attention to either the impact that their forests, NFPs and plantations had on the landscape, or to the wildlife living on their properties. Sylvia Crowe was appointed around 1963/4, as a consultant on landscaping, and was to guide the FC on the layout of new plantations in harmony with local scenery, as well as improving the appearance of existing forests. The *Annual Report* of 1964 saw her vision as unique and valuable, allowing the FC to start "blending good forestry practice with a proper regard for the beauty of the countryside".[55] Two years later, she was praised again, for she had "emphasised the need for contrast between planted and open ground; for avoidance of harsh outlines in new plantations; and for the shaping of clear-felled areas within the landscape pattern".[56] More importantly, whilst Crowe's work was often criticised as only being of a cosmetic nature, her appointment to advise the FC surely marks the very beginning of the aesthetic landscape education of the organisation's staff. Similarly, in 1964, the FC appointed a Divisional FC Officer to the new post of Wildlife Officer, who was to work with the Nature Conservancy and other nature conservation organisations to be responsible "for improving and coordinating practice throughout the Commission on wild life management and forest protection"; the ultimate goal of the FC being, "to harmonize the conservation of wildlife with the needs of timber production", not, it appears, recreation.[57] The FC took no real action on the visual impact of their forests or nature conservation prior to the mid-1960s. They provided a more acceptable definition of what a NFP was in 1960: "The Commission claim that, as the forests mature, they will be seen for what they are; at once an economic asset and a source of positive pleasure to the eye and spirit". This *Annual Report* did, quite rightly, go on to say just what an important recreational resource the NFP had become:

> "There is thus growing up a generation of young people who have come to accept the Commission's forests as places where, quite simply, they can enjoy themselves, and in return learn how to protect the forests and help foresters by an understanding of their work."[58]

The 'protection' spoken of here, was more to do with vandalism and the fire threat, than the conservation of forest flora and fauna. In March 1948, the Advisory Committee had discussed the possible provision of leaflets to inform visitors and holidaymakers about Glenmore NFP, but the committee later abandoned this idea, and in 1949 asked John Walton to edit a guidebook with contributions from experts in the fields of social and cultural history, forestry, folklore and natural history. The first NFP Guide for Glenmore was published by HMSO in May 1949; a third edition came in 1960, a fourth edition in 1966 and a much expanded fifth edition in 1975.[59] It was noted that 4,000 copies of the guidebook were sold in its first year,[60] and the guide remained one of the only publicity tools that the FC used to sell Glenmore NFP to the public, believing that the facilities on offer were already well known to those Scots interested in countryside recreation, or members of an outdoor organisation. In 1951, in an attempt to widen NFP publicity the FC in Scotland decided to sell the attractions of NFPs to factories and workshops, through bodies such as the Employers Federation.[61] In retrospect it is perhaps odd that, although over the period 1949 to 1975 the FC asked well known and respected Cairngorm naturalists (Seton Gordon and Roy Dennis come to mind) as well as other academic authorities to write sections of the guidebook, these people were never included in the committee that shaped the destiny of Glenmore NFP. That was placed in the hands of nominated representatives of youth, recreational and tourist organisations, many of whom would merely be reluctant staff sent along to meetings from headquarters across the Central Belt. The future of the NFP was overwhelmingly decided from Edinburgh.

At the same time as the Glenmore NFP was born, the Central Council of Physical Recreation (CCPR), with the support of the Scottish Education Department, opened the Scottish Centre of Outdoor Training at Glenmore Lodge in September 1948. B.H. Humble suggests the impetus for this came from the success of military training in the Cairngorms over the war years, and the popularity of a first CCPR outdoor training course at Loch Lomond Youth Hostel over Easter 1946, with boating on the loch and an ascent of Ben Lomond. The idea of an outdoor youth training centre in the northern or eastern Highlands was picked up by Lord Douglas Hamilton, giving birth to what Humble calls a great industry of outdoor recreation.[62] In a promotional book about Glenmore Lodge, written by Catharine Loader as early as 1952, the object of the training centre was described thus:

"to use the excellent natural surroundings offered by mountain, loch and forest, to experiment with forms of education which will assist the individual to discover his or her physical, mental and spiritual potentialities ... initiative, observation, courage and humility are qualities demanded from a good citizen as well as from the intelligent exponent of open air activities."

In 1950, a Glenmore Club was formed in Edinburgh, reflecting the urban roots of many of the children and adults who stayed at the Lodge; in 1950, it was estimated that around 40% of visitors were keen members of a youth or university recreation society. Over 1951 and 1952, Glasgow Education Authority decided to initiate a series of Glenmore reunions, at which mountaineers like Douglas Scott and Tom Weir spoke, and the SMC were on hand to offer advice and recruit members.[63] In 1959, the outdoor training centre moved into a new purpose-built building and the old Lodge became a youth hostel, opening in 1961. The Lodge built a new boathouse on Loch Morlich in 1967.[64] The NFP and Glenmore Lodge were seen to complement each other; for that reason the FC leased the old shooting lodge to the CCPR in 1948, it being no longer needed by foresters. Visitor numbers to Glenmore Lodge, and the SYHA Loch Morlich property have been tabulated below to give a flavour of the growing recreational interest in the area from the late 1940s to the mid-1960s.[65]

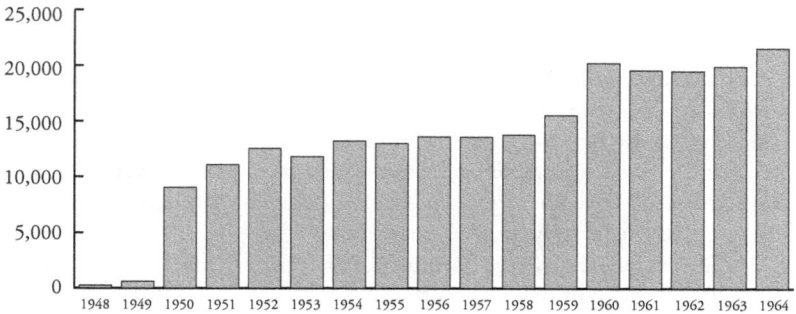

Chart 2. Visitor numbers at Glenmore Lodge (CCPR/SCPR) 1948–1964
(Source: FC 9/2, FC 6-1)

1961	11,906
1962	14,681
1963	14,884
1964	17,866

Table 6. Visitors to SYHA Loch Morlich 1961–1964
(Source: FC 9/2, FC 6-1)

Visitor Numbers and Visitor Management at the National Forest Park

The first holidaymakers arriving at Glenmore NFP in 1948 would have found a public camping ground, a reserved area for youth organisations' camps, a wet weather shelter and the improved Norwegian Huts. As early as November 1946, the Advisory Committee had decided that these huts should only be used by boys' organisations, having had problems with 'mixed' groups from Elgin Academy and Birmingham University. This segregation of the sexes had frustrated the Director of Physical Education at Birmingham University, who as late as April 1949 was still complaining that such a move could mean that "the widest possible use cannot be made of the facilities at Glenmore". There was something of a moral tone to the FC's provision of recreation in these huts, and they decided to hold firm on the single sex occupancy rule, confident that the huts were booked up in the 1948 season for four week-long periods and five weekends, and for eleven week-long periods and two weekends in the 1949 season.[66] It is delightful to note that the FC moral crusade had evolved by March 1951 to subject adults staying in the Norwegian Huts to the same rules; they could stay "provided the parties were confined to members of the one sex".[67] Over the 1950s, small tourist infrastructure developments occurred, but very much in an *ad hoc* fashion; three car parks were built in 1950/51; in 1958, the FC grant for the upkeep of the Glenmore road was raised from £7,568 per annum to £10,000.[68] The FC always tended to react to growing visitor numbers, rather than have the facilities in place beforehand. In the first years of the 1950s, there was some friction between the FC and the youth organisations over issues of maintenance. In March 1951, a SYHA delegation at an Advisory Committee meeting in Edinburgh asked it to address the "question of the upkeep of the paths on the higher slopes above the plantations". The FC quite obviously were not willing to put money into the upkeep of paths on rough unplantable ground where they felt so few people ventured. They replied (via F.C. Handford) that "it was part of the Commission's policy to keep the National Forest Parks as near to nature as possible",[69] which was a deviously convenient answer (indeed, an escape route).

During the 1950s and 1960s, Loch Morlich and the camping grounds and associated low-level forest trails were seen by the FC as the focus (the honey-pot) for recreational activity at the park; this despite a scare in 1953/54, when Loch Morlich was declared "unsafe to all but the strongest swimmers" and warning notices were erected around the lochside and in car parks.[70] It should be stressed that from 1950 to 1970 the FC took great satisfaction in being the leading provider of countryside recreational facilities in the UK, and they took every opportunity to show off the NFP scheme; in July 1956 a party of delegates from the Supreme Soviet toured the Queen Elizabeth NFP; later in October 1956, the first committee meeting to set up a Border NFP met in Newcastle.[71] Much of the expansion of the scheme post-1955, seems to have been boosted by a final decision taken on the wrangle over NPs and NFPs. The Scottish National Committee of the FC issued a statement in early December 1954, drafted by Sir Samuel Strang Steel (Chairman) and J.M. Bannerman, that from now on, "the Commissioners favoured creating National Forest Parks rather then including forest areas in National Parks".[72]

As visitor numbers to Glenmore began to rise steeply in the mid-1950s, so the problem of litter became worse, the first documented statement about a 'litter problem' being in 1956.[73] This was a widespread problem. In 1961, at all NFPs the FC removed 750 tons of litter, and noted that 22,500 milk bottles had been left behind by irresponsible campers. The FC freely accepted that this was a direct result of "a rapid increase in the number of campers, and in too many instances a lowering of their standards".[74] The FC did strengthen some visitor regulations in the 1960s and 1970s, but it was hard to do so in the face of such enthusiasm for the relaxed atmosphere at a NFP like Glenmore, as recorded in the *Annual Report* for 1959:

> "There is evidence in the form of appreciative letters that the facilities provid-
> ed – such as shower rooms and cooking shelters – and the absence of all but
> essential rules, met a real need for which the Commission will have to continue
> to cater on an increasing scale."[75]

In an interesting international comparison, A.P. Snyder (a District Forest Ranger in the Sierra National Forest in California) wrote in the mid-1960s that recreational forests in the USA were suffering irreparable trail erosion, and were similarly being buried beneath a litter problem, "a can pile". Snyder felt that these were the two greatest challenges to the 'new breed of forest administrators', conceding that (rather like Scotland) the US Forest Service only woke up to the pressures of a recreational demand on its land around 1950. He concluded in 1966 that foresters should now be aware "that wilderness is of great concern to large numbers of educated, interested, loquacious, dedicated, and often highly opinionated people".[76] The British FC perhaps lagged behind a little, but had awoken to the complexities of forest management by the late 1960s. Total visitor numbers for all the NFPs, certainly show a steep rise over the period 1960 to 1972, as recorded below:[77]

1948	1949	1950	1951	1952	1953	1954
c.15,000	18,775	42,691	53,600	c.50,000	c.64,000	c.75,000

1960	1961	1963	1964	1969*	1970	1972
267,000	250,000	c.250,000	354,000	470,000	850,000	c.1,000,000

Table 7. Overnight Stays on all NFP Sites in UK 1948–1972
* plus 300,000 under permit in the New Forest. (Source: FC 10)

New charges were introduced at Glenmore in 1960, but the FC were determined that they were not to be on the high side. A holiday with a car and tent or a caravan would cost 4/– per night, or 24/– per week; a walker with a tent would pay 1/– per night or 6/– per week.[78] Little is recorded of the type of visitor that used Glenmore NFP in the 1950s and 1960s, aside from the fact that it attracted youth organisations, school parties, families, and lone hillwalkers. The FC appeared surprised in 1950 that Glenmore was drawing in mountaineers and winter sports enthusiasts and noted this down as "an interesting development",[79] obviously unaware that the Glenmore and Cairngorms area had attracted recreational climbers from the 1880s, and even some skiers in the 1920s and 1930s. It must not be forgotten that the NFP scheme was also a profit-making venture, and any success hinged on the number of visitors who came to stay. They came to Glenmore in their thousands after 1948, as the following table reveals:[80]

	1948	1949	1950	1951	1952	1953
Public Camping Ground	794	1,050	2,388	2,673	3,685	5,175
Juvenile Camping Ground	261	472	772	1,707	1,098	1,172
Norwegian Huts	1,500	1,650	3,517	3,720	5,625	5,551
Total	2,558	3,172	6,677	8,100	10,408	11,898
	1954	1955	1956	1957	1958	1959
Public Camping Ground	5,464	13,950	9,614	9,868	9,571	16,283
Juvenile Camping Ground	1,574	446	988	3,622	1,133	2,402
Norwegian Huts	6,784	7,085	6,831	5,148	7,288	6,509
Total	13,822	21,481	17,433	18,638	17,992	25,194
	1960	1961	1962	1963	1964	
Public Camping Ground	16,272	14,468	17,225	35,751	51,613	
Juvenile Camping Ground	1,002	1,043	653	2.858	2,362	
Norwegian Huts	8,932	8,870	8,722	8,208	7,743	
Total	26,206	24,381	26,600	46,817	61,718	

Table 8. Annual Visitor Totals ('person-nights') for all parts of Glenmore NFP 1948–1964
(Source: FC 9/2, FC 6-1)

It therefore seems odd that the FC did not appoint Recreational Planning Officers to most regional offices (including Glenmore) until 1974.[81] They were aware of the growing pressure placed on their NFPs by increasing visitor numbers, for they had predicted that the summer season of 1961 "would test the capacity of the sites to the utmost", and that in Scotland it would soon have to be ordered that any caravan could only remain in a NFP for a maximum of fourteen days.[82]

In early December 1958, at a meeting of the Scottish NFP Advisory Committee in Edinburgh, some decisions were taken for the coming decades. The old Glenmore Lodge was to be turned over to the SYHA to develop, as their aims "would be in accord with the general purpose for which the National Forest Parks were created", reconfirming the purely recreational focus of Glenmore NFP at that time. It was agreed that a privately-run tea-room and shops might have to be provided or 'allowed' during the 1960s, but that no commercial development of hotel facilities would be tolerated within the park boundaries, to compete with the FC facilities.[83] At an Advisory Committee meeting in January 1960, with Glenmore NFP almost twelve years old, the FC was congratulated by Mr. Ferris of the STB, "for providing the National Forest Parks and for taking an active interest in their maintenance and development". He was "confident that the facilities provided were much appreciated by those who used them". Mrs. Robertson of the SRoWS drew the committee's attention to a path inside the NFP that the FC had erected a fence over, "which prevented the use of the path by pony trekkers". John Walton again tried to suggest that a small museum "of local geological, topographical and natural history interest" might be provided in all the NFPs, principally because he thought that, as they stood, the parks were just rural playgrounds and that "those using the Parks were largely ignorant of the work of the Commission and indeed of the Park areas generally".[84] His suggestion met with little support in 1960, although it is timely to record that almost all of Walton's early ideas would be incorporated in the new Visitor Centre at Glenmore opened on 12 April 1991 by Ian Grant, Chairman of the STB.[85] In understanding from the outset (1936) that countryside recreation ran hand in hand with nature conservation interests and youth education, John Walton was a prophet ahead of his time.

Glenmore 1950–1980: The Future Plans?

Almost ten years into the life of Glenmore NFP, in February 1957, the NFP Advisory Committee agreed that they should try to meet at least once a year to discuss Glenmore, but that they had successfully achieved all their aims, and "there may not be any major developments to discuss".[86] The years from 1957 to 1967 may be classed as inactive years. The Scottish NFP *Progress Reports* for Glenmore over that decade talk only of new stone block fireplaces (1960), increased toilet accommodation (June 1960), electric razor sockets (refused in 1961), new sewage works (1962), fire extinguishers, first aid boxes and an additional area for camping (1963, but hindered by bad weather).[87] Although the FC did decide in December 1963 to approve a proposal that a planner should be engaged to advise on the future development of Glenmore,[88] it is apparent that the FC had lost impetus and direction over the NFP issue. Indeed, they appeared hopelessly lost. A series of remarkably clueless letters passed between FC offices in London and Edinburgh in January 1966, after the Estate Management section of the FC in Edinburgh asked where the original NFP idea had come from. L.H. Grinsted of the Secretariat (FC London) replied that "the extent of our knowledge" about NFPs, was that a committee was set up in "about 1935" [in fact, 1936] for Argyll, and that "in about 1946" this committee turned its attention to all of Scotland. That was all the information he could provide.[89] The Edinburgh FC office knew no more, replying to Grinsted that "the only file in our possession is utterly silent on the question", although they did correctly state that the first Scottish NFP Advisory Committee meeting was on 14 February 1946, but reported that "nothing is recorded on the constitution, terms of reference or tenure and termination of appointments". It was a great mystery, especially as the committee did not meet over 1965.[90] Out of such a muddle, a new vision struggled to emerge.

In an internal report of December 1962 *Public Relations and the Forestry Commission*, the FC accepted its need to be more accountable to the general public for the £12m that it annually received from the Exchequer, and that its services had to be "socially desirable, reasonably remunerative and efficiently executed". They also accepted the inadequacy of their own public relations service, and asked how many Scottish MPs had toured NFPs and FC plantations: "We generally take the attitude – 'well if they are interested, they will come to us'", the report concluded.[91] This was the first expression that the FC, especially in Scotland, were struggling to find a vision for the future, some new initiatives to break the stalemate and a better public image. The first six NFPs were in place by 1950, and covered 237,750 acres; three were in Scotland, one in Wales, one in England and one partly in Wales and England. The *Annual Report* for 1961, spoke of how the FC needed to take the broadest possible view of their responsibilities, recognising that although their "primary duty must be to establish and manage plantations effectively for the production of timber", they must also make future plans for "improving and enlarging public opportunities for enjoyment".[92] To that end the Scottish NFP Advisory Committee did express considerable disappointment that plans to establish another NFP in Glencoe as a proposed joint venture with the NTS (at a total cost of £50,000), with a £37,500 investment in a camping ground at Achnacon Farm, fell through in May 1969, when the HIDB pulled out of the venture.[93]

In June 1966, the Scottish National Committee of the FC considered one option before them: to focus resources better into favoured recreational projects, one of which was Glenmore. This committee visited Glenmore on a tour in early June, and met later in the High Range Hotel in Aviemore to mull over their £25,000 development proposal for the NFP, which appeared rather inadequate when other "commercial interests were investing £4m in hotels primarily to enjoy the facilities now available in the Forest Park".[94] This was a critical time for the future of Glenmore. By the mid-1960s the Cairngorm mountains were being keenly exploited and appreciated as a recreational resource. The ski road from Coylumbridge, past Loch Morlich to the upper ski-slopes of Cairn Gorm had been built in 1960; during 1966/67 this road was widened to a two-lane highway. The hillwalker, climber, skier and naturalist were now joined by growing numbers of motorised tourists; Nigel Pears noted that 3.9m bus and coach tour passengers came to the Cairngorms in 1960; this had risen to 5.8m by 1963. On Easter Monday 1962, over 5,000 people were estimated to be on Cairn Gorm alone.[95] The ski facilities, easier access, and a growing demand for leisure and recreational pursuits saw Glenmore NFP and the FC deeply involved in the Cairngorms tourist industry by 1966. The meeting in Aviemore in June 1966, decided on the following course of action, as money became available: to provide a warden's hut and information centre, to construct a tea-room, to make general caravan and campsite improvements (the site was reorganised in 1968), to build more car parks, to improve the water and sewage infrastructure, to introduce limited sailing facilities on Loch Morlich, and to replace the Norwegian Huts with a new building (a Norwegian Hostel was opened in 1970 with room for around fifty people).[96]

With this momentum, the Scottish National Committee held a meeting 'to Review the Future Development of Glenmore Forest Park' in April 1967; it was convened in Inverness, an important statement by the (more responsive) FC to local and regional community and leisure interests. It was decided that "any development at Glenmore must be beyond reproach and that a fair amount of capital investment will be necessary". Three phases of development were outlined, with the third phase crucially indicating that the FC were still willing "to react to changing circumstances", in the face of further Cairngorms tourist development. The FC committee sought to support a village development at Glenmore, to remove Army personnel from public camp sites and to set up an Advisory Council of local representatives of interested groups. It was envisaged that Inverness County Council would take over the liability for existing water and drainage services, and that the SYHA would now take over and develop the Norwegian Huts.[97] One of the first alterations that the FC had to seek was a reduction in the speed limit in the NFP from 40 mph to 20 mph, following the tragic death of a young boy on the Glenmore road in the summer of 1968.[98] The Inverness meeting in 1967 seems to have been a small part of a FC attempt to refine and streamline all NFPs and the Commission's role in recreational provision across the UK. In January 1968, the Scottish National Committee met to discuss a national memo, 91/67 'Public Recreation and the Forestry Commission', where it was stated that although public recreation must be regarded as important, it would always come second to growing timber. From that premise, other conclusions were reached; that all development plans for NFPs should now be prepared in consultation with the Scottish Development Department and local authorities; that all types of shooting should be banned from NFPs; that commercial private developers should now be invited to investigate the possibility of holiday chalets in NFPs; and that (late in the day) nature conservation should be encouraged as "there is no doubt about the increasing importance of this work".[99] This redistribution of resources was evident in the *Annual Report* for 1969, which at last gave an indication of a structured future policy:

> "In general, the Commission intends in future to concentrate their available resources on recreational developments in areas where the greatest use will be made of them and where they will benefit the largest numbers of people."

There was a new feel to this *Annual Report*. The FC seemed aware, as it entered the 1970s, that new forms of organised sport and recreation were jostling for position in NFPs and other Commission forests. The Report spoke of orienteering; approved motor car rallies with "large international entries and considerable numbers of spectators"; windsurfing was introduced on Loch Morlich in 1978. The FC also reflected on its considerable recreational portfolio across the UK, revealing that by Spring 1969 it had 8 organised camp sites with resident wardens (in season), 23 youth camp sites, 105 picnic areas, 94 forest walks and 107 prepared car parks.[100] Indeed, the 1970s would see a notable change in the way that the FC responded to the new recreational challenge. Instead of only the FC providing facilities for other leisure organisations to use, the organisations and sports bodies themselves began to make specific recreational requests of the FC, especially in the hosting of large mass participation sporting events. A Scottish Orienteering Association (SOA) was born in June 1962 in Perthshire, and by 1963/64 it was making plans to hold orienteering instructors' courses at Loch Morlich SYHA property; by 1980, an interest in ski-orienteering was developing.[101] To anticipate these coming changes, a new Conservation and Recreation Branch was set up at the FC in London, the Commission believing that their forests had a "greater capacity for absorbing recreation without impairing the environment, than other forms of land use".[102] It does appear that the FC in Scotland were aware of the diversification of leisure pursuits on NFPs as early as 1961, their own *Annual Report* speaking of "sectional interests" such as pony trekking, orienteering, natural history study groups and training for the Duke of Edinburgh award scheme; the Report also concluded that with the new ski road, "skiing at Glenmore has been embarrassingly popular".[103] As part of this restructuring programme the FC in Scotland revealed themselves to be willing to release unplantable land for profit, or to allow further recreational development to occur under the auspices of another organisation. In 1954 at Glenmore, they sold 5,361 acres of mountain land to the Nature Conservancy for an undisclosed sum, the area including 56 acres of uneven aged Scots Pine *Pinus sylvestris* and 809 acres of plantable land.[104] In 1971, the Secretary of State for Scotland and the FC agreed on the transfer of almost 6,000 acres of land in the upper section of Glenmore NFP into HIDB control, with Clause 12 of the Feu Charter granted to the HIDB stating that, "the said disponee will be bound to agree to the area of ground being designated as lying within Glenmore Forest Park"; Clause 9 of the charter re-enforced people's right to enjoy this land as they pleased, "to allow the public free access on foot to the said area of ground for the purposes of recreation". R.D. Watson has provided compelling tabulated evidence that the resulting confusion as to whether the HIDB land was still a part of Glenmore NFP, has generated numerous contradictory statements in maps, guide books and commissioned reports from 1971 to 1991.[105] It is interesting that the NC had to buy their share of the NFP in 1954, but the HIDB acquired their section by free transfer, perhaps reflecting relative political indifference to nature conservation interests in the mid-1950s, although the Scottish Office may have dictated the financial terms.

In this period, the FC never really undertook any internal visitor management recreation surveys on their NFP properties. In 1968, W.E.S. Mutch published the results of his own investigations into recreational habits in state forests, concluding that there were two distinct types of visitors: the first group wanted only the basic facilities provided, so as not to impinge on the wilderness quality of the forest; the second group demanded toilets, car parks and children's play areas as a visible sign of their needs being catered for.[106] Members of this second group were less keen to wander on waymarked trails or paths, and more often than not did not stray far from their car; rather, they sought the sanctuary of a visitor centre, tea-room, or picnic site. In 1964, the FC in Scotland had decided that in future years they would look to building more picnic sites "at those forests which are most visited by the public", anticipating "an increasing demand for the facilities offered in the Forest Parks".[107] It was for the education of this second group of visitors that the FC opened a small visitor centre at Glenmore in 1971.

It was left to a geography student at the University of St. Andrews, Conal Ruddock (in July and August 1979), to conduct the most comprehensive visitor survey of the lower parts of Glenmore NFP over this period, concentrating most of his research in the Loch Morlich area. Ruddock concluded, after interviewing 239 groups of visitors, that the management policies at Glenmore were too passive, and that the FC were still reluctant to spend time and money on important recreational management projects. To raise revenue, Ruddock suggested that a toll be introduced as visitors entered the park, which, if levied in the 40p per adult range, could have raised as much as £100,000 each year "to fund a more intensive recreation management strategy". Ruddock's findings suggest that at Glenmore the FC entered the 1980s still with a great deal to learn about visitor management and the provision of recreation. As in the USA, Ruddock believed, "the public will have to become used to paying for such facilities" when on a day visit.[108] In the Spring of 1980, the FC in Scotland issued an attractive leisure map detailing all of their NFPs, picnic sites (over 450), car park viewpoints, campsites and forest trails, targeted at both the day-tripper and the holidaymaker.[109] This map was part of a growing recognition within the FC in the late 1970s and 1980s of the importance of the day visitor to recreational forests, outside of the NFP holiday scheme. In March 1980, a public information booklet was launched, *The Forestry Commission and Recreation* as Policy and Procedure Paper No. 2. It spoke of a desire to continue to maintain the "special status" of the NFPs, but conceded that the main emphasis of the coming decade would be in the provision of facilities for day visitors: "those who want to spend a day in the country … they come mainly from towns, usually by car, and their principal requirement is for somewhere to park, to picnic and to walk for fairly short distances". The recreational development remit of the 1980s would be focused on car parks, picnic places, viewpoints and short forest walks, "particularly where they are readily accessible to visitors from towns and holiday centres".[110] Late in the day, as the fourth paper in this series, the FC published *The Forestry Commission and Conservation* (March 1980),[111] in which a promise was made to safeguard FC woodlands as wildlife habitats, and to liaise with nature conservation organisations over special site designations in the coming years. In 1992, Forest Enterprise declared Glenmore a Caledonian Forest Reserve, 44 years after it had become a recreational playground. In an ambitious plan, a Regeneration Zone ($^2/_5$ of the forest) has been identified where all the non-native conifers will be removed by 2000, and it is hoped that existing areas of natural Scots Pine will regenerate. In a Restoration Zone, the felling of other conifers will continue until 2034 in small areas chosen to improve the look of the forest, and to improve its value as a wildlife habitat. Forest Enterprise hope to plant local Scots pine seedlings and some native deciduous trees to add variety in this scheme to manage the woodland in harmony with public recreation.

An Historical Perspective on Planting

The section above has ended on a positive note for the future, blending nature conservation, forestry practice and recreation in the twenty-first century at Glenmore. This is, however, a new initiative. Before becoming a NFP in 1948, Glenmore was viewed purely in terms of timber production. The FC had, after all, been established under the Forestry Act of 1919 simply to establish and harvest a natural resource of timber.[112] What has not been thoroughly investigated is to what extent this continued at Glenmore after 1948. In May 1952, the FC produced a 'Forest Profile' of Glenmore that, in the briefest possible terms, talked of an "extensive planting" regime with Scots pine, Lodgepole pine *Pinus contorta*, Norway spruce *Picea abies*, Sitka spruce *Picea sitchensis*, European larch *Larix decidua*, Japanese larch *Larix kaempferi* and Douglas fir *Pseudotsuga menziessi*. By 1952, 2,476 acres were described as being "under tree crops", and 824 acres remained to be planted: most of the plantings were done at 1,000/1,500ft.[113] There was nothing controversial about the planting of these exotic alien conifers in the years from 1924 to 1933 (the first phase of planting at Glenmore) because there was no vocal environmental lobby in Scotland to protest about blanket afforestation, the mixing of native and non-native trees, or monotonous dark regimented plantations with low bio-diversity. Issues of visual amenity were rarely publicly articulated in Scotland pre-1960, whereas in England the FC had already by 1935 been pressed into setting up a joint committee with the CPRE, to discuss issues of aesthetic landscape protection. In the much-admired Wordsworthian Lake District and also in Snowdonia in Wales, there had been anti-FC rhetoric over mass Sitka spruce plantings from as early as the 1920s and on into the 1930s. Here the FC were forced into an agreement not to plant in certain key areas of cherished visual beauty. Chris Smout has shown that the FC cared little for, indeed were openly hostile to, nature conservation interests in Scotland in the 1940s and 1950s, fearing the widespread establishment of nature reserves and the subsequent sterilisation of land that they coveted.[114] Donald Mackay has shown that to Roy Robinson, who single-handedly directed the course of British forestry for twenty-five years, "Scotland was a resource of planting land and not much more".[115] Recreation managed to carve a niche for itself in post-war reconstruction, but nature conservation and visual amenity generally remained the enemy of the professional forester in Scotland. This is not to say that within the UK Forestry Commission staff there were not emerging voices of protest against a national forest strategy dictated by purely economic, strategic and social factors (rampant blanket planting, rural employment and the growth of forest villages). It would be wrong to say that all foresters despised Nature. Some had originally joined the staff of the FC after 1950 to be able to work outdoors close to the natural world. Other early nature conservationists sat on NFP committees in an advisory role. Over time, their ideas about forestry on an ecological basis developed. Their influence, although present, was certainly not pervasive or well received in the highest levels of the organisation, nor did it begin to have any impact on policy until the 1980s. Men such as Don MacCaskill, Affleck Gray, John Walton, Herbert Edlin, M.L. Anderson, John Davies, D. Henderson, D.M.B. Yorke and Warwick Deal should perhaps be seen as the roots of a tradition within British state forestry that criticised the dreadful monoculture of Sitka spruce, and saw forests and woodlands as places for humans and wildlife alike.

There had been considerable fellings at Glenmore during both World Wars. Henry Alexander in 1920 had bemoaned the loss of each Scots pine at the hands of the Canadian Lumber Corps, who had arrived in Glenmore in November 1916 and had felled 50,000 trees in the Sluggan glen by Autumn 1917, plus an additional 76,000 trees around Loch Morlich from July 1917 to 1919. Only the Duke of Richmond and Gordon's intervention prevented a clean cut, and guaranteed that seed trees were left "to secure natural regeneration of the forest".[116] During the Second World War, access to Glenmore forest was considerably improved, with the building of new forest roads and the use of Bailey bridges, which would have eased the toil of the twenty men working as foresters there by May 1952 (living in six houses and a worker's hostel). There was very little planting during the 1940s (some Sitka spruce in 1941 and 1948 only) and during the 1945–1950 period when the NFP was born, giving an impression that recreational provision had won the day. Indeed, the Scottish Home Department in its 'Programme of Highland Development' published in 1950, praised the visionary establishment of NFPs as part of a wider scheme by government to support and develop the Highland tourist economy.[117] Glenmore NFP had been running just two years then.

A second wave of the planting of exotic conifers began in 1950 and ran on until 1973. The rapid planting programmes (many on private land) of the 1960s came about as the FC were now urged by government to make forestry more commercially successful and to seek more end-users for their timber product. The emergence in this decade of a UK wood-processing industry reinforced the need for sylvan monoculture on a grand scale, and a rapid turnover of trees to guarantee a supply for continual processing. The Solly Zuckerman report on *Forestry, Agriculture and Marginal Land* (1957)[118] further called for the justification of state forestry to change from the now outdated need for a strategic reserve of timber (for pit props) in case of war to a more hard-nosed purely commercial venture, attractive to outside private investment and client forestry developers. Better site preparation, the technical development of ploughing techniques over the period 1950–1970, and large scale mechanical cultivation methods had radically changed the face of British forestry practice post 1945. In the 1960s, few in Scotland spoke out against the FC planting programmes, although W.H. Murray in his influential report to the National Trust for Scotland did criticise the FC at Glenmore for destroying the beauty of the landscape with their plantings, and for allowing the construction of the ski road through the forest in 1960 which made "an ugly scar" on Cairn Gorm's north face.[119] This was 1961/62, but Murray was a minority voice of aesthetic protest. It is also apparent from W.H. Murray, and FC records, that over the 1950s the FC in Scotland tried to muscle in on the Caledonian pinewoods of Rothiemurchus, they themselves admitting that by 1959 there had been, "intermittent negotiations with the owner, Colonel Grant, to acquire areas but without success". The FC seemed particularly interested in Rothiemurchus land to the south-east of Loch Morlich and on Pityoulish Hill, after the Spey Survey of 1951 had shown to them only 6,448 acres of plantable land, which they hoped to boost by a second FC survey. Grant contended that the FC did not pay high enough rents for long leases; he would not consider an offer of less than 10/– an acre for plantable ground from the FC. W.H. Murray concluded that "a close watch on the actions of the Forestry Commission in this region of the Cairngorms is needed".[120] The FC campaign to take control of the Rothiemurchus pinewoods for both felling and planting purposes comes from before the creation of the Cairngorms NNR in 1954; the FC tried to maintain this campaign in the late 1950s on land outside the NFP boundaries.

The planting of exotic conifers amongst Scots pine – dating from the beginning of the nineteenth century on some Highland estates – ran on into the late 1980s under the FC, in direct contravention of accepted public wisdom that had come to see the Sitka spruce plantation of the 1970s, and most certainly the 1980s, as an unacceptable blot on the Cairngorm landscape. A growing environmental awareness about the mixed planting of alien species and even non-native Scots pine seed through the 1970s was disregarded by the FC at Glenmore; indeed, the FC planted Sitka spruce by the Glenmore road in 1984; around the campsite in 1986; and even more remarkably, were still planting Sitka spruce in 1989. To the list of alien species declared in 1952 as part of the planting regime, Western hemlock *Tsuga heterophylla* and hybrid larch *Larix x eurolepis* can now be added.[121] It has led to what Jim Crumley has called "plantation-stifled Glenmore".[122] Basil Dunlop has revealed that although a scientific and spiritual appreciation of native woodlands was alive in the 1970s (indeed, it can in fact be traced back to the 1930s), it achieved far greater recognition in the early 1980s with the passing of the Wildlife and Countryside Act of 1981. This coincided with a growing public recognition over the late 1970s and across the 1980s that the afforestation of upland areas had gone too far, and had now irrevocably changed some cherished landscapes, especially in Scotland. A forestry company planted Lodgepole pine at Abernethy in 1981, behaving with the same cavalier attitude in the search for financial gain that the FC continued to display at Glenmore throughout the 1980s and indeed past the 1987 publication by the NCC of a national inventory of ancient, long-established and semi-natural woodland. In the Badenoch and Strathspey survey for that inventory, it was revealed that the "conversion to planting has caused the greatest loss of natural woodland this century", with almost 42% of the woodland resource under exotic conifers.[123]

The full story of the FC planting regime at Glenmore will probably never be known, especially in its most controversial aspects. To the FC, recreation always came a distinct second behind the need to plant and fell trees, and nature conservation issues were not confronted until the late 1970s and 1980s, and then not always whole-heartedly.

However, the FC had put much effort into providing forest recreation in Scotland from the mid-1930s onwards. NFPs were also being discussed in Scotland by the Association for the Preservation of Rural Scotland (APRS) in Edinburgh as early as the summer of 1929, at the same time as discussions over the creation of 'a national trust' for Scotland, and a National Park for Scotland. At an APRS meeting in May 1929, Sir John Stirling-Maxwell asked members to note that the "hinterlands of the Forestry Commission's properties" might be disposed of for the nation to enjoy as the land "was of an un-plantable character".[124] Roger Muhl, Forest District Manager for Inverness, believes that the history of Glenmore up to 1970 was free from conflict and controversy, and in many instances he is correct. J. Stirling-Maxwell privately confessed to J.P. Grant of Rothiemurchus in March 1929 that "the Glenmore Forest brings us into constant collision with tourists and the net revenue is very small". Indeed, he stated that the FC had actively sought a buyer for part of the forest in the late 1920s and had agreed a price with Hamborough that included Glenmore Lodge in the deal, ostensibly because the whole shooting rent of around £900 was eaten up each year by costly repairs to the Lodge, rates, taxes and staff wages. The FC, he said, "has no hesitation whatever about selling superfluous land to private individuals ... we have strong motive for wishing to sell unplantable land unless it brings in good revenue". The sale to Hamborough fell through in 1929.[125] They became providers of popular outdoor recreation to gain that much needed revenue.

Public conflict between nature conservation, recreation and forestry only came with the later ski-development, the transfer of the upper part of the NFP to HIDB control (who delayed until 1987 to produce a management plan for their new Cairngorm Estate), and has persisted as an awareness of nature conservation values in Scotland, particularly of native woodlands, has been raised.[126] In the final analysis, Glenmore has given a great deal of enjoyment to thousands of people since 1948 in organised recreational provision, but this has been at a cost to the area's flora and fauna, quite apart from the damage to the native pinewood. Over the 1920s, the greenshank *Tringa nebularia* had its largest breeding density in Strathspey on the shores of Loch Morlich; from 1949 to 1951, they had declined to four pairs; by 1963 there was just one pair. By the 1970s the Glenmore greenshank population had collapsed.[127] The FC did not even notice this.

Notes to Chapter 7

1 R.D. Watson, 'The History and Development of the Glenmore National Forest Park', A Critique Commissioned from Landwise Scotland by Save the Cairngorms Campaign (SCC, Inverness, January 1993).

2 Donald Mackay, *Scotland's Rural Land Use Agencies* (Scottish Cultural Press, Aberdeen, 1995); John Sheail, *Nature in Trust: The History of Nature Conservation in Britain* (Blackie and Son, London, 1976); John Sheail, *Rural Conservation in Inter-War Britain* (Clarendon Press, Oxford, 1981).

3 John Lightfoot, *Flora Scotica* (B. White, London, 1777), Vol. II, pp. 588-589.

4 'Glenmore' (pseud. Donald Shaw), *Highland Legends and Fugitive Pieces of Original Poetry* (John Lindsay, Edinburgh, 1869), first published in 1859, pp. 42–62, 122–134.

5 H.M. Steven and A. Carlisle, *The Native Pinewoods of Scotland* (Oliver and Boyd, Edinburgh, 1959: this reprint edition by Castlepoint Press, Dalbeattie, 1996), pp. 125–129.

6 John Eaton, 'In a Pine Wood', *The Deeside Field*, No. 7, 1935, pp. 21–25.

7 Eric Simms, *A Natural History of Britain and Ireland* (J.M. Dent and Sons, London, 1979), pp. 197–210.

8 Lars Kardell, 'Recreation Forests – A New Silviculture Concept?', *Ambio*, Vol. 14, No. 3, 1985, pp. 139–147.

9 Warwick Deal, *A Guide to Forest Holidays in Great Britain and Ireland* (David and Charles, Newton Abbot, 1976), pp. 45–56; Francis Thompson, *Discovering Speyside* (John Donald, Edinburgh, 1990).

10 The archives of the Forestry Commission are held in West Register House, the Scottish Record Office (SRO), Edinburgh at FC. See SRO: FC 4-12, *Forestry Act 1927* (HMSO, London, 1927), p. 2.

11 Anon., 'Glenmore: A National Forest', *Cairngorm Club Journal*, Vol. 11, No. 62, September 1924, pp. 82–86.

12 David Turnock, *The Historical Geography of Scotland since 1707 – Geographical Aspects of Modernisation* (Cambridge University Press, Cambridge, 1982), pp. 246–261.

13 Sheail 1981, *op. cit.*, pp. 170–192.

14 J.P.D. Dunbabin, 'Book Review – John Sheail *Rural Conservation in Inter-War Britain* (1981)', *The English Historical Review*, Vol. XCIX, No. 391, April 1984, pp. 469–470.

15 See SRO: GD 325-1/422, Letter from Roy Robinson, Chairman FC to G. Erskine Jackson, SLPF, dated 17 January 1936.

16 SRO: GD 325-1/422, Copy of article from *The Scotsman*, dated 12 February 1936.

17 SRO: GD 325-1/422, 'Minutes of the first meeting of the Argyll National Forest Park Advisory Committee', Edinburgh, 14 February 1936.

18 SRO: GD 325-1/422, 'Minutes of the meeting of the Argyll National Forest Park Advisory Committee', Edinburgh, 20 November 1936.

19 See the comprehensive 'Minutes of the Argyll NFP Advisory Committee' held in SRO: GD 325-1/384 and SRO: GD 325-1/301.

20 SRO: GD 325-1/384, 'Minutes of the Argyll NFP Advisory Committee', Edinburgh, 10 March 1938. This Committee had grown in 1937 and early 1938, to include a wide range of recreational and youth organisations, including the Camping Club, the Girl Guides, the National Playing Fields Association, the Scottish Rights of Way Society, the Boy Scouts Association, the Ramblers Federation, the Scottish Central Council of Juvenile Organisations, the Parks Department of Glasgow Corporation and the Scottish Youth Hostels Association. It was suggested in March 1938 that Folk Dancing Societies should be asked to join.

21 SRO: GD 325-1/384, Argyll National Forest Park – Short Report for Year ending 31 December 1937, signed by F.C. Handford, Secretary of Argyll NFP Advisory Committee, January 1938.

22 SRO: GD 325-1/301, Argyll National Forest Park – Short Report for Year ending 31 December 1938; Herbert L. Edlin (ed.), *Forestry Commission Guide: Argyll Forest Park* (HMSO, Edinburgh, fifth edition 1976), first published in 1939.

23 SRO: GD 325-1/301, Letter from Professor J. Walton, University of Glasgow to F.C. Handford, Secretary of Argyll NFP Advisory Committee, dated 12 March 1939.

24 SRO: GD 325-1/301. 'Minutes of the meeting of the Argyll NFP Advisory Committee', Edinburgh, dated 4 April 1939.

25 SRO: FC 7-71, Forest Profiles (North Scotland) – Queen's Forest, Glenmore, dated 5 May 1952.

26 SRO: FC 7-68, Forest Profiles (North Scotland) – In[s]chriach, Inverness, dated 5 May 1952. See also SRO: FC 3-18, for details of Inshriach section of 1937, and Invereshie section of 1954.

27 Sheail 1981, *op. cit.*, p. 187.

28 SRO: GD 325-1/301, *Memo* from F.C. Handford, to all members of the Argyll NFP Advisory Committee, dated 25 March 1942.

29 FC, *Report of the National Forest Park Committee – Glentrool* (HMSO, London, 1943). John Sutherland chaired this FC Committee appointed on 22 October 1943.

30 SRO: GD 325-1/301, 'Minutes of the meeting of the Argyll NFP Advisory Committee', Edinburgh, 2 May 1942.

31 SRO: GD 325-1/301, Letter from F.C. Handford, FC Edinburgh, to Michael Lorimer WS, Scottish Land and Property Federation, dated 3 October 1946.

32 SRO: FC 4-1, 'Minutes of the 194th meeting of the Forestry Commission', London, 17 April 1941.

33 FC, *Report of the National Forest Park Committee – Forest of Dean* (HMSO, London, 1938). J.C. Wynne Finch chaired this FC Committee appointed on 25 March 1938.

34 FC, *Post-War Forest Policy – Report by H.M. Forestry Commissioners*, Cmd. 6447 (HMSO, London, 1943), pp. 77–80, 85.

35 SRO: FC 3-15, 'Minutes of the meeting of the Scottish National Committee of the FC', Edinburgh, 12 October 1945.

36 SRO: FC 3-15, 'Minutes of the meeting of the Scottish National Committee of the FC', Edinburgh, 11 April 1946.

37 SRO: FC 3-15, 'Minutes of the meeting of the Scottish National Committee of the FC', Edinburgh, 10 October 1946.

38 Sheail 1981, *op. cit.*, Mackay 1995, *op. cit.*, p. 35.

39 Sheail 1976, *op. cit.*, pp. 107–108.

40 SRO: FC 6-1, 'Minutes of the meeting of the Scottish National Forest Parks Advisory Committee', Edinburgh, 14 November 1946. Aside from the FC, those attending were Scottish Ramblers' Federation, Scottish Education Department, the Camping Club of Great Britain and Ireland, the National Playing Fields Association, The Boys' Brigade, Scottish Land and Property Federation, the Boy Scouts Association, the Scottish Standing Conference of Voluntary Youth Organisations, Scottish Tourist Board, Girl Guide Association, Automobile Association, the Association for the Preservation of Rural Scotland, Cyclists Touring Club, Scottish Girls' Training Corps.

41 SRO: FC 9/2, Letter from F.C. Handford, FC Scotland, Edinburgh to D.M. MacPhail, Dept. of Health for Scotland, dated 23 November 1946.

42 SRO: FC 9/2, 'Minutes of the meeting of the Scottish National Parks Committee', Edinburgh, 26 November 1946.

43 SRO: FC 3-15, 'Minutes of meeting of Scottish National Committee of FC', Edinburgh, 12 December 1946.

44 SRO: FC 3-15, 'Minutes of meeting of Scottish National Committee of FC', Edinburgh, 13 February 1947.

45 SRO: FC 3-15, 'Minutes of meeting of Scottish National Committee of FC', Edinburgh, 5 June 1947.

46 Anon., 'Scotland opens third Forest Park', *Take Note* (Magazine of the Scottish Tourist Board), July 1948, p. 4.

47 Anon., 'Planning for 1997', *Take Note*, May 1947, pp. 4–5.

48 SRO: FC 6-1, 'Minutes of the meeting of the Scottish NFP Advisory Committee', Edinburgh, 11 March 1948.

49 SRO: FC 6-1, Letter from F.C. Handford, FC Scotland, Edinburgh to Professor J. Walton, Department of Botany, University of Glasgow, dated 1 April 1948.

50 SRO: FC 6-1, 'Minutes of the meeting of the Scottish NFP Advisory Committee', Edinburgh, 7 April 1949.

51 SRO: FC 3-15, 'Minutes of the meeting of the Scottish National Committee of the FC', Edinburgh, 10 June 1948.

52 SRO: FC 4-12, 'Glenmore National Forest Park Byelaws – Byelaws made by Forestry Commissioners in pursuance of the Forestry Act, 1927', dated 11 August 1948, signed by F.W. Hamilton, Secretary, Forestry Commission. An initial batch of 1,200 were printed.

53 FC, *Forestry Commission Byelaws 1971*, No. 997, 1 July 1971 (HMSO, London, 1971), p. 3.

54 SRO: FC 10-1/28, FC, *28th Annual Report of the Forestry Commissioners for the Year Ending September 30 1947* (HMSO, London, 1948), pp. 14–15.

55 SRO: FC 10-1/45, FC, *45th Annual Report of the Forestry Commissioners for the Year Ending September 30 1964* (HMSO, London, 1965), pp. 10–11. Sylvia Crowe was a former President of the Institute of Landscape Architects.

56 SRO: FC 10-1/47, FC, *47th Annual Report of the Forestry Commissioners for the Year Ending September 30 1966* (HMSO, London, 1967), p. 8.

57 SRO: FC 10-1/45, *loc. cit.*

58 SRO: FC 10-1/40, FC, *40th Annual Report of the Forestry Commissioners for the Year Ending September 30 1959* (HMSO, London, 1960), pp. 9–10.

59 John Walton (ed.), *National Forest Park Guides: Glen More – Cairngorms* (HMSO, Edinburgh, 1960); D.A. Woodburn (ed.), *Forestry Commission Guide: Glen More Forest Park – Cairngorms* (HMSO, Edinburgh, 1975).

60 SRO: FC 6-1, 'Minutes of the meeting of the Scottish NFP Advisory Committee', Edinburgh, 8 March 1951.

61 SRO: FC 3-15, 'Minutes of the meeting of the Scottish National Committee of the FC', Edinburgh, 12 April 1951.

62 B.H. Humble, 'The Glenmore Story', *Climber and Rambler*, August 1975, pp. 380–383; B.H. Humble, *On Scottish Hills* (Chapman and Hall, London, 1946), pp. 100–108; Anon., 'School for Climbing', *Take Note*, February 1948, p. 4.

63 Catharine M. Loader, *Cairngorm Adventure at Glenmore Lodge* (William Brown, Edinburgh, 1952). Catharine Loader was the Technical Representative of the CCPR. In 1952, the Scottish section of the Central Council of Physical Recreation became the Scottish Council of Physical Recreation, which in 1972 became the Scottish Sports Council.

64 Pamphlet, 'Glenmore Lodge: The Scottish Centre of Outdoor Training – Aviemore, Inverness-shire, Outdoor Training Programme, 1969'.

65 These figures are taken from a range of source materials held in SRO: FC 9/2; FC 6-1.

66 SRO: FC 9/2, National Forest Parks in Scotland – Progress Report, Edinburgh, April 1949.

67 SRO: FC 6-1, 'Minutes of the meeting of the Scottish NFP Advisory Committee', Edinburgh, 8 March 1951.

68 SRO: FC 3-16; FC 6-1.

69 SRO: FC 6-1, 'Minutes of the meeting of the Scottish NFP Advisory Committee', Edinburgh, 8 March 1951.

70 SRO: FC 6-1, 'Minutes of the meeting of the Scottish NFP Advisory Committee', Edinburgh, 12 January 1954.

71 SRO: FC 3-16, 'Minutes of the meeting of the Scottish National Committee of the FC', Edinburgh, 17 July 1956. The first meeting of a Border NFP Advisory Committee was held in Newcastle on 4 October 1956.

72 SRO: FC 3-15, 'Minutes of the meeting of the Scottish National Committee of the FC', Edinburgh, 7 December 1954.

73 SRO: FC 10-1/37, FC, *37th Annual Report of the Forestry Commissioners for the Year Ending September 30 1956* (HMSO, London, 1957), pp. 62–63.

74 SRO: FC 10-1/42, FC, *42nd Annual Report of the Forestry Commissioners for the Year Ending September 30 1961* (HMSO, London, 1962), p. 14.

75 SRO: FC 10-1/40, FC, *40th Annual Report of the Forestry Commissioners for the Year Ending September 30 1959* (HMSO, London, 1960), p. 25.

76 A.P. Snyder, 'Wilderness Management – A Growing Challenge', *Journal of Forestry*, Vol. 64, July 1966, pp. 441–446.

77 These figures are taken from SRO: FC 10.

78 SRO: FC 3-16, 'Minutes of the meeting of the Scottish National Committee of the FC', Edinburgh, 9 February 1960. A motor cycle and tent was charged at 2/6d. per night, or 15/– per week.

79 SRO: FC 10-1/31, FC, *31st Annual Report of the Forestry Commissioners for the Year Ending September 30 1950* (HMSO, London, 1951), p. 45.

80 These figures have been extrapolated from a wide range of sources held in SRO: FC 6-1; FC 9/2.

81 SRO: FC 10-1/53, FC, *53rd Annual Report of the Forestry Commissioners for the Year Ending September 30 1974* (HMSO, London, 1975).

82 SRO: FC 6-1, 'Minutes of the meeting of the Scottish NFP Advisory Committee', Edinburgh, 1 February 1961.

83 SRO: FC 6-1, 'Minutes of the meeting of the Scottish NFP Advisory Committee', Edinburgh, 4 December 1958.

84 SRO: FC 6-1, 'Minutes of the meeting of the Scottish NFP Advisory Committee', Edinburgh, 27 January 1960.

85 Glenmore National Forest Park Visitor Centre, *pers. obs.*

86 SRO: FC 6-1, 'Minutes of the meeting of the Scottish NFP Advisory Committee', Edinburgh, 22 February 1957.

87 SRO: FC 6-1, Scottish National Forest Parks – Progress Report, January 1962.

88 SRO: FC 6-1, 'Minutes of the meeting of the Scottish NFP Advisory Committee', Edinburgh, 4 December 1963.

89 SRO: FC 6-1, Letter from L.H. Grinsted, Secretariat, FC HQ London to Estate Management, FC Edinburgh, dated 12 January 1966.

90 SRO: FC 6-1, Letter from M. Nicholson, Asst. Senior Officer, FC Scotland, to L.H. Grinsted, Secretariat, FC, HQ London, dated 17 January 1966.

91 SRO: FC 3-17, Internal Report: *Public Relations and the Forestry Commission*, Edinburgh, dated December 1962.

92 SRO: FC 10-1/42, FC, *42nd Annual Report of the Forestry Commissioners for the Year Ending 30 September 1961* (HMSO, London, 1962), p. 14.

93 See SRO: FC 3-18.

94 SRO: FC 3-18. Notes on the Scottish National Committee of the FC tour, 7/8/9 June 1966.

95 Nigel V. Pears, 'Man in the Cairngorms: A Population –Resource Balance Problem', *Scottish Geographical Magazine*, Vol. 84, 1968, pp. 45–55.

96 SRO: FC 3-18.

97 SRO: FC 3-18. 'Minutes of the meeting of the Scottish National Committee of the FC to review the future development of Glenmore Forest Park', Inverness, 12 April 1967.

98 SRO: FC 3-18, 'Minutes of the meeting of the Scottish National Committee of the FC', Edinburgh, 5 June 1968. The Chairman of the FC in London personally wrote to Inverness County Council to ask for this change.

99 SRO: FC 3-18, Scottish National Committee – Notes of Discussions on Memo 91/67, 'Public Recreation and the Forestry Commission', Edinburgh, January 1968.

100 SRO: FC 10-1/49, FC, *49th Annual Report of the Forestry Commissioners for the Year Ending March 1969* (HMSO, London, 1970), p. 14.

101 Bob Climie, *History of the Scottish Orienteering Association* (SOA/private publ., Elgin, 1990).

102 SRO: FC 10-1/51, FC, *51st Annual Report of the Forestry Commissioners for the Year 1970–1971* (HMSO, London, 1971), pp. 8, 15.

103 SRO: FC 10-2/23, *Annual Report – Forestry Commission (Scotland) 1961*, paragraph 16, 'Amenity and Access to the Countryside'.

104 SRO: FC 3-18.

105 R.D. Watson, *op. cit.*, pp. 7–19, 17. See his Table, 'References to the Extent of the Boundaries of the Glenmore National Forest Park (GNFP)', p. 17.

106 W.E.S. Mutch, *Public Recreation in National Forests: A Factual Survey* (HMSO, London, 1968); D.N. McVean and J.D. Lockie, *Ecology and Land Use in Upland Scotland* (Edinburgh University Press, Edinburgh, 1969), pp. 98–102.

107 SRO: FC 10-2/26, *Annual Report – Forestry Commission (Scotland) 1964*, paragraph 16, 'Amenity and Access to the Countryside'.

108 Conal Ruddock, 'Visitors and Visitor Management in Glen More Forest Park', Unpublished dissertation for the degree of M.A. (Hons.), Department of Geography, University of St. Andrews, January 1980, Thesis No. 334.

109 FC Map, 'See Your Forests – Scotland', Spring 1980.

110 SRO: FC 13-8, FC, *The Forestry Commission and Recreation*, Policy and Procedure Paper No. 2 (FC, Edinburgh, March 1980), reprinted April 1984 and May 1988.

111 FC, *The Forestry Commission and Conservation*, Policy and Procedure Paper No. 4 (FC, Edinburgh, March 1980).

112 Herbert L. Edlin, *Forestry in Great Britain – A Review of Progress to 1964* (FC, London, May 1964).

113 SRO: FC 7-71, Forest Profile (North Scotland) –Queen's Forest, Glenmore, dated 5 May 1952.

114 T.C. Smout, 'Scottish Native Woodlands in Historical Perspective', in D. Mollison (ed.), *Sharing The Land* (John Muir Trust, Musselburgh, 1994), pp. 1–6.

115 Mackay 1995, *op. cit.*, pp. 60–61.

116 Henry Alexander, 'The Canadian Lumber Camps in the Cairngorms', *Cairngorm Club Journal*, Vol. X, No. 55, July 1920, pp. 1–11; V.A. Firsoff, 'The Forests of the Cairngorms', *Take Note*, April 1954, pp. 12–13.

117 Scottish Home Department, *A Programme of Highland Development*, Cmd. 7976 (HMSO, Edinburgh, 1950), pp. 17–18.

118 Prof. Sir Solly Zuckerman, *Forestry, Agriculture and Marginal Land – A Report by the Natural Resources (Technical) Committee* (HMSO, London, 1957).

119 W.H. Murray, *Highland Landscape – A Survey* (NTS/Aberdeen University Press, Aberdeen, April 1962), pp. 52–54.

120 W.H. Murray, *Ibid.*, p. 16; SRO: FC 3-16, 'Minutes of the meeting of the Scottish National Committee of the FC', Edinburgh, June 1959. Material taken from various communiqués and reports, 'Rothiemurchus Estate'.

121 'FC Stock Map: Inverness FD Map No. 228, Queen's Forest, Glenmore, Inverness', dated 1989, revised 1992, issued by the Conservator, FC Inverness, scale 1:10000.

122 Jim Crumley, *A High and Lonely Place – The Sanctuary and Plight of the Cairngorms* (Jonathan Cape, London, 1991), p. 100.

123 B.M.S. Dunlop, 'The Woods of Strathspey in the Nineteenth and Twentieth Centuries', in T.C. Smout (ed.), *Scottish Woodland History* (Scottish Cultural Press, Edinburgh, 1997), pp. 176–189; NCC, *Inventory of Ancient, Long-established and Semi-natural Woodland, Badenoch and Strathspey* (NCC, Peterborough, 1987).

124 The archives of the Association for the Preservation of Rural Scotland (APRS) are privately held at Gladstone's Land (3rd floor), 483 Lawnmarket, Edinburgh; 'Minutes of the Meeting of the Executive Committee of the APRS', Edinburgh, 3 May 1929.

125 See NRA(S) 102:399, Letters from Sir J. Stirling-Maxwell, Addison Committee member and Forestry Commissioner to Lt. Col. J.P. Grant of Rothiemurchus, Rothiemurchus Estate, dated 13 March 1929 and 18 March 1929. Extensive investigations have failed to identify the buyer named 'Hamborough'. It may have been a member of the Hambro's banking family.

126 Roger G. Muhl, Forest District Manager, Forest Enterprise, Inverness, *pers. comm.*

127 Desmond Nethersole-Thompson and Adam Watson, *The Cairngorms – Their Natural History and Scenery (Collins, London, 1974), p. 138.*

8

'Our natural playground':
The Cairngorms National Park Ideal

In 1950, the National Parks Commission set up in England and Wales under the National Parks and Access to the Countryside Act of 1949, set about the task of designating parks for their intrinsic scenic beauty and the recreational possibilities that they afforded. Scotland had been left out of this park legislation, for a number of key reasons, and the issue of National Parks (NP) in Scotland has remained an emotive and controversial issue across the ensuing years. When National Parks were first mooted for Scotland, the Cairngorms area was in the vanguard of a popular campaign to preserve Scotland's scenic grandeur and to promote its widespread recreational facilities. A Cairngorms National Park was always seen as primarily a recreational playground, along the model provided by National Parks in the USA after 1872.

Other commentators have analysed well the political, economic and social background to the British National Park movement, most notably John Sheail, H.C. Darby, Gordon Cherry and Ann and Malcolm MacEwen.[1] There has been a bias towards England and Wales in this work because NPs were ultimately created there, and the Scottish situation has often remained peripheral to the main argument. Within the Scottish situation, the Cairngorms story has remained untold, although it provides a timely and useful case study of the pros and cons for a NP on the ground, in the Highlands of Scotland. This chapter then, will not retell the history of National Park legislation in its wider application,[2] but rather will discuss how different interests responded to the challenge of potential NP status for the Cairngorms area. In particular, it will reveal the concerted opposition from local landowners from 1930 onwards, which played a fundamental role in shaping the debate. This was far more central to the Cairngorms situation than the national issue of the development of Highland glens by the North Scotland Hydro-Electric Board, as proposed by government from 1942 in a Scottish Office committee.[3]

The Earliest Demands for a Cairngorms National Park 1900–1930

The National Park concept in Great Britain is often traced back to William Wordsworth in the English Lake District, especially his call for all visitors to "testify that they deem the district a sort of national property, in which every man has a right and interest, who has an eye to perceive and a heart to enjoy".[4] In Scotland (and for the Cairngorms also) the NP issue was first raised in 1904 by Charles Stewart, in the journal *Nineteenth Century and After*. For Stewart, a National Park in Scotland should have two objectives; the preservation of fine scenery and the conservation of certain 'useful' species of native flora and fauna: the rabbit *Oryctolagus cuniculus*, "in spite of his pleasant little personality", was an undesirable. Stewart felt that either Jura or Rhum would make a "glorious National Park" and much of his interest was concentrated on the west coast of Scotland, although he did concede that there were estates, and very grand scenery in Ross-shire and Inverness-shire (in which the Cairngorms lie) from which a NP could be constructed. Just as town parks and open spaces had provided succour and recreation to "rich and poor, and especially the guttersnipes", so a NP would prove popular to scientists, tourists (an hotel should always be provided) and agriculturists: "the Government that has the courage and the spirit to undertake and carry through its accomplishment will deserve and will receive an ample meed of gratitude".[5] The NP ideal for Scotland lay dormant until the late 1920s, although John Sheail has shown that the Society for the Promotion of Nature Reserves (SPNR), in their 1915/16 survey of wildlife sites across the UK, found Glen Clova in Angus (on the southern fringes of the Grampian Mountains) to be worthy of special NP status for its botanical interest.[6]

The specific idea of having a Cairngorms National Park emerged properly in the autumn of 1928 in *The Scots Magazine*. The editor first printed an article by the access campaigner Ernest A. Baker in October 1928, stating that he would then devote much of the November and December issues to this debate. In 1923, Baker had already made a name for himself with stinging criticism against absentee landlordism in the Highlands, and radical support for the access question, "as the moors and forests of Scotland have been converted into a private park, with public access only to the mere fringes". He likened this "social evil", to the closing of the Alps to the people of Europe. In the early 1920s, Baker did not call for NPs as such, rather for the opening up of areas like the Cairngorms "as a pleasure-ground for the urban population of Britain" by an "epoch-making development".[7] By October 1928 Baker felt that no area in Britain, "by its configuration and the charm of its untouched solitudes", was better "for the purposes of a great natural park", than was the Cairngorms. He urged that the fairest mountain areas in Scotland should be nationalised, "and for the first time in history [become] useful possessions". His vision was for controlled and regulated recreation, with limited tourist development, fearing that "there will inevitably be a demand, sooner or later, for a rack-railway up Cairngorm".[8] A prophetic voice from history: that demand was to come, but not until the mid-1990s.

Baker was supported, in a moral lesson for this month delivered by a 'Self-Thinking Scotsman to his Father', concerned that Scots should take a keen responsibility for their landscape heritage, especially in the Cairngorms, where often litter (a by-product of professional "litter-ary society" climbers in the area) revealed the thoughtlessness of some visitors.[9] Alan Graeme in the pages of *The Scots Magazine* called for the purchase of the Cairngorms as an ideal 'National Domain' that, with low land prices in the late 1920s, would cost only the price of a battleship. He felt that the Cairngorms would become self-regulating hills, protecting themselves from a "jazz-bandy advance" of tourists and developers. It is interesting that Graeme also cites some of the anti-NP rhetoric from the late 1920s; namely that nobody would visit the area because it was too remote; that too many people would spoil the Cairngorms anyway; that deer stalking would be ruined, and that tourism could run rampant.[10] The battle lines between those in favour of a Cairngorms NP and those against, had been drawn at the earliest possible juncture in the debate.

Professor J.W. Gregory, a geologist and former President of the SSC from 1910 to 1913 presented a strong argument in December 1928 for a Cairngorm NP as a means of encouraging tourism, with the opening of a well-planned holiday resort, and the development of winter sports. The central location of the mountains appealed to Gregory, as did the scenery, but his vision was also of a recreational paradise on cheaply acquired mountain slopes.[11] Alex Inkson McConnochie spoke of a spiritual park in the Cairngorms, "where the winds carry healing in their wings", and welcomed the gradual influx of visitors that NP designation would guarantee. The entire project was "a magnificent idea", McConnochie enthused, but warned that it must remain geographically and financially manageable – he felt that the first step could be to make Glenmore "the nucleus of a National Park", and then to expand from there. A map of the Cairngorm Area was issued with this volume, defining the region as bounded by the Rivers Dee, Geldie, Feshie and Spey; eight estates could contribute land to the Cairngorm National Domain, namely the Mackintosh of Mackintosh part of Glen Feshie, Rothiemurchus, Glenmore, Abernethy, Glenavon, Invercauld, Mar and the Macpherson-Grant owned part of Glen Feshie. A total of 173,000 acres was mapped out.[12]

This NP propaganda continued to be aired in the pages of *The Scots Magazine* in the spring of 1929, with a notable contribution from the nationalist Erskine of Marr. He wanted a "National Forest of the Cairngorms" (which the

FC in part created at Glenmore in 1948), to be "a National Sanctuary – a sort of serpentless Eden", a place of solitude and tranquillity and "innocent bodily recreation". How wrong he then was to conclude his essay with a firm belief that Cairngorm landowners, "would be patriotic enough to come into the plan, provided of course any little sacrifice it may involve them in were suitably gilded".[13] Former Prime Minister Ramsay MacDonald declared himself in favour of a Cairngorms NP in an interview published in January 1929. MacDonald sought protection for the flora and fauna of the region in any proposed plan, and expressed concern about the infrastructure needed to develop a winter sports industry in the area, fearing "the spectacle of the Cairngorms spotted with miscellaneous erections and buildings", which would surely "interfere with the complete pleasure of the mountain lover and admirer". J.I. Macpherson wanted any scheme to have the goodwill of all the people, and spoke of preserving the area for future generations of Scots within the ideal "to conserve the dignity and grandeur of our native hills".[14]

Reacting to this written support for a NP in the Cairngorms, the Association for the Preservation of Rural Scotland (APRS), which had only been founded over 1926/27, called a conference on the subject for public interest, in Glasgow at the Highlanders' Institute on 4 June 1929. Invited organisations came from a primarily recreational open-air movement background namely the Cairngorm Club, the SMC, the SRoWS, the Dundee Ramblers, the Glasgow and West of Scotland Ramblers Federation and the APRS. Public and private landowning interest was represented by the FC and the SEFS; the Royal Scottish Geographical Society also sent a delegate. There was general support for the idea of a Scottish National Park, and the Cairngorm mountains were seen as the first choice. The APRS pressed for the formation of a Scottish Forest Reserve Committee "to inquire into, and report on, the matter in all its bearings". The Chairman was Sir J. Douglas Ramsay of Bamff. This committee later proposed the formation of a Scottish-based National Trust, a reserve to preserve flora and fauna in Glen Affric and the purchase of lands in the Cairngorms for "a Recreational Park".[15] The Scottish Forest Reserve Committee reported its findings to the Christopher Addison governmental committee on 22 January 1930, via Douglas Ramsay and the Rev. A.E. Robertson. In that month, the *Cairngorm Club Journal* carried a short article looking back on the progress made to date, and cited the promotional role that *The Scots Magazine* and later the *Glasgow Herald* (to a much smaller degree) had played in the last two years of the 1920s. These two publications had been used as a valuable forum for discussion on a Cairngorms NP within Scotland. This article also praised the role of Aberdeen Town Council who accepted a report drafted by Henry Alexander and George Roberts in January 1930 in favour of a recreational park in the Cairngorms; the area nominated here covered 282 square miles at a cost of £354,000, with cheaper costing alternatives available down to £195,000. The battle would be to strike a balance between recreational developments (chalet inns and refuge huts were proposed) and the preservation of mountain scenery.[16] Henry Alexander presented this report to the Addison Committee on 23 May 1930, although it is recorded that Aberdeen Town Council refused to contribute financially to a NP scheme in the Cairngorms, oddly maintaining "the area is not near enough to Aberdeen to be of local importance".[17] Why then had they commissioned a report?

Around 1930 there was widespread popular literary support for a Cairngorms NP, with many commentators appearing convinced that the designation would soon become a reality. In 1931 John Bulloch predicted that the next evolutionary step after the break-up of the great estates of Badenoch would see them "take the form of national parks".[18] A year later, as James Baikie mused on *Things Seen in the Scottish Highlands*, he envisaged this for the Cairngorms:

> "It may be hoped that in the fulness of time the movement which has been hinted at, if not actually started, of securing the Cairngorms as a National Park will be carried out ... within the next half-century." [19]

As the mid-1930s approached, the access campaigner Ernest Baker considered a Cairngorms NP to have many benefits:

> "The real economic value will be in the infinite opportunities for healthy exercise and unfettered access to nature at her grandest. Scotland will be richer, England will be richer, when this great piece of our natural playground is restored to the one purpose for which it is obviously fitted."

Baker did fear rampant tourism in the region, sensing that "there is sure to be a demand, sooner or later, for a railway to the top of Cairn Gorm and into the Larig Ghru", but the recreational potential of the scheme far outweighed any doubts that sentimental 'mountain-lovers' might harbour. To support the scheme, he declared, was an act of patriotism. Baker wisely concluded that the success of this NP scheme, would depend "largely on the friendly or the unfriendly attitude of the owners or trustees of these properties [the great Cairngorm estates]".[20]

It is important to mention that Lord Bledisloe, when Parliamentary Secretary to the Ministry of Agriculture in the mid-1920s, is usually credited with starting the National Park mania in England and Wales; the Scottish and wider UK NP campaigns had different roots. Lord Bledisloe visited North American NPs in 1925, and reported favourably on how they catered for wildlife and people alike, in his campaign to attract the government's attention to this question in 1928. By 1929, Bledisloe had the support of the Council for the Preservation of Rural England (CPRE), the Council for the Preservation of Rural Wales (CPRW) and the newly-founded APRS. This growing national rallying call went unheeded by the Conservative government of Stanley Baldwin from Nov 1924 to June 1929 – as natural allies of the landed classes they were unwilling to disturb the rural status quo by supporting anything as radical as land nationalisation. However, the following Labour government of J.Ramsay MacDonald was more responsive to the idea, and appointed the Addison Committee in the autumn of 1929.

The First Phase of Discussion 1929–1930

In early May 1929, a full four months before J. Ramsay MacDonald appointed the Addison Committee, a number of organisations prompted by newspaper speculation over the creation of a NP in the Cairngorms, began to gather their thoughts on the issue. The SRoWS were among the first to declare themselves in favour of a 'Public Park', A.W. Russell believing that, "Glen More at the base of Cairngorm, taking in Cairngorm itself on the one side and the Buachaille on the other is one of the most ideal that we have". Russell went on to confirm that the area held considerable attractions for winter sports enthusiasts (a view to which not all subscribed), and that any camping facilities had to be planned better than in the USA ("I have not actually camped in America" he apologised): "Americans as well as Canadians are much more in the habit than we are of going in great flocks and do not perhaps so much mind camping just beside their neighbour as I think the majority of our people would".[21] The APRS did not even mention the Cairngorms as a potential NP in a circular sent out by Sir Ian Colquhoun of Luss to interested organisations in late May; they focused their initial attention on Arran and Kintail as sites, and the possible future call for hotels, mountain railways and camping sites, or what they preferred to call "a Nature Reserve proper".[22]

In May and June 1929 during an exchange of letters between Arthur Russell of the SRoWS and Lawrence W. Chubb of the National Playing Fields Association, Russell put forward his own definition of what a 'Cairngorm Park' could become, "as opinion is at present rather indefinite for the acquisition of a National or Public Park". Here lay the crux of the matter. A National Park should be "where nature could mainly be preserved wild and unspoilt". A Public Park would be "where camping would be allowed and possibly refreshment houses provided". Russell also added that a weakness in the whole NP scheme was the absence of a National Trust in Scotland[23]; to which Chubb suggested an approach be made to the National Trust (NT) in England, who could hold property in Scotland if they so desired.[24] Certainly in June 1929, Arthur Russell was convinced that come "the probable formation later of a National Trust for

Scotland" it should be the body to hold a Cairngorm NP.[25] Chubb congratulated him on this vision, adding: "It will be a magnificent achievement if you can manage to save the Cairngorms". It is an indication of how widely the scheme was being discussed, that these words of support were sent from Belgrave Road in London.[26] In September 1929 the Directors of the SRoWS formally submitted their evidence to the Scottish Forest Reserve Committee and the APRS. In a long submission, they saw in the Cairngorms both the creation of a "true nature reserve for animal, bird and plant life" on "tracts of country of wild and varied nature well removed from centres of population", alongside a "Reserve or Park suitable for camping or a holiday ground" on "tracts of country ... less rugged and within reasonable distance of large centres of population". There was some confusing interchange of terminology here, but the basic conclusion was that the Cairngorms were the only single area that could "meet all the varying requirements". They expressed a concern that the expense of acquiring such large tracts of land in the area "might be so serious as to unnecessarily delay and prejudice the whole project". Could the Carnegie Trust not be approached about a sizeable financial donation, they asked.[27] In their final evidence to the Addison Committee on 22 January 1930 (but drafted in memorandum form on 10 January by J. Douglas Ramsay) the Scottish Forest Reserve Committee (SFRC) and the APRS felt that it was impractical to combine a nature reserve and a recreational park in the Cairngorms, and so favoured the latter. They also felt the climate in the region was "too treacherous" to permit the establishment of a winter sports industry.[28]

At the first meeting of the SFRC on 7 August 1929 the Chairman, J. Douglas Ramsay, had sought to canvass opinion on the desirability of creating a NP in the Cairngorms, and had urged all interested organisations to report on the feelings of their membership, and club membership numbers. The next meeting was scheduled for 2 October, when Douglas Ramsay wanted to discuss if the land should be "acquired by purchase and held in trust for the nation", or if it should be just, "scheduled but left in the hands of its present owners, access to the land being free to all".[29] They later concluded that outright purchase of the land would be necessary in the case of a Cairngorms recreational park. SRoWS member John Bartholomew gave evidence on behalf of the Royal Scottish Geographical Society, who favoured a National Park in Scotland on "the Cairn Gorm plateau north of the Feshie-Dee furrow and the plateau extending south-eastward from Lochnagar and forming the watershed between these systems and Glen Clova and Glen Isla on the South". It would be an area not only for "wholesome recreation" but also for geographical education, and could see the re-establishment of a high level meteorological station (perhaps on Cairn Gorm itself) to replace the much regretted loss of the Ben Nevis Observatory.[30]

By July 1930 the Forestry Commission (FC) had thrown its hat into the ring, and offered the unplantable land in Glenmore Forest as a NP, providing the entire scheme was self-financing and that the FC would receive compensation for the subsequent loss of sporting rights there. The FC sought the right to control access to the 'National Park experiment', and even gave the Addison Committee a projected list of costs (an initial capital expenditure of £9,000, and an annual maintenance bill of £1,500) should they assume control of the scheme, which was probably Sir John Stirling-Maxwell's (Forestry Commissioner) desire.[31]

The Opposition of the Cairngorm Landowners 1930–1931

It is apparent that in late January 1930, Stirling-Maxwell (a Forestry Commissioner, who also sat on the Addison Committee) was forced to defend himself against the wrath of the Cairngorm landowners over the NP scheme. From his letter to the laird of Rothiemurchus, it is evident that he had been labelled as one "of the ring leaders in the National Parks", and that he had supposedly advocated "that land should be taken for a National Park" if an agreement was not reached with a landowner. He hotly denied both these accusations, adding that he had often sympathised with the laird of Rothiemurchus "when the public were discussing in the newspapers whether they ought to have merry-go-rounds in your forest or only bathing pools and a golf course". He also defended the actions of the FC who, by offering Glenmore as an alternative, had annoyed J.P. [Iain] Grant of Rothiemurchus, who called them "a bad neighbour". Stirling-Maxwell tried to calm Grant's fears by privately asserting, of the Addison Committee, that "none of them are very keen about the project and I feel pretty sure that the report will be mainly devoted to questions of finance and administration (and regional planning), without any attempt to define or even suggest, specific areas".[32] Stirling-Maxwell was the first of many prominent figures in the NP campaign in the 1930s and 1940s who would be criticised and, at times, insulted by the Cairngorm landlords. Their counter-attack began at the start of 1930, with the laird of Rothiemurchus appearing to muster the troops in February by calling for the formation of an Owners' Committee within the Cairngorms area "to exchange views with the idea of formulating a common policy".[33] As well as working together to thwart the scheme, the landowners also agreed to bombard the Addison Committee with long individual letters of outrage and complaint, "stating their unqualified opposition to the Cairngorm proposals".[34]

To bolster their campaign further the landowners began to seek support in England, by contacting absentee landlords who held some of the smaller Cairngorm estates. An indignant Stuart W. Clark wrote from Banbury in Oxfordshire, that he would not have recently purchased his estate "had I had any idea that there was a chance of the Cairngorms being made into a National Park ... it would quite spoil the privacy of the place and the shooting would be useless". Clark asserted that the scheme would incur "a heavy expense to the country and I think would benefit very few"; the cost of fencing and wardens for the NP, plus the cost of sporting rights and heavy estate taxation would "fall on the public in the event of the National Parks becoming proprietors", he argued. A Cairngorms NP would drive him out: "I should be compelled to sell if the place became a national park as it would be useless to me".[35] This was just the sort of English ally that the local Cairngorm landowners sought, and he remained loyal and supportive to the cause throughout. In February 1930, Clark reported that he had talked with Lord Bledisloe and asked him bluntly "who is to blame for the national park mania?", revealing that Bledisloe believed Sir J. Stirling-Maxwell to be "at the bottom of all the trouble". Clark added: "The Country hasn't money to spare for all these things – and the Parks are not wanted".[36]

The estate owners first met as a group on 15 March 1930 in the Strathspey Estate Office in Grantown-on-Spey, where it was decided to have plans prepared and circulated showing the boundaries of all the estates that would fall inside the proposed NP scheme.[37] The minutes of this meeting show that Grant of Rothiemurchus was appointed Chairman, and was urged to become a member of the Sub-Committee that would deal directly with the Addison Committee to ascertain its remit and the level of representation that the Cairngorm landowners would receive. Present at this meeting were Sir George Macpherson Grant of Ballindalloch and his Factor, Lady Seafield's Trustees, representatives of the Duke of Richmond and Gordon, Colonel A.H. Farquharson of Invercauld, J.B. Hosie (the Commissioner of Fife Estates), a representative of Mackintosh of Mackintosh, and the Aberdeen Advocate John Murray.[38] This attendance must have pleased J.P. Grant of Rothiemurchus who, in a private circular note to all local landowners, had called for 'a community of interest' to prevent the Cairngorms being "over-run by tourists during the stalking season much to the detriment and depreciation in rateable value". Grant was still angry with the FC, who were not invited to the meeting as they had already acted on this issue "without consulting neighbouring proprietors".[39]

It was during the month prior to this meeting that the most extreme aspects of the landowners' campaign had surfaced. In February 1930, the threat to landed interest by the creation of a NP in the Cairngorms became a matter in which King George V was a player, kept informed by what can best be described as courtier gossip. In a letter sent by Sir Frederick Ponsonby from the Privy Purse Office at Buckingham Palace to W.H. Bonham-Carter (and then duplicated for the Cairngorm landowners), it was stated that Sir Douglas Ramsay of Bamff (a former Commissioner at Balmoral) had privately informed the King that the Cairngorm estates were worthless and that "there was no stalking done there", so the "owners would be well advised to give their consent to the Scheme". The letter also stated that the Duke of Richmond and Gordon and The Mackintosh had already "consented to part with their land". John Murray communicated the contents of this letter to Grant of Rothiemurchus on 17 February 1930,[40] and all hell broke loose. The Duke of Richmond and Gordon was livid and wrote to Lord Stamfordham asking that the truth of the matter be put before King George V; he also ordered Douglas Ramsay to approach the King and to declare himself a devious liar. The Duke would tolerate "no nonsense of this kind, more especially as he has no doubt his name was used in order to induce the Mar Estates to fall in with the scheme".[41] The Duke himself wrote in anger to Rothiemurchus Estate from Goodwood (Chichester) abusing Douglas Ramsay as "a mischievous liar" in thinking that the Duke would part with Glenavon, and speaking of "the wiseacres who have set the scheme afoot" as having no understanding of deer or Highland stalking.[42] Sir Frederick Ponsonby continued to take a keen interest in fanning the flames of rumour from Buckingham Palace, writing to the Duke of Richmond and Gordon that he had heard Douglas Ramsay suggest that, should the Cairngorm proposal fall through, then a more comprehensive scheme would be decided upon "and the Government will ride rough shod over any sporting right". George V was reportedly outraged to hear that an Addison Committee member had even suggested Lochnagar as a NP, which would have "made Balmoral quite impossible for the King".[43] As the Duke had observed "this cackhanded scheme" would see a "proposed invasion" of the Cairngorms.[44] He wrote in defiant mood to Grant of Rothiemurchus in early March: "Personally I don't intend to budge and if it comes to hard hitting I shall use every weapon I can lay my hand on! It is a pity H[is] M[ajesty] has been brought into it."[45]

This whisper campaign left J. Douglas Ramsay out in the cold. He was shunned by Cairngorm and fellow landowners who had once been his associates. From late February 1930 Douglas Ramsay protested his innocent role as Chairman of the SFRC, but his words fell on deaf ears. His long letters to his former friend J.P. Grant of Rothiemurchus have an almost tragic edge to them as he sought to rebuild bridges of trust and friendship, all along claiming that he had been misrepresented, humiliated and personally rebuked by the King. He claimed he had actually been persuaded by Iain Colquhoun of Luss (a noted figure in the early history of the APRS and NTS) to serve as Chairman, to put "the brake on the extremists", and had expected some to call him "a blackleg – a traitor etc.", but had, "never expected that the first stone would come from an old friend". He confessed: "Personally I don't want a National Park anywhere – and I think there is every chance that the whole thing will fall through", even suggesting that Grant should tell the Addison Committee to "Go to Hell".[46] Another letter spoke of Douglas Ramsay's attempts to curb some enthusiasts on the SFRC, warning the laird of Rothiemurchus, "but look out all the same, for public opinion crystallizes on the central Cairn Gorms more and more daily". It is apparent that Douglas Ramsay did receive abusive letters from some Cairngorm landowners some of whom he had not met, and subsequently hoped he never would. He did show some sympathy with the highest egalitarian ideals of a NP, if it could be "used not as a Lunar Park or Coney Island, but as a place to which less fortunate people than ourselves, who like to be alone in large spaces, can go for a rest without let or hindrance".[47] The Duke of Richmond and Gordon continued to attack Douglas Ramsay in March 1930, "for having taken his name in vain with a definite purpose".[48] It should not be forgotten that Douglas Ramsay was a part of the Scottish landowning class himself (holding Bamff Estate, near Alyth in NE Perthshire). He was being vilified for having broken ranks; for stepping outside the expected social and political role that landowners saw for themselves in that era. He stood accused by his very own class of siding with socialists in London, and in the eyes of the landed elite he had lost all sense of his inherited duty and honour.

On 8 March Douglas Ramsay, in a last-ditch attempt to curry favour with the Cairngorm landowners, broke the trust of his fellow committee colleagues and allowed J.P. Grant of Rothiemurchus a pre-publication look at SFRC evidence. He knew he was behaving in an unprofessional and rash manner and begged Grant to read the document and return it immediately, adding:

> "you can understand that were any part of it to get out and become public, and forestall the Government Committee in any way, I should get into a Hell of a row."

He concluded that the SFRC were utterly against any crass commercial exploitation of a recreational NP, even by new road schemes, and that "we are trying to damn the 'Winter Sports' crowd – and the Access to Mountains Bill. We are not as black as we are painted!"[49] His views on the skiing industry would have endeared him to The Mackintosh of Mackintosh who curtly wrote to J.P. Grant: "Winter sports on the Cairngorms are impossible. Not skiing ground. Too rocky and no long slopes."[50]

In a sense, this angry and accusatory letter exchange between the various protagonists over February and March 1930 did distract from the issue at hand, namely how the Cairngorm landowners were going to fight the NP proposals. However, at the same time, these letters allowed all interested participants to understand how the enemy might argue, and to refine their own arguments. The letters acted as a dress rehearsal for the main event, which was the visit of the Addison Committee to the Aviemore Hotel on 23–24 May 1930. The Sub-Committee of the Cairngorm landowners met on 19 May at Grantown-on-Spey to plan their arguments against the scheme.[51] Just prior to this meeting Grant of Rothiemurchus scribbled some personal notes to himself, as an *aide-*

mémoire, to refine his own viewpoints and steel himself for the battle ahead. The crux of his argument was to be "the inutility of the Cairngorms as the most suitable locus for a Park likely to serve the interests of the great bulk of the population". This line of argument was to form part of the strategy selected by the Cairngorm landowners in early May 1930, and they were confident that this would work, and that financial issues were likely to stop the scheme anyhow. Grant's notebook reveals that his major grievance was that a NP designation would see the estates lose their sporting value without any compensation, and that public discussion of the scheme was bound to frighten off future sporting tenants. The 'public aspect' of the NP worried him also; he would not stand aside and let the Cairngorms become "a Glasgow Park". He felt that the public were already given sufficient recreational facilities in the area, and that they often abused that privilege, citing broken bothies, fires, disturbance during the stalking season, and litter at the Corrour Bothy and Marquis' Well. Should the ideal stay alive, the landowners' immediate problem was what steps to take to stop the particular scheme dead. Grant proposed that they should always present a common front; protest to the Press, the APRS and the SLPF; and that they should urge all the past and present sporting tenants on Rothiemurchus, Glenavon, Invercauld, Glen Feshie and Abernethy Estates to join ranks with them against the scheme.[52]

The meeting between the Addison Committee and the landowners in Aviemore confirmed the worst fears of the Cairngorm Owners' Committee: they felt Dr. Addison had already made up his mind to recommend this area, and that his committee members "knew nothing of the local conditions and importance of the sporting value in this area". This was reiterated in a conversation reported between Col. Farquharson and Dr. Addison in June, where Addison put another nail in Douglas Ramsay's coffin by quoting him as very much "in favour of the scheme".[53] There was talk of a proposed meeting ('conference') in London between the Cairngorm landowners and the Addison Committee to be held in early June, but the estate owners saw no gain in this and decided to abandon the idea, especially as their agents had been refused entry to the Addison Committee evidence session in Edinburgh.[54] To his credit, Christopher Addison sought to find some compromise with the landowners, and extended an invitation for a second meeting over the late summer of 1930, but this met with no enthusiasm.[55]

With the publication of the Addison Committee report in April 1931, which recommended that an American style recreational NP should be set up in the Cairngorms, archival evidence on the actions of the Cairngorm landowners falls silent. They had shown themselves to be very willing to come together in a display of strength and common purpose to defeat the Cairngorms NP scheme, and the laird of Rothiemurchus had displayed vigour as their co-ordinator and spokesman. In a sense, they were also making a political statement against the Labour government of the day, a defiance that Sir Frederick Ponsonby at Buckingham Palace was determined to promote:

> "The whole project is very tiresome, but with a Labour Government in power it is essential that all landowners in Scotland should pull together, and that the Government should not have any excuse for pushing through a drastic scheme and riding rough shod over all sporting rights." [56]

The latter part of this letter confused the Duke of Richmond and Gordon as to whether the landowners should "all agree to the scheme lest 'worst befall us' ", or "all unite in opposing it". [57] They elected to fight on. The wider National Park ideal was kept alive over the 1930s at a time of severe financial crisis for the country. The Addison Committee evidence laid the foundations for years of debate between supporters and critics of the scheme, but produced no firm action. By the later 1930s, tourism (including countryside recreation) was beginning to be seen to have a role in the planned future industrial and economic development of Scotland as a whole, and its remoter regions in particular. [58] In the search for economic improvement in the Highlands though, one government committee in 1938 felt that any NP designation "would tend to concentrate tourist traffic on one district", when the tourist trade needed to be spread as widely as possible. [59] The debate raged on into the 1940s.

A Decade of Reports and Committees 1940–1950

In the early 1940s, the NP ideal across the UK was seen as an important component of the national landuse plan for post-war reconstruction; "a search for a clear picture of a better world which lies ahead and which, if plans are drawn up and the essential preparations made in advance, can be achieved after this struggle is over", urged Lord Justice Scott's Committee in August 1942, adding that "the establishment of National Parks in Britain is long overdue". [60] There was talk of the establishment of a central Land Commission, and the merits of public acquisition by purchase of land for all types of development. [61] In England and Wales, the extensive Dower report of May 1945 defined what a NP would be, and set about the task of selecting suitable areas and discussing how the project should be financed. Dower believed, although his remit did not extend to Scotland, that for every three NPs established in England and Wales, one should be designated in Scotland, suggesting the Highlands as holding the best options. [62] A later report on NPs in England and Wales, prepared by the Arthur Hobhouse Committee in July 1947, provided Parliament with a short historical outline of the NP movement in Scotland, and decided to include the eight areas recommended in the 1945 *Report of the Scottish National Parks*

Survey Committee (Cmd. 6631) on an enclosed map, "to complete the picture of National Park proposals for the whole of Great Britain".[63] On the initiative of the APRS a Scottish Council for National Parks (SCNP) was formed in 1943; just a year earlier, in a report to Tom Johnston (Secretary of State for Scotland) by the Committee on Hydro-electric Development in Scotland, it was stated that the designation of a NP on aesthetic grounds alone would sterilise the area chosen and create unemployment and piecemeal economic prosperity, should Hydro-electric schemes be excluded.[64] The matter was to be carried forward by a Scottish National Parks Survey Committee (SNPSC) set up in 1944 under the chairmanship of the hapless J. Douglas Ramsay, "to advise upon the selection of four or five areas in Scotland which might be suitable for National Parks", and to conduct site visits and surveys.

At the first meeting of the SNPSC on 10 February 1944, the committee sought to identify various criteria by which each area should be assessed. Of foremost importance were 'Aesthetic criteria' and 'Recreational Facilities'. Lower down the list came 'Local Attitudes', 'Access', 'Educational/Cultural/ Social Interests', 'Accommodation', 'Weather' and 'Rural Reconstruction'. No mention was now made of wildlife. A tentative selection of suitable areas was made (which included the Cairngorms), and thanks were given to the APRS for help in compiling this list. The SCNP were also thanked for their list of proposed sites from November 1943, which featured the Cairngorms.[65] By March 1944 a final list of sites for survey had been completed, with some areas such as the Cuillins, Arran, Rhum and Glen Clova/Glen Esk being dropped for failing in a variety of criteria reasons.[66] At a SNPSC meeting in July 1944, it was decided that the Cairngorms area should be visited and surveyed by F. Fraser Darling and Arthur Geddes (Survey Officer).[67]

As part of their investigations Fraser Darling and Geddes made an appointment to see J.P. Grant of Rothiemurchus on 18 July 1944, although Grant records this meeting as having taken place a day earlier. They did not arrange to meet with any other Cairngorm landowners it appears; indeed, Grant asked for copies of minutes of the meeting to be given to him (as 'informal spokesman') for confidential distribution amongst his fellow proprietors. Some hand-written notes by Grant reveal that the SNPSC dealings with him can actually be traced back to February 1944. A prodigious and precise recorder of all conversations and meetings that he had on the NP issue in the 1930s and 1940s, the laird of Rothiemurchus noted that he was approached by J. Douglas Ramsay in Edinburgh and learned that the Cairngorms region was on Ramsay's list but was not a first choice, due to the region's distance from centres of population. However, Ramsay warned Grant that visitor numbers would continue to grow, so it "would be wise to consider selling while the going is good". At a chance meeting of the laird, Douglas Ramsay and Arthur Geddes in the Highland Club in Inverness during April 1944, this advice to sell was again urged upon Grant who, "indicated clearly that I was not in favour of taking their advice". At the July meeting in Rothiemurchus, Grant gave his reasons for opposing the scheme, which had not changed over the fourteen years since the Addison Committee investigations. His most pressing concern was the destruction of sporting rights and the increased fire risk, along with the deterioration of letting values of all farms in the district that would come with a NP designation.[68] Geddes took official notes at this meeting, and recorded that Grant did not understand that sporting values were falling across Scotland even in areas where there was little recreational activity, or that a "future park authority" would ensure that a NP designation would not interfere with the prosperity of local agriculture and forestry. Fraser Darling and Grant met a second time at Rothiemurchus on 26 July when little of worth was achieved, although Darling did tell the laird that he might have to provide a camping ground in the forest, although it was hoped that visitors to a Cairngorms NP would prefer the high tops.[69] The SNPSC met a day after this meeting to consider the 'Report on the Cairngorm Area', and decided without much debate to recommend an area of 180 square miles as a suggested National Park[70], emphasising the varied recreational opportunities in the mountains, their educational interest, the good weather and ample hotel and hostel accommodation available nearby; it is also an area "of outstanding beauty", concluded their final report of 1945.[71]

The SNPSC findings opened the way for the creation of a Scottish National Parks Committee (SNPC) in January 1946, that would focus on continued investigations into the named sites, and questions of finance and administration. It held its first meeting in Edinburgh on 21 February 1946, with J. Douglas Ramsay as its Chairman, to be guided by the following working definition of what a National Park should be:

> "an extensive tract of country of outstanding natural beauty, preferably also of scientific, cultural or historic interest, owned or controlled by the Nation, accessible to all as a matter of right under suitable regulations, and administered by or on behalf of the Nation to the end that its distinctive values may be preserved unimpaired for the enjoyment and recreation of this and future generations."[72]

At that inaugural meeting, Douglas Ramsay urged his fellow committee members to now assume, "that there are to be National Parks in Scotland", and that a central authority would be set up to establish them. They were not to be put off by landowner opposition for "there will be a solution of the problem of compensation and betterment". For a man who declared himself in 1930 to be secretly against NPs, there was a good deal of campaigning zeal in this opening speech. As NPs in the UK would be a new experiment, the work of the SNPC would be, "as something of a laboratory experiment – the construction of a 'pilot plant' on which to test opinion before embarking on the full programme of National Parks". It was at this meeting that Douglas Ramsay arranged for the creation of a Sub-Committee to be called the Scottish Wild Life Conservation Committee (SWLCC) to consider the issue of nature conservation both inside and outside of the proposed NP sites [see Chapter 9].[73]

During the course of its investigations, the SNPC chose not to visit the Cairngorms area and focused instead on three particular sites: the Loch Lomond/Trossachs area (which Douglas Ramsay had identified as the priority site in February 1946), the Ben Nevis/Glen Coe/Blackmount area and Glen Affric. The Cairngorms featured little in the discussion process, principally because the committee members now knew of the FC proposal to create a National Forest Park at Glenmore which, for some, would suffice as the recreational park in that district. As regards the projected cost of land acquisition at the sites, the Cairngorms came out the cheapest at £200,000, a full £100,000 less than the Loch Lomond or Loch Torridon sites. An internal SNPC note gave further details on the cost of the 199,808 acres recommended by the SNPSC in the Cairngorms. The estimated value was initially set at £249,760 including all buildings, timber and sporting rights, based on a value of 25s. per acre. However, independent advice from a valuer had considered the hill land in the Cairngorms only to be worth in the range of 12–13s. per acre.[74] In their final report of 1947, the SNPC recommended the establishment of a distinct National Parks Commission for Scotland under the control of the Scottish Secretary, with local group committees representing each NP area. In what was already a decade of surveys, committees and reports, the SNPC urged the need for more detailed surveys and investigations on each proposed site, and a further period for consultation with government and local authorities. No action should be taken yet; the discussion period was destined to continue. The committee concluded that it was desirable that five NPs (including the Cairngorms) should be designated within ten years of any NP legislation.[75] This was the only sense of urgency that they displayed.

The next step was taken by Arthur Woodburn (Secretary of State for Scotland) who called a meeting of all interested organisations on 9 July 1948 at St. Andrews House, Edinburgh, after pressure from the Scottish Council for National Parks. At this meeting it was decided to form another group, the Scottish National Parks Working Party (SNPWP) who would further "examine in detail what positive schemes for development were practicable".[76] The lukewarm response of the local authorities to a NP scheme was well expressed at this meeting by Sir D.W. Cameron of Lochiel (Inverness County Council) who felt that their provision was not an urgent matter, especially in light of the Forestry Commission action at Glenmore National Forest Park; what the Highlands needed more "were water supplies and housing". Arthur Woodburn also spoke, "in general agreement", that the five priority areas should become NPs, but that there should be no subsequent attempt "to 'Butlinize' the Park areas", nor should they become merely "a wilderness or a Whipsnade". He urged that their development "should be in harmony with Highland needs and traditions and should not involve the loss of good agricultural land".[77] He was, in a fashion, predicting the future ambiguities inherent within the development of National Parks south of the border. The FC took a more active role on this SNPWP committee than they had over the past, spurred on by the success of their National Forest Park scheme in Scotland which they were keen to differentiate from a National Park ideal. They appointed L.A. Newton as their representative, and he was immediately called before Henry Beresford-Peirse (Director of the FC in Scotland) so he would understand the party line.[78] Both Newton and F.C. Handford were told bluntly by Peirse that they as FC staff, "need not be in any way enthusiastic about setting up National Parks". Newton was to sit on the SNPWP and "make certain that the maximum forestry development is allowed for within the Park areas", and that the FC would be left alone to carry out their agreed forestry operations without meddling interference.[79] The mindset of the FC had not changed from January 1944 when they had discussed the Dower report in London; J.M. Bannerman thought that report to be inconsistent, "the effect of the recommendations would be to sterilise large sections of the countryside". The Chairman spoke of how NPs would make it impossible for the FC to conduct their timber operations, and (speaking for the populace) concluded that John Dower had, "entirely missed the point that there was much more of interest in walking through a wood than over a bare hillside".[80]

From 1948 to 1952, the membership of the SNPWP included a diverse range of opinions derived from government agencies, voluntary heritage and recreation bodies, local authorities and tourism agencies.[81] The Chairman was G.H. Kimpton (Department of Health for Scotland). After a first preliminary meeting in Edinburgh in July 1948, the SNPWP held its first official meeting on 23 September, against the backdrop of Article 5 of the Town and Country Planning (Scotland) Order of 1948, which had designated the five Douglas Ramsay priority areas (Loch Lomond/the Trossachs, Glen Affric area, Ben Nevis and Glen Coe, the Cairngorms, Loch Torridon area) as National Park Direction Areas. The post-war Labour government believed this could satisfy demands for a NP north of the border, and not openly anger landed interest. Now the Secretary of State for Scotland was to be notified of all planning applications within the five areas. Having discussed and seen reports on three of the areas from September 1949 to December 1950, the SNPWP at their seventh meeting on 8 December 1950, "agreed that the Cairngorms area should be considered next".[82] Mrs B.L.C. Moira was appointed Cairngorms Survey Officer, with D.M. McPhail providing secretarial support; both were from the Department of Health for Scotland, a body that seemed both to dominate the functioning of the SNPWP and define its pro-recreation and tourism outlook. In the spring of 1949, the Department of Health had canvassed opinion from the recreation and youth organisations in Scotland on the NP issue. Alex Gray of the Scottish Committee for Camping Legislation wrote to McPhail with two resolutions; that camping be widely permitted over all the NP areas, and that "the interests of the people be not placed secondary to those of the wildlife of the country". This letter mysteriously fell into the hands of the FC in Scotland, and H.G. Beresford-Peirse scribbled angry pencil notes across it, furious that free open access could bring sanitation problems, pollution of water supplies and an increased fire risk to FC plantations.[83] H.A. Rendel Govan, a Planning Consultant with Ross and Cromarty County Council wrote to McPhail in April 1949, expressing the view widely held by Scottish local authorities that National Parks in the Highlands (if created) should be born of a wise determination to seek the economic rehabilitation of the areas concerned, and should "not be developed solely for the benefit of the Townsman ... the benefit of holiday-makers". This was a thoughtful letter, stressing that, in the wider picture, "the whole of our small but beautiful countryside is rightly to be regarded as our single National Park". The particularism of the NP scheme would not solve the varied social and economic problems of the Highlands; that would in part be achieved "through the repopulation and better cultivation of the land", suggested Govan. The countryside had to be seen as a whole, "where beauty and usefulness are interwoven together".[84] There was an important message here, in the middle of a century that in retrospect can be seen as having given us a British countryside peppered with site designations. In the 1940s, even F. Fraser Darling, who became one of the most respected environmental thinkers in Scotland, called for the creation of NPs for their social value and "to serve as museum pieces in a countryside ... as national lungs". He listed the Cairngorms, the English Lake District and Snowdonia as his first choices in 1943, in the only published account of his declared support for the NP ideal.[85] In 1945, the highly influential nature conservationist and botanist A.G. Tansley sought support for something akin to NPs to be designated in southern and eastern England, feeling that the uplands of Scotland and northern England had hijacked the debate. He urged the creation of a new site designation to be called 'Scheduled Areas', to protect regions of southern Britain outside of the current NP scheme that possessed a high scenic, scientific and amenity value. Part of his plea for safeguarding "habitats of great ecological value", holds the origins of the modern SSSI designation.[86]

The National Park Ideal Slips Away 1950–1980

From around 1951, and the election of a Conservative government, "the heart went out of the National Park movement in Scotland".[87] There was still some unfinished business from the late 1940s, namely the SNPWP reports on the Cairngorms area and the Loch Torridon/Loch Maree/Little Loch Broom area, which would run on until February 1952. Scotland had not been included in the National Parks legislation for England and Wales in 1949 and, in that sense, an opportunity had been lost. There is a sense that a separate Bill was considered for Scotland; in July 1947, J.D. Fairgrieve (civil servant in the Scottish Home Department) confided to a internal memo sheet that any National Park legislation would not cover the whole UK, and that government were proposing "a separate Bill for Scotland in 1949–1950 or later".[88] In fact, the case for a NP in the Cairngorms had been strongest in the early 1930s, when land prices were lower, but when the opposition of local landowners was also at its strongest. Indeed, the Cairngorm landowners were never again quite able to organise themselves as well as they had in 1930 to oppose the NP scheme. Although the Cairngorms area had always been seen as a suitable site for a recreational park, from 1955 onwards the focus of all discussion was on how tourism could be promoted in the area, to serve the needs of the local population and boost the economic profile of the region. Both the amenity and recreational organisations, and government, concentrated their efforts on tourism in the later 1950s – almost exclusively in the early years of the 1960s. The Cairngorm landowners, now that the threat of a NP seemed to have passed, also had a key role to play in this [see Chapter 6].

Tourism and regional economic development in the Cairngorms were to the fore as early as June 1951 in the final report to the SNPWP by B.L.C. Moira; an earlier draft report of May 1951 was considered at the SNPWP meeting in Edinburgh on 16 May 1951.[89] The report included extensive statistical analysis of the use of SYHA facilities in the area, the number (and trading seasons) of local hotels and B & B accommodation, and comments put forward by numerous youth and recreation bodies interested in a proposed Cairngorms NP. The Board of Trade stated they could see no scope "for over-ambitious developments aimed at making a 'Scottish Switzerland' of the Cairngorms", adding that the expected appeal of a NP would be with students and climbing clubs, although some high-class hotels should be provided for some wealthier sportsmen. The content of this report was, however, strongly developmental: bridges, bothies, lodges, shelter huts for skiers, ski-tows, long-distance footpaths and the Glen Feshie road scheme were all demanded in the evidence of the various outdoor bodies to the SNPWP. There was no talk here of a Cairngorms National Park being a wilderness area, nor were any nature conservation issues discussed; in their evidence the Scottish Committee of the Nature Conservancy appeared undecided as to whether the NP area would need a warden, while the FC evidence was solely concerned with the number of milking cows at Glenmore NFP being insufficient to meet demand.[90] In their consideration of the Moira report (as action which might be taken in the Cairngorms area), the SNPWP committee listed over twenty proposals, with roads, footpaths and bridges as the top priorities, followed by signposts and, remarkably, the provision of buoys on Loch Morlich. In line with American National Parks, they suggested park entrance kiosks with Information Officers throughout the area, backed up by major visitor centres in Braemar and Aviemore; a youth voluntary service should be established; public telephones should be placed on every road in the area. The penultimate proposal dealt with the protection of wildlife, suggesting that just "some of the Old Caledonian forest in the area should be preserved", perhaps under Tree Preservation Orders from Aberdeen and Inverness County Councils.[91]

The pro-development aspects of the Douglas Ramsay proposals, and especially the way they were voraciously taken forward in evidence given to the SNPWP, worried some observers. In April 1950, J.K.W. Dunn attacked his own climbing club, the Scottish Mountaineering Club (SMC) for their casual dismissal of NPs as "a planner's pipe-dream". The inactivity of the SMC on this issue was "ludicrously myopic" declared Dunn, who identified the North of Scotland Hydro-Electricity Board and the FC as the agents of destructive change in the Highlands; only a NP authority in Scotland could halt their pillaging of the landscape, he declared. Unless the SMC gave up its neutral stance soon and supported the NP ideal, then the Highlands would be given over, "not to sheep and deer, which have nearly depopulated them, but to the new monopolies of hydro-electricity and the marching conifers".[92] A rebuttal came immediately from SMC member John Osborne, outraged that Dunn had envisaged a National Park Commission acting as "a Scottish Parliament ... perhaps even a dictatorship is implied". Osborne added that the SMC had little or no interest in NPs, whatever individual club members might feel, and that the primary focus of comment on the issue should be only to safeguard the interests of their sport. A National Park designation anywhere in the Highlands, he argued, could bring a plethora of rules and regulations designed to restrict and impede climbers and hill-walkers. A note attached to this article explained that neither the editor of the *SMC Journal* nor the club would be held to ransom by these viewpoints; the club committee alone decided policy.[93]

Good evidence that the NP ideal was slipping away in the mid-1950s can be seen in the March 1957 decision taken by the Scottish Council for National Parks (founded in 1943) publicly to restate their objectives, both in the press and to other interested organisations:

"to establish and press for the establishment of National Parks in Scotland and to do anything else which may contribute towards that end." [94]

The momentum and desire for a Cairngorms NP had slowed sometime in the first half of the 1950s, probably between 1952 and 1955. Indeed, in a letter to the FC in April 1956, the SCNP stated that they would now focus all their energy on the proposed Loch Lomond/the Trossachs NP, and invited all County Councils, landowners and other bodies to co-operate with them. The SCNP hoped that the Forestry Commission could be in favour of the establishment of a National Park.[95] It became more obvious over the period 1955-1965 that the Cairngorms area was going to be developed into a recreational year-round playground by government, philanthropic industrial magnates and voluntary bodies. In 1950, the Scottish Landowners' Federation had re-organised themselves to represent better the views of their members, and it was thus unlikely that the Cairngorm landowners would ever have to fight alone as they did in 1930, now that a national organisation would speak on their behalf. In the mid-1960s, the SLF circulated a statement, 'Notes on National Parks', to all members, just in case a Cairngorms NP ideal was born out of the development craze in the area. It was strikingly similar to the evidence given to the Addison Committee over 34 years ago by the laird of Rothiemurchus and his fellow proprietors. The main threats from a Cairngorms NP were fire risk, a loss of sporting values, damage to estate property, and the need to regulate access which was not an acute problem at present, but would become so under any plans to open up the area as a NP. The notes concluded that the existing National Forest Park scheme could be profitably expanded to meet any demand for National Parks, and that instead of seeking to muscle in on private estates, the government should "show the way on property which they already own".[96] In October 1964, the Advisory Panel on the Highlands and Islands under Lord Cameron, reported that although agriculture and forestry remained the key support to the Highland economy, recreation was rapidly assuming a position of great importance, especially in the eastern Highlands where the Cairngorms area was an obvious choice for the planned, comprehensive study and development of tourism and recreation. Lord Cameron's committee saw no need for NPs in the Highlands, as the NFP scheme was so commendable and successful. He felt that the FC "would be justified in making charges for access and for car parks" at NFPs.[97]

The Cairngorms area was used as a case study in the November 1965 London conference, 'The Countryside in 1970'. Study Group No. 9 on Countryside Planning and Development in Scotland, describing the area as "hitherto lonely and superbly beautiful", felt that some check was needed on the rapid development of the mountains as a national winter sports resort, but did not feel that a NP designation was called for, reserving that solely for the Loch Lomond/the Trossachs site. It was at this conference that the call for establishing a 'Countryside Commission' in Scotland was publicly declared; with the Countryside (Scotland) Act of 1967, the Countryside Commission for Scotland (CCS) became a reality in April 1968, satisfying the NTS (especially Lord Wemyss and J. Stormonth-Darling) who had been calling for such a body from the mid-1960s. Group No. 9 also concluded that the concept of NPs was a very limiting one that, by its definition, ignored many other areas of countryside, and tended to imply overuse and thus a perceived deterioration in the landscape and traditional agriculture, sporting rights and forestry in the designated area. The wider UK vision for the 1970s was to be that National Parks should be recognised "as just one element in the recreational needs of the nation". A SCNP member called for the future establishment of any body that would balance recreational demands and countryside needs, "and engender an atmosphere of positive action" in the Scottish NP debate.[98] This suggested a current period of lethargy. There was a belief at the start of the 1970s that the 'Countryside in 1970' conferences and the creation of CCS, could see a resolution of the NP question in Scotland, especially as regards the mechanisms by which they would be managed and financed. In reality, the Scottish aspects of these conferences had been just a sideshow in what was predominantly an English exercise.

In 1974, CCS published *A Park System for Scotland*, after two years of consultation with voluntary bodies and landuse agencies (NCC, FC, HIDB, NTS, SLF, Crofters Commission, Scottish Sports Council, STB). This should now be seen as an attempt to re-activate many of the issues of the 1930s and 1940s, although the term 'National Park' was felt to be too controversial and so was abandoned in favour of new terminology. The Cairngorms were nominated to receive 'Special Park' status, along with some other Douglas Ramsay priority sites; this was conceptually similar to NPs in England and Wales, and was directed towards the development and control of recreational facilities within the areas in an attempt to satisfy the needs of urban visitors.[99] Again this proved to be a missed opportunity, despite the 1974 report being a forward thinking countryside paper; NPs of some sort could have been created if CCS had not decided to hold out for planning powers in their proposals. The local authorities, spurred on by COSLA, were determined not to relinquish any of their planning powers to a parks authority. The report was sidelined and, "once again the national park ideal in Scotland had been submerged".[100] There had been such a determination from within CCS to avoid use of the loaded term 'National Park', that the ultimate proposals had been too feeble on the issue and had successfully been challenged by the campaigning force of local authorities, whose interest in NPs had waxed and waned over the preceding decades.

The largely ineffective National Park Direction Areas were abolished in 1980, being replaced by National Scenic Areas (NSA), the largest of which actually was the Cairngorms NSA. The Scottish Secretary now had the ability to support CCS if they opposed a development in the NSA that had been given planning permission by the local authority.[101] It is worth recalling here that James Bryce had called for landscape protection akin to NSA designations over eighty years before, in his lecture to the Cairngorm Club in Aberdeen [see Chapter 3]. In 1990, in *The Mountain Areas of Scotland*, CCS recommended that the Cairngorms, because of their high heritage value and an ongoing attrition of their landscape qualities, should be designated as a National Park, with an administrative system based on an independent planning board. Legislation was needed, "to make an early start on the establishment of National Parks in Scotland".[102] Such spirited urgency had been displayed repeatedly by report writers from 1930 onwards, but the talking was destined to continue. This came to nothing, and CCS was submerged into SNH the following year. The new body took a lead from Scottish Office ministers not to press for National Parks.

Scotland was left out of the NP legislation in the 1949 Act, but was included in the nature conservation legislation. From April 1951 to April 1957, ten National Parks were designated in England and Wales, and then the movement appeared content with its achievements. No subsequent Act giving Scotland NPs was forthcoming, although it is a possibility that it was intended to have a separate Act for Scotland; but legislative time was not found for such a complex question before the Labour government fell. Under the subsequent Conservative ministries from 1951 into the early 1960s, landed interest would once again have a relevant voice in opposing NP legislation for Scotland.

There is still little public understanding of why there are no NPs in areas like the Cairngorms, or for that matter, in Scotland. The role of regional landowners in thwarting a NP designation in the Cairngorms has now been explained in greater detail by using the Grant of Rothiemurchus correspondence. They played a key role in the NP debate in Scotland, and this study has documented how bitter and deep was their opposition. The Hydro-electricity debate had no impact on the Cairngorm glens; but it was a central issue to the NP debate, most markedly in the west of Scotland and Glen Affric. In the 1940s and after, Secretaries of State for Scotland (such as Tom Johnston) were never willing to contemplate NP designations that they felt would obstruct the development of certain glens by the new Hydro Board. From the mid-1930s and the establishment of the NFP scheme, the FC played out their chosen role as a blocking organisation. The obvious popular success of National Forest Parks guaranteed that organised opposition to a Cairngorms National Park, as well as the FC themselves, would cite Glenmore as an example of satisfactory recreational provision in place, negating any need to resort to NP designation.

Problems of access were not felt to be particularly acute in the Cairngorms in the 1940s and 1950s, and had certainly relaxed from the decades of battle between the SRoWS and landowners in the 1880s and 1890s. Those arrayed in favour of a NP in the Cairngorms were, in reality, a small lobbying force, composed of far too many organisations with too few members in the 1930s and 1940s. The public spirit of recreational provision which fuelled the NP debate was modified by the late 1950s to embrace mass tourism development in the Cairngorms. The NP ideal was lost within a new doctrine that linked tourism with regional economic regeneration. In reality, there is no easy answer as to why there is no NP in the Cairngorms, nor why the NP idea seemed to slip away in the early 1950s out of public debate. In a letter held in the NC archives (and put before its Scottish Committee) H.R. Smith of the Scottish Office reported that by late 1952 Inverness County Council had been officially informed "that there was no prospect of a National Park in the near future" in the Cairngorms, and that they should now focus their attention on discussing the merits of a Cairngorms nature reserve instead.[103]

Notes to Chapter 8

1   John Sheail, *Nature in Trust – the History of Nature Conservation in Britain* (Blackie and Son, London, 1976); John Sheail, *Rural Conservation in Inter-War Britain* (Clarendon Press, Oxford, 1981); John Sheail, 'The Concept of National Parks in Great Britain 1900–1950', *Transactions of the Institute of British Geographers*, No. 66, November 1975, pp. 41–56; John Sheail, 'Nature Reserves, National Parks, and Post-war Reconstruction in Britain', *Environmental Conservation*, Vol. 11, No. 2, Spring 1984, pp. 29-34; H.C. Darby, 'British National Parks', *Advancement of Science*, Vol. 20, No. 83, November 1963, pp. 307–318; Gordon E. Cherry, *Environmental Planning 1939–1960, Volume II: National Parks and Recreation in the Countryside* (HMSO, London, 1975); Ann MacEwen and Malcolm MacEwen, *National Parks: Conservation or Cosmetics* (Allen and Unwin, London, 1982); Ann MacEwen and Malcolm MacEwen, *Greenprints for the Countryside?: The Story of Britain's National Parks* (Allen and Unwin, London, 1987).

2   See the archives of the Scottish Home and Health Department held in the Scottish Record Office, Edinburgh at HH. See especially SRO: HH41-303; HH41-304; HH41-305; HH41-306 which all contain information on the National Parks and Access to the Countryside Bills and Act of 1949.

3   Peter L. Payne, *The Hydro* (Aberdeen University Press, Aberdeen, 1989); Scottish Office, *Report of the Committee on Hydro-electric Development in Scotland*, Cmd. 6406 (HMSO, Edinburgh, 1942), p. 26.

4   William Wordsworth, *A Guide Through the District of The Lakes, In The North of England, With a Description of The Scenery, for the Use of Tourists and Residents* (Hudson and Nicholson, Kendal, fifth edition 1835), p. 88.

5   Charles Stewart, 'A National Park for Scotland', *Nineteenth Century and After*, Vol. LV, No. 327, May 1904, pp. 822–826.

6   Sheail 1975, 'The Concept of National Parks in Great Britain 1900–1950', *op. cit.*, pp. 41–42.

7   Ernest A. Baker, *The Highlands with Rope and Rucksack* (H.F. and G. Witherby, London, 1923), pp. 11–54, 'Introductory'.

8   Ernest A. Baker, 'The Cairngorms as a National Park', *The Scots Magazine*, New Series, Vol. 10, No. 1, October 1928, pp. 1–6.

9   John Scot, 'Letters of a Self-Thinking Scotsman to his Father', No. IV, Legacy and Litter, *The Scots Magazine*, New Series, Vol. 10, No. 1, October 1928, pp. 38–40.

10 Alan Graeme, 'Hills of Home – The Spiritual Claim for a National Park', *The Scots Magazine*, New Series, Vol. 10, No. 2, November 1928, pp. 89-96.

11 J.W. Gregory, 'The Claim for a National Park', *The Scots Magazine* , New Series, Vol. 10, No. 3, December 1928, pp. 173–177.

12 Alex Inkson McConnochie, 'The National Nature of the Cairngorms', *The Scots Magazine*, New Series, Vol. 10, No. 3, December 1928, pp. 178–183, with map of 'The Cairngorm Area'.

13 Ruaraidh Erskine of Marr, 'The Claim for a National Park', *The Scots Magazine*, New Series, Vol. 10, No. 6, March 1929, pp. 416–420.

14 J. Ramsay MacDonald (in an interview), 'Why I Support the Cairngorm National Park Scheme', *The Scots Magazine* , New Series, Vol. 10, No. 4, January 1929, pp. 251–252; J.I. Macpherson (in an interview), 'The Scheme Appeals to Me', *The Scots Magazine*, New Series, Vol. 10, No. 4, January 1929, pp. 252–253.

15 See APRS, *Annual Report of the APRS, 1929*, pp. 6–8.

16 Anon., 'The Cairngorms as a National Park', *Cairngorm Club Journal*, Vol. 12, No. 69, January 1930, pp. 163–164. The Alexander and Roberts report was prepared by a Sub-Committee of the Links and Parks Committee of Aberdeen Town Council, that must have been appointed late in 1929. Henry Alexander presented this report to the Addison Committee on 23 May 1930, on behalf of Aberdeen Town Council. A copy can also be found in NRA(S) 102:399 in the papers of the lairds of Rothiemurchus.

17 *Report of the National Park Committee*, Cmd. 3851 (HMSO, London, April 1931), p. 97.

18 John Malcolm Bulloch, *Sporting Visitors to Badenoch*, Highland Handbook V (Robert Carruthers and Sons, Inverness, 1931), p. 27.

19 James Baikie, *Things Seen in the Scottish Highlands* (Seeley, Service and Co., London, 1932), pp. 53–54.

20 Ernest A. Baker, *On Foot in the Highlands* (Alexander Maclehose and Co., London, 1933), p. 106–131. Additional phrase in brackets not in original.

21 See SRO: GD 335-40, Letter from A.W. Russell, Scottish Rights of Way Society, Edinburgh to Sir Ian Colquhoun of Luss, dated 6 May 1929.

22 SRO: GD 335-40, Circular letter from Sir Ian Colquhoun of Luss, Chairman of Executive Committee, Association for the Preservation of Rural Scotland, Edinburgh, dated 21 May 1929.

23 SRO: GD 335-40, Letter from Arthur Russell, Scottish Rights of Way Society, Edinburgh, to Lawrence Chubb, General Secretary, National Playing Fields Association, dated 23 May 1929.

24 SRO: GD 335-40, Letter from L.W. Chubb to A.W. Russell, Scottish Rights of Way Society, dated 27 May 1929. Chubb's logic on the National Trust (NT) holding property in Scotland was based on the fact that the University of Edinburgh sat on the Council of the NT, which suggested that the remit of the NT should extend to Scotland.

25 SRO: GD 335-40, Letter from A.W. Russell, Scottish Rights of Way Society, Edinburgh, to L.W. Chubb dated 5 June 1929.

26 SRO: GD 335-40, Letter from L.W. Chubb, National Playing Fields Association, Belgrave Road, London to A.W. Russell, dated 6 June 1929.

27 SRO: GD 335-40, Minutes and Submission of the Meeting of the Directors of the Scottish Rights of Way Society, Edinburgh, dated September 1929.

28 See NRA(S) 102:399, Scottish Forest Reserve Committee – Memorandum, signed by J. Douglas Ramsay, Chairman, dated 10 January 1930; see also *Report of the National Park Committee*, Cmd. 3851, *op. cit.*, pp. 86–87.

29 SRO: GD 335-40, Letter from Rev. A.E. Robertson, Scottish Rights of Way Society Representative on Scottish Forest Reserve Committee, Cluny Gardens, Edinburgh, to A.W. Russell, Scottish Rights of Way Society, dated 10 September 1929; SRO: GD 335-40, Letter from Kenneth Ferguson, Organising Secretary, Association for the Preservation of Rural Scotland, Edinburgh, to Secretary of Scottish Rights of Way Society, Edinburgh, dated 5 October 1929 and reply dated 15 October 1929.

30 SRO: GD 335-40, Memorandum of Evidence Prepared by the Council of the Royal Scottish Geographical Society, Edinburgh, dated January 1930.

31 *Report of the National Park Committee*, Cmd. 3851, *op. cit.*, pp. 126–128, Appendix VI, 'Proposals for Utilising Glenmore Forest', Forestry Commission, dated 10 July 1930.

32 NRA(S) 102:399, Letter from John Stirling Maxwell, member of the Addison Committee to Lt. Col. J.P. Grant of Rothiemurchus, Rothiemurchus Estate, dated 30 January 1930.

33 NRA(S) 102:399, Letter from Angus Cameron, Commissioner representing His Grace the Duke of Richmond and Gordon, Richmond and Gordon Estate Office, Fochabers, Moray-shire, to Lt. Col. J.P. Grant of Rothiemurchus, Rothiemurchus Estate, dated 4 February 1930.

34 NRA(S) 102:399, Letter from A. Mitchell, Lady Seafield's Trustees, Strathspey Estate Office, Grantown-on-Spey, to Lt. Col. J.P. Grant of Rothiemurchus, dated 25 June 1930. These letters reached the Addison Committee in June and July 1930.

35 NRA(S) 102:399, Letter from Stuart W. Clark, Banbury, Oxfordshire, to Lt. Col. J.P. Grant of Rothiemurchus, Rothiemurchus Estate, dated 8 February 1930.

36 NRA(S) 102:399, Letter from Stuart Clark, Banbury, Oxfordshire, to Grant of Rothiemurchus, dated 13 February 1930.

37 NRA(S) 102:399, Letter from Lt. Col. J. Grant Smith, Lady Seafield's Trustees, Strathspey Estate Office, Grantown-on-Spey to Lt. Col. J.P. Grant of Rothiemurchus, Rothiemurchus Estate, dated 17 March 1930.

38 NRA(S) 102:399, 'Minute of the Meeting of Proprietors and their Representatives interested in the Proposal to form the Cairngorms into a National Park', held in the Strathspey Estate Office, Grantown-on-Spey on Saturday 15 March 1930 at 11.30 a.m. The Sub-Committee formed was Lt. Col. J.P. Grant of Rothiemurchus, Charles Mackenzie (Factor at Ballindalloch) and Lt. Col. J. Grant Smith (Lady Seafield's Trustees) who was to act as Secretary.

39 NRA(S) 102:399, Private Letter to all Proprietors, from J.P. Grant of Rothiemurchus, Rothiemurchus Estate, Aviemore, no date, probably February 1930.

40 NRA(S) 102:399, Letter from John Murray, Aberdeen to J.P. Grant of Rothiemurchus, Rothiemurchus Estate, dated 17 February 1930.

41 NRA(S) 102:399, Letter from Angus Cameron, Commissioner of Duke of Richmond and Gordon Estate, Estate Office, Fochabers to Lt. Col. J.P. Grant of Rothiemurchus, Rothiemurchus Estate, dated 25 February 1930.

42 NRA(S) 102:399, Letter from Duke of Richmond and Gordon, Goodwood, Chichester to Lt. Col. J.P. Grant of Rothiemurchus, Rothiemurchus Estate, dated 21 February 1930.

43 NRA(S) 102:399, Letter from Sir Frederick Ponsonby, Privy Purse Office, Buckingham Palace, London, to the Duke of Richmond and Gordon, dated 24 February 1930.

44 NRA(S) 102:399, Letter from Duke of Richmond and Gordon, Goodwood, Chichester, to Lt. Col. J.P. Grant of Rothiemurchus, dated 26 February 1930.

45 NRA(S) 102:399, Letter from Duke of Richmond and Gordon, Goodwood, Chichester, to Lt. Col. J.P. Grant of Rothiemurchus, dated 2 March 1930.

46 NRA(S) 102:399, (Private and Confidential) Letter from Sir J. Douglas Ramsay, 69 Great King Street, Edinburgh, to Lt. Col. J.P. Grant of Rothiemurchus, Rothiemurchus Estate, dated 28 February 1930.

47 NRA(S) 102:399, (Private) Letter from Sir J. Douglas Ramsay, Edinburgh, to Lt. Col. J.P. Grant of Rothiemurchus, dated 27 February 1930. Douglas Ramsay thought he knew who was behind the whisper campaign: "This storm in a teacup has arisen between the Keeper of the Privy Purse and the Solicitor to the Mar Estates. Trust Mar to misunderstand and mismanage".

48 NRA(S) 102:399, (Private) Letter from Sir J. Douglas Ramsay, Edinburgh, to Lt. Col. J.P. Grant of Rothiemurchus, dated 3 March 1930. Douglas Ramsay continued to try to defend his honour: "but I want you to realise that I am not the villain His Grace would have you believe, but simply that some Genius in Buck[ingham] Ho[use] has given a garbled account of my words to someone else who has probably

only heard half, and repeated that half still further garbled. But you cannot accuse people in that position – so at present I am whipping boy!"

49 NRA(S) 102:399, Letter from J. Douglas Ramsay, Edinburgh, to Lt. Col. J.P. Grant of Rothiemurchus, Rothiemurchus Estate, dated 8 March 1930.

50 NRA(S) 102:399, Letter from The Mackintosh of Mackintosh to Lt. Col. Grant of Rothiemurchus, dated 20 February 1930.

51 NRA(S) 102:399, 'Minutes of Meeting of Committee of Cairngorm Owners' held at Grantown-on-Spey on 19 May 1930. The Addison Committee had fixed the meeting for Friday 23 May in the Aviemore Hotel at 4 p.m. The landowners agreed to meet there before at 2.30 p.m.

52 NRA(S) 102:399, Personal private notes made by Lt. Col. J.P. Grant of Rothiemurchus, no date, probably Spring 1930. The notes were made under various headings namely, 'reasons for calling meeting', 'joint interest', 'my views on public aspect', 'private aspect', 'conclusion'. See also NRA(S) 102:399, letter from Lt. Col. J. Grant Smith, Lady Seafield's Trustees, Strathspey Estate Office, Grantown-on-Spey, to Lt. Col. J.P. Grant of Rothiemurchus, dated 5 May 1930.

53 NRA(S) 102:399, Letter from Lt. Col. J. Grant Smith, Strathspey Estate Office, Grantown-on-Spey, to Lt. Col. J.P. Grant of Rothiemurchus, Rothiemurchus Estate, dated 2 June 1930.

54 NRA(S) 102:399, Letter from Lt. Col. J. Grant Smith, Strathspey Estate Office, Grantown-on-Spey, to Lt. Col. J.P. Grant of Rothiemurchus, dated 4 June 1930.

55 NRA(S) 102:399, Letter from Geoffrey G. Barnes, Secretary to the Addison Committee, Treasury Chambers, Whitehall, London, to Lt. Col. J.P. Grant of Rothiemurchus, Rothiemurchus Estate, dated 18 June 1930.

56 NRA(S) 102:399, Letter from Sir Frederick Ponsonby, Privy Purse Office, Buckingham Palace, London, to the Duke of Richmond and Gordon, Goodwood, Chichester, date 26 February 1930.

57 NRA(S) 102:399, Letter from Angus Cameron, Commissioner of Duke of Richmond and Gordon Estate, Estate Office, Fochabers, to Lt. Col. J.P. Grant of Rothiemurchus, Rothiemurchus Estate, dated 4 March 1930.

58 Scottish Economic Committee, *Scotland's Industrial Future: The Case for Planned Development* (McCorquodale and Co., Glasgow, 1939), pp. 11, 44–45, 122–124. This Committee was appointed by the Scottish Development Council in consultation with Sir Godfrey Collins (Secretary of State for Scotland) in April 1936. The Chairman was Sir Steven Bilsland.

59 Scottish Economic Committee, *The Highlands and Islands of Scotland: A Review of the Economic Conditions with Recommendations for Improvement* (Robert Maclehose, Glasgow, 1938), pp. 139–142.

60 *Report of the Committee on Land Utilisation in Rural Areas*, Cmd. 6378 (HMSO, London, 1942), pp. vi, 59.

61 *The Control of Land Use*, Cmd. 6537 (HMSO, London, 1944), pp. 7–9, 14.

62 *National Parks in England and Wales – Report by John Dower*, Cmd. 6628 (HMSO, London, 1945), p. 13.

63 *Report of the National Parks Committee (England and Wales)*, Cmd. 7121 (HMSO, London, 1947), pp. 7, 13.

64 *Report of the Committee on Hydro-electric Development in Scotland*, Cmd. 6406 (HMSO, Edinburgh, 1942), pp. 32–34.

65 See SRO: FC 9-2, 'Minutes of the first Meeting of the Scottish National Parks Survey Committee', Edinburgh, dated 10 February 1944. This was a small committee composed of Sir J. Douglas Ramsay (Chairman), F. Fraser Darling, D.G. Moir (Hon. Sec. of SYHA and Royal Scottish Geographical Society), Peter Thomsen (who died in September 1944), Arthur Geddes, A.B. Taylor and D.M. McPhail (Secretaries).

66 SRO: FC 9-2, 'Minutes of Meeting of the Scottish National Parks Survey Committee', dated 15 March 1944.

67 SRO: FC 9-2, 'Minutes of Meeting of the Scottish National Parks Survey Committee', dated 11 July 1944.

68 NRA(S) 102:398, Handwritten Private notes made by Lt. Col. J.P. Grant of Rothiemurchus, dated 1944.

69 NRA(S) 102:398, Typed page of Minutes, 'National Parks: Cairn Gorm Area, Note of interviews between Colonel J.P. Grant of Rothiemurchus, Dr. F.F. Darling and Dr. A. Geddes, on 18 July 1944, and between Colonel Grant and Dr. Darling on 26 July 1944'. Signed by Arthur Geddes and F. Fraser Darling and submitted as evidence to Scottish National Parks Survey Committee. These notes were sent to J.P. Grant of Rothiemurchus for his files on 31 July 1944, although a minor deletion was made on 3 August 1944.

70 SRO: FC 9-2, 'Minutes of Meeting of the Scottish National Parks Survey Committee', dated 27 July 1944.

71 *National Parks – A Scottish Survey*, Report by the Scottish National Parks Survey Committee, Cmd. 6631 (HMSO, Edinburgh, 1945), pp. 16–17, 'The Cairngorms', listed as region 4 on priority list.

72 *Ibid.*, p. 5.

73 SRO: FC 9-2, 'Minutes of first Meeting of the Scottish National Parks Committee', Edinburgh, dated 21 February 1946.

74 SRO: FC 9-2, Scottish National Parks Committee: 'Note on estimated capital values of five priority areas', IV Cairngorms Area.

75 *National Parks And The Conservation of Nature in Scotland*, Report by the Scottish National Parks Committee and the Scottish Wild Life Conservation Committee, Cmd. 7235 (HMSO, Edinburgh, 1947), pp. 6–22.

76 SRO: FC 9-4, Letter from the Department of Health for Scotland, St. Andrews House, Edinburgh, to Secretary, Forestry Commission, Edinburgh, dated 14 July 1948.

77 SRO: FC 9-2, 'Minutes of Meeting to discuss National Parks in Scotland', held at St. Andrews House, Edinburgh, on 9 July 1948.

78 SRO: FC 9-4, FC internal memo, from H.G. Beresford-Peirse, Director of Forestry Commission in Scotland, to L.A. Newton, dated 19 July 1948.

79 SRO: FC 9-4, Internal Forestry Commission memo from H.G. Beresford-Peirse to F.C. Handford, dated 31 July 1948.

80 SRO: FC 9-1. 'Extract from Minutes of Meeting of Forestry Commission to discuss the Dower Report', London, held on 19 January 1944.

81 SRO; FC 9-4. The membership of the Scottish National Parks Working Party came from delegates from the following organisations; the Department of Health for Scotland, Argyll County Council, Dunbarton County Council, Inverness County Council, Ross and Cromarty County Council, the National Trust for Scotland, the North of Scotland Hydro-electric Board, the Scottish Tourist Board, the Forestry Commission, the Department of Agriculture for Scotland, the Scottish Education Department, the Scottish Home Department and the Scottish Council for National Parks. Late in joining were Stirling County Council and the Joint Committee for Scottish Open Air Organisations. The Chairman was G.H. Kimpton from The Department of Health for Scotland, with Secretaries taken from the same organisation.

82 SRO: FC 9-4, 'Minutes of the seventh Meeting of the Scottish National Parks Working Party', Edinburgh, dated 8 December 1950.

83 SRO: FC 9-4, Letter from Alex Gray, Honorary Secretary, Scottish Committee for Camping Legislation to D.M. McPhail, Department of Health for Scotland, Edinburgh, dated 27 March 1949. This letter also contains pencil notes by H.G. Beresford-Peirse, Forestry Commission in Scotland, date unknown.

84 SRO: FC 9-4, Letter from H.A. Rendel Govan, Planning Consultant, Ross and Cromarty County Council, to D.M. McPhail, Department of Health for Scotland, Edinburgh, dated 29 April 1949.

85 F. Fraser Darling, *Wild Life of Britain* (Collins, London, 1943), pp. 41–44.

86 A.G. Tansley, *Our Heritage of Wild Nature – A Plea for Organized Nature Conservation* (Cambridge University Press, Cambridge, 1945), pp. 46–50.

87 Donald Mackay, *Scotland's Rural Land Use Agencies* (Scottish Cultural Press, Aberdeen, 1995), p. 145.

88 SRO: HH41-8, see the minute and memo sheets in this file of the Scottish Home and Health Department.

89 SRO: FC 9-4, 'Report on Proposed Cairngorms National Park', Confidential, dated 20 June 1951, compiled by B.L.C. Moira for the Scottish National Parks Working Party.

90 SRO: FC 9-4, 'Proposed Cairngorms National Park Reports, Scottish National Parks Working Party', dated May 1951 and 20 June 1951.

91 SRO: FC9-4, *loc. cit.*, Moira Report, June 1951.

92 J.K.W. Dunn, 'National Parks in Scotland', *The Scottish Mountaineering Club Journal*, Vol. 24, No. 141, April 1950, pp. 216–221.

93 John G. Osborne, 'National Parks in Scotland – Another View', *The Scottish Mountaineering Club Journal*, Vol. 24, No. 142, April 1951, pp. 312–315.

94 SRO: FC 9-2, 'Public statement of the aims of the Scottish Council for National Parks', dated March 1957.

95   SRO: FC 9-2, Letter from Kenneth Macrae, Scottish Council for National Parks to A.H.H. Ross, Director, Forestry Commission in Scotland, Edinburgh, dated 18 April 1956.

96   SRO: GD 325-2/174, 'Notes on National Parks', no date, but presumed to be mid-1960s as the rest of the file relates to that period.

97   Department of Agriculture and Fisheries for Scotland, *Land Use in the Highlands and Islands*, Report by The Advisory Panel on the Highlands and Islands (HMSO, Edinburgh, 1964), pp. 61–65; Anon., 'Cairngorm Area', *Cairngorm Club Journal*, Vol. 17, No. 93, 1968, pp. 248–251.

98   *Countryside: Planning and Development in Scotland*, Report by Study Group No. 9 at 'The Countryside in 1970' Second Conference, London, 10 to 12 November 1965 (Royal Society of Arts/NC, London, 1965), pp. 8-19; Malcolm Payne, 'Countryside Planning and Development in Scotland 1962–1987: The National Parks Legacy', Unpublished essay, dated October 1989.

99   CCS, *A Park System for Scotland* (CCS, Perth, 1974), pp. 4–8, 18, 23, 36. J.R. Crabtree, 'National Park designation in Scotland', *Land Use Policy*, Vol. 8, No. 3, July 1991, pp. 241–252; George Dickinson, 'National Parks – Scottish needs and Spanish experience', *Scottish Geographical Magazine*, Vol. 107, No. 2, 1991, pp. 124–129.

100   Mackay, *op. cit.*, p. 152.

101   CCS, *Scotland's Scenic Heritage* (CCS, Perth, 1978).

102   CCS, *The Mountain Areas of Scotland* (CCS, Perth, 1990), p. 38; CCS, *The Mountain Areas of Scotland (Conservation and Management) – A Report on Public Consultation* (CCS, Perth, February 1991).

103   The archives of the Nature Conservancy and Nature Conservancy Council are held in the Scottish Record Office (SRO), Edinburgh, at SNH. See SRO: SNH 1-1, 'Minutes of Meeting of the Scottish Committee of the Nature Conservancy', dated 27 November 1952, under 'Proposed Reserves, Action in 1953'.

9

From Aspiration to Designation: The Origins of the Cairngorms National Nature Reserve

Before 1990, there had been few noteworthy attempts to trace the history of nature conservation in Great Britain in its widest sense, or to outline the historical development of individual nature reserves. In the modern era, the pioneers of this documentary-based environmental history have been Dudley Stamp and, more substantially, John Sheail.[1] All subsequent work owes a great deal to this early initiative and scholarship.[2] Scotland has led the way in the compiling of the history of individual nature reserves. The most noted contributions have been Graeme Whittington's edited study of Tentsmuir NNR in Fife,[3] Paul Ramsay's SNH-commissioned history of Creag Meagaidh NNR from its designation in 1985,[4] Magnus Magnusson's history of the island of Rhum which includes an historical appreciation of nature conservation practices there,[5] and Tim Clifford and Andrew Forster's study of woodland management policy on Britain's first NNR at Beinn Eighe from 1944 to 1994 (although the NNR was not designated until 1951).[6] English Nature sponsored Peter Marren's 1994 study of NNRs in England,[7] and there have been recent historical ecology texts on Wicken Fen NNR and Moccas Park NNR[8] and a study of the founding father of British nature reserves, Charles Rothschild.[9]

This growing interest in writing on the history of nature reserves has coincided with the fiftieth anniversary of the nature conservation legislation in the 1949 Act. This study of the history of the largest NNR in Britain is equally timely, not just because of the high international profile of the Cairngorms[10] or because such a history has not been written before, but also because an understanding of the history of this NNR prior to 1980 sets the scene for many of the public conflicts between competing landuse interests in that area, which were to become so widespread during the 1980s and 1990s. A history of the Cairngorms NNR highlights how ill-equipped the NC staff were from 1954 to protect the unique flora and fauna of the reserve in the face of the expanding (but inherently traditional) use of the Cairngorm forests and high tops as a recreational resource. Visitor management became the overriding concern of the NC, once they had woken up to the existence of such a problem. As the upland ecologist Adam Watson concluded in 1996, this has been to the detriment of long-term intensive research, where NC staff have achieved little, where most work has been done from "spare-time studies by amateurs and scientists", and there has been little research into land management practices on both private estates and state-owned land.[11]

The Earliest Calls for British Nature Reserves

The nature reserve movement in Britain can be traced back to the establishment of the Society for the Promotion of Nature Reserves (SPNR) in 1912, at a time when legislation to protect Britain's wildlife against cruelty and exploitation was seen to be the pressing need. The sanctuary ethos of a nature reserve scheme for the country did not become fashionable until the early 1940s; in that sense the SPNR was 30 years ahead of its time.[12] The efforts of the SPNR to urge organisations like the National Trust to purchase and manage nature reserves for the nation met with some support even in the 1910s; in December 1912, *The Times* applauded the aims of the Society, stating that, "the only effective method of protecting nature is to interfere with it as little as possible; and this can be done only by forming a large number of local reserves – to safeguard the varying species and types of scenery on their native ground". A second editorial, urged all students and lovers of nature to flock to join the SPNR whose campaign should only be met with "wide and sympathetic support".[13] The *Journal of Ecology* in 1913 ran a short piece on the SPNR, and the role that all naturalists in the UK should take in helping to select nature reserves, citing the RSPB's Watchers' scheme as a step on the road to establishing bird sanctuaries.[14] The journal *Nature* added its voice to the call for nature reserves in March 1914, as a way of reserving beautiful land that had not yet been "irretrievably befouled", although E. Ray Lankester was keenly aware of the pressure that people could put on these reserves, proposing only the "occasional admission of visitors". He urged all "lovers of the wilderness, all worshippers of uncontaminated nature", to communicate with the SPNR and contribute to the promotion of "its most worthy national objects".[15] It would be the 1940s before the movement gathered steam again, and then it sought to move beyond the mere definition of what a nature reserve should be, into the more complex arena of site selection.

Thoughts on a Cairngorms Nature Reserve 1929–1947

In the SPNR survey of 1912–1916 to select nature reserves in the UK, the Cairngorms was not investigated as a nationally important site, although the southern foothills of the Grampian mountains at Caenlochan and Glen Doll were included as areas worthy of protection.[16] In December 1929, urged on by the CPRE, the British Correlating Committee (for the Protection of Nature) born in January 1924, gave evidence to the Addison Committee of areas where nature reserves were most required: Glen Doll and Caenlochan were named again, this time alongside Rothiemurchus Forest; thus here lies the first call for a Cairngorms area nature reserve. The British Correlating Committee was composed of representatives from zoological societies, the national museum service, the BOU, NT, RSPB, Linnaean Society, SPNR and international fauna preservation societies. Fearful of passing on sensitive information to egg collectors and plant collectors, the Committee published only the briefest outline of why each site was chosen. Rothiemurchus was deemed worthy of protection for its mammals, birds and plants, but was seen (in retrospect, mistakenly) to have no geological or entomological value. In the Addison report, James Ritchie (zoologist and Keeper of Natural History at the Royal Scottish Museum) proposed the Cairngorms area as a National Park, and thought all areas secured by the FC (plus the Killin/Kenmore mountainous area) should become nature reserves: "a sanctuary for the scientific care, study and preservation of all wild plant and animal life within its limits", he enthused.[17]

This concern over the impact of collectors on the fauna and flora at a site such as Rothiemurchus is documented well into the 1940s. In March 1946, J.A. Macmillan wrote from Gordonstoun School in Elgin to the laird of Rothiemurchus, asking if groups of boys might be allowed to camp or stay overnight in the boathouse on Loch Morlich, as a base for exploring the forest and high tops. They were granted permission, but the laird spoke of the district being "plagued by careless or ignorant people who cause forest fires, and professional collectors of rare birds eggs who cater for well-to-do amateur collectors". The Gordonstoun boys were asked to act as informal forest wardens against these unscrupulous marauders, to "help stop these abuses and if possible bring offenders to justice". Grant of Rothiemurchus hoped the boys would gain a good deal of, "field-craft and bird lore, as well as doing a bit of useful public work".[18]

In 1928, the British Ecological Society had proposed an amateur and scientific study of the flora of Britain from mountain top down to the coast.[19] The Cairngorms area was later recognised for its rare and unique Alpine flora by the Botany School at Cambridge University, which held summer expeditions to the area in 1938 and 1939, under the leadership of Alex Watt. The hallmark of these studies of the mountain *Callunetum* and the *Empetrum-Vaccinium* zone was meticulous observation of dynamic relationships between plant communities and their ecosystem, and the effect of altitude and exposure on vegetation patterns. This work spawned the three 'Ecology of the Cairngorms' articles in the *Journal of Ecology* over 1948 to 1951; publication had been held up by the war.[20] It built on the tradition of botanical observations in the area that began with James Robertson in 1771, and was continued over the nineteenth century.

It was during the first half of the 1940s that English-based nature conservation charities and investigation committees first came to recognise the importance of a habitat reserve in the Cairngorms. However, there was still considerable ignorance in the southern English heartland of these bodies about the precise status of flora and fauna in the northern Highlands. In 1942 the businessman, field naturalist and sportsman Geoffrey Dent, in his RSPB sponsored investigations (over 1940/41) as evidence for the Nature Reserves Investigation Committee (NRIC), regarded both the Cairngorms and Rothiemurchus to be of special importance as future bird sanctuaries, and outlined the importance of "mountain areas in Scotland and old pine forests such as the Spey Valley" within any contemplated national scheme of sanctuaries.[21] Dent's view was later supported in 1945, by those redoubtable ladies of Scottish ornithology, Evelyn Baxter and Leonora Rintoul, who wrote to Joseph Westwood (the Secretary of State for Scotland), asking that any National Park scheme for Scotland include a sanctuary for nature in "an area in the Cairngorms from the highest tops to the pine forests", ostensibly to protect the unique avifauna of snow bunting *Plectrophenax nivalis*, dotterel *Charadrius morinellus*, ptarmigan *Lagopus mutus*, Scottish crossbill *Loxia scotica* and crested tit *Parus cristatus*: "These birds are so typically Scottish and so very local in their breeding area as to call for special care", they pleaded.[22] George Waterston (Edinburgh printer, and Director of the RSPB in Scotland until 1972), in a letter to Fraser Darling in April 1946, agreed with the ladies and offered his support for a Cairngorms nature reserve taking in both Rothiemurchus and Glenmore, and containing "the remnants of the ancient indigenous Caledonian Forest with its interesting fauna and flora which should be preserved at all costs". Waterston also declared himself in favour of a Field Studies Centre at Glenmore Lodge, fearful that, should the SYHA get their hands on it, the local wildlife would suffer from hordes of recreational visitors attracted by cheap accommodation, without any responsibility or guidance. The forests should be used solely as a regulated educational resource, he concluded.[23]

Running parallel to Sir William Jowitt's appointed NRIC in 1942, was a British Ecological Society (BES) venture to identify sites of ecological importance across Great Britain, and to represent the views of amateur and professional ecologist alike in the crucial task of site selection. British ecologists had become increasingly frustrated over the 1920s and 1930s by a lack of field sites for research. The BES Nature Reserves Committee included the botanist and academic A.G. Tansley, civil servant and ecologist Cyril Diver and animal ecologist C.S. Elton (leading figures in the nature conservation movement at this time), and took a dynamic and constructive stance in the nature reserves debate, deliberately using the phrase 'conservation' and discarding the backward-looking term 'preservation' which so typified the older fauna reports for the British Empire. In its recommendations of 1943, the BES considered the Cairngorms as being worthy of Scheduled Area status, which sought to protect "large samples of the most important and characteristic tracts of country", primarily to maintain scenic beauty and not just to satisfy the research needs of ecologists. It was notable that there was a bias of these Scheduled Areas towards the better known south-east corner of England;[24] A.G. Tansley was to ask for this in 1945, to counter-balance the National Park movement's preference for remote northern mountainous areas.[25] However, the thrust of this report was the search for living outdoor laboratories where fundamental scientific research could be carried out by the new breed of scientists, the ecologists. The primacy of the scientific basis for nature reserves lies here; the 1940s were a time of growing public and political recognition and respect for ecological science and its practitioners. The BES report also proposed that rare and localised species, including the crested tit, were worthy of special consideration and long-term scientific study within habitat reserves: by implication, this suggests a Spey Valley site. After hearing of continued tree fellings in the Rothiemurchus woods in September 1947, James Ritchie voiced his concern (as Chairman of the Scottish Wild Life Conservation Committee) that "adequate provision must be made for the protection of the crested tit".[26] By the mid-1940s, the Cairngorms area was gaining more official recognition in England for its rarest flora and fauna. It was also declared to be of geological importance in May 1944 by M. MacGregor of the Geological Survey Office in Edinburgh, who considered the mountains to have "striking glacial and drainage phenomena", unique moraine configurations and wide spreads of fluvio-glacial deposits: "It provides also many illustrations of the effects of glaciation in modifying topographical features and in influencing drainage", his report concluded.[27] However, ecologists had now assumed the leadership of the British nature reserve movement.

The Role of the Scottish Wild Life Conservation Committee 1946–1949

By the second half of the 1940s, the nature reserve movement was wholly tied to the National Park movement in Britain. There was official recognition, though, that nature conservation had to be dealt with in distinct government reports and by separate committees, and the Scottish situation was to be examined in isolation, as England and Wales were investigated by J.S. Huxley's committee which reported in July 1947.[28] To that end, at an Edinburgh meeting of the Scottish National Parks Committee in February 1946, J. Douglas Ramsay formally appointed a special committee (the Scottish Wild Life Conservation Committee) having been "asked to arrange for the examination of this matter by a small body of experts". This committee, which comprised zoologist James Ritchie, Fife landowner and ornithologist John Berry, Perthshire landowner

Douglas Ramsay, the naturalist and author Frank Fraser Darling, botanist James Matthews and geologist Murray MacGregor, was to have an advisory role to the SNPC, but was to address the conservation of wildlife in Scotland as a whole, and not just within the proposed National Park areas.[29] As the NRIC had not investigated the Scottish situation, the SWLCC committee had, essentially, to begin from scratch in gathering information about wildlife in Scotland, digging deep into their own personal scientific knowledge as a starting point. Education, they believed, was central to the success of any nature conservation message. In June 1946, they met with John Laird, a Kirkcudbright representative of the Directors of Education in Scotland, and he was asked by James Ritchie: "How best can we encourage interest in wildlife in the school and so eventually help conservation in the country?". In the ensuing discussion Fraser Darling felt that young farmers should be targeted, as they would be "interested if they were told what the birds they had killed had been eating". John Berry proposed school natural history classes based on the food chain, "to start at the insect end rather than the bird end ... one may graduate to the binocular stage, but we ought to start with emphasising the inter-relationships of the different forms of nature".[30] Later, in April 1955, members of the SWLCC were invited to attend 'Field Studies in Education' events organised by the Scottish Field Studies Association in Glasgow, Edinburgh and Aberdeen.[31]

They held a less convivial meeting that same day with A.H. Gosling of the FC in Scotland. He argued that all woodland in the country would do best if managed by the FC, be it inside or outside a nature reserve or National Park. Argument ensued over SWLCC concerns about the FC shooting black grouse *Tetrao tetrix* in some plantations, and the SWLCC declared themselves much in favour of an increase in woodpeckers *Picus sp/Dendrocopos sp*, capercaillie *Tetrao urogallus* and pine marten *Martes martes*, much to Gosling's chagrin. Gosling fought his corner well though, keen to stress that had good sense prevailed and the FC been given Glen Affric, "without any question of National Parks", then they would have managed "a good section of those woods to maintain their present character rather than to run them entirely as a commercial proposition". Gosling appeared angered that nobody recognised that the FC was here to help nature conservation interests; "In many respects our interests are the same", he explained.[32] As part of their investigations into the international experience of National Parks and nature reserves, John Berry, Robert Grieve (Technical Officer of the SDD) and birdwatcher and writer R.S. Fitter were sent to Switzerland by the Scottish Office in July 1946, following an invitation from the Swiss League for the Protection of Nature. Grieve, in his report and discussion in September with E.M. Nicholson and Lord Chorley, believed that the principal lesson to be learned from Switzerland was how to use publicity and propaganda "in training the public to respect nature". He felt there were superb natural advantages in Scotland (citing "the excellent system of Deer Forest paths in the Highlands") but that "insufficient publicity was given to these assets".[33] The Scottish Landowners' Federation would surely have found that statement ominous.

The first report of the SWLCC in June 1947 did not name any sites, but supported the establishment of 'National Nature Reserves' outside of the National Park scheme. Such 'National Reserves' would be intrinsically Scottish, reflecting "outstanding geological features, or plant and animal communities typical of particular conditions ... [they would] be under constant and close scientific scrutiny". Much of this report addressed the desire of the SWLCC to have a 'Biological or Wild Life Service in Scotland', to begin the arduous task of planning effective nature conservation measures.[34] In the second SWLCC report of March 1949, viewed earlier by the Scottish National Parks Committee on 14 December 1948 in Edinburgh, a list of recommended nature reserves was produced. High ground (over 2,500 ft.) in the central Cairngorms fell under a proposed 'National Park Reserve', which would be administered by a Scottish National Parks Commission. However, in the event that a National Park was not created in the Cairngorms, then the proposed site would transfer immediately to 'National Nature Reserve' status. The SWLCC proposed state ownership of these reserves, although in rare cases a proprietor could be allowed to enter into an agreement with the proposed 'Scottish Committee of the Nature Conservation Board', and thus maintain his ownership of the land. The Cairngorms were listed in the report as 'National Park Reserve 2', held to be important "as a centre for the study of plants and animals existing under arctic-alpine conditions". Within the wider Cairngorms area, other sites listed were the Valley of Quoich, Glen Doll, the Moss of Dinnet and Dinnet oakwood; most importantly, the extensive Cairngorm plateau was felt to be unique for its plants, insects, birds and geological features.[35] In nominating 38,336 acres of the Cairngorms as a 'National Park Reserve', the SWLCC ran headlong into the thorny question of access to the proposed reserve, especially as this might have to be controlled (or denied) to wildlife sanctuaries that fell within recreational National Parks. James Matthews said a permissive clause could be used to safeguard sensitive breeding sites, but in all likelihood there would be no question of excluding the public. Robert Grieve was justly concerned that "difficulties might arise from any suggestion of limited access or implied exclusion from such a popular and extensive area", D.G. Moir having previously raised this as a point of principle in the SNPC meeting, with particular reference to the central block of the Cairngorms.[36] These difficulties arrived in the first years of the 1950s.

The New Nature Conservancy and the Cairngorms 1949–1954

The 'Biological or Wild Life Service' proposed by the SWLCC in 1947 had, by November 1948, evolved into the Nature Conservancy (NC), with the botanist A.G. Tansley as Chairman, and field naturalist Capt. Cyril Diver as the first Director-General. Dr John Berry had already been personally appointed by the Secretary of State, Tom Johnston, as Director-designate for the NC in Scotland, probably because of his senior post on the North of Scotland Hydro-Electric Board and (being a Fife landowner) his working familiarity with the concerns of lairds and sportsmen. It remained for nature conservation to carve a niche for itself within national government, both in the political and financial spheres. Earlier, in April 1947, John Berry and Sir Norman Duke had spoken about the creation of two committees (one for England, one for Scotland) under the guidance of a 'Nature Conservation Board for Great Britain'. Berry was pleased that there would be a wide degree of freedom of operation for the Scottish Committee, and perhaps greater opportunities for research north of the border. He also urged that the new body must "avoid coming under the aegis of the Agricultural Research Council [set up in 1930]", and would instead prefer to work under the protection of the Scottish Home Department.[37] However, civil servants in the Scottish Home Department remained unconvinced of the need for a possible continued role for the SWLCC or the creation of a new official body. J.D. Fairgrieve minuted concerns to W.H. Hansford on an internal memo sheet on 8 May 1947: (a) was government really prepared to pay for this kind of service under present financial circumstances?; (b) how far should such a service be made to be self-supporting or to produce economic results?; (c) how far is the cost of a nature conservation scheme desirable or justifiable to the public?; (d) how far was the whole affair just a job-finding scheme for scientists? Fairgrieve continued to be hostile to the idea of a government protecting nature above dealing with other more pressing human issues. In December 1947, responding to the SWLCC idea of a new committee to look into a comprehensive Wildlife Protection Bill for GB as a whole, he warned colleagues that the Prime Minister (Clement Attlee) had instructed "that the number of new Committees should be restricted", as there were more urgent matters confronting the nation.[38]

Under the auspices of the National Parks and Access to the Countryside Act of 1949 and its Royal Charter, the Nature Conservancy was given the dual function of research and nature conservation via the designation of NNRs. The first meeting of the Scottish Committee of the NC was on 2 April 1949 in Edinburgh, where J.R. Matthews (Chairman) urged that the committee build on the good work done by the SWLCC and perhaps start with surveys of proposed reserve sites. The Cairngorms were discussed at this meeting by John

Berry who reported that the Scottish Education Department wished to host courses for school natural history at Glenmore Lodge with the full collaboration of the NC, who it hoped would make "an ecological survey of this property". Again it was reiterated that any nature reserve in the Cairngorms must take into account, "the importance of this area to outdoor recreational activities", especially if bye-laws had to be drawn up.[39] Site selection was put on hold, as the second SWLCC report had only just been published, and committee members needed time to digest its proposals.

Over 1949 and 1950, the new NC sought to forge links with amateur and professional scientists in the UK who had worked on Scottish research projects for universities, research institutes or government departments, primarily to establish lines of discussion and co-operation.[40] The NC was well aware that changing circumstances on some of the proposed SWLCC reserves, first looked at in 1946–1948, demanded quick action as regards site designation. At the bare minimum, the sites needed to be revisited by scientists "before further decisions were taken as to reserve status".[41] To that end, in January 1952, John Walton and J. Grant Roger were dispatched to the Cairngorms "to report on sites specially suitable for conservation, within and outside the National Forest Park". The catalyst for this investigative visit was a letter written by Capt. Desmond Nethersole-Thompson (County Councillor and RSPB Watcher for the Spey Valley) to J.R. Matthews, urging that a Cairngorm reserve be established with all haste.[42] During 1952 Nethersole-Thompson carried out a survey of the birds of Rothiemurchus and the Central and Western Cairngorms for the NC, and he had met J. Grant Roger informally to draw up tentative boundaries for a nature reserve in the area. Two years later, Nethersole-Thompson and the NC were estranged over the boundary issue, which he believed should take in only the land that the NC had purchased at Invereshie, or instead take in Glen Feshie and Inchrory Forest, with the bird rich areas of low ground at Inverdruie and Loch Morlich. He actually tried to halt the designation in May 1954, forcing the RSPB to write to the Minister of State for Scotland, the Earl of Home, to distance themselves from their rogue employee's views, and to urge the early declaration of a large reserve.[43]

Committee discussion would not focus in on the Cairngorms fully until 1953, with the agriculturist and forester Arthur Duncan stating his support for a large scale nature reserve there late in 1952, and Fraser Darling not envisaging any problems with local Cairngorm landowners over sporting rights or felling issues, neither of which the NC need interfere with. The Cairngorms were officially listed under 'Proposed Reserves, Action in 1953' in November 1952.[44] The key issue over 1953/54 would be how quickly the NC could negotiate Nature Reserve Agreements with the landowners, and at what cost to the integrity and aspirations of the NC. State ownership was not being considered.

In late January 1953, John Berry first outlined the possible boundaries of a Cairngorms NNR before the NC Scottish Committee, after he and R.Aylmer Haldane (NC Administrative Officer) had represented the NC at a meeting on 20 January 1953 in Inverness with landowners and the local authorities, "at which unanimous agreement was reached that such a reserve should be set up over a wide and varied area". D. Nethersole-Thompson proposed the resolution at this meeting "urging the Scottish Committee of the Nature Conservancy to establish a NNR in the Cairngorms without prejudice to the climbing public and to the ultimate formation of a National Park". On this invitation, the NC would make the first approaches to landowners. The boundaries of the proposed NNR would run across the estates of Rothiemurchus, Mar and Inshriach. The access question, National Park versus National Nature Reserve was clearly going to pose a problem over the next year. On 9 July 1953, J. Grant Roger (Senior Scientific Officer, NC Edinburgh) despatched maps of the proposed NNR for D.M. McPhail in the Department of Health for Scotland to circulate to other Departments for comment and approval (such as Ministry of Works, Ministry of Transport, Scottish Command, Air Ministry, County Clerks).

A Year of Controversy and Debate 1953–1954

The negotiation and discussion period over 1953 was to throw up a number of challenges which the NC Scottish Committee should have expected, yet for which they seem to have been unprepared. The FC representative on the committee, Sir Henry Beresford-Peirse, remained openly sceptical about a NC-run Cairngorms reserve. He cited a FC and Department of Agriculture survey from the early 1950s which proposed that a considerable part of the Spey catchment area "should be put under trees", in particular areas of bare land on Rothiemurchus, Inshriach, Invereshie and Glen Feshie; this, he suggested, would be a far better use of the land. He felt that the NC could simply negotiate with the FC for some nature conservation privileges at Glenmore National Forest Park, and be satisfied with that.[45] Later in the year, the Director of the FC in Scotland, wrote to the SDD saying his organisation could not agree to any proposals which would hinder forestry developments, whilst hoping that "the setting up of this NNR will not adversely affect any forestry interests whether the land is state or privately owned". The North of Scotland Hydro-Electric Board chose not to object, but did cite their 1943 development scheme, which had identified possible future power projects on the Rivers Feshie, Dee, Tilt, Shie, Ardle and Garry. There were "certain streams within the NNR we might wish to use, and powers to transmit electricity in or across the area must remain".[46] There was a wide range of opinion on how best to proceed with the landowners.

Some members felt that all the landowners must eventually acquiesce to the NC demands not to shoot ptarmigan and black grouse on the reserve; some felt the NC should restrict all felling on the reserve, and pay compensation; some considered that a threat of compulsory purchase should be made clear to the landowners should they break the agreements; some felt that the NC might fail to get the owners' participation in the project if they drove too hard a bargain; some disliked the idea of a token payment for land; some felt that the estates should be allowed to continue to burn heather as they wished. A NC Estates and Acquisitions Sub-Committee was constituted to advise the Scottish Committee on matters of finance and legal issues for such a reserve.[47]

Not until May 1953, with the committee debate still ongoing, did Jamie V. Johnstone (Assistant Land Agent NC) report that negotiations with the landowners were up and running, and that the next logical step would be the production of draft Nature Reserve Agreements. Some modifications to the reserve boundaries were called for by James Ritchie, who asked that the NNR run along the northern shores of Loch Gamhna and Loch-an-Eilein (and not through the middle of them). Inverness County Council pressed to have the NNR take in areas of low ground at Ord Ban, Coylumbridge and Loch Morlich, probably because of the commercial tourism potential of these sites close to roads. There was also discussion about whether the NNR should take in a part of the Duke of Fife's Mar estate to the south-east past the Linn of Dee; Aberdeen botanist J.R. Matthews thought this to be ill-judged, as he knew the area swarmed with tourists, and was far better suited to any future National Park designation. E. Max Nicholson (ornithologist and Director-General of the Nature Conservancy 1952–1966) also felt this land to be an undesirable extension to the proposed NNR, as the Duke's trustees were keen to engage in commercial forestry activities which would bring them into direct conflict with the NC.[48] A 'model' standardised formal procedure for negotiations over Nature Reserve Agreements was put in place only in late May 1953; all negotiations for NNRs prior to that had been drafted as the NC went along.[49] This seems to tally with the experiences of the NC in England over its earliest dealings with landowners. John Sheail's work reveals that at times the NC took on more than it could deal with, and it "lacked the staff of sufficient standing to handle the delicate negotiations required".[50] The NC in Scotland regularly claimed it had far too few staff to achieve its goals, most vocally in October 1954 when James R. Matthews complained to Max Nicholson that staff were "dangerously overworked", and Scotland's staff allocation, "was meagre in view of the complexity and extent of conservation problems in the Highlands".[51] The Scottish Committee was still very concerned about staff shortages in 1969 and 1973, when H.A. Maxwell (Chairman) argued that a major weakness in the NC's overall organisation was a shortage of staff, "particularly in Scotland",[52] at a time when the creation of the new Nature Conservancy Council was being debated.

As part of the build-up to the establishment of a Cairngorms NNR, the NC in Scotland took an unusual but refreshingly inter-disciplinary outlook in October 1953, when (albeit haphazardly) they began to collect historical and bibliographical information on the Cairngorms. Much of the investigative work for this 'Cairngorms Brief' was done by R.A. Haldane and Muriel Longmire, although they sought guidance from the Cairngorm landowners over the identification of books written about the Cairngorms and individual estates from around 1800. Haldane's circular letter to the landowners concluded: "It is a great pleasure to us to see the Cairngorms proposal progressing, and we are all keenly looking forward to its becoming an accomplished fact". A list of books was produced by Haldane, including works by naturalists such as Seton Gordon, Richard Perry, Frank Fraser Darling and John Harvie-Brown, as well as social and cultural writing by Thomas Dick Lauder and Elizabeth Grant of Rothiemurchus. He also thought that the most important early tours of the area would contain information, principally Colonel Thornton's 'Sporting Tour'. Listing museums, public and university libraries as sources for all this material, Haldane catalogued journal articles of interest, suggesting that the *Cairngorm Club Journal* "proved to contain much worthwhile information", alongside *The Deeside Field*, the *SMC Journal* and the *Scottish Geographical Magazine*. Some very basic conclusions were drawn from this research, but it appears as if the larger part of Haldane's work remained unfinished. How useful it could have been to NC staff (if completed) by identifying historical links between people and nature in the Cairngorms, and offering a thorough bibliographical survey![53]

At the start of 1954, the NC Estates Sub-Committee gave the Scottish Committee the go ahead to purchase Invereshie estate in the Cairngorms from the FC. An area of 5,329 acres was bought at a purchase price of £3,625. The NC told the FC that they aimed to protect a woodland area east of the deer fence of around 600 acres,[54] just in case the FC sought to meddle in its future management. The NC became angered with the FC in March, when the condition of purchase revealed a clause forcing the control of vermin (undefined) into the hands of the nature conservation agency.[55] The NC also inherited the sporting rights of this property which they continued to let commercially. To this day (2000), Invereshie-Inshriach remains the only part of the Cairngorms NNR (about $1/_8$th) owned by Scottish Natural Heritage.

Agreements with the landowners were concluded over 1953 and the first months of 1954, although the laird of Rothiemurchus held up the process by remaining unconvinced about offering a protection area on his estate for ptarmigan. This bargaining prompted A.B. Duncan to minute his belief that the landowners should reveal that they were "demonstrably giving sufficient in exchange for the benefits they would be receiving".[56] Money was central to the Nature Reserve Agreements with the landowners; it is apparent that Inshriach was obtained for £25 annual compensation for 25 years; Mar was obtained for a £30 annual contribution to the Headkeeper's wages and a further £17 towards rates; Rothiemurchus came into the NNR for compensation of £100 per annum over 25 years, which suggests the importance the NC attached to its full participation in the scheme. These financial arrangements were not based on the acreage of land each estate contributed, but were more probably founded on sporting values and woodland values.

The Public Access Question

Over Autumn 1953 and Spring 1954 there were reports as far afield as the *Manchester Guardian*, the *Aberdeen Press and Journal* and the *Dundee Courier and Advertiser*, that the NC proposed severely to restrict access to the NNR. This issue would prove a big headache for the NC, and led to a year of suspicion, distrust and animosity. A Department of Health memo of July 1953 urged that the NC should be made to reveal now if they did plan ever to close or restrict public access to certain areas in the interests of scientific research. Other civil servants expressed similar disquiet over the size of the proposed reserve which could surely not be wardened effectively, nor could the NC make the project workable unless they started to meet and work with outdoor interests. If the NNR did, as claimed, contain the "cream of the Cairngorms area", then access restrictions would have to be made through bye-laws. This, in the eyes of the Department of Health, would be "a most sinister proposal". There was bound to be debate on this issue by the public and press. The first anti-NC press comments came in August 1953, focusing on access and the fear that a recreational National Park would not come to the region if a large NNR were declared. As a response, Inverness County Council started to push for National Park legislation to achieve tourist development in the area, but Aberdeen County Council refused to join in the fray, considering that only a small bit of land beyond the Linn of Dee was involved from their side. The SYHA spoke of their concerns over access restrictions. James Grigor of Stockton on Tees wrote in anger directly to the Secretary of State for Scotland on 30 August 1953:

> "As a Scot and Cairngorm lover, I deplore any possible action which might restrict a Scotsman's right to walk and climb the hills, and would like to protest in the strongest possible manner against any part of the Cairngorm country being singled out for classification as 'Nature Reserve' with access restricted according to the whims of any committee."

By September 1953 both Inverness-shire and Banffshire County Council Planning Committees had turned down the NNR project, believing it would "seriously jeopardise the possibility of having a National Park set up". They urged that a national decision should be taken on this landuse conflict, and vowed to protect public rights in the area. Inverness County Council then fell strangely quiet on the subject for 6 months. The *Highland News* of 12 September carried an article by Desmond Nethersole-Thompson who was now against the NNR as proposed, because it would render a National Park decision null and void, and was ill-conceived. Lord Lovat, supporting a National Park, declared the NNR plans "as representing a jig-saw puzzle". The *Manchester Guardian* (from a city well known for its rambling clubs) spoke of "the ugly thought that officialdom will try to keep climbers off the hills, botanists out of the forests, and birdwatchers away from the lochs." This was a scaremongering article, bound to rouse passions, with premature talk of permits, bye-laws and the horrors of restricted access. Meanwhile, in the *Glasgow Herald*, the naturalist Richard Perry asked if the National Park ideal for the Cairngorms had finally been rejected.[57]

The Department of Health continued to put pressure on the NC to meet with open-air interests, and eventually succeeded with an Edinburgh meeting held on 14 December 1953. Here concerns over public access restrictions and boundaries were raised, alongside the need to protect rights of way and camping out overnight in the hills. A. Cromar of the Scottish Ski Club thought it 'unfortunate' that the NC should set up a NNR before a National Park was established. Max Nicholson argued against this by stating that a nature reserve would lie within a National Park in Snowdonia, and no clash of interests was expected there. W.M. Duff of the Cairngorm Club proposed that a Consultative Committee be set up for the area. This pressure on the NC from the Department of Health, led to formal complaints from the NC (in Oct/Nov 1953) that the Department was consistently going behind its back in communicating with outdoor interests, and was deliberately giving misleading information to local planning authorities. Civil servants denied these charges of interference. By May 1954, the Director of the NC in Scotland wrote in anger to H.R. Smith of the Department of Health that some in the Scottish Office obviously did not appreciate that the NC was one of the Secretary of State's 'official family' in Scotland and thus could claim direct access to him. The NC was tired of being pushed around or dictated to by other Departments or by Inverness County Council, which had asked the NC to be given a share in the management of the NNR (they were refused).[58] From this December meeting sprang the NC invitation, by an open letter from R.A. Haldane in January 1954, to set up a Cairngorms Consultative Panel with three County Councils and outdoor interests.[59] Richard Perry and the mountaineer Tom Weir had already argued in *The Scots Magazine* about the access question on a Cairngorms NNR, with Weir urging that the forest of Rothiemurchus should be the whole reserve and that the high tops should be left to the climbers.[60] The Consultative Panel idea obviously won over the mountaineering fraternity, as both the Cairngorm Club and the SMC later reported the designation of the NNR with enthusiasm, eventually content that freedom of access to the hills would not be lost.[61] The Panel first met in Aberdeen on 28 June 1954 (just before the NNR was declared) and represented a diverse cross-section of recreational and tourism agencies and organisations in Scotland, to the almost total exclusion of nature conservation interests. The meeting discussed mountain rescue initiatives, public access questions and facilities, and the thorny issue of access bye-laws for the reserve (which never materialised). The Panel agreed to meet regularly, but there is no further record of its meeting again.[62] The NC may have let the idea die, feeling swamped by such a forceful pro-recreation discussion group. Had this Panel been continued, some of the difficult visitor management problems that the NC faced in the 1960s and 1970s might have been reduced.

Over 1954, the arguments born of the National Park versus nature reserve debate had rumbled on. In April 1954, two County Councils (Aberdeen and Inverness) urged the Scottish Office to halt the designation, these "irrecoverable final steps", and asked for an audience with the Minister of State. Throughout, the Department of Health had remained unconvinced of the need for a large NNR in the Cairngorms, H.R. Smith confiding that "it is a pity, perhaps, that the NC have taken such a large view of their functions." It was difficult for civil servants to see the justification for reserving such a huge area in the face of other competing landuses, when no obvious economic benefit was derived. They were also very aware that relations remained sour between the NC and Inverness County Council, an internal memo of March 1954 even noting that "what Dr Berry would like is something which would enable him to say to the County Councils that there is very little likelihood of National Park legislation." They certainly refused to help the NC; an attached note urged all Scottish Office staff to be as non-committal as possible about the National Park issue. For his part, John Berry, stressed the alternative value of a large NNR which, he suggested:

> "should in practice provide a great deal of what the National Parks' people appear to want. I much hope…that almost all of those who are at present apprehensive or critical will find that they have lost nothing and gained much for which they have been asking."[63]

Berry was keenly aware that the Scottish Office had displayed a clear reluctance to forge ahead and grasp the National Park nettle. The Scottish Office despatched the Minister of State (Earl of Home) to Inverness on 20 May 1954 to meet with Inverness County Council and discuss their objections to the Cairngorms NNR. The Minister stopped off at Rothiemurchus Estate *en route* where he canvassed the thoughts of the laird. He reported that J.P. Grant was very much in favour of preserving wildlife, and welcomed the role and assistance of the NC on his property. Grant was furious at the meddling role of Nethersole-Thompson in the whole affair, but was most concerned that his estate should avoid falling under a National Park designation in the future. The Earl of Home calmed his fears, clearly stating that the government had other uses for the money that this scheme would need.[64] At the meeting at Inverness County Buildings, attended by the Minister, the NC, Lord Lovat, Capt. Nethersole-Thompson, A.W. Mackenzie and F.W. Walker, the County Council identified their concerns as the boundaries of the NNR, the date of declaration, the wider prospects for National Parks, and the defence of public rights. Once again, the NC offered full assurances that they would not interfere with the rights of public access, or obstruct the National Park ideal for the region. The Earl of Home spoke of how well he thought nature reserves and National Parks sat with each other in England, and that really the Secretary of State, not the NC, had ultimate sanction over public access issues, as he had to approve any draft bye-laws they proposed. This conciliatory face-to-face meeting between government, NC and County Council seemed to finally clear the way for the launch of the NNR.

Just before the declaration, the NC produced a brief for the Scottish Office (14 May) outlining why they wanted a NNR in the Cairngorms, and what they had learnt over the last few years. Naturally, it identified the scientific value of the site, but also spoke of the danger of any postponement as landowners, with fewer estate staff than ever before, clearly could no longer provide adequate supervision to protect against fires and egg-collectors. The lesson of the previous year was that if the NC wanted to designate 45 to 50 NNRs by 1959 and perform their statutory function, then they had to be protected by government from interference, obstruction, and intrusion by County Councils who sought to question scientific urgency or vary proposed boundaries.[65]

The Launch

The Cairngorms NNR was declared on 9 July 1954 at 39,689 acres, being made up of the NC-owned Invereshie section, plus 17,500 acres of Mar Estate, 2,290 acres of Inshriach Estate and 14,500 acres of Rothiemurchus Estate.[66] Some of the Nature Reserve Agreements were not finalised until after the NNR had been introduced to the nation by the Director General of the Nature Conservancy, E. Max Nicholson, in Edinburgh.[67] In October 1953, John Berry had suggested that the Duke of Edinburgh might open the NNR during the annual Royal presence at Balmoral, but the Scottish Office considered this ill-advised, due to the controversy over the access issue. Later, the Earl of Home was similarly advised by civil servants to make an excuse on 'geographical reasons' to stay away from the launch; because of the "doubts about the Cairngorms project in local authority and open-air circles" he was urged by D.M. McPhail in early June to keep a more or less detached attitude until it was seen how the NNR actually worked in practice. In the end, the NC simply hosted a luncheon on 10 July at Nethybridge Hotel for landowners and County Councillors.[68]

The *Glasgow Herald* presented full coverage of this NNR launch. Nicholson praised the landowners for historically having looked after their land "as if it were a nature reserve", and congratulated them for willingly entering into agreements with the NC which were, in fact, "the first nature reserve agreements to be concluded with private proprietors anywhere in Britain". They had promised to dedicate their estates "to the object of nature conservation", and Nicholson announced that research work would begin on the regeneration of Scots pine, high altitude meteorology and mountain ecology. Sporting rights would not be challenged by the NC, deer stalking and grouse shooting would continue on the reserve, but ptarmigan would be protected in special zones and the only bird of prey to be shot would be sparrowhawks *Accipiter nisus*. All collecting of eggs and plants was to be outlawed, the primary object of the reserve being "to safeguard its characteristic Highland wildlife". It was at this launch that Nicholson made his now oft-quoted statement (which surely came back to haunt him many times): "We do not want to see the area opened up to charabancs and helicopters and whatever future horrors there may be".[69] Editorials in the *Glasgow Herald* that day praised the public-spirited co-operation of the landowners and County Councils in the admirable venture, although one writer predicted landuse conflict in the future if "the traffic through the area increases considerably, or relatively large numbers of visitors transgress the common code of behaviour on the hills". Countryside education was seen as the way forward, to instruct "the ordinary citizen in the elements of natural history, so that he may respect his obligations as well as his rights when he gets into the countryside". The writer had little confidence in the future behaviour of tourists, climbers and skiers.[70] The launch was also covered by *The Times*,[71] and reported by the SPNR.[72] The legal land aspects of the NNR were announced under Section 19 of the 1949 Act in the *Scotsman* on 12 July, and maps were lodged for public inspection in Inverness, Kingussie, Aberdeen, Edinburgh and London.

The twenty-fifth meeting of the NC Scottish Committee in October 1954 provided an opportunity for reflection on past achievements in NNR and Local Nature Reserve (LNR) designation. The NC owned three NNRs in Scotland at Beinn Eighe (1951), Morton Lochs (1952) and Tentsmuir Point (1954), alongside the Cairngorms NNR held with Nature Reserve Agreements. One LNR, at Aberlady Bay, had been declared in 1952 by agreements with East Lothian County Council. J.R. Matthews continued to express concern that public understanding of the NC role in the Cairngorms was poor, and "much more work must be done" to convince visitors that they would not be locked out of the NNR. The NC must undertake publicity (via lectures, press statements and radio interviews) to quash such misunderstanding, Matthews warned, as he handed this job over to John Berry (NC Director in Scotland 1948–1967) and J. Grant Roger (NC Senior Scientific Officer). Matthews also asked that "a short paper setting forth the financial implications of the Cairngorm Agreements be circulated to members". Possible extensions to the NNR were even discussed at this meeting, with Glen Feshie, Glenavon and Glen Quoich/Glen Lui high on the wish list, although E.M. Nicholson preached caution over the matter, worried that "the NC would no doubt be urged to add still other areas".[73] Only in December 1954, did J. Grant Roger submit the first proposals for scientific research on the Cairngorms NNR to the Scottish Committee. The early focus would be on climatology, muirburn and moorland plant communities.[74]

Notes to Chapter 9

1 John Sheail, *Nature in Trust: The History of Nature Conservation in Britain* (Blackie and Son, London, 1976); Dudley Stamp, *Nature Conservation in Britain* (The New Naturalist, Collins, London, 1969); John Sheail, *Seventy-five Years in Ecology: The British Ecological Society* (Blackwell Scientific Publications, Oxford, 1987); John Sheail, *Natural Environment Research Council – A History* (NERC, Swindon, 1992).

2 David Evans, *A History of Nature Conservation in Britain* (Routledge, London, second edition, 1997); Donald Mackay, *Scotland's Rural Land Use Agencies* (Scottish Cultural Press, Aberdeen, 1995); Norman W. Moore, *The Bird of Time: The Science and Politics of Nature Conservation* (Cambridge University Press, Cambridge, 1987); R.A. Haldane, *A Short Review of the Protection Afforded to Wild Life in Scotland* (NC, Edinburgh, 1966).

3 Graeme Whittington (ed.), *Fragile Environments: The Use and Management of Tentsmuir NNR, Fife* (Scottish Cultural Press, Edinburgh, 1996).

4 Paul Ramsay, *Revival of the Land: Creag Meagaidh National Nature Reserve* (SNH, Battleby, 1997).

5 Magnus Magnusson, *Rum: Nature's Island* (Luath Press, Edinburgh, 1997).

6 Tim Clifford and Andrew Forster, 'Beinn Eighe National Nature Reserve: Woodland Management Policy and Practice, 1944–1994', in T.C. Smout (ed.), *Scottish Woodland History* (Scottish Cultural Press, Edinburgh, 1997), pp. 190–206; A.N. Forster, 'A Report on the Woodland Management Policy at Beinn Eighe National Nature Reserve, 1951–1970', Unpublished essay, completed 28 October 1991, for NCC Inverness.

7 Peter Marren, *England's National Nature Reserves* (English Nature/T. and A.D. Poyser, London, 1994).

8 Laurie E. Friday (ed.), *Wicken Fen – the Making of a Wetland Nature Reserve* (Harley Books, Colchester, 1997). Paul T. Harding and Tom Wall (eds.) *Moccas: an English*

Deer Park – the History, Wildlife and Management of the first parkland NNR (English Nature, Peterborough, 2000).

9 Miriam Rothschild and Peter Marren, *Rothschild's Reserves: Time and Fragile Nature* (Balaban/Harley Books, Colchester, 1997).

10 Horst Wirth (ed.), *Nature Reserves in Europe* (Jupiter Books, London, 1981), p. 154; Kai Curry-Lindahl, *IUCN Survey of Northern and Western European National Parks and Equivalent Reserves* (United Nations Environment Programme, Nairobi, 1974), Report on Great Britain, pp. 1-20.

11 Adam Watson, 'Internationally Important Environmental Features of the Cairngorms, Research, and Main Research Needs', *Botanical Journal of Scotland*, Vol. 48, Pt. 1, 1996, pp. 1–12.

12 Society for the Promotion of Nature Reserves, *Handbook 1962 – 45th Annual Report* (SPNR, British Museum of Natural History, London, 1962).

13 *The Times*, December 18 1912, p. 7, leader article; *The Times*, December 18 1912, p. 9, editorial comment.

14 Wilfrid M. Webb. 'The Nature Reserve Movement in Britain', *Journal of Ecology*, Vol. 1, 1913, p. 46.

15 E. Ray Lankester, 'Nature Reserves', *Nature*, Vol. XCIII, No. 2315, 12 March 1914, pp. 33–35.

16 Sheail, 1976, *op. cit.*, pp. 127–135.

17 *Report of the National Park Committee*, Cmd. 3851 (HMSO, London, 1931), pp. 66–71, 89–90; James Ritchie, *The Influence of Man on Animal Life in Scotland* (Cambridge University Press, Cambridge, 1920).

18 NRA(S) 102:398, Letter from Jas. A. Macmillan, Gordonstoun School, Elgin, to J.P. Grant of Rothiemurchus, dated 8 March 1946. Reply from J.P. Grant of Rothiemurchus, dated 17 March 1946.

19 E.J. Salisbury, 'A Proposed Biological Flora of Britain', *Journal of Ecology*, Vol. 16, 1928, pp. 161–162.

20 Sheail, 1987, *op. cit.*, p. 167, photograph Plate 18; Alex S. Watt, 'The Ecology of the Cairngorms, Part 1: The Environment and the Altitudinal Zonation of the Vegetation', *Journal of Ecology*, Vol. 36, 1948, pp. 283-304; G. Metcalfe, 'The Ecology of the Cairngorms, Part II: The Mountain *Callunetum*', *Journal of Ecology*, Vol. 38, 1950, pp. 46–74; Alan Burges, 'The Ecology of the Cairngorms, Part III: The *Empetrum-Vaccinium* Zone', *Journal of Ecology*, Vol. 39, 1951, pp. 271–284.

21 Sheail, 1976, *op. cit.*, pp. 137, 141.

22 SRO: FC 9/3, Letter from Evelyn B. Baxter and Leonora Jeffrey Rintoul, Upper Largo, Fife to Hon. Joseph Westwood, Secretary of State for Scotland, Edinburgh, dated 12 December 1945.

23 SRO: FC 9/3, Letter from George Waterston, Edinburgh, to F. Fraser Darling, dated 30 April 1946, entitled 'Nature Reserves in Scotland'.

24 British Ecological Society Nature Reserves Committee, 'Nature Conservation and Nature Reserves', *Journal of Ecology*, Vol. 32, No. 1, May 1944, pp. 45–82. This

report was approved by the BES Council in October 1943, and then published. An additional 750 individual copies were also sold; see Sheail, 1987, *op. cit.*, pp. 134–138; Stephen Bocking, 'Conserving Nature and Building a Science: British Ecologists and the Origins of the Nature Conservancy', in Michael Shortland (ed.), *Science and Nature – Essays in the History of the Environmental Sciences* (British Society for the History of Science/The Alden Press, Oxford, 1993), pp. 89-114.

25 A.G. Tansley, *Our Heritage of Wild Nature – A Plea for Organized Nature Conservation* (Cambridge University Press, Cambridge, 1945), pp. 46–50.

26 SRO: FC 9/3, Minutes of the meeting of the Scottish Wild Life Conservation Committee, Edinburgh, dated 29 September 1947.

27 SRO: FC 9/3, Report, 'Geological Survey – Scotland: Cairngorm Massif', by M. MacGregor, Geological Survey Office, Edinburgh, dated 31 May 1944.

28 *Conservation of Nature in England and Wales*, Cmd. 7122, Report of the Wild Life Conservation Special Committee (HMSO, London, 1947).

29 SRO: FC 9/2, Minutes of the meeting of the Scottish National Parks Committee, Edinburgh, 21 February 1946.

30 SRO: FC 9/2, Minutes of Scottish Wild Life Conservation Committee meeting with John Laird, Representative of Directors of Education in Scotland, held in Edinburgh, 26 June 1946.

31 The archives of the Scottish Home and Health Department are held in the Scottish Record Office, Edinburgh at HH. See SRO: HH41-6, Invitation.

32 SRO: FC 9/2, Minutes of Scottish Wild Life Conservation Committee meeting with Mr. Gosling, Representative of the FC in Scotland, held in Edinburgh, 26 June 1946

33 SRO: FC 9/2, Minutes of Scottish Wild Life Conservation Committee meeting, Edinburgh, 30 September 1946, and discussion on report by R.S.R. Fitter, R. Grieve and J. Berry on visit to Swiss National Parks, 30 June–7 July 1946. At this meeting, the SWLCC expressed frustration that P.A. Clancey had been collecting crested tits on Speyside for research purposes in 1946.

34 *National Parks and the Conservation of Nature in Scotland*, Cmd. 7235, Report by the Scottish National Parks Committee and the Scottish Wild Life Conservation Committee (HMSO, Edinburgh, 1947), pp. 57–72.

35 *Nature Reserves in Scotland*, Cmd. 7814, Final report by the Scottish National Parks Committee and the Scottish Wild Life Conservation Committee (HMSO, Edinburgh, 1949), pp. 12–13.

36 SRO: FC 9/2, Minutes of the meeting of the Scottish National Parks Committee, Edinburgh, 14 December 1948, 'Consideration of Final Report of Scottish Wild Life Conservation Committee'. Discussion on this issue is also held in SRO: HH41-6.

37 SRO: HH41-7 'Notes on telephone conversation between Sir Norman Duke and Dr John Berry, 29 April 1947.'

38 See SRO: HH41-7, HH41-8, especially the minute sheets and memo notes to other civil servants in the Scottish Home and Health Department.

39 The archives of the Nature Conservancy and Nature Conservancy Council in Scotland are held in the Scottish Record Office (SRO), Edinburgh at SNH. See SRO: SNH 1-1, Minutes of the first meeting of the Nature Conservancy – Scottish Committee, at St. Andrews House, Edinburgh, Saturday 2 April 1949, 10 a.m. Present at this inaugural meeting were J.R. Matthews (Chairman), C. Diver (Director-General), J. Berry (Director-designate Scotland), A. Anderson, H.G. Beresford-Peirse, F. Fraser Darling, A.B. Duncan, A.D. Peacock, J. Ritchie, J. Walton, Sir B. Neven-Spence, F. Bath (Secretary), D.M. McPhail, A.M.D. Chalmers, with apologies from Lord Wemyss and G.M. Yonge.

40 SRO: SNH 1-1, Minutes of the meeting of the Nature Conservancy – Scottish Committee, 12 Hope Terrace, Edinburgh, 25 February 1950, under 'Scientific Work'.

41 SRO: SNH 1-1, Minutes of the meeting of the Nature Conservancy – Scottish Committee, Edinburgh, 20 May 1950.

42 SRO: SNH 1-1, Minutes of the meeting of the Nature Conservancy – Scottish Committee, Edinburgh, 24 January 1952; Anon., 'Spey Valley, Scotland', *Bird Protection 1951 – 61st Annual Report of the RSPB*, p. 35.

43 SRO: DD12/892, Report by Capt. Desmond Nethersole-Thompson 'Ornithological Consequences of Present Cairngorms Reserve Boundaries' dated 15 May 1954. Letter from PE Brown, Secretary RSPB London, to The Earl of Home, Minister of State for Scotland, Scottish Office, dated 19 May 1954.

44 SRO: SNH 1-1, Minutes of the meeting of the Nature Conservancy – Scottish Committee, Edinburgh, 27 November 1952.

45 SRO: SNH1-1, Minutes of meeting of NC Scottish Committee, Edinburgh, 29 January 1953.

46 SRO: DD12/891, Letter from Director of FC in Scotland to SDD dated 8 September 1953. Response of North of Scotland Hydro-Electric Board sent to SDD, dated 10 September 1953; they cited the Development Scheme under the Hydro-Electric Development (Scotland) Act 1943.

47 SRO: SNH 1-1, Minutes of the meetings of the Nature Conservancy – Scottish Committee, Edinburgh, 29 January 1953, 26 March 1953; Minutes of a preliminary meeting of the Nature Conservancy Estates and Acquisitions Sub-Committee for Scotland, Edinburgh, 26 March 1953.

48 SRO: SNH 1-1, Minutes of the meeting of the Nature Conservancy – Scottish Committee, Edinburgh, 28 May 1953.

49 SRO: SNH 1-1, Minutes of the meeting of the Nature Conservancy Estates and Acquisitions Sub-Committee for Scotland, Edinburgh, 28 May 1953.

50 John Sheail, 'From Aspiration to Implementation – the establishment of the first National Nature Reserves in Britain', *Landscape Research*, Vol. 22, No. 1, 1996, pp. 37–54.

51 SRO: SNH 1-1, Minutes of the meeting of the Nature Conservancy – Scottish Committee, Edinburgh, 7 October 1954.

52 SRO: SNH 1-3, Minutes of the meeting of the Nature Conservancy – Scottish Committee, Edinburgh, 19 January 1973.

53 The archives of the Nature Conservancy and the Nature Conservancy Council for the Cairngorms area are held at the Aviemore SNH office as Achantoul SNH. See Achantoul SNH, Handwritten file, 'Interim Report on Cairngorm Brief', dated around October 1953, compiled by R.A. Haldane and M. Longmire.

54 SRO: SNH 1-1, Minutes of the meeting of the Nature Conservancy Estates and Acquisitions Sub-Committee for Scotland, 12 Hope Terrace, Edinburgh, 21 January 1954; Minutes of the meeting of the Nature Conservancy – Scottish Committee, Edinburgh, 21 January 1954.

55 SRO: SNH 1-1, Minutes of the meeting of the Nature Conservancy – Scottish Committee, Edinburgh, 25 March 1954.

56 SRO: SNH 1-1, Minutes of the meeting of the Nature Conservancy – Scottish Committee, Edinburgh, 5 November 1953.

57 SRO: DD12/891. See letters, memo and minute sheets, and newspaper cuttings on the proposed NNR access question.

58 SRO: DD12/891, Minutes of the meeting of the NC Scottish Committee and Open-Air Interests, dated 14 December 1953. See also memo and minute sheets. Letter from John Berry to H.R. Smith, dated 4 May 1954.

59 SRO: SNH 1-1, Minutes of the meetings of the Nature Conservancy – Scottish Committee, Edinburgh, 5 November 1953 and 21 January 1954; NC, *Report of the Nature Conservancy for the Year Ended 30th September 1953* (HMSO, London, 1953), pp. 13–14. See also SRO: DD12/891 for discussion.

60 Richard Perry, 'A Cairngorm Nature Reserve – The Urgent Need for Protection', *The Scots Magazine*, New Series, Vol. LX, No. 2, November 1953, p. 134; Tom Weir, 'A Cairngorm Nature Reserve – Why Not Rothiemurchus?', *The Scots Magazine*, New Series, Vol. LX, No. 2, November 1953, p. 135.

61 Alastair Hetherington, 'The Cairngorms Nature Reserve', *The Scottish Mountaineering Club Journal*, Vol. 25, No. 146, May 1955, pp. 387–389, with Map produced by the Nature Conservancy in 1954; Anon., 'The Cairngorms Nature Reserve', *Cairngorm Club Journal*, Vol. 17, No. 89, 1954, pp. 21–24, with Map produced by the Nature Conservancy in 1954.

62 Anon., 'The Cairngorms Nature Reserve Consultative Panel', *Cairngorm Club Journal*, Vol. 17, No. 89, 1954, p. 49; Dick Balharry, 'The History of the Cairngorms NNR – with particular reference to its Management', Unpublished essay, dated 31 July 1992, p. 4. The members of the Panel were listed as Inverness County Council, Aberdeen County Council, the Association of Scottish Climbing Clubs, the SMC, the Cairngorm Club, Moray Mountaineering Club, the Grampian Club, the Etchachan Club, the Scottish Ski Club, the STB, the Mountain Rescue Committee, the NC, APRS, SYHA, SCPR, SRoWS, Scottish Council for National Parks, the Camping Club of Great Britain and Ireland, the British Caravanners' Club, Scottish Canoe Association, Scottish Caravan Club, the Woodcraft Folk –Scottish Section. This list provides ample evidence of the huge recreational interest in the Cairngorms,

running far ahead of nature conservation interests by the mid-1950s. It is odd that the NTS and FC were not represented.

63 SRO: DD12/891. See memo and minute sheets from March 1954. Letter from John Berry, NC Edinburgh, to H.R. Smith, Department of Health for Scotland, dated 1 April 1954.

64 SRO: DD12/892. Notes of meeting between Colonel Grant of Rothiemurchus and the Minister of State, The Earl of Home, at Rothiemurchus on 20 May 1954.

65 SRO: DD12/892, Nature Conservancy brief to Scottish Office, dated 14 May 1954.

66 J.C. Arbuthnott and J.G. Roger, 'Management Plan – Cairngorms National Nature Reserve', Prepared February-December 1958, Appendix VII, 'Detailed Particulars of Properties', pp. 1–11.

67 Achantoul SNH, 'Cairngorms NNR – Reserve Agreements'. For instance; Agreement between John Raffles Flint Drake and the Nature Conservancy, dated 3 July 1954, registered 20 August 1954; Agreement between Lieutenant-Colonel John Peter Grant MBE, Younger of Rothiemurchus and the Nature Conservancy, *circa.* 28 July 1954. Due to the obvious sensitive nature of each of the Nature Reserve Agreements, I was only allowed a sight of the front cover of each to record the dates of signature and registration. The historian can only speculate as to the contents of these documents, and how they influenced the history of management policy on the Cairngorms NNR.

68 This is described in SRO: DD12/891 and 892.

69 *Glasgow Herald*, Friday July 9 1954, p. 8, 'Britain's Newest and Largest Nature Reserve'.

70 *Glasgow Herald*, Friday July 9 1954, p. 6, 'Cairngorms Nature Reserve', Editorial; *Glasgow Herald*, Friday July 9 1954, p. 6, 'Work of the Nature Conservancy'.

71 *The Times*, July 9 1954, p. 8, 'Cairngorms Nature Reserve – New Status Today'.

72 Society for the Promotion of Nature Reserves, *SPNR – Handbook 1954* (SPNR, London, September 1954), p. 25.

73 NC, *Report of the Nature Conservancy for the Year Ended 30th September 1954* (HMSO, London, 1954), pp. 42–43; SRO: SNH 1-1, Minutes of the meeting of the Nature Conservancy – Scottish Committee, Edinburgh, 7 October 1954.

74 SRO: SNH 1-1, Minutes of the meeting of the Nature Conservancy – Scottish Committee, Edinburgh, 7 December 1954. Glen Feshie, Glenavon and Glen Quoich-Glen Lui were put into Phase III of the 'Five Year programme of Reserves', to be looked at in 1957/58.

10

Balancing Science, Nature and People:
The Management of the Largest National Nature Reserve in Britain

The National Nature Reserve Infrastructure

After the formal declaration of the National Nature Reserve (NNR) in July 1954, it seems odd that the search for a regional/reserve headquarters did not begin in earnest until March 1959. Indeed, F.H.W. Green (NC Principal Scientific Officer for Climatology) drafted a memo to the Nature Conservancy (NC) Scottish Committee on 20 March 1959, titled 'Proposed Speyside Field Station', but his proposal was not formally completed until 1 June. A headquarters on Deeside was never considered as an option, but the memo urged quick action, and if possible, on Speyside:

> "The desirability of having a Field Station in the vicinity of the Cairngorms Nature Reserve has been in view ever since the Reserve was acquired; the matter is now becoming urgent for the following reasons:"

The reasons presented were 'Red Deer', 'Meteorology', and 'General Research'. On the Deer issue, Green asked the NC to think ahead to the probable location of the proposed Red Deer Commission (RDC), suggesting that Inverness would be the likely base, and that the NC should respond to that and locate its scientists and stalkers (who would be working closely with the RDC) on Speyside.[1] Under the heading of 'General Research', Green envisaged the Field Station as a centre of research excellence under immense scientific demand from outside and within the NC. The station should aim to get effective research done in the Cairngorms Reserve, by having "adequate field facilities", and "accommodation for visiting scientists working on long assignments in the Highlands". Green's memo attempted to urge the Scottish Committee to consider Grantown-on-Spey as a suitable location for such a Field Station. He regarded Aviemore as "not so desirable as Grantown as a place for resident staff to live at", and likely to be plagued by "curiosity callers, as distinct from serious visitors, through being absolutely on road A9, Edinburgh to Inverness".[2] The NC Scottish Committee nevertheless pressed the Director-General (Max Nicholson) and the Director in Scotland (John Berry) to visit Aviemore and select a building, which they did on 21 June 1959.[3]

The final selection of the property named Achantoul seems appropriate, as the house had been bought by the naturalist and wildlife photographer Seton Gordon in the Spring of 1923 as a residence close to his beloved Cairngorm mountains. The building is described by Raymond Eagle as, "a stone house, built on a slight bank on the west side of the road, with a magnificent view of the Cairngorms, particularly of the Lairig Ghru pass, which it faces directly".[4] It appears that Berry and Nicholson were initially looking only for a property to lease, and the NC did place advertisements to that end in the local press. Achantoul was chosen because of its purchase price of £2,500, with only an additional £400 needing to be spent on the property (£100 for internal decoration, £100 for contingencies and £200 to purchase a generator for the private electricity supply). It was envisaged that this expenditure should put the house in order for immediate use, and plans could now go ahead for its future development as a Field Station.[5] The NC took over ownership of Achantoul on 24 July 1959, and it was to be ready for occupation on 1 October 1959 – initially by only the Deer and Climatology units, though with the possibility that other staff from Edinburgh would be sent to this new station.[6]

The first two wardens of the NNR in late 1954 were Archie MacDonald (a former gamekeeper) based at Achnagoichan Cottage on Rothiemurchus, who was responsible for the Speyside part of the reserve, and Malcolm Douglas, based at Linn Cottage, Inverey, Braemar who looked after the Deeside part. The NC had leased Achnagoichan from the laird of Rothiemurchus in October 1953 for an annual rent of £10. By the end of 1955, the Deeside warden had moved into Lilybank Cottage in Braemar, which the NC purchased in November 1954 for £1,000. Cairngorms NNR Reserve signs were first purchased and erected in 1955, as part of the wardening information service. The wardening staff on the NNR grew in line with extensions to the NNR made in January 1963 and May 1966. A wooden hut was also erected near Derry Lodge in 1955 for the use of the wardening staff as an overnight shelter. The use of Summer (seasonal) wardens was suggested only in September 1969, as a late response to growing numbers of visitors in the Aviemore area.[7] This short section of the chapter shows the administrative mechanics necessary to get a reserve up and running with a headquarters and wardens and staff in post; it is noticeable that the wardening staff were put in place well before the NC scientific staff were given a Field Station from which to work. It will be revealed later that the NC were generally slow to react to the challenges of visitor management in the area; however, as the first Management Plan of 1958 suggested, the NNR was not created to be a visitors' playground, rather its primary focus was the conservation of native woodlands and mountain habitats, "so that these may persist and develop naturally with a minimum of interference … but controlled to some extent by scientific management based on observation, experience and experiment". There would be some attempt to rehabilitate areas of felled woodland and to observe levels of natural regeneration in the pinewoods. The NNR was to be an open-air laboratory for all types of meteorological, geological and biological research and experiments.[8]

Early Scientific Research and Management 1954–1966

An early aspect of NC research in the NNR was the climatological work of F.H.W. Green, who had brought this specialist knowledge to the Aviemore Field Station, which was under his directorship. The tradition of meteorological observations in the Cairngorms dates back to the establishment of a weather station at Braemar in 1855 on the initiative of Prince Albert, and the formation of the Scottish Meteorological Society in that year. Daily observations did not begin at Balmoral until February 1906, but it has been suggested that Castle Newe in Strathdon began recording weather data in 1833.[9] A Cairngorms Weather Survey by Cambridge and London Universities and Scout groups took place in 1953, and as a result of this work the fledgling NC presence in the Cairngorms inherited over 25,000 observations from five sites in the mountains, alongside temperature values from stations at Glenmore Lodge, Dalwhinnie and Braemar. In 1954, the NC had sponsored other meteorological recordings on Ben Lawers and on Beinn Eighe NNR. The focus of this work was recording temperature values and ranges, and linking this to plant growth.[10] Writing in 1955, Green saw his early research as defining the climatic environment of the Cairngorms, in terms of micro/macro-climatology, and in particular providing evidence of the factors that inhibited Scots pine growth; as well as mapping the indices of 'maritime-ness' which he believed increased as one ascended mountains. He championed the ceaseless comparison of results from other upland areas with the Cairngorms NNR results, to ascertain the effects of climate and altitude on flora and fauna.[11] Much of this work was of a pioneering nature, especially the evaporation studies at Achnagoichan from 1955, along with daily records there of rain or snowfall, vapour pressure, relative humidity and wind speed. The information gathered in these long-term studies over the decades after 1953 has been used by animal and plant ecologists on upland sites across the UK. It has been the "high-altitude ironmongery" assembled on the summit of Cairn Gorm over 1975/77 by the Meteorological Office and Heriot-Watt University, that has witnessed the most public use of scientific research from the Cairngorms: mountaineers, hillwalkers, naturalists and the operators of the chairlift still rely heavily on hourly recordings from this weather station, which has given "documentary evidence for the contention that the weather of our hills for their height, is amongst the most testing in the world".[12]

Reindeer

An early experiment inherited by the NC on the Cairngorms NNR was the re-introduction of reindeer *Rangifer tarandus*, a project first conceived by Swede Mikel Utsi on a visit to Scotland in 1947. Their re-introduction as mere curiosities had been attempted as far back as the eighteenth century in Atholl forest, and in 1820 on Mar. In the late 1940s, Utsi identified certain lichens in the Cairngorms as an ideal food source upon which to base the first experimental phase of the reindeer programme, using animals from his own Lapland herd. The first animals arrived in 1952, with further additions in 1954, 1955 and 1961. The early formation of the Reindeer Council of the United Kingdom in 1949, was probably instrumental in securing the long-term future of a reindeer herd, despite the fact that they were initially restricted to unsuitable fenced ground for two years, and did not start to breed successfully until May 1955.[13] Earlier in September 1952, the NC Scottish Committee had discussed the original importation of eight reindeer to the Cairngorms in the light of the deaths of three animals. There were quarantine health worries for the Scottish Committee to consider, and they urged that any dead reindeer should now be subjected to thorough post-mortems.[14] Over the early 1950s the NC had a lukewarm enthusiasm for the entire reindeer programme, and in May 1953 the Scottish Committee refused to give further approval to the project until a probationary period was over, around Spring 1955. J. Grant Roger (Senior Scientific Officer) reported that he had attended an examination of the stomach contents of a reindeer, and had observed that it contained no lichens, but a variety of grasses, sedges and the leaves of young willows and birches,[15] which suggests the animals did slow the regeneration levels of some tree species.

The reindeer were held on fenced grazing land below Moormore, leased from Grant of Rothiemurchus, and on a small fenced plantation in Glenmore by Sluggan road, which had been deliberately chosen in 1953 to demonstrate to doubters that the animals would not browse Scots pine seedlings and thus clash with nature conservation values. By 1956, the Department of Agriculture for Scotland had recognised that reindeer could live and breed in the Cairngorms, and this opened the way for a British Reindeer Company to start to build up a free-ranging commercial herd, continue basic research on the species and allow tourists access to the animals. In 1957, there were 16 reindeer; by 1971, the herd was over 90 strong; 280 reindeer were born in the Cairngorms from 1963–1975. The Reindeer caused the NC in Aviemore a number of problems, stemming from the fact that the animals wandered at will up onto the Cairngorms plateau, and drew in visitors. Over the 1950s and 1960s, the reindeer often grazed on Cairn Gorm and Ben MacDhui in the Summer, and in the Winter they could be found near the new ski slopes searching for scraps. John Walton had advised in January 1954 that the reindeer must be kept away from all areas "of outstanding botanical interest", and should not be on unfenced land adjacent to the proposed NNR.[16] In the 1960s, the NC became irritated by a public misunderstanding that linked the animals to the NC's nature conservation work. An amusing example of this problem of reindeer within the NNR occurred in March 1965, as warden John Forsyth noted in his monthly report:

> "On March 20th I spoke to an Oxford student who had camped the previous night at Corrour Bothy. He stated that he had some difficulty in keeping his tent up because of reindeer pestering for titbits of food. I have heard of several instances recently of reindeer kicking out at visitors to Cairngorm and have seen a reindeer raking about the car park there, looking for scraps like a mongrel dog. Some people link the reindeer with the Nature Conservancy, which I feel is unfortunate." [17]

The reindeer problem never went away, and as the public's awareness of these animals grew over the 1970s and 1980s the herd became a major tourist attraction which, during the winter when the animals were unfenced, had a physical impact on the NNR.

The Native Pinewoods

From the mid-1950s, the protection and regeneration of the native pinewoods was viewed as "the most important conservation requirement", and scientific work to achieve this was called for in the 'Management Plan' of 1958. This built upon a call to "secure woodlands as Nature Reserves before they disappeared", made by botanist James R. Matthews, Chairman of the NC Scottish Committee in November 1953. At the same meeting Donald McVean (Scientific Officer) urged a new exchange of expertise and scientific knowledge regarding Highland woodlands, between the NC and FC.[18] In January 1957, the NC Scottish Committee discussed Highland pinewoods on two fronts – research and conservation. Although preaching the need for economy in planning fencing lines, the committee agreed "that research on natural regeneration was a legitimate subject of research for the Conservancy"; however, it was important to begin soon to put "actual trees on the ground".[19] The committee was running somewhat behind operations on National Nature Reserves, as experimental regeneration work had begun at Beinn Eighe NNR in 1953 and on the Cairngorms NNR in 1955. At the wetter Beinn Eighe NNR there was concern that the pinewood might not be able to regenerate naturally, giving rise to a debate over the 1950s about the level of intervention needed. On the drier Cairngorms NNR this debate appears not to have taken place, as pinewoods such as Rothiemurchus were viewed as being able to regenerate naturally – as was indeed noted in the first Management Plan. The bulk of NC research done on Scots pine in this period was conducted by D.N. McVean (then Senior Scientific Officer at Anancaun Field Station, Kinlochewe). In the mid-1950s the emphasis was placed on re-establishing trees on sites where wartime felling had taken place, by active management based on seed collection and spot sowing. In 1955, McVean began spot sowing on Invereshie and in Glen Einich. In March 1956, J. Grant Roger explained to NC Assistant Land Agent, J.C. Arbuthnott, that experimental fencing was to be erected in Glen Derry. Two woodland plots were fenced against grazing animals, one to be dug over, the other burnt, the object of this experiment being "the study of Scots pine regeneration under the conditions mentioned". Two additional areas of pasture on the Derry 'flats' were to be fenced, manured and one was sown with grass seed, "to study the effects on the growth and composition of the pasture and to investigate the possibility of improving the grazings".[20] Spot sowing was also undertaken in 1956 on Invereshie and Rothiemurchus, over 2,000 spots recording an 80% success rate. All the experimental plots were closely monitored by NC staff and McVean in these early years of experimentation, and rock phosphate was added to some seedlings; seedling size and light intensity measurements were taken to compare results with Beinn Eighe in the west. In September 1956, a morning was spent demonstrating the results of certain plots on Rothiemurchus to the laird, who must have taken a keen interest in this work, for in 1958 he allowed the NC to create seedling beds at Achnagoichan, and later a tree nursery there in 1962.[21]

The Achnagoichan tree nursery remained in seedling production until 1975; in 1972, it recorded its maximum annual production of 20,000 plants. The bulk of the nursery was devoted to Scots pine *Pinus sylvestris*, but rowan *Sorbus aucuparia*, alder *Alnus glutinosa* and birch *Betula spp* seedlings were planted out in small quantities. In March 1959 at the start of this venture, the NC warden cut a hundred square feet of nursery beds, a half of which was to be supplied by an eight-volt soil heating unit.[22] Ownership of Invereshie allowed the NC to concentrate their planting and experiments there, and in June 1961 Kenneth M. Wallace wrote of the success of the conservation planting to NC Edinburgh. He noted that "the protection from grazing provided by the fencing had caused an upsurge of natural regeneration of pine and birch on the lower slopes especially, with some patches of rowan and clumps of willow also recovering", which he felt fully justified the expense of fencing and maintenance. There had been some damage to seedlings in the upper plots of Invereshie by hares *Lepus spp*, but "the abundance of natural regeneration showing" was very encouraging.[23] In May 1963, Donald McVean looked back on the success of his Glen Einich experimental plot from 1955, conceding that it was a small-scale undertaking which had proved that spot sowing gave seedlings a better start than broadcast sowing on heather sward. The Einich seedlings came above the heather (at six inches tall) after five or seven years, but some superphosphate and potash fertiliser was needed on some spot sowings. In the 1960s, the regeneration experiments on the NNR became more elaborate, although Inshriach was little used, as it was seen primarily as a wintering ground for deer. McVean published the results of much of his work in the *Journal of Ecology*, and these papers, along with H.M. Steven and A. Carlisle's *The Native Pinewoods of Scotland* (1959), still have great scientific value for current conservation management of native pinewoods. By 1963, McVean was urging the NC to use only locally collected seed in their regeneration work, to plant up gaps in open forest and extend pine stands by sowing and planting, and to continue fencing off potential regeneration sites.[24] In the long run these efforts have maintained and established Scots pine on parts of the NNR where none would have developed had an interventionist approach not been taken. It was important that these young plantations were of local and native provenance, and McVean's call for this practice in 1963 was somewhat ahead of its time. Of course, another view is that this pro-active management has damaged the natural integrity of the NNR, and that the use of enclosures for forest regeneration has just delayed the need to confront the real causes of poor regeneration, namely high deer numbers and overgrazing. In 1975/6, the Achnagoichan nursery was formally closed down. During the 1970s, limited experimental work was done solely in Glen Feshie, with four fenced plots installed in 1975, holding collections of Scots pine and juniper *Juniperus communis* seed there.

Of course, a key issue in all NC/NCC native pinewood research and policy was ownership of the land. In January 1981, the NCC Scottish Advisory Committee read a paper on native pinewood conservation in the NNR, which identified only four woods (covering just 959 hectares) that the NCC owned, alongside a further 5,591 hectares held under Nature Reserve Agreement (NRA) schemes with landowners. Over 1,525 hectares of these woods were subject to the owners' right to fell, with an option for the NCC to purchase the timber (a costly exercise) within 14 days after an intent to fell had been lodged. It was a poor situation for the NCC to be in, and whilst they realised the national importance of increasing the proportion of Deeside/Speyside pinewoods, which they knew could be best achieved on Rothiemurchus where natural regeneration levels were good, they had to try and push nature conservation requirements within a private landowner's wider commercial land management strategy. In the balancing act between nature conservation and production needs in the 1970s and 1980s, the NCC turned to Capital Transfer Tax (CTT) exemptions as a way to dissuade landowners from felling, through compensation and tax breaks. "It is hoped to secure the national interest in the land, but leave the maximum flexibility in management terms with the owners", the paper concluded.[25]

Extensions to the NNR 1963–1970

As early in the life of the NNR as October 1954, discussions started as regards extensions to the reserve. The period of actual expansion began in January 1963 with the addition of 19,133 acres of Glen Feshie by NRA with Sir Ewen Macpherson-Grant of Ballindalloch. This brought the total area of the NNR to 52,822 acres, "reinforcing its status as one of the most important Nature Reserves in Europe".[26] Formal discussions to obtain Glen Feshie had begun in 1961, but over 1962 encountered adverse comment from Scottish Office Departments, planners and County Councils. A Department of Health memo of February 1962 noted that a Glen Feshie extension would mean that over half of the long-proposed Cairngorms National Park area would now fall within the NNR, and that would surely lead to a conflict of interests. Additionally, the Glen Feshie road project (Kingussie to Braemar) had been revived in June 1961; with a subsequent realignment of plans by the Roads Division of Inverness County Council to give access to possible skiing corries in the glen being drawn up in May 1962. SDD civil servant F.J. Evans, suggested that part of the NNR should be included in a development plan for Glenmore National Forest Park, to meet coming tourist requirements. Evans feared that a larger NNR meant a larger area of 'dead ground', with restrictions on tourist and infrastructure development. He was supported by R. Wallace (Clerk of Inverness County Council) who wrote to the Department of Health seeking assurances that a Glen Feshie extension, "would not prejudice the development of the area as part of the National Park and would not restrict the provision of suitable facilities for tourists".

The Feshie road project slipped away again in Summer 1962, after B.S. Thomson of the SDD Roads Division costed the scheme at £1m, and urged that new road projects be undertaken elsewhere. It is apparent that the NC maintained an open mind about the road, as W.J. Eggeling communicated to I.R. Duncan of the SDD in March 1965. He suggested that the NC would not object to a through road with few stopping places on what could be a key tourist route, nor would they object to discreet ski-tows on the sides of the glen. However, since 1962 the NC had stood firmly against a chairlift being erected in the glen; on 30 May 1962 John Berry, J.C. Arbuthnott (NC Land Agent in Scotland) and Tom Huxley (NC Senior Scientific Officer for Conservation) met in Edinburgh with Robert Grieve of the SDD to discuss this fear. Grieve explained that as the primary resource of the Highlands was attractive scenery, then tourism, wider access and National Park status should be pushed above all other issues, to ensure the rehabilitation of rural economies. Development, he felt, was essential in an area like Glen Feshie. He warned the NC that whereas the aim of conservation in England was mere preservation in a highly urbanised landscape, in Scotland economic development and human communities mattered more, and thus a huge and growing NNR in the Cairngorms "could become irreconcilable" with wider government policy on National Parks or tourism.

The NC line was to give vague development assurances and to state clearly that the privately-owned glen would only come into the NNR scheme via a NRA if the landowner so desired; the NC could not afford to purchase the glen outright. However, in Spring 1966 the NC did make some move to purchase Glen Feshie, clearing this with various government departments and agreeing to all Scottish Office conditions for multi-purpose use of the land. A last minute objection by the Scottish Office killed the purchase, and the failure to secure the glen was a major setback to the NC research programme (especially deer) in Scotland. W.G. Pottinger (SO Assessor) could offer no better explanation to the NC/NC Scottish Committees than to say that the government decision to halt the acquisition was an ad hoc one, which Lord Howick of Glendale (NC Chairman) thought a very weak reason indeed.[27] The concerns over the growth of land in the Cairngorms devoted principally to nature conservation in the 1960s – at the root of this Scottish Office intervention – were captured in anonymous comments on a SDD minute sheet in February 1962. It was a question of the difference between a nature reserve and a National Park: "With a National Park public access should be actively encouraged and developed, whereas with a nature reserve public access is necessarily looked upon without enthusiasm." Where the NNR was big, the 'deadening effect' it created on the land was big, and any potential future economic development was prejudiced.[28]

In May 1966, a second extension was made under NRA to obtain 5,296 acres of Glen Avon, owned by Major George Seton Wills, giving a new total NNR area of 64,118 acres.[29] Over 1970, the NC purchased Inshriach Estate which they merged with Invereshie as a single management unit, keeping the hill ground for the NNR, but selling off the arable land for profit. In January 1971, J. Morton Boyd (Director NC/NCC in Scotland 1970–1985) told the Scottish Committee that ownership of Inshriach "strengthened the Conservancy's hand in the Cairngorms area".[30]

Scientific Research and Management 1966–1980

NNR Management Policy

There is a real sense that once the NNR is established, the NC Scottish Committee turns its attention to the important selection and consideration of other sites. The first revision of the NNR Management Plan was made in 1967 to cover only the years up to 1971 and it appears that the NC/NCC did not have a new management scheme operational until 1987. This suggests that from 1971 to 1987 at least, the NNR was functioning outside of the guidelines of a management structure, or that the 1967 Management Plan was simply extended to last twenty years. Dick Balharry (SNH Aviemore) has suggested that both the Nature Conservancy and Nature Conservancy Council did mean to update the 1967 Management Plan but never got beyond the discussion stage in the 1970s. In 1976 a 'Perpetuation and Appreciation' objective emerged which sought to protect the biological and physical features of the NNR with a minimum of human interference, and to encourage the appreciation and study of the flora and fauna without destroying the natural qualities of the area.[31] In 1977, the NCC produced a draft NNR Management Plan discussion document, which Lord Dulverton (owner of Glen Feshie) responded to by outlining his own historical review of operations in the glen. The premise of the NCC document had been that the fulfilment of nature conservation in the Cairngorms NNR could not be achieved without a substantial reduction in red deer numbers, and that the conservation of pinewoods in the reserve also depended on this reduction. Dulverton argued that such a cull of deer would be catastrophic to all landowning interests in the region and would be impossible to achieve within the lifetime of the present planning prospectus. As an alternative, he suggested more fencing for areas showing good regeneration so that, after a century of such management, substantial areas of re-afforested land would appear as a mosaic throughout the reserve.[32] In November 1977, J. Morton Boyd wrote to Bob Boote (Director NCC in London) that he was hoping to meet with landowners in the NNR to discuss current management policies and possible new policy proposals, as well as allowing the FC, CCS, RDC and SLF into the wider discussion process.[33]

Discussions over a Management Plan revision dragged on from early 1978 to Autumn 1979 at least. Landowners tended to slow the process down. By September 1979, Morton Boyd complained that 50% of the NRA landowners had not yet responded to the NCC draft plan. At a NCC Scottish Advisory Committee meeting in January 1978, Boyd spoke out that the NCC must now demonstrate some dynamic short-term successes for nature conservation interests in the Cairngorms, and that staff "should not be too apologetic about pushing nature conservation interests first", even though restricted resources meant that the whole NNR could not be protected. He also suggested that the rise of "unacceptable human pressures in the area" was as important as the deer management issue. Overall, he maintained, they needed to reconcile nature conservation with the "practicalities of economic factors of local estate management within the NNR, and with the financial resources available for the implementation of the NCC's policies on the NNR". There was a recognition at this meeting that conflict with landowners was inevitable, but how much should NCC compromise, asked the Chairman Sir David Montgomery, in order to gain the necessary support and agreement with estates in the NRA scheme?[34] This meeting, and J.M. Boyd later, also felt that there was a clear 'lack of sympathy' towards nature on the part of the Highlands and Islands Development Board, and that as a key player in the region they should show more appreciation of the role of nature conservation in rural landuse policy. Over a year later (25 April 1979) the same committee sought to redefine NNR management policies. The red deer problem, especially the issue of compensation to landowners who culled and lost revenue, was seen as a top priority but also a major financial undertaking. Once again, the need for short-term visible public successes was reiterated, with a suggestion to step up planting and rotational fencing schemes in order to aid natural regeneration of the native pinewoods. The meeting also spoke of the pressures and demands that would come with growing visitor numbers to the NNR over the 1980s, in particular concerning wardening, NCC local staff levels, access points and financial constraints (the NCC Treasury budget had risen from £5.2m in 1976/77 to £6m in 1977/78, with a reserve acquisition fund of just £350,000 in 1978). The NCC was the only body with a general responsibility for the whole of the Cairngorms NNR, and they were therefore in a unique position to influence all management policies, but they had to face up to the enormous challenges and questions this posed. The problem in 1979 was how to perform the balancing act between nature conservation, traditional estate management and greater public access to and enjoyment of the NNR.[35] The inability of the NC/NCC to respond fully to new environmental, political and recreational developments in the area after 1967, by producing regular updates of the management strategy, must be seen as a failure on their part.

Red Deer

In 1959, when the Speyside Field Station was opened one of the first units to come north from Edinburgh was the Deer Research and Survey team under V.P.W. Lowe, who were to play a "full part in informing and advising the Red Deer Commission on scientific aspects of the work".[36] Although the bulk of the NC's research on red deer *Cervus elaphus* would take place on Rhum after 1957,[37] the Cairngorms NNR saw the NC involved in both deer management, control and research. In 1954, part of the Mar Estate in the NNR at Glen Ge-usachan was set aside as a Deer Sanctuary from which visitors were excluded between August and November, so as not to disturb the estate stalking. In the period 1954–1976 the NC/NCC managed first Invereshie and then Invereshie-Inshriach as a traditional sporting estate. The number of stags taken by a shooting tenant was determined by tradition, not science, and the venison was sold on, raising around £130 a year in the mid-1960s. The hinds were shot by NC staff. However, a change of policy came in 1976, on the initiative of Dick Balharry, which sought to 'control' deer numbers on this land by reducing the deer population to a level that would allow natural regeneration of the forest.[38] From 1976, the number of deer annually shot on Invereshie was doubled compared with the former sporting management policy, and the effectiveness of this policy change has been revealed in high levels of pine regeneration at the site. The scientific impulse for the new management strategy dates back to 1966 and the creation of the NC Range Ecology Group, based until 1974 in Glen Feshie. The landowner, Lord Dulverton had graciously suggested to the NC in 1966 that they could conduct deer research in the glen both inside and outside the NNR, as long as they did not oppose a road through the glen or discourage public use of the area for recreation. This was obviously an unsat-isfactory arrangement from the outset, but it was the best deal the NC could get on the mainland. NC Principal Scientific Officer, David Jenkins, warned in committee in April 1967, that such doubtful security of tenure was destined to highlight tensions between traditional sporting estate management, forestry and NC scientific research. The success of this scheme largely depended upon goodwill on both sides and proper liaison at all levels, especially after October 1966 when Lord Dulverton openly declared his primary landuse aims to be timber and deer production, plus grouse, salmon and farm stock.[39] The NC's second progress report, covering 1969–1971, revealed scientific proof that the natural regeneration of birch *Betula spp* and pine *Pinus spp* would not occur, until the deer population on the NNR was drastically reduced. Most of the damage to seedlings was done by grazing, but some were uprooted or trampled. Of 150 seedlings planted at different sites in the glen in 1969, only 11% remained a year later; all "tall and conspicuous seedlings" (the most healthy) were taken. Over the years 1968–1971, the NC, with Glen Feshie Estate and the RDC were shooting the traditional cull of 120 stags and around 250 hinds, out of a total glen deer population of c.2,360.[40] Some of this range research was of a basic nature, and it did not take into account any sporting, economic or landuse considerations facing the landowner, but the research did challenge the validity of previous deer management policies on the NNR. It also brought the conflicts between landowners and the NC/NCC out into the open by the mid-1970s. The NC Scottish Committee recognised the limitations of Glen Feshie as a place for their experimental studies in July 1969, and called for the acquisition of another mainland deer forest which they could own.[41] A month prior to this they had outlined the nature of their working relationship with Glen Feshie Estate through an agreement with West Highland Woodlands, which granted facilities for deer research in the glen co-ordinated by a Management Committee. The NC also spoke of financial constraints in its research budgeting in the late 1960s which "may affect the nature and magnitude of the manpower available for deer range research at Glenfeshie". They looked forward to the 1970s and a better understanding of the principles governing "the inter-relations between deer and their habitat, as a foundation for the future management of Highland environments in the long-term".[42]

Visitor Management

The Management Plan of 1967 invoked a new role for the NNR in the late 1960s and into the 1970s, that of "a wilderness zone in the wider Cairngorms area". This was done to protect the reserve from the rapid tourism development in the Aviemore area during the early 1960s; the NC was not going to allow any development to take place within the NNR boundaries. Indeed, the NC would maintain a ban on camping, increase fire-fighting precautions and outlaw certain recreational activities.[43] Here was confirmation that a nature reserve originally established as a representative example of a unique upland environment and a place for potential research, was now forced to confront a new challenge, that of tourism and visitor management, which arguably came to dominate the life of the NNR to the present day. The management of recreation was to become far more time-consuming for NC/NCC staff than the promotion of new nature conservation initiatives.

The first Management Plan of 1958 makes little mention of public access to the reserve, although visitors were given open access at all times of year, except on to the Mar Estate during the stalking season. Certain rights of way such as the Lairig Ghru and Lairig an Laoigh were identified, but all permission to camp had to be sought from the NC or landowners. Some limited advice was given on mountain safety, derived from the public consultation for the 1957 Inverness-shire Police Committee pamphlet, *The Price Paid*.[44] It was not felt necessary in the late 1950s to establish any fenced or prohibited areas on the NNR as a safeguard against the effects of visitor access, presumably because the NC were uncertain of just how many visitors would come, although a visiting tradition going back to the nineteenth century should have warned them. They made no formal provisions, and were caught off guard as early as 1962.

The warden's monthly/annual reports to Edinburgh headquarters show the start of this problem. The Summer of 1960 brought "birdwatchers, students and hikers", and whilst these individuals behaved responsibly, organised parties of the Military and SCPR were criticised for taking liberties with training in the area. Witness Archie MacDonald:

> "In my opinion there is far more disturbance caused to wildlife at certain times of the year by these large organised parties than there is from small parties of people who go for the love of the hills, or to observe wildlife and plants in their natural conditions."

MacDonald added that this was a developing situation that "I respectfully suggest will have to be looked into in the future".[45] In 1962, MacDonald reported that litter was becoming a problem, especially at the popular Loch an Eilein.[46] Restricting access was not considered an option. Indeed, the NC Scientific Officer, J. Grant Roger, praised the recreational potential of the NNR in September 1962, confident that visitors were not yet interfering with scientific research or with wildlife:

> "elsewhere in the Highlands grouse shooting activities often deter hillwalkers, so, for the large number of people who normally take their holidays in August, the Cairngorms Reserve, being predominantly a deer forest, does have great amenity value."[47]

Warden John Forsyth recorded high numbers of visitors in August 1964, and found great difficulty in removing campers from quieter parts of the reserve; "One often hears the protest, 'But we don't like the official sites. They're too crowded'. This, in August, is certainly true and there is no doubt that additional camping and caravanning sites will shortly be required in this area". During August 1964, Forsyth had cause to stop and challenge the following; some long-distance runners around Loch an Eilein; a bugler practising on Creagan-bun-Suinn; pony-trekkers and cycling clubs and people in several small boats on Loch an Eilein.[48] A wide diversity of recreational interest is represented here, but Forsyth probably found these visitors a shade less eccentric in their pursuits than the family he had encountered in July.

> "One man, a member of the British Safari Club, appeared to think that he was entitled to take his landrover anywhere he pleased and was obviously out looking for 'giants to kill'. He stated that he and his family went 'on safari' every weekend. He was checked, while attempting to force a crossing by the stream between Loch-an-Eilein and Loch Gamhna."[49]

Such pressure on the NNR was bound to force a response from the NC, and it came in late 1964, prompted by a series of meetings. J. Grant Roger came to Aviemore in October to meet with the wardens to discuss "the whole question of the tourist", in light of the projected holiday developments in the area.[50] The NNR warden, Archie MacDonald appears to have taken the visitor management issue to heart over the 1960s, and regularly warned NC Edinburgh that continued inaction on the subject would prove disastrous in the long run. In November 1964, a serendipitous meeting of MacDonald, Major Drake of Inshriach and Grant of Rothiemurchus at Aviemore rail station resulted in an hour-long discussion on Cairngorm tourism. MacDonald wrote of this to J.G. Roger, that "it was pleasing to hear the whole Tourist Board outlook on the Highlands politely shot for six". He added a caveat; "one thing I do know, as long as we manage the Cairngorms Nature Reserve as a RESERVE, the answer is simple … it's only when we let other interests turn it into a playground or a National Park that it becomes difficult".[51] Ten years after the creation of the NNR, the NC were waking up to the issue of visitor management and were realising that access to the reserve would be linked inexorably to the accommodation infrastructure in the wider Cairngorms area and burgeoning tourism developments in Strathspey. Forsyth drafted a memo in November 1964, 'Public Facilities – Cairngorms NNR', where he proposed that the NC adopt the 'honeypot area' solution to visitor management, predicting the possibility of restricted access in the years to come: "our efforts should be concentrated on channelling the public to certain areas and that it might be a good plan to accustom the public to the idea of restricted access before this becomes a necessary fact". He also concluded that signposting the reserve from regional roads was undesirable, as it would "inevitably attract people out of sheer curiosity, thereby adding to public pressure on the area".[52] The end of 1964 saw the first NC visitor survey, conducted on Rothiemurchus. Interviews with nine visitors revealed that all came to the NNR for "peace and quietness"; seven of the nine were professional people; all were Scots; two had known the area since 1926, two others from before 1939; two visitors were skiers; four visitors described themselves as casual photographers, and all enjoyed seeing wildlife. All displayed a strong sense of the aesthetic, as Forsyth explained:

> "Six expressed an abhorrence of developments in connection with tourists and skiers in the Loch Morlich/Cairngorm area. Four compared it with Blackpool and two said they would never go back on Cairngorm. All stated that they would not like to see better access for motor vehicles, and all felt that Glen Einich should remain closed to traffic."[53]

Discussions began in 1965 with a view to publishing and marketing a visitor pamphlet for the NNR; this was eventually published in 1966, after liaison with landowners and recreation organisations. Its launch was linked to the NC display at the White Lady Shieling on Cairn Gorm, in a joint venture with the National Trust for Scotland to highlight the fragile ecosystem of the mountains.[54]

By the mid-1960s the decision to make Rothiemurchus (in particular, Loch an Eilein) the focus for visitor management had spawned the idea of a regulated Nature Trail on the NNR. It was conceived on the existing tradition of visitor concentration on the Rothiemurchus Estate, and built along the 1832 carriage road constructed there by the Duchess of Bedford. Opened in June 1965, it proved a very successful venture, hosting around 35,000 visitors over the period 1965–1969. An indication of its popularity can be derived from visitor counts and/or take-up of a trail leaflet, priced at 6d. in 1969, as displayed below.[55]

Monthly Totals		Annual Totals	
Month	Number of leaflets sold	Year	Number of leaflets sold or visitors
June 1967	1,268	1965	c.5,000
June 1968	1,674	1966	c.7,500
June 1969	1,298	1967	c.8,000
1971 (3 weeks)	5,123 (cars)	1968	8,139
		1969	c.7,000
		1970	7,327
		1973	10,370
		1975	c.18,000 (visitors)
		1976	c.20,000 (visitors)

Table 9. Visitors to the Loch an Eilein Nature Trail 1965–1976
(Source: Achantoul SNH)

In July 1965, the NC put together, for the STB holiday festival at the Aviemore Centre, an exhibit blending wildlife with human history and recreation in the Cairngorms, entitled 'Man and Nature in Speyside'. The obvious popularity of structured visitor facilities on the NNR forced the NC to consider expanding the nature trail idea; in July 1967, Joe Eggeling (former NC Conservation Officer, and now Director for Scotland) and J.G. Roger proposed the construction of an Achlean Nature Trail in Glen Feshie, intended also to keep people on the lower ground and thus away from the sensitive dotterel *Charadrius morinellus* breeding area on the high tops. An observation platform was to be constructed to give visitors a panoramic view of the glen, and to allow them to observe red deer.[56] The recreational watching of deer species had been instigated by the Forestry Commission at Grizedale (in Westmorland) during the late 1960s and proved a popular and diverse use of forest land. The trail was opened by the landowner, Lord Dulverton, on 11 June 1970 and, in its short life, recorded these visitor numbers in what is a more remote part of the NNR: [57]

Year	AnnualTotals Number of visitors or leaflets sold
1970	836
1971	c.3,000 (visitors)
1973	2,450

Table 10. Visitors to the Achlean Nature Trail 1970–1973
(Source: Achantoul SNH)

The Achlean Nature Trail was closed in the Summer of 1975, due to the inability of the Nature Conservancy Council (NCC), the local crofter and Lord Dulverton to agree on a visitor management strategy for the site. The NC/NCC had also become concerned about visitor over-use of the valuable fragile remnant of Scots pine at Badan Mosach, as people came to view the beautiful waterfall there. Surprisingly, the observation tower was not removed until July 1978, after Lord Dulverton complained to the NCC that visitors were wandering all over Glen Feshie searching for it, and footpath erosion on the route to the tower was getting worse. Dulverton was angered that there appeared to be no NCC management whatsoever at the site. [58]

In 1969, the NC and Rothiemurchus undertook an unofficial review of public facilities within the NNR, after warden David Holland had identified a new focus for the litter problem at the Shelter Stone and on the plateau, and had questioned the role of organised parties within the reserve, in particular 'Highland Guides'; "these guided parties may prove to be the biggest danger from the public pressure aspect", he warned. [59] During September 1969, Ted Hammond (Assistant Regional Officer, NC Aviemore) met with J.P. Grant of Rothiemurchus to discuss the future wardening strategy on the NNR. Both felt that a passive visitor information service, based on leaflets and nature trails, could no longer cope, and that a new line of thought was needed. Hammond suggested, "the provision of a first class information service in terms of information centres coupled to a seasonal wardening service", to run alongside the present system. The laird of Rothiemurchus seemed to like this change in policy, and offered the NC the use of an old cottage at Loch an Eilein, which in 1964 he had wanted to convert into a 'tea and refreshment' place, although he had withdrawn the proposal in 1965 under NC pressure. The NC obtained a lease for the cottage in 1970, and a visitor centre was opened on 1 July 1972 by naturalist and author Sir Frank Fraser Darling, together with an associated exhibition, 'The Native Pinewoods'. Hammond also spoke of the importance of linking the NC visitor facilities with those in the wider Cairngorms area, as the NC seemed slow to involve itself in the public relations work associated with nature conservation. Anti-vandalism measures had now to be a part of the NNR visitor management strategy, due to the "changing pattern of the type of visitors now using Speyside". The wardening service must strike at the heart of the problem for the first time, "nearest to the greatest density of visitors". His final warning to NC headquarters stands even today as a prophetic statement on the conflicting demands of nature conservation and recreation:

> "It is my considered opinion that if the Conservancy do not soon take a more positive approach in the field of visitor reception, control and education on the Cairngorms, all the previous years work in promoting conservation in the area will evaporate in the face of growing tourist and commercial pressures and eventually compromise the very existence of this, the largest Reserve." [60]

During the 1970s the NC/NCC made some limited advances in the provision of visitor services, often linking these to the growing demand for environmental education. They also conducted further visitor surveys to ascertain popular perceptions and expectations of the NNR. The future visitor policy was laid out in the Management Plan of 1967, where "priority of interest will be given to a programme in which foci of interest are provided for the public at the main access points and in the zones most vulnerable to damage. Away from these points it is proposed that little or no development should take place". [61] With this a new line was taken in selling nature conservation to the public through the high-profile wardening service, guided walks and information centres. To boost the public image of the NC and NNRs, a Speyside Wildlife Group was founded in 1972, but it had been abandoned as a forum to lessen landuse conflict by 1977, due to the competing landuse interests of its member organisations. The NCC established their own internal discussion group on visitor management in 1974, called the Cairngorm Users, which sought to blend official nature conservation policies with the wishes of other interested organisations. It met during 1975/76 but was considered unnecessary with the appointment, in 1977, of a seasonal (May to October) NCC Countryside Conservation Officer based in the Aviemore Tourist Board Office. [62] Nature conservation was learning that it had to live alongside popular recreation in a region of expanding tourism activity.

The Glen Einich Water Scheme

The quickening pace of development and tourism provision on Speyside in the mid-1960s created infrastructure demands on its environs from the burgeoning centre of Aviemore. One of the most pressing concerns was the water supply to the town, and this had important ramifications for the NNR and recreation in the area. In 1964, Inverness County Council put forward a proposal to make use of Loch Einich on Rothiemurchus under a Spey Valley Water Scheme, in an attempt to run slightly ahead of all proposed development in the region and thus already "have under consideration the question of the provision of water supply for the large hotel and tourist development at Aviemore and Coylumbridge". The scheme, using Loch Einich as a source, would cost around £600,000 and offer the local communities about three times the amount of water they then received.[63] A central figure in the coming debate was the landowner, J.P. Grant, who had been initially approached earlier in 1964 by the County Water Engineer for permission to allow a survey to be made. Grant was caught in a dilemma because he was a supporter of regulated tourist development in the area, but also held a Nature Reserve Agreement with the NC. In discussions with the County Council, Grant asked that the route of the proposed pipeline should be brought near the northern shore of Loch an Eilein, to supply his proposed venture of a teashop as well as houses on the Feshie Bridge to Aviemore country road.[64] The estate was not to miss out on the bounty of piped water from its own loch, especially if others would fund the scheme.

The proposal caught the NC by surprise, as in fact did Grant's suggestion of a tearoom at Loch an Eilein. Land Agent John Arbuthnott was bemused:

> "Food for thought indeed. If Loch Einich is to be a water supply it should certainly never be the terminal of a dead-end road! What about this 'tea and refreshment' place at Loch-an-Eilein? Have we heard of this before?"[65]

NC headquarters felt that a line of communication had broken down, and that they had been left in the dark about development proposals that would affect the NNR. The Regional Officer in NE Scotland, J. Grant Roger, was reprimanded:

> "You must keep us better informed. I note from Colonel Grant's letter that he informed you of this project 'some time ago'. The Chairman is particularly anxious that no projected development in the Cairngorms should escape our notice or consideration at the earliest possible stage."[66]

By mid-December 1964, Inverness County Council via the SDD had decided to divide the projected scheme into distinct stages, with a first phase priced at £110,000, whereby the pipes would not be taken right up to Loch Einich, but instead a temporary intake would be made at the Am Beanaidh below its confluence with the Allt Druidh.[67]

This readjustment of the magnitude of the scheme seemed to satisfy the NC and they rapidly gave formal agreement to the interim project (in January 1965), but reserved their position as regards the entire project. At no stage was any mention made by the NC that they felt the scheme to be damaging to the integrity of the NNR, or that nature conservation values were having to accommodate an intrusion into an NNR because of new resource infrastructure demands from the neighbouring tourism industry. Work began on phase one of the Einich Water Scheme in 1966 and the whole project was finished by 1975. The pipeline carrying the water was buried to a depth of one metre and was identified with concrete surface markers. The extraction pipeline ran six miles down the glen to heading tanks, where pressure was built up to push the water onwards. Over the late 1970s and 1980s the scheme was dogged with structural and pressure problems and the NCC found the whole situation to be intolerable. However, in any proposed new work on the pipeline, the water authorities have played on the strength of their legislation to act in the public interest above legislation promoting nature reserves.[68]

An Overview

The creation of National Nature Reserves (NNRs) was a unique designation held by the Nature Conservancy (NC) alone. The reserves were set up before Sites of Special Scientific Interest (SSSIs) were given any teeth, and the NC in the years after 1949 was looking for representative sites to reflect a broad range of habitats in the UK. There were two goals in these early years when rapid site acquisition was to the fore, namely, to preserve fauna and flora on the NNR and to conduct scientific research.[69] In the late 1940s there was a real concern amongst ecologists that the best examples of wild Britain would not survive long into the 1950s, indeed there had been some attrition in the quality of certain nominated nature reserves over the 1940s, as the political nature reserves debate matured. Different NNR acquisition philosophies developed in England and Scotland. Where nature and people were clearly separated in England, more smaller sites were acquired. In remote rural Scotland, the NC chose much larger sites. Scottish NNRs have always needed to support both human and natural communities (but often were unable to do this), and for a site designation to work the NC/NCC had to rely on the willingness of local communities, landowners and other landuse interests to be a part of the conservation scheme. The key issue was ownership of the land. If the NC purchased and thus owned the NNR then they were able to undertake all the scientific and management projects they wished. However, if they had to enter into Nature Reserve Agreements with landowners to create the NNR, their presence was weakened from the outset. Although NRAs were never intended to be a major method by which the Nature Conservancy could acquire sites, they did enable the NC (especially in Scotland) to obtain an enormous acreage on the cheap for nature conservation interests in the countryside. Additionally, estateowners in Scotland seemed willing to come into NRA schemes with the NC, especially as landowning, farming and forestry interests were so well represented on the NC Scottish Committee (in the quota nominated by the Scottish Office), and within the NC operational staff in Edinburgh, some of whom (John Berry, A.B. Duncan and J.C. Arbuthnott) often negotiated the terms of NRA agreements with owners and the SLF. Certainly, in the 1950s the NC took a very hesitant, at times apologetic line with landowners; a booklet of 1954 explaining the role of NNRs was little more than an apologia to farmers and landed interest.[70] The NC/NCC owned only a small part of the Cairngorms NNR and it is apparent that, under the existing agreements with landowners, neither body was able to deliver a sustainable future for the visions and objectives inherent in the original reserve designation. Endless discussion and debate with landowners slowed down policy initiatives enormously after 1954. For the NC/NCC real strength over the wise management of the NNR depended on their ownership of it, or at least substantial powers to ensure good, sympathetic management practice for nature conservation by the landowners through the voluntary principle.[71] However, in 1954 the NC could not be blamed for embarking down the road of Nature Reserve Agreements with landowners, as this was the only option open to them, and it was the first time in Scotland that such agreements had been tried. The Swedish biologist Kai Curry-Lindahl examined the issue of statutory powers of compulsory purchase held by the NC/NCC in Great Britain and concluded (in 1974) that they had been wise to avoid utilising this power. Had they done so, few NNRs would have been established. Indeed, in 1954 it was politically impractical for the NC to invoke compulsory purchase of land in the Cairngorms. However, by 1988 Curry-Lindahl had changed his mind, and now cited the Cairngorms NNR as an example of a situation "where the ultimate line of defence has to be put in action", and compulsory acquisition should occur to protect such a valuable area. He concluded by stating that it must now be desirable that the largest and most important NNRs in Great Britain "could be taken over entirely as soon as possible by a single authority such as the NCC". Only then would the long-term interests of nature conservation be best served.[72]

As they stood, we do know that the Nature Reserve Agreements left all traditional sporting estate management in the hands of the landowners. The agreements gave the NC/NCC only limited rights on the NNR, allowing them to appoint wardens, to carry out and control scientific research and to erect reserve signs. There were some restrictions imposed on landowners (for which compensation was given) as regards muirburn, the use of fertiliser and the shooting of pest or game species: this last condition established a contentious protection zone for ptarmigan on Rothiemurchus. In the wider scheme of things the NC/NCC had few powers to control forestry operations or the culling of red deer on the NNR, and estates that chose to pursue purely game or forest management policies were not willing to abandon these rights. If a landowner wished to clear-fell some native pinewoods on his estate within the NNR for profit (as J.P. Grant of Rothiemurchus sought to do with 1255 cubic metres over 1980/81) then, under the NRA agreement, the NCC had just 14 days in which to respond by offering to purchase the standing timber (through difficult emergency access to funds, by claiming a national conservation interest in the land). The NRA agreements meant that landowners could effectively blackmail the NC/NCC, as happened on many SSSIs after the 1981 Wildlife and Countryside Act.[73] However, the NC/NCC did not lead by example. They managed the land that they owned at Invereshie-Inshriach (12% of the NNR) as a traditional sporting estate, and Dick Balharry of SNH has spoken of how the first NNR wardens were selected from a gamekeeping background so as to consolidate NC/NCC control of stalking rights and venison sales over the period 1954–1976; this must be seen as a failure in the pure conservation management of a high profile NNR.[74] Indeed, the Cairngorms NNR has not lived up to what the public would expect of a nature reserve, principally because of the NC/NCC's lack of control over the issue of overgrazing by deer and sheep. The damage done to native pinewoods on Mar and in Glen Feshie has been substantial, and continued unchecked after 1954, made worse by the estates' willingness to put out winter feed for red deer (often well into the summer months). It is worth recalling that as early as August 1946, the Scottish National Parks Committee warned that the deer population of the Highlands was "probably twice as high as it should be".[75] However, on Rothiemurchus, natural regeneration has been locally quite good. Along with traditional sporting management have come bulldozed estate access tracks into the heart of the NNR and the fragile Arctic plateau ecosystem; this was particularly evident in the late 1960s and early 1970s in Glen Feshie and up onto Moine Mhor. Other constraints on management for nature conservation have come from the statutory rights of other bodies: most importantly, of the water authorities in Glen Einich, and the FC's own agreements with landowners – which resulted in the planting of alien conifers in Glen Feshie over the 1970s under a Forestry Dedication Scheme.

The worst human impact has been damage to vegetation, soil erosion and the widening of footpaths, and some disturbance to breeding birds caused by dogs off the lead. The most damage to wildlife is often done by those who cherish it the most: amateur naturalists, birdwatchers and photographers tend to stray well off footpaths onto the sensitive plateau and so disturb breeding birds on the nest or trample rare upland plants.[76] Research has proved that dotterel *Charadrius morinellus* have suffered little from easier human access onto the Cairngorm high tops, but the ptarmigan *Lagopus mutus* has failed as a breeding bird near the ski area, due to disturbance, to birds being killed by flying into ski-tows and to egg predation by gulls *Larus spp* and crows *Corvus spp* attracted up the mountains by human refuse. There have been winners and losers amongst the wildlife of the Cairngorms; the snow bunting *Plectrophenax nivalis* has done well as a breeding bird on Cairn Gorm over the 1970s and 1980s, due to our propensity to drop scraps of food.[77] In the forests below, recreational disturbance and fatal collisions with deer fencing have led to a substantial decline in capercaillie *Tetrao urogallus* numbers. Recreational development around the edges of the Cairngorms NNR (and within it, at Rothiemurchus) has proved unstoppable; short of a 'no go' policy which would have been politically unpalatable in the 1960s and after, there has been little that the NC/NCC could do, save to attempt to steer visitors away from the most sensitive nature conservation sites. In Spring 1977, the NCC fought off a planning application for a helicopter service on Cairn Gorm, as they had earlier strictly regulated flights by the BBC and NTS over St Kilda and Rhum, to protect breeding seabirds and the white-tailed (sea) eagle *Haliaeetus albicilla* reintroduction project from continuous disturbance.[78] It truly was a stroke of bad luck for the NC/NCC that having established the NNR in 1954, just ten years later it sat directly alongside the remarkable development of Aviemore and the Spey Valley into Britain's only year-round holiday resort. Perhaps, though, they should have better anticipated this, and had a contingency plan to hand before the mid-1960s. As it was, the sterilisation and restriction that NNR status was perceived to bring to the countryside, proved incompatible with the mass tourism, regional economic regeneration and local industrial development that government saw as the way to solve the economic and social ills of the 1960s 'Highland Problem'. By the 1970s, this confrontation of landuse interests led directly to the adversarial relationship between developers/planners and conservationists in the Highlands. Nature conservation was seen as an impediment to landuse change, and was locally viewed as an 'imposed' landuse, forced on remote rural areas by scientists in London or Edinburgh.

Adam Watson has outlined how the potential of the NNR has not been achieved due to a lack of long-term scientific field work and enormous gaps in the research programme, concluding that quality "research must underlie conservation policy". He presents an exhaustive list of work that should have been done on the NNR.[79] However, with the division of the Nature Conservancy (in 1973) into the Nature Conservancy Council (which would acquire and manage nature reserves as well as having a promotional and educational function) and the Institute of Terrestrial Ecology (which would undertake the bulk of ecological research), there has been less emphasis on science in nature conservation management in Britain. The loss of this research function was more crucial in Scotland, as upland conservation issues such as grouse and deer, by their very nature are complex intertwined ecological and land management problems. The bulk of the NCC's work has been on habitat management and visitor management, and this is certainly true of the Cairngorms NNR. Under the NC in the 1950s and 1960s some research work was neglected because of a lack of staff and research experience, despite the NNR being founded on the cornerstone of pioneering scientific research in various subjects.

The importance of the Cairngorm mountains and forests as a biological site has never been in doubt. Derek Ratcliffe (NCC Chief Scientist 1973–1989) best articulated this in 1977 by listing 39,200 hectares of the Cairngorms across three counties as a Grade I nature conservation site of international importance.[80] There have, of course, been other nature reserves/site designations close to the central Cairngorms and Spey Valley, most importantly in the Scottish Wildlife Trust Pass of Ryvoan reserve in 1976, the RSPB Insh Marshes Reserve in 1973, their Abernethy Reserve in the 1980s, and the Eastern Cairngorms SSSI in 1971. In 1964, Joe Eggeling wrote that we have both a national and personal responsibility to protect an area like the Cairngorms, but overall nature conservation values have generally appeared weak when directly challenged by other landuses. As Eggeling warned:

"Man's reach is in danger of exceeding his grasp, and nowhere is this more obvious than when he seeks to develop, use and abuse the land around him."[81]

This point about nature conservation values was brought out after Rawdon Goodier (NC Regional Officer for North Wales, Bangor) toured Eastern Scotland with J. Grant Roger in June 1969, before he was posted to Edinburgh. Goodier wrote on 18 June to J. Morton Boyd, then Assistant Director (Conservation) in Edinburgh, about the "possibilities and problems" offered by the Cairngorms NNR: "The management problems of all the other Reserves within the region seem quite simple and orthodox by comparison", he believed. He observed that the position of the NNR was both unique and challenging, set as it was within a much larger area of comparable value, and mainly held by NRAs with landowners. He felt it deserved very special treatment, and urged that a great deal of thought must be given to its possible future role in the wider region, when NC policies could so easily be affected by policymaking within other organisations in the area. Goodier had this to say about the East of Scotland:

"This is the part of Britain where it is still possible to consider that nature conservation could have a major role to play among the dominant landuses, both on its own account and also in conjunction with the use of the land for Forestry and Recreation."[82]

Morton Boyd's frank reply to these initial observations by Rawdon Goodier, is worthy of reproduction in full, and concludes this chapter well:

"The Cairngorms gives you the best example of how comparatively feeble the Conservancy's impact has been within a large development area in which nature conservation, if not playing a dominant role, is a concept in common usage by the planners and managers of the land. The dominance of nature conservation will be in many ways proportionate to the massiveness of the personalities promoting nature conservation in the Cairngorms. The closer you come to study the situation, however, the more you will come to realise that unless we are supermen, it will take more than an organisation of our size to create and sustain the dominance of conservation."[83]

Notes to Chapter 10

1   F.H.W. Green was right. The archives of the Red Deer Commission (RDC) are held in the Scottish Record Office (SRO), Edinburgh at RDC. See SRO: RDC 1-1, The Red Deer Commission was formally constituted on 1 October 1959 under the Deer (Scotland) Act of 1959. The headquarters were located at Elm Park, Island Bank Road, Inverness.

2   Achantoul SNH, memo from F.H.W. Green, NC Aviemore to the Nature Conservancy – Scottish Committee, dated 20 March 1959 and 1 June 1959.

3   Achantoul SNH, Memo from Miss P.M. Read, NC London to F.H.W. Green, NC Aviemore, dated 17 June 1959.

4   Raymond Eagle, *Seton Gordon – The Life and Times of a Highland Gentleman* (Lochar Publ., Moffat, 1991), p. 93.

5   Achantoul SNH, Office note, 'Speyside Field Station', dated 7 July 1959.

6   Achantoul SNH, Minutes of the joint meeting of the Nature Conservancy and the Nature Conservancy – Scottish Committee, dated 24 July 1959, Item 5, 'Speyside Field Station'. Also in memo from T. Sexton, Executive Officer, NC London, to F.H.W. Green, NC Aviemore, dated 29 July 1959.

7   J.C. Arbuthnott and J.G. Roger, 'Management Plan', 1958, *loc. cit.*; J.G. Roger and E.M. Matthew, 'Management Plan – Cairngorms National Nature Reserve', First Revision 1967–1971, compiled 1967.

8   J.C. Arbuthnott and J.G. Roger, *ibid.*, pp. 3, 19.

9   G. Manley, 'Meteorological Observations on Royal Deeside', *Weather*, Vol. 23, 1978, pp. 457–459.

10 M.W. Dybeck and F.H.W. Green, 'The Cairngorms Weather Survey, 1953', *Weather*, Vol. 10, 1955, pp. 41–48.

11 F.H.W. Green, 'Climatological Work in the Nature Conservancy', *Weather*, Vol. 10, 1955, pp. 233–236; Frank D.N. Spaven, 'Obituary: F.H.W. Green', *Scottish Geographical Magazine*, Vol. 99, No. 2, September 1983, p. 120. Green had served

as a meteorologist in World War II with the RNVR. He was known in the NC for his characteristic blend, "of rigorous scientific discipline in tackling a specific regional problem with illuminating its practical outcome by inter-regional comparison". He died in early 1983.

12 J.S. Barton, 'Wind and Weather on Cairn Gorm Summit', *The Scottish Mountaineering Club Journal*, Vol. 33, No. 175, 1984, pp. 52–56.

13 Anon., 'The Future of Reindeer in Scotland', *Nature*, Vol. 179, No. 4572, 15 June 1957, pp. 1233–1234.

14 SRO: SNH 1-1, Minutes of the meeting of the Nature Conservancy – Scottish Committee, Edinburgh, 25 September 1952.

15 SRO: SNH 1-1, Minutes of the meeting of the Nature Conservancy – Scottish Committee, Edinburgh, 28 May 1953.

16 SRO: SNH 1-1, Minutes of the meeting of the Nature Conservancy – Scottish Committee, Edinburgh, 21 January 1954.

17 Achantoul SNH, John Forsyth, NC Aviemore, 'Report for March 1965 – Reindeer', dated 16 April 1965.

18 SRO: SNH 1-1, Minutes of the meeting of the Nature Conservancy – Scottish Committee, Edinburgh, 5 November 1953; J.C. Arbuthnott and J.G. Roger, 'Management Plan', 1958, *loc. cit.*, pp. 19–20; NC, *Report of the Nature Conservancy for the Year Ended 30th September 1959* (HMSO, London, 1959), pp. 4–8.

19 SRO: SNH 1-2, Minutes of the meeting of the Nature Conservancy – Scottish Committee, Edinburgh, 24 January 1957.

20 Achantoul SNH, Memo from J. Grant Roger, NC Edinburgh to J.C. Arbuthnott, NC Land Agent, dated 21 March 1956, 'Experimental Fencing in Glen Derry – Some Details of Requirements and Aims'.

21 Achantoul SNH, NC Internal memos from D.N. McVean, dated 5 June 1956 and 1 October 1956, relating to visits to Cairngorms NNR during May and September 1956.

22 Achantoul SNH, NC Internal memo from D.N. McVean, dated 24 March 1959, relating to visit to Cairngorms NNR during March 1959.

23 Achantoul SNH, Letter from Kenneth M. Wallace, NC Aviemore, to J. Eggeling, J.G. Roger and A. MacDonald, NC Edinburgh and Aviemore, dated 1 June 1961.

24 Achantoul SNH, NC Internal memo, from D.N. McVean to J.G. Roger, dated 10 May 1963, 'History of pine sowings in Glen Einich experimental plot'; D.N. McVean, 'Ecology of Scots Pine in the Scottish Highlands', *Journal of Ecology*, Vol. 51, No. 3, November 1963, pp. 671–686; H.M. Steven and A. Carlisle, *The Native Pinewoods of Scotland* (Oliver and Boyd, Edinburgh, 1959); J.G. Roger and E.M. Matthew, 'Management Plan', 1967, *loc. cit.*, pp. 41–44.

25 In SRO: SNH 5-10, Papers submitted to the NCC Scottish Advisory Committee, Edinburgh. See debate over 'Rothiemurchus Pinewoods' 23 January 1981, and paper 'Native Pinewood Conservation- Rothiemurchus'.

26 NC, *Report of the Nature Conservancy for the Year Ended 30th September 1963* (HMSO, London, 1963), pp. 42–43; Achantoul SNH, 'Notes for the Press Conference given by the Scottish Committee of the Nature Conservancy on Publication of 1963 Annual Report', Press Office, St. Andrew's House, Edinburgh, dated 4 December 1963.

27 SRO: SNH 1-2, Minutes of the joint meeting of the NC and NC Scottish Committees, 28 April 1966.

28 See the Scottish Office minute sheets and comments, letters and communications held in SRO: DD12/892.

29 Anon., 'The Cairngorms National Nature Reserve', *Cairngorm Club Journal*, Vol. 17, No. 93, 1968, p. 278; Achantoul SNH, 'Cairngorms NNR – Reserve Agreements', Agreement between Major George Seton Wills/David Seton Wills of Ramsbury, Marlborough, Wiltshire and of Inchrory Lodge, Tomintoul and the Natural Environment Research Council, dated 14 April 1966, registered 21 September 1966; Achantoul SNH, NC Press Release – Nature Reserves, no date, but after 1966.

30 SRO: SNH 1-3, Minutes of the joint meeting of the Nature Conservancy and the Nature Conservancy – Scottish Committee, London, 28 January 1971.

31 Dick Balharry, 'History of the Cairngorms NNR', *loc. cit.*, pp. 10–11.

32 Papers of J. Morton Boyd at ms38449/Box File 9. Letter from Boyd to R.E. Boote (Director NCC, London), Sir David Montgomery, Prof F.G.T. Holliday, dated 20 September 1977 regarding 'Policy Document Discussions with Lord Dulverton.'

33 Papers of J. Morton Boyd at ms38449/Box File 9. Letter from Boyd to R.E. Boote, NCC London, dated 1 November 1977.

34 SRO: SNH3-1, Minutes of NCC Scottish Advisory Committee meeting, Edinburgh, 17 January 1978. See discussion on Cairngorms NNR, Management Plan- Second Revision, Management Policies.

35 SRO: SNH3-1, Minutes of NCC Scottish Advisory Committee meeting, Edinburgh, 25 April 1979. See debate on Cairngorms NNR- Statement of Policies.

36 NC, *Report of the Nature Conservancy for the year Ended 30th September 1959* (HMSO, London, 1959), pp. 45, 70–71.

37 NC, *A Short Review of Research in Scotland* (NC, Edinburgh, 1966), pp. 9-11.

38 R. Balharry, 'History of the Cairngorms NNR', *loc. cit.*, pp. 14–17; Achantoul SNH, Nature Conservancy – Scottish Committee, Cairngorms NNR – 6th Progress Report, 1964; Achantoul SNH, Nature Conservancy – Scottish Committee, Cairngorms NNR – 7th Progress Report, 1965.

39 SRO: SNH 1-2, Minutes of the meetings of the NC Scottish Committee, Edinburgh, 6 October 1966, and 17 April 1967.

40 D. McCowan/NC Edinburgh, 'Glen Feshie – Progress Report 1969–71, Range Ecology Research'. For Restricted Circulation.

41 SRO: SNH 1-3, Minutes of the joint meeting of the Nature Conservancy and Nature Conservancy – Scottish Committee, London, 18 July 1969.

42 Achantoul SNH, Proposal for Research at Glenfeshie, 'The Aims of Research and Development at Glenfeshie', dated June 1969.

43 J.G. Roger and E.M. Matthew, 'Management Plan', 1967, *loc. cit.*, p. 50.

44 J.C. Arbuthnott and J.G. Roger, 'Management Plan', 1958, *loc. cit.*, p. 25.

45 Achantoul SNH, 'General Report for Summer and Autumn 1960', by Archie MacDonald, Achnagoichan Cottage, Rothiemurchus, dated January 1961.

46 Achantoul SNH, 'Report for August 1962', by Archie MacDonald, Rothiemurchus.

47 Achantoul SNH, letter from J.G. Roger, NC Edinburgh, to Archie MacDonald, Rothiemurchus, dated September 1962.

48 Achantoul SNH, 'Monthly Report – August 1964', Sections on 'Visitors' and 'Removal of Campers', by John Forsyth, NC Aviemore.

49 Achantoul SNH, 'Monthly Report – July 1964', by John Forsyth, NC Aviemore.

50 Achantoul SNH, 'Monthly Report – October 1964', by Archie MacDonald, NC Rothiemurchus/Aviemore.

51 Achantoul SNH, Letter from Archie MacDonald, Kinakyle, NC Aviemore, to J.G. Roger, NC Edinburgh, dated 9 November 1964. The emphasis is in the original.

52 Achantoul SNH, NC memo, 'Public Facilities – Cairngorms NNR', by John Forsyth, Achnagoichan, Rothiemurchus to J.G. Roger, NC Edinburgh and A. MacDonald, NC Aviemore, dated 2 November 1964.

53 Achantoul SNH, 'Report, Cairngorms Nature Reserve – Rothiemurchus Section: notes on Visitors', by John Forsyth, Achnagoichan, Rothiemurchus, dated 5 December 1964.

54 Achantoul SNH, Letter from J.G. Roger, NC Edinburgh to F.H.W. Green, NC Aviemore, dated 3 December 1965, 'Pamphlet for Cairngorms NNR'. This visitor information leaflet was updated and expanded in 1978 and 1989 by the NCC. They reflected a distinctly more professional approach to visitor information services by the NCC, being well illustrated, educational as well as informative.

55 Achantoul SNH, numerous sources.

56 Achantoul SNH, Proposal, 'Cairngorms NNR – Achlean Nature Trail', from J.G. Roger and J. Eggeling, NC Edinburgh to K.M. Wallace, NC Aviemore, dated 5 July 1967.

57 Achantoul SNH, numerous sources.

58 Dick Balharry, *pers. comm.*, and Interview, dated 23 June 1995, Aviemore SNH office.

59 Achantoul SNH, 'General Report – June 1969', by D.B. Holland, NC Aviemore.

60 Achantoul SNH, Letter from Ted Hammond, NC Aviemore, to J.G. Roger, NC Edinburgh, dated 9 September 1969, 'Information Service/Summer (Seasonal) Wardening Service'.

61 J.G. Roger and E.M. Matthew, 'Management Plan – Cairngorms National Nature Reserve', 1967, *loc. cit.*, pp. 60–65.

62 Dick Balharry, 'History of the Cairngorms NNR', *loc. cit.*, p. 21. The post of NCC Countryside Conservation Officer existed from 1977 to 1982.

63 Achantoul SNH, Letter from F.J. Evans, Regional Planning Officer, Scottish Development Department, Edinburgh, to W.J. Eggeling, NC Edinburgh, dated 14 December 1964.

64 Achantoul SNH, Letter from J.P. Grant of Rothiemurchus, Rothiemurchus Estate to H.D.V. Forsyth, County Water Engineer, Inverness County Council, dated 26 July 1964.

65 Achantoul SNH, NC memo from J.C. Arbuthnott to J.G. Roger and W.J. Eggeling, NC Edinburgh, dated 27 July 1964.

66 Achantoul SNH, NC memo from J.C. Arbuthnott to J. Grant Roger, dated 28 July 1964. Underlining is in original.

67 Achantoul SNH, Letter from F.J. Evans, SDD Edinburgh, to W.J. Eggeling, NC Edinburgh, 14 December 1964.

68 David Carstairs, Aviemore SNH, *pers. comm.*

69 *The Nature Conservancy* (HMSO, London, 1950), pp. 2–3; Cyril Diver, 'The Work of the Nature Conservancy', *Transactions of the Royal Institution of Chartered Surveyors*, Vol. LXXXV, Pt. II, Session 1952/53, pp. 1–11.

70 NC, *Nature Reserves and Sites of Special Scientific Interest*, Information Leaflet No. 1 (HMSO, London, 1954).

71 Dick Balharry, *pers. comm.*

72 Kai Curry-Lindahl, 'The Cairngorms National Nature Reserve (NNR), the Foremost British Conservation Area of International Significance', in J.W.H. Conroy, A. Watson, A.R. Gunson, *Caring for the High Mountains– Conservation of the Cairngorms* (ITE/Centre for Scottish Studies, Aberdeen, 1990), pp. 108–119.

73 SRO:SNH 3-1, Minutes of the NCC Scottish Advisory Committee, 7 November 1980.

74 Dick Balharry, *pers. comm.*

75 This statement can be found at SRO: FC 9-2, 'Minutes of meeting of the Scottish National Parks Committee', Edinburgh, dated 27 August 1946.

76 Roy H. Dennis, *pers. comm.*, and author *pers. obs.*

77 Adam Watson and Robert Rae, 'Dotterel Numbers, Habitat and Breeding Success in Scotland', *Scottish Birds*, Vol. 14, No. 4, Winter 1987, pp. 191-198; Adam Watson, 'Human Induced Increases of Carrion Crows and gulls on Cairngorms plateaux', *Scottish Birds*, Vol. 18, No. 4, Winter 1996, pp. 205–213; Adam Watson, 'Dotterel *Charadrius morinellus* numbers in Relation to Human Impact in Scotland', *Biological Conservation*, Vol. 43, 1988, pp. 245–256; NCC, *Nature Conservation in the Cairngorms – Defence of the Northern Corries* (NCC, Edinburgh, no date, but presumably late 1980s); Adam Watson, 'Habitat Use by Snow Buntings in Scotland From Spring to Autumn', *Scottish Birds*, Vol. 19, No. 2, Winter 1997, pp. 105–113; Adam Watson, 'Bird and Mammal Numbers in Relation to Human Impact at Ski Lifts on Scottish Hills', *Journal of Applied Ecology*, Vol. 16, 1979, pp. 753–764.

78 The papers of J. Morton Boyd, ms 38449/Box File 9. See letters to R.E. Boote, Director NCC, London dated 17 February 1977, and 5 May 1977 on 'Helicopters on NNRs- A Policy Statement'.

79 Adam Watson, *Botanical Journal of Scotland*, 1996, *op. cit.*

80 Derek Ratcliffe (ed.), *A Nature Conservation Review – Volume II, Site Accounts* (Cambridge University Press, Cambridge, 1977), pp. 268–269; see also John Morton Boyd, 'Nature Conservation', *Proceedings of the Royal Society of Edinburgh*, Vol. 84B, 1983, pp. 295–336.

81 W.J. Eggeling, 'Nature Conservation in Scotland', *Transactions of the Royal Highland and Agricultural Society of Scotland*, Sixth Series, Vol. 8, 1964, pp. 1–27.

82 Papers of J. Morton Boyd at ms38449/Box File 9, Letter from Rawdon Goodier, NC North Wales, to J. Morton Boyd, NC Edinburgh, dated 18 June 1969. Underlining is in original.

83 Papers of J. Morton Boyd at ms38449/Box File 9, Letter from J.M. Boyd, NC Edinburgh, to Rawdon Goodier, NC Bangor, dated 19 June 1969.

11

Postscript

This 'Postscript' builds upon the original conclusions drawn from the individual chapters of the book and offers brief but broad-ranging conclusions on the overall history and development of nature conservation and recreation in the Cairngorms. 1999 saw the fiftieth anniversary of the 1949 National Parks and Access to the Countryside Act which established not only National Parks in England and Wales but also a Nature Conservancy (NC) with powers to create National and Local Nature Reserves. There has been too casual an acceptance in Great Britain that recreation and nature conservation are purely twentieth century phenomena, and this has led to ignorance of their importance before the 1949 Act, and a subsequent neglect of the role that history could have in guiding future policy for land-managers and policymakers. If we are ever fully to understand current landuse conflicts and attitudes in the UK, or indeed, Western Europe and North America, then it is critical to realise that the past holds the origins and has shaped the course of many of the bitter contemporary environmental and developmental debates in the countryside.

There have been a number of key players in the historical development of nature conservation and recreation in the Cairngorms. The Forestry Commission (FC), born in 1919 with a remit to boost Britain's strategic reserve of trees, have done little to forward the cause of nature conservation. They have, however, been wise and generous providers of recreational facilities at Glenmore from the second half of the 1940s, and their National Forest Park scheme, which made use of otherwise unplantable ground, has met with much public praise. This provision of a recreational playground in the heart of an upland ecosystem has been at a cost to any nature conservation ideals; the greatest losers have been the wading birds (greenshank *Tringa nebularia*, common sandpiper *Actitis hypoleucos*, ringed plover *Charadrius hiaticula*, curlew *Numenius arquata*, lapwing *Vanellus vanellus* and oystercatcher *Haematopus ostralegus*) which formerly bred around Loch Morlich during the twenty years after 1930, but were absent by the mid-1980s, following human disturbance from recreational pursuits on shore and loch, habitat destruction and egg-predation by scavenging carrion/hooded crows *Corvus corone corone/cornix*. No other loch shore in the

Cairngorms (not even Loch Insh) has been developed so extensively as Loch Morlich, and it is unlikely that such dramatic declines in breeding bird numbers will have occurred at other less disturbed Cairngorm area lochs. Historically, the Forestry Commission have too often played a role as a blocking organisation when confronted by conservation and recreation initiatives of others, and in the inter-war years sought themselves to be the virtual National Park authority in the UK. Only after 1992 at Glenmore, have they started to forward the cause of nature conservation in the Cairngorms, by establishing Regeneration and Restoration Zones in the forest to encourage at last natural regeneration and the sustainable management of Glenmore. This project marks the watershed between afforestation in its conventional mode, and a new benign type of forest policy.

The Cairngorm landowners have been important to the evolution of nature conservation and recreation across the nineteenth and twentieth centuries. The most striking examples of landuse conflict in this study relate to their concerted campaign of opposition to the establishment of a National Park in the Cairngorms in 1930/31 (no socialist government in London was going to have their estates!), and to a lesser degree to their opposition to the National Park ideal on an individual basis during the 1940s. Their eventual involvement in a Cairngorms National Nature Reserve scheme in the mid-1950s could be seen as an attempt on their part to support the lesser of two evils, especially as the Nature Conservancy appeared willing to offer financial compensation for their involvement in the scheme and would allow them to maintain a firm control over traditional sporting and land management rights. Indeed, by the mid-1950s many landowners were finding it financially difficult to run their estates and were short on estate personnel. A Nature Reserve Agreement with the NC not only gave them money, but also some control and use of wardening staff appointed by the NC to the National Nature Reserve in which their estates fell. John Berry (first Director of the Nature Conservancy in Scotland) has suggested that estate owners also came into the scheme because legal advisors to the Scottish Landowners' Federation had cleared the financial arrangements and declared the NC's negotiations as 'fair and just'. In a sense, these NRAs were a 'good deal' for some landowners.[1] From the 1960s, many of the landowners offered support to the governmental and philanthropic provision of wider recreational facilities in the Spey Valley, and this is especially true of the Grants of Rothiemurchus. In general, recreation has not benefited traditional landuses; indeed, in the second half of the nineteenth century, recreational/access/rights of way bodies had to negotiate (or fight) for the privilege of walking or climbing on mountain or moorland. The exception to this has been Rothiemurchus Estate. Here, there has been a tradition of coming to the estate that can be traced back to the 1770s at least, and this became more widespread over the course of the nineteenth century. There were squabbles over rights of way, principally fuelled by the Edinburgh-based Scottish Rights of Way Society who selected Rothiemurchus as the Highland backdrop for one of their most public campaigns, but consensus over recreational access to the estate began to be reached in the first half of the twentieth century. Nature conservation and recreation worked together most successfully at Rothiemurchus as early as the 1880s and 1890s, when visitors came to view the Loch an Eilein osprey *Pandion haliaetus* nest. This must be seen as a direct forerunner of the RSPB osprey watchpoint set up at Loch Garten in 1959, which also blended nature conservation with recreation. The traditional sporting estates of the Cairngorms still maintain a dominance over landuse in the area, but in recent times this has begun to crumble, with Mar Lodge Estate passing into the hands of the National Trust for Scotland in 1995. Rothiemurchus Estate still combines traditional sporting landuse with important recreational, nature conservation and environmental education provisions; Glen Feshie Estate remains as a traditional sporting estate.

Traditional sporting estates have contributed to the most serious obstacle to nature conservation and ecological restoration in the Cairngorms – the red deer *Cervus elaphus* overgrazing issue. The worst examples of damage to the upland and forest ecosystems have come from those landowners who have been unwilling to learn the lessons of the last thirty years. Overgrazing on Mar and in Glen Feshie over the nineteenth and early twentieth centuries, ensured that natural regeneration of native pinewoods was practically absent when the Nature Conservancy brought these two estates into the National Nature Reserve scheme in the 1950s and 1960s. There has been little or no improvement in that situation to the present day. Again, Rothiemurchus Estate was different. Single family ownership, and a deep social and economic tie to the health of the Rothiemurchus pinewoods over the past few centuries, ensured that natural regeneration levels of Scots pine, though variable, have been at least locally quite good in the modern era. The wave of popular recreation at Rothiemurchus from the 1960s onwards has not had an overtly detrimental effect on the flora and fauna of the estate, although the modern management problems of soil and footpath erosion are apparent in places.

It could be argued that, prior to the battles and public inquiries of the 1980s and 1990s over the Cairngorms, the landowners and developers had their own way. Full Nature Conservancy ownership of the Cairngorms National Nature Reserve would have forwarded the cause of nature conservation in the area, but the Nature Reserve Agreements with the landowners and the 'voluntary principle' meant that the NC could not compel the landowners to take action on behalf of nature conservation. In general, the NC in Scotland in the 1950s and 1960s declared some vast National Nature Reserves and staked a claim over substantial areas of land, a claim which they were never able to substantiate in the Cairngorms. Compared with the NC in England at the time, the Edinburgh-based office of the NC had poor finances and too few staff to manage effectively such large and remote nature reserves in the Highlands. As each year went by in the 1950s, the NC in Scotland declared more reserves, and the resource situation worsened relative to the area to be managed. However, the NC took the only step open to them in 1954, to secure the area as a nature reserve by entering into relatively weak Nature Reserve Agreements. Had they not done this, it it is perhaps reasonable to speculate that the area would probably be neither better nor worse than it is today. The fact that so large an area was declared an NNR so soon at least helps to establish that nature conservation has a strong moral claim to prior consideration as a landuse over the area so designated, now and in the future.

As it is, the loser in the twentieth century does appear to have been nature conservation; by the 1990s, recreation has emerged as a powerful landuse, especially when it is directly associated with the economic activity of tourism. Although both nature conservation and recreation evolved together from historic roots back in the eighteenth and nineteenth centuries, recreation has always been seen to benefit more people directly, and to lead to economic and social development by providing jobs and bringing in more people to the area. Nature conservation in the UK has not been seen to have an economic or financial benefit to local people, and the establishment of a nature reserve has often led to accusations of the sterilisation and waste of good farming or forestry land. The Cairngorms area provides an exception to this accepted wisdom, in the ospreys at Loch Garten. Here the RSPB Centre and nature reserve, hosting 1,923,638 visitors by the end of 1999, have demonstrated that nature conservation can provide money and local jobs, stimulating the creation of a zone of holiday cottages for let, B&B accommodation and small-scale service industries associated with tourism. This form of pioneering UK eco-tourism from the 1960s highlighted the link between recreation and a sustainable and clean environment. More interesting is the fact that it has built on the first popular aesthetic and admiring observations of ospreys (for their own intrinsic worth) made at Rothiemurchus Estate in the last two decades of the nineteenth century. A 'new' RSPB Osprey Centre was opened on 19 July 1999 by Jim Wallace MP (Deputy First Minister of Scotland), and is dedicated to George Waterston. National membership of the RSPB soared from 87,448 in 1971 to 1,011,000 in 2000.[2] Over Spring 2000, Professor Ian Levitt (Department of Historical and Critical Studies at the University of Central Lancashire) was engaged in a research project listing all the Scottish papers presented to the Cabinet in London from 1917 to 1966. His initial findings suggest that the majority of papers that dealt with 'environmental' topics were largely about exploitation, not preservation. He believes that only in the 1960s did nature conservation appear as a legitimate topic of Scottish concern, but this was paralleled by further attempts to exploit the countryside (mainly the Highlands) for tourism development, especially around Aviemore and the Cairngorms.[3]

It is timely to draw a comparison here between nature conservation and scenic conservation. Recreational development in the Cairngorms has been far less damaging to mountain birds, for example, than was first envisaged. It has brought millions of visitors to the area, especially after the skiing and holiday centre developments of the early 1960s, but the ecological damage has been restricted to vegetation and soil erosion at the most popular visitor locations. However, whilst there have been some attempts to protect wildlife in the area, there has been a substantial neglect of landscape conservation. Beauty in the British countryside has not enjoyed the same level of official protection as nature, and when a Countryside Commission for Scotland was created in the late 1960s it had a predominantly recreational management remit. Popular culture in the twentieth century (and back into the nineteenth century) has been far more interested in scenic beauty than in biodiversity, yet scenic conservation practice in the Cairngorms (and the UK) has been undervalued. Recreation had a dramatic effect on scenic conservation in the Cairngorms area, with the damage on the visual amenity of the region being perpetrated by the skiing infrastructure on Cairn Gorm, water sports centres and the Aviemore Mountain Resort complex. In June 1961, the mountaineer W.H. Murray was appointed by the National Trust for Scotland to undertake a landscape survey of the Highlands, to identify areas of outstanding natural beauty, to report on the distinguishing characteristics of these areas, and to assess change within them. His resulting publication, *Highland Landscape – A Survey* (1962), is one of the most important books of the twentieth century about rural Scotland; his findings form the basis of the National Scenic Areas today. Sadly, the NTS who commissioned the study saw the final report as little more than a recreational guide to the Highland counties; the Chairman of Council, the Earl of Wemyss and March believing that 'Murrays' would soon rank alongside 'Munros' and that "no able bodied person – resident or visitor – will be content until he or she has penetrated every one". In a succinct synopsis of the state of the Cairngorms in 1961/62, Bill Murray wrote of the loneliness of Loch Avon; the "unmitigated wildness" of Upper Glen Feshie; the "singular loveliness" of Rothiemurchus, and the "scene of devastation, like a World War 1 battlefield" where the Forestry Commission had ploughed for the planting of conifers at Glenmore and in Lower Glen Feshie. The appeal of the Cairngorm mountains was not an obvious one he admitted, but they held one distinctive quality, "a majesty great enough to cast a spell on man's mind". Murray's survey revealed that the face of the Highlands was changing greatly, and he blamed the Forestry Commission, hydro-electric projects, landowners, county councils, local authorities, industry and the fashion for new developments for mass recreation.

The new ski road, he felt, was an ugly scar on the north face of Cairn Gorm. Murray's survey remains a challenging and thought-provoking document 40 years on. His eloquent plea for an urgent recognition of the need for scenic conservation went unheeded in the 1960s and 1970s:

> "The ugliness that has grown up in so many of our towns arrived there insidiously, creeping in by degrees through lack of over-all direction, foresight, or control. The same situation is arising in the Scottish Highlands. The outstanding beauty of the Highland scene, which is one of the nation's great natural assets, has been haphazardly expended and no account kept. The wasting away of this asset is bound to continue and to accelerate..."[4]

The Cairngorms National Nature Reserve begins on Cairn Gorm just 450 metres from a ski-tow. The bulldozed estate tracks of traditional sporting estates (especially on Mar and Glen Feshie) have left ugly lines on the landscape, and the use of ATV vehicles by the estates has led to soil erosion and landslips. Plantation forestry has also contributed to a lessening of the scenic grandeur of the Cairngorms. Plans now to construct a funicular railway up Cairn Gorm will lead to further recreation-induced constructions on the mountain, which will continue to present the summer visitor to the area with a desperately ugly and contaminated view; winter snow seems to somewhat soften the visual impact of the ski road and ski-tows. There is much work still to be done on the history of countryside recreation if we are ever to understand the dynamics of modern rural Great Britain, especially with the dramatic increase in leisure as a human activity after World War II, and the impact that recreation can have as a competitive landuse.

Consideration of the intrinsic scenic beauty of the Cairngorms scene brings to mind the issue of 'wilderness', both here in the UK and in the USA. In the 1964 Wilderness Act, the 88th Congress defined (and legislated) for the promotion and protection of 'wilderness areas' within the USA. They were to be places untouched by human hands, where man was to be a transient visitor. The land was to be wholly undeveloped and was to be kept in its natural state. Of course, those areas were held for the nation by the Federal government.[5] Such a definition of wilderness would be utterly impractical in Great Britain, for a remote and beautiful Cairngorms glen is at best a semi-natural environment. It is not surprising that in the mid-1960s the USA government sought to define formally what wilderness should be, for the early designation of Yellowstone National Park in 1872 had established a firm link between the concept of wilderness and the American psyche. In Great Britain, and in Europe as a whole, wilderness is so far removed from our historical and cultural traditions that we have little understanding of what it should be in its purest form. Additionally, any thoughts of state-owned National Parks in Scotland aroused widespread hostility from the conservative forces of landed interest, and pro-development bodies, who all feared the nationalisation and subsequent sterilisation of the land. Had a National Park come to the Cairngorms in the 1950s instead of the establishment of the NNR, then it would probably have meant the importation of the English/Welsh National Park system which has resulted in little real nature conservation benefit. Had the Cairngorms National Park ideal come to fruition in the early 1930s, then control of it might have been given to a National Park Commission, to the Department of Agriculture, or perhaps even to the Forestry Commission. This, however, is counter-factual history and mere speculation on what might have happened. Such a National Park, if based on the American model would have been a recreational development. Both USA National Parks and the English National Parks of the Lake District and Peak District have suffered considerable erosion of their wilderness and scenic qualities in the decades after 1960. High population densities in the hinterlands of those two English National Parks (within an hour's drive away) have ensured high visitor numbers, bringing considerable management problems. In 1963 the Peak District National Park hosted 7m visitors; by 1995 this had soared to 22.5m visitors each year. Over 17m people reside within 60 miles of this NP, and 95% of visitors to the National Park come by car. The annual average daily traffic flow in the NP has risen from 3,000 vehicles in 1980 to 5,000 vehicles in 1995. Around 10% of footpaths in the Park are now unusable; the cost of footpath maintenance (3,000km of paths) has gone up by 200% since 1990. The Peak District is clearly being 'loved to death'. On reflection, a Cairngorms National Park would probably not have been subject to the same visitor numbers, due to its more remote location away from large centres of population, but it would still have been a popular National Park, attracting holidaymakers more than day-visitors.

With the election of a Labour government in May 1997, and the establishment of a devolved Scottish Parliament in May 1999, the National Park ideal has returned to the political scene. The ground rules for all of Scotland's proposed National Parks were provided in the National Parks (Scotland) Act of 2000, where plans to conserve and enhance the natural and cultural heritage of the areas sat alongside calls for the sustainable use of natural resources, the promotion of recreational facilities, and economic and social development for local communities. SNH was asked by Scottish Ministers to consult the people of Scotland on the details of the proposed Cairngorms National Park, and in particular on the area of the park and how it should be run. This consultation period was to be completed by April 2001. A Cairngorms National Park could become a reality in the first years of the twenty-first century, almost 75 years after it was first mooted.

The last century has pointed out the importance of nature conservation and recreation as landuses in the Cairngorms area, but time has not solved the question of the balance between them, nor how to achieve this balance along with a strengthening of the economic prosperity of the region, without which any future designation would not be sustainable in the long run.

Notes to Postscript

1   Dr John Berry of Tayfield, *pers.comm.*

2   Source: RSPB *Birds* magazine 1970–2000.

3   Letter, from Prof. Ian Levitt, Dept of Historical and Critical Studies, University of Central Lancashire, Preston, to Prof. TC Smout, University of St. Andrews, dated 8 March 2000.

4   W.H. Murray, *Highland Landscape – A Survey* (Aberdeen University Press/NTS, Aberdeen, April 1962). Murray's reconnaissance was funded from the NTS Mountainous Country Funds, money which had been anonymously donated by an NTS supporter and mountaineer. Bill Murray (1913–1996), eventually resigned from the NTS because he felt they were breaking the 'natural management' wishes of the NTS benefactor and mountaineer, Percy Unna. With family money, Unna set up the Mountainous Country Fund to acquire land for the NTS, who were to undertake "that the land be maintained in its primitive condition for all time with unrestricted access to the public." Unna died when out walking in December 1950.

5   In October and November 1994, I visited the Law School library at Cornell University, NY USA, where I was able to consult Acts of Congress relating to wilderness, wildlife and National Parks. The Act "to establish a National Wilderness Preservation System for the Permanent Good of the Whole People, and for Other Purposes" was made on 3 September 1964.

Bibliography

Primary Sources

Archives

Archives of the Grants of Rothiemurchus, privately held at the Doune of Rothiemurchus, by Aviemore, Inverness-shire, but catalogued in the Scottish Record Office (SRO), Edinburgh at NRA(S) 102.

Archives of The Mackintosh of Mackintosh held in the Scottish Record Office (SRO), Edinburgh at GD 176.

Archives of the Scottish Landowners' Federation (SLF) held in the Scottish Record Office (SRO), Edinburgh at GD 325.

Archives of the Scottish Rights of Way Society (SRoWS) held in the Scottish Record Office (SRO), Edinburgh at GD 335.

Archives of the Scottish Development Department (SDD) held in the Scottish Record Office (SRO), Edinburgh at DD.

Archives of the Scottish Home and Health Department held in the Scottish Record Office (SRO), Edinburgh at HH.

Archives of the Department of Agriculture and Fisheries for Scotland held in the Scottish Record Office (SRO), Edinburgh at AF.

Archives of the Highlands and Islands Development Board (HIDB) held in the Scottish Record Office (SRO), Edinburgh at HDB.

Archives of the Forestry Commission (FC) held in the Scottish Record Office (SRO), Edinburgh at FC.

Archives of the Aviemore Station Hotel Company held in the Scottish Record Office (SRO), Edinburgh at GD 387/9. Formerly held in SRO at NRA(S) 3017.

Archives of the Doune of Rothiemurchus Hotel held in the Scottish Record Office (SRO), Edinburgh at GD 387/11.

Archives of the National Trust for Scotland (NTS), privately held at 28 Charlotte Square, Edinburgh as NTS.

Archives of the Royal Society for the Protection of Birds (RSPB), privately held at The Lodge, Sandy, Bedfordshire as RSPB.

Archives of the Nature Conservancy in Scotland (NC) and the Nature Conservancy Council in Scotland (NCC) held in the Scottish Record Office (SRO), Edinburgh at SNH.

Archives of the Nature Conservancy (NC) and the Nature Conservancy Council (NCC) for the Cairngorms area held at the Scottish Natural Heritage (SNH) Aviemore Office as Achantoul SNH. This archival deposit is uncatalogued and kept in some disarray.

Archives of Badenoch Printers, privately held by the Johnstone family, Kingussie but catalogued in the Scottish Record Office (SRO), Edinburgh at NRA(S) 2081.

Archives of the Red Deer Commission (RDC) held in the Scottish Record Office (SRO), Edinburgh at RDC.

Archives of the Association for the Preservation of Rural Scotland (APRS), privately held at Gladstone's Land (3rd floor), 483 Lawnmarket, Edinburgh as APRS.

Personal papers of Seton Gordon held in the National Library of Scotland (NLS), Edinburgh at Acc 5640, 7451, 9176, 9377, 9990, 10166.

Personal papers of J. Morton Boyd held in the University of St. Andrews Library, St. Andrews at ms 38449.

Archives of the Scottish Mountaineering Club (SMC) held in the National Library of Scotland (NLS), Edinburgh at Acc 11538.

Archives of the Mountaineering Council of Scotland (MCS), held in the Scottish Record Office (SRO), Edinburgh at GD 429.

Photographic and Map Archives

The Cairngorm Club Lantern Slides held in the University of Aberdeen Library, Aberdeen at ms 3405.

The Burn-Murdoch Stereoscopic Slides held in the Department of Archives and Manuscripts, University of Dundee, Dundee at ms 104.

The R.M. Adam Collection held in the Photographic Collection of the University of St. Andrews Library, St. Andrews.

The J.E.A. Steggall Collection held in the Photographic Collection of the University of St. Andrews Library, St. Andrews.

The Valentine Collection held in the Photographic Collection of the University of St. Andrews Library, St. Andrews.

Archival Maps and Plans

A number of original maps, plans and posters were consulted from the Register House Plans (RHP) Collection in the Scottish Record Office (SRO), Edinburgh. They are referenced as SRO: RHP.

Parliamentary Papers and Government Publications (HMSO)

A Programme of Highland Development. Cmd.7976. Scottish Home Department (HMSO, Edinburgh, 1950).

British Sessional Papers, House of Commons Bills – Public, 1884, 1884-1885, 1886, 1887, 1888, 1889, 1890, 1890-1891, 1892, 1897, 1898, 1900, 1908.

Cairngorms Working Party, *Common Sense and Sustainability: a Partnership for the Cairngorms* (HMSO Scottish Office, Edinburgh, 1992).

Cherry GE, *Environmental Planning 1939–1969, Volume II: National Parks and Recreation in the Countryside* (HMSO, London, 1975).

Conservation of Nature in England and Wales. Cmd.7122, Report of the Wild Life Conservation Special Committee (HMSO, London, 1947).

Edlin HL (ed), *Forestry Commission Guide: Argyll Forest Park* (HMSO, Edinburgh, fifth edition 1976). First published in 1939.

Edlin HL, *Forestry in Great Britain – A Review of Progress* (FC, London, May 1964).

Edlin HL (ed), *Forests of North-East Scotland* (HMSO, Edinburgh, 1976).

FC, *Post-War Forest Policy – Report by HM Forestry Commissioners.* Cmd.6447 (HMSO, London, 1943).

FC, *Report of the National Forest Park Committee – Glentrool* (HMSO, London, 1943).

FC, *Report of the National Forest Park Committee – Forest of Dean* (HMSO, London, 1938).

FC, *Forestry Commission Byelaws 1971.* No.997 (HMSO, London, 1971).

Hansard Parliamentary Debates, III Series (Feb–Mar 1884), IV Series (May–June 1892), IV Series (May 1900), IV Series (May 1908), IV Series (May–June 1908).

Land Use in the Highlands and Islands. Report by The Advisory Panel on the Highlands and Islands (HMSO, Edinburgh, 1964).

Mutch WES, *Public Recreation in National Forests: A Factual Survey* (HMSO, London, 1968).

National Parks in England and Wales – Report by John Dower. Cmd.6628 (HMSO, London, 1945).

National Parks – A Scottish Survey. Cmd.6631. Report by Scottish National Parks Survey Committee (HMSO, Edinburgh, 1945).

National Parks and the Conservation of Nature in Scotland. Cmd.7235. Report by the Scottish National Parks Committee and the Scottish Wild Life Conservation Committee (HMSO, Edinburgh, 1947).

National Parks and Access to the Countryside (HMSO, London, no date, presumably c. 1950).

Nature Reserves in Scotland. Final Report by the Scottish National Parks Committee and the Scottish Wild Life Conservation Committee. Cmd.7814 (HMSO, Edinburgh, 1949).

NC, *Nature Reserves and Sites of Special Scientific Interest.* Information Leaflet No.1 (HMSO, London, 1954).

Report of the National Park Committee. Cmd.3851 (HMSO, London, April 1931).

Report of the Committee on Land Utilisation in Rural Areas. Cmd.6378 (HMSO, London, 1942).

Report of the Committee on Hydro-Electric Development in Scotland. Cmd.6406. The Scottish Office (HMSO, Edinburgh, 1942).

Report of the National Parks Committee (England and Wales). Cmd.7121 (HMSO, London, 1947).

Report of the Departmental Committee To Enquire and Report with Regard to Lands in Scotland Used as Deer Forests. Cmd.1636 (HMSO, Edinburgh, 1922).

Scottish Development Department, *Cairngorm Area – Report of the Technical Group on the Cairngorm Area of the Eastern Highlands of Scotland* (HMSO, Edinburgh, 1967).

The Control of Land Use. Cmd.6537 (HMSO, London, 1944).

The Nature Conservancy (HMSO, London, 1950).

Walton J (ed), *National Forest Park Guides: Glen More – Cairngorms* (HMSO, Edinburgh, 1960).

Woodburn DA (ed), *Forestry Commission Guide: Glen More Forest Park-Cairngorms* (HMSO, Edinburgh, 1975).

Forestry, Agriculture and Marginal Land – A Report by the Natural Resources (Technical) Committee (HMSO, London, 1957).

Agency/Organisation Reports and Publications

Aitchison J, *The History of the Use of Film and Video by the Royal Society for the Protection of Birds, 1933–1989* (RSPB, Sandy, 1988/89).

APRS, *Annual Reports*

ASH Consulting Group, ITE, Ruth Tillyard, *Cairn Gorm Summit Tourism Management Programme* (ASH, Edinburgh, April 1994).

Aviemore and Spey Valley Tourist Board, *Area Profiles and Information Sheets*

British Ecological Society Nature Reserves Committee, 'Nature Conservation and Nature Reserves', *Journal of Ecology*, Volume 32, No.1, May 1944, pp.45–82.

Cairngorms Partnership, *The Cairngorms Assets – A Cairngorms Partnership Working Paper* (CPB, Grantown-on-Spey, 1996).

CCS, *A Park System for Scotland* (CCS, Perth, 1974).

CCS, *Scotland's Scenic Heritage* (CCS, Perth, 1978).

CCS, 'Cairngorm Recreation Survey – A Brief for Prospective Consultants', June 1987.

CCS, *The Mountain Areas of Scotland* (CCS, Perth, 1990).

CCS, *The Mountain Areas of Scotland (Conservation and Management) –A Report on Public Consultation* (CCS, Perth, February 1991).

Centre for Leisure Research, *Aviemore and Spey Valley Visitor Survey –A Report to HIDB* (CLR, Edinburgh, March 1989).

Countryside: Planning and Development in Scotland. Report by Study Group 9, 'Countryside in 1970' Conference, London (Royal Society of Arts/NC, London, 1965).

Curry-Lindahl K, *IUCN Survey of Northern and Western European National Parks and Equivalent Reserves* (United Nations Environment Programme, Nairobi, 1974).

FC, *Annual Reports*

FC Scotland, *Annual Reports*

FC, Map: *See Your Forests – Scotland* (FC, Spring 1980).

FC, *The Forestry Commission and Recreation. Policy and Procedure Paper No.2* (FC, Edinburgh, March 1980).

FC, *The Forestry Commission and Conservation. Policy and Procedure Paper No.4* (FC, Edinburgh, March 1980).

Francis Frith Collection plc, 'The Francis Frith Collection: Frith on Fiche, Brochure', Andover 1988.

Getz D, *The Impact of Tourism in Badenoch and Strathspey* (Report to HIDB and STB, dated May 1982).

Haldane RA, *A Short Review of the Protection Afforded to Wild Life in Scotland* (NC, Edinburgh, 1966).

Highlands and Islands Enterprise, *Economic Updates*

HIDB, *Area Profiles for Moray, Badenoch and Strathspey Local Enterprise Area.*

Mackay Consultants, *Cairngorm Visitor Survey – Summer 1987.* Report to CCS, HIDB, Highland Regional Council, NCC, September 1988.

Moira BLC, *Highland Landscape – A Report on Landscape Appraisal and Building in the Countryside.* Commissioned by Highland Regional Council, Inverness, 1979.

NC, *Annual Reports*

NC, *A Short Review of Research in Scotland* (NC, Edinburgh, 1966).

NCC, *Inventory of Ancient, Long-established and Semi-Natural Woodland: Badenoch and Strathspey* (NCC, Peterborough, 1987).

NCC, *Nature Conservation in the Cairngorms – Defence of the Northern Corries* (NCC, Edinburgh, no date but presumably late 1980s).

NTS, *Yearbooks*

NTS, Map: *Getting Off the Road – Speyside and Cairngorm* (Caledonian Press, Edinburgh, 1965).

NTS, 'The National Trust for Scotland and The Mar Lodge Estate – A Message for NTS Members' (Edinburgh, August 1995).

NTS, 'A Background Note for Newer Members' (Edinburgh, January 1995).

Rowan-Robinson J, Gordon WM, Reid CT, *Public Access to the Countryside – A Guide to the Law, Practice and Procedure in Scotland* (SNH/COSLA, Battleby, no date, c.1992).

RSFS, *Scottish Forestry Journal – Being the Transactions of the Royal Scottish Forestry Society*, Volume 50 (1936) and Volume 51 (1937).

RSPB, 'Film Hire Catalogue', no date, c. early 1970s.

RSPB, *Annual Reports*

Russell G, 'The National Trust for Scotland: The Formative Years, 1929–1939' (NTS, Edinburgh, 1990).

Save the Cairngorms Campaign, *Manifesto for the Cairngorms* (SCC, Inverness, 1992).

Save the Cairngorms Campaign and Scottish Wildlife and Countryside Link, *The Northern Corries: An Alternative Approach* (SCC/SWCL, Inverness and Perth, 1996).

Scottish Economic Committee, *Scotland's Industrial Future: The Case for Planned Development* (McCorqoudale and Co., Glasgow, 1939).

Scottish Economic Committee, *The Highlands and Islands of Scotland: A Review of the Economic Conditions with Recommendations for Improvement* (Robert Maclehose, Glasgow, 1938).

Scottish Rights of Way Society, Map: *The Cairngorm Passes* (SRoWS, Edinburgh, no date, post-1971).

Scottish Tourist Board, *Tourism and the Scottish Environment* (STB/Tourism and Environment Taskforce, June 1993).

SPNR, *Handbooks –Annual Reports*

Miscellaneous Unpublished Material

Arbuthnott JC and Roger JG, 'Management Plan: Cairngorms National Nature Reserve', Compiled February–December 1958.

Arnott JMS, 'James Bryce 1838–1922', Internal SNH essay. No date, c.1990s.

Balharry R, 'The History of the Cairngorms NNR – with particular reference to its Management', Personal Document, dated 31 July 1992.

Bassett P, 'A List of the Historical Records of the Royal Society for the Protection of Birds' August 1980.

Cairngorm Chairlift Company, Three documents entitled 'Cairngorm Chairlift Company – A Short History', 'Economic and Social Impact', 'Cairngorm Recreation Trust'. No date.

Clay A, 'History of the RSPB Film Department', Unpublished essay, 1974.

FC Stock Map: Inverness FD Map No.228, 'Queens Forest, Glenmore, Inverness'. Dated 1989, revised 1992. Issued by the Conservator, FC Inverness.

Forster AN, 'A Report on the Woodland Management Policy at Beinn Eighe National Nature Reserve, 1951–1970', Unpublished essay, completed 28 October 1991, for NCC Inverness.

'Glenmore Lodge: The Scottish Centre of Outdoor Training – Aviemore, Inverness-shire, Outdoor Training Programme', 1969.

Gordon J, 'History of the Insh Marshes Nature Reserve and Surrounding Area', Unpublished essay, dated 6 July 1994.

NC in Scotland, 'Bound Volume of Cairngorm Photographs by R.M. Adam, J.G. Roger, C.S. Elton', From period 1924–1958. Also with same views retaken from April–May 1996 by P.R. Moore, SNH Aviemore Office.

NC/McCowan D, 'Glen Feshie – Progress Report 1969–1971'. Range Ecology Research, NC Edinburgh, 1971.

Payne M, 'Countryside Planning and Development in Scotland 1962–1987: The National Parks Legacy', Unpublished essay, dated October 1989.

Roger JG, 'Management Plan: Craigellachie National Nature Reserve', Compiled October 1961.

Roger JG and Matthew EM, 'Management Plan: Cairngorms National Nature Reserve (First Revision, 1967–1971)', Compiled 1967.

Smart RN, 'Robert Moyes Adam', Unpublished short biography to accompany exhibition, May 1996.

'The Doune Of Rothiemurchus – Promotional Brochure', dated c.1935.

'The Doune of Rothiemurchus Hotel – Road Sign', dated 1938.

Watson RD, 'The History and Development of the Glenmore National Forest Park', Commissioned from Landwise Scotland by Save the Cairngorms Campaign, Inverness, dated January 1993.

Secondary Sources

Books

Alexander H, *The Cairngorms* (Scottish Mountaineering Club, Edinburgh, 1950). First published in 1928.

Allen DE, *The Naturalist in Britain – A Social History* (Allen Lane, London, 1976).

Anderson G and Anderson P, *Guide to the Highlands and Islands of Scotland Including Orkney and Zetland, Descriptive of their Scenery, Statistics, Antiquities, and Natural History. . .* (A and C Black, Edinburgh, 1850).

Automobile Association, *AA Hotels: England, Wales and Scotland* (AA, London, 1953).

Baikie J, *Things Seen in the Scottish Highlands* (Seeley, Service and Co., London, 1932).

Baker EA, *The Highlands With Rope and Rucksack* (HF and G Witherby, London, 1923).

Baker EA, *On Foot in the Highlands* (Alexander Maclehose, London, 1933).

Baxter C, *Experience Scotland – Cairngorm and Speyside* (Richard Drew, Glasgow, 1986)

Baxter C, *Scotland – The Nature of the Land: Photographs of National Nature Reserves in Scotland* (Colin Baxter Photography/NCC, Biggar, 1988).

Baxter C and Goodier R, *The Cairngorms – The Nature of the Land* (SNH/Colin Baxter Photography, Grantown-on-Spey, 1998).

Borthwick A, *Always A Little Further* (Eneas Mackay, Stirling, 1947).

Brander M, *The Hunting Instinct: The Development of Field Sports over the Ages* (Oliver and Boyd, Edinburgh, 1964).

Brander M, *A Hunt Around the Highlands – On the Trail of Colonel Thornton* (The Standfast Press, Gloucester, 1973). First published in 1961.

Brendon P, *Thomas Cook – 150 Years of Popular Tourism* (Secker and Warburg, London, 1992).

Brown J, *A Brief Account of a Tour of the Highlands of Perthshire, July 1818* (Ogle, Allardice and Thomson, Edinburgh, 1818).

Brown L, *Birds and I* (Michael Joseph, London, 1947).

Brown P and Waterston G, *The Return of the Osprey* (Collins, London, 1962).

Bulloch JM, *Sporting Visitors to Badenoch*. Highland Handbook V (Robert Carruthers, Inverness, 1931).

Burton JH, *The Cairngorm Mountains* (William Blackwood, Edinburgh, 1864).

Calderwood WL, *The Salmon Rivers and Lochs of Scotland* (Edward Arnold, London, 1909).

Campbell A, *The Grampians Desolate, A Poem* (Vernor and Hood, London, 1804).

Campbell A, *A Journey from Edinburgh Through Parts of North Britain; Containing Remarks on Scottish Landscape. . .* (John Stockdale, London, new edition in two volumes 1811). First published in 1802.

Caufield C, *Thorne Moors – With a Photographic Essay by Fay Goodwin* (Sumach Press, St. Albans, 1991).

Christian G, *While Some Trees Stand – Wild Life in our Vanishing Countryside* (Newnes, London, 1963).

Climie B, *History of the Scottish Orienteering Association* (SOA/private publication, Elgin, 1990).

Cockburn Lord H, *Circuit Journeys* (David Douglas, Edinburgh, 1888).

Collie W, *Memoirs of William Collie* (Sands and McDougall, Melbourne, Australia, 1908; photographic reprint by Highland Printers, Inverness, 1992).

Collinge WE, *The National Importance of Wild Birds* (RSPB Pamphlet, London, 1927).

Collis JS, *The Vision of Glory* (Cardinal/Sphere Books, London, 1989). First published in 1972.

Conroy JWH, Watson A, Gunson AR, *Caring for the High Mountains – Conservation of the Cairngorms* (ITE/Centre for Scottish Studies, Aberdeen, 1990).

Cook HK, *Over the Hills and Far Away: Three Centuries of Holidays* (George Allen and Unwin, London, 1949).

Coward TA, *The Birds of the British Isles and their Eggs* (Frederick Warne, London, 1930).

Cross E, *Short Walks In The Cairngorms* (Luath Press, Barr, 1994).

Cross E, *Walks In The Cairngorms – Near Aviemore* (Luath Press, Barr, 1992).

Cross E, *The Speyside Holiday Guide* (Luath Press, Barr, 1993).

Crumley J, *A High and Lonely Place– The Sanctuary and Plight of the Cairngorms* (Jonathan Cape, London, 1991).

Crumley J, *The Heart of the Cairngorms* (Colin Baxter Photography, Grantown-on-Spey, 1997).

Curry-Lindahl K, Watson A, Watson RD, *The Future of the Cairngorms* (The North East Mountain Trust, Aberdeen, 1982).

Darling FF, *Wild Life of Britain* (Collins, London, 1943).

Deal W, *A Guide to Forest Holidays in Great Britain and Ireland* (David and Charles, Newton Abbot, 1976).

Dennis M, *A View From The Croft* (Colin Baxter Photography, Lanark, 1990).

Dennis R, *Ospreys* (Colin Baxter Photography,Grantown-on Spey, 1992).

Dennis R, *The Birds of Badenoch and Strathspey* (Colin Baxter Photography, Grantown-on-Spey, 1995).

Dickson JH and Henderson DM (eds), *A Naturalist in the Highlands: James Robertson, His Life and Travels in Scotland, 1767–1771* (Scottish Academic Press, Edinburgh, 1994).

Dougall R, *In and Out of the Box* (Fontana, Glasgow, 1975).

Dougall R, *A Celebration of Birds* (Collins and Harvill, London, 1978).

Douglas RM, *The Scots Book* (EP Dutton, New York, 1935).

Duff D (ed), *Queen Victoria's Highland Journals* (Lomond Books, London, 1994).

Eagle R, *Seton Gordon – The Life and Times of a Highland Gentleman* (Lochar, Moffat, 1991).

Else R and McNeish C, *The Edge – One Hundred Years of Scottish Mountaineering* (BBC Books, London, 1994).

Evans D, *A History of Nature Conservation in Britain* (Routledge, London, 1997).

Firsoff VA, *The Cairngorms on Foot and Ski* (Robert Hall, London, 1949).

Firsoff VA, *On Ski in the Cairngorms* (W and R Chambers, Edinburgh, 1965).

Fladmark JM (ed), *Heritage – Conservation, Interpretation and Enterprise* (Donhead Publ., London, 1993).

Fraser H, *Amid the High Hills* (A and C Black, London, 1923).

Friday LE (ed), *Wicken Fen – the Making of a Wetland Nature Reserve* (Harley Books, Colchester, 1997).

Gilpin W, *Observations on the Highlands of Scotland* (Richmond Publ., Surrey, 1973). First published in 1789.

Glasgow Herald, *Motoring In Scotland – A Touring Guide* (George Outram, Glasgow, 1935).

'Glenmore'(pseud. Donald Shaw), *Highland Legends and Fugitive Pieces of Original Poetry* (John Lindsay, Edinburgh, 1869). First published in 1859.

Gordon S, *The Cairngorm Hills of Scotland* (Cassell, London, 1925).

Gordon S, *Days With the Golden Eagle* (Williams and Norgate, London 1927).

Grant E, *Abernethy Forest: Its People and Its Past* (The Arkleton Trust, Nethybridge, 1994).

Grant IF, *Along a Highland Road* (Shepheard-Walwyn Publ., London, 1980).

Grant of Rothiemurchus E, *Memoirs of a Highland Lady* (John Murray, London, 1898).

Grant of Rothiemurchus E, *Memoirs of a Highland Lady – Volumes I and II* (Canongate Classics, Edinburgh, 1992).

Gray A, *Legends of the Cairngorms* (Mainstream Publ, Edinburgh, 1987).

Gray A, *The Big Grey Man of Ben MacDhui* (Birlinn Ltd, Edinburgh, 1994).

Green D (ed), *Cobbett's Tour In Scotland, By William Cobbett, 1763–1835* (Aberdeen University Press, Aberdeen, 1984).

Haldane ARB, *The Drove Roads of Scotland* (Thomas Nelson, London, 1953).

Hammond N (ed), *RSPB Nature Reserves* (RSPB, Sandy, 1984).

Harley DC and Hanley ND, *Economic Benefit Estimates for Nature Reserves: Methods and Results*. Discussion Paper in Economics 89/6 (Department of Economics, University of Stirling, 1989).

Harris P, By Appointment: *The Story in Pictures of Royal Deeside and Balmoral* (The Press and Journal, Aberdeen, 1988).

Hart-Davis D, *Monarchs of the Glen – A History of Deer Stalking in the Scottish Highlands* (Jonathan Cape, London, 1978).

Harvie-Brown J and Buckley TE, *A Vertebrate Fauna of the Moray Basin – II Volumes* (David Douglas, Edinburgh, 1895).

Harvie-Brown J, *A Vertebrate Fauna of the Tay Basin and Strathmore* (David Douglas, Edinburgh, 1906).

Holloway S, *The Historical Atlas of Breeding Birds in Britain and Ireland, 1875–1900* (T and AD Poyser, London, 1996).

Hosking E and Lowes H (eds), *Masterpieces of Bird Photography* (Collins, London, 1947).

Hudson D, *Highland Deer Stalking* (The Crowood Press, Marlborough, 1989).

Humble BH, *On Scottish Hills* (Chapman and Hall, London, 1946).

Hume Brown P (ed), *Early Travellers in Scotland* (David Douglas, Edinburgh, 1891).

Hunter J, *On The Other Side Of Sorrow: Nature and People in the Scottish Highlands* (Mainstream, Edinburgh, 1995).

Jenkins D (ed), *Land Use in the River Spey Catchment* ACLU Symposium No. 1 (Aberdeen Centre for Land Use, Aberdeen, 1988).

Johnston JL, *Scotland's Nature in Trust– The NTS and its Wildland and Crofting Management* (Poyser Natural History/NTS, London, 1999).

Jolly W, *The Life of John Duncan, Scotch Weaver and Botanist* (Kegan Paul, Trench and Co., London, 1883).

Kerr J, *Old Grampian Highways* (The Atholl Experience, Blair Atholl, 1984).

Knox AE, *Autumns On The Spey* (John Van Voorst, London, 1872).

Lambert RA (ed), *Species History in Scotland: Introductions and Extinctions since the Ice Age* (Scottish Cultural Press, Edinburgh, 1998).

Lansdale MH, *Scotland– Historic and Romantic, Volume II* (HT Coates, Philadelphia PA, USA, 1902).

Lauder TD, *Highland Rambles, And Long Legends to Shorten the Way* (A and C Black, Edinburgh, 1837).

Lauder TD, *Scottish Rivers* (Edmonston and Douglas, Edinburgh, 1874).

Lightfoot J, *Flora Scotica– Volume II* (B White, London, 1777).

Linklater E, *The Lion and the Unicorn* (George Routledge and Sons, London, 1935).

Loader CM, *Cairngorm Adventure at Glenmore Lodge* (William Brown, Edinburgh, 1952).

Lynch M, *Scotland— A New History* (Pimlico, London, 1993).

McConnell J and Conroy JWH (eds), *Environmental History of the Cairngorms*, Special Issue of Botanical Journal of Scotland, Volume 48, Part 1 (Edinburgh University Press/BSS, Edinburgh, 1996).

McLean AC, *The Highlands and Islands of Scotland* (Crescent Books, New York, 1976).

McVean DN and Lockie JD, *Ecology and Land Use in Upland Scotland* (Edinburgh University Press, Edinburgh, 1969).

Macculloch JD, *A Description of the Scenery of Dunkeld and Blair in Atholl* (Joseph Mallett, London, 1823).

Macculloch JD, *The Highlands and Western Isles of Scotland, Containing Descriptions of their Scenery and Antiquities . . .* (Longman *et al*, London, 1824).

MacDonald JA, *The Burgh of Kingussie 1867–1967* (Kingussie Town Council, Badenoch, 1966).

Macdonald A and Macdonald P, *Granite and Green – Above NE Scotland* (Mainstream, Edinburgh, 1992).

MacEwen A and MacEwen M, *National Parks: Conservation or Cosmetics* (Allen and Unwin, London, 1982).

MacEwen A and MacEwen M, *Greenprints for the Countryside?: The Story of Britain's National Parks* (Allen and Unwin, London, 1987).

MacGillivray W, *The Natural History of Dee Side and Braemar* (Printed for private circulation by Bradbury and Evans, London, 1855).

MacGillivray W, *Descriptions of the Rapacious Birds of Great Britain* (Maclachlan and Stewart, Edinburgh, 1836).

MacGillivray W, *A History of the Molluscous Animals of the Counties of Aberdeen, Kincardine and Banff* (Cunningham and Mortimer, London, 1843).

Mackay D, *Scotland's Rural Land Use Agencies* (Scottish Cultural Press, Aberdeen, 1995).

Maclagan D, *Nugae Canorae Medicae: Lays by the Poet Laureate of the New Town Dispensary* (Thomas Constable, Edinburgh, 1850).

Macleod A (ed), *The Songs of Duncan Ban Macintyre* (Oliver and Boyd for the Scottish Gaelic Texts Society, Edinburgh, 1952).

Macmillan H, *Rothiemurchus* (JM Dent, London, 1907).

MacNally L, *Highland Deer Forest* (Pan Books, London, 1973).

Macpherson A, *Glimpses of Church and Social Life in the Highlands in Olden Times* (William Blackwood, Edinburgh, 1893).

Magnusson M and White G (eds), *The Nature of Scotland— Landscape, Wildlife and People* (Canongate/Scottish Post Office Board, Edinburgh, 1991).

Magnusson M, *Rum: Nature's Island* (Luath Press, Edinburgh, 1997).

Marren P, *England's National Nature Reserves* (English Nature/T and AD Poyser, London, 1994).

Marsh GP, *Man and Nature: Or Physical Geography as Modified By Human Action* (Sampson Low, London, 1864).

Marshall M, *The Travels of Tramp-Royal . . .* (WM Blackwood, Edinburgh, 1933).

Martin V and Inglis M (eds), *Wilderness, The Way Ahead* (Findhorn Press, Forres, 1984).

Marzaroli O, *One Man's World: Photographs 1955–1984* (Third Eye Centre and Glasgow District Libraries, Glasgow, 1984).

Mawman J, *An Excursion to the Highlands of Scotland, and the English Lakes, with Recollections, Descriptions and References to Historical Facts* (T Gillet, London, 1805).

Mitchell A, *Vacation Notes in Cromar, Burghhead and Strathspey* (Neill and Co., Edinburgh, 1875).

Mollison D (ed), *Sharing the Land* (John Muir Trust, Musselburgh, 1994).

Moore NW, *The Bird of Time: the Science and Politics of Nature Conservation* (Cambridge University Press, Cambridge, 1987).

Morton HV, *In Scotland Again* (Methuen, London, 1933).

Muir E, *Scottish Journey* (Mainstream, Edinburgh, 1996). First published in 1935.

Murray WH, *Highland Landscape–A Survey* (Aberdeen University Press/NTS, Aberdeen, 1962). Commissioned by NTS.

Murray of Kensington S, *A Companion and Useful Guide to the Beauties of Scotland . . . . to Which is added, A more Particular Description of Scotland, Especially that part of it Called the Highlands* (George Nicol, London, 1799).

Murray of Kensington S, *A Companion and Useful Guide to the Beauties in the Western Highlands of Scotland, And In the Hebrides . . . to Which is added, A Description of Part of the Main Land of Scotland* (W Bulmer, London, 1803).

Nethersole-Thompson D and Watson A, *The Cairngorms – Their Natural History and Scenery* (Collins, London,1974).

Nethersole-Thompson D and Watson A, *The Cairngorms – Their Natural History and Scenery* (Melven Press, Perth, II edition and enlarged 1981).

Nicol J, *Guide to the Geology of Scotland . . .* (Oliver and Boyd, Edinburgh, 1844).

Nicol J, *The Geology and Scenery of the North of Scotland: being two lectures given at the Philosophical Institution, Edinburgh* (Oliver and Boyd, Edinburgh, 1866).

Parke H, *Scottish Skiing Handbook* (Luath Press, Barr, 1989).

Peel JHB, *More Country Talk* (Robert Hale, London, 1973).

Plumb C, *Walking In the Grampians* (Alexander Maclehose, London, 1935).

Porter J and Porter M, *Missed Pictures– 22 Memories of the Lairig Ghru* (Way-Walkers Series, Inverness, 1991).

Poucher WA, *A Camera In The Cairngorms* (Chapman and Hall, London, 1947).

Quigley H, *The Face of Britain– The Highlands of Scotland* (BT Batsford, London, 1936).

Quigley H, *The Highlands of Scotland* (BT Batsford, London, 1949).

Ramsay P, *Revival of the Land: Creag Meagaidh National Nature Reserve* (SNH, Battleby, 1997).

Ratcliffe D, *A Nature Conservation Review– The Selection of Biological Sites of National Importance to Nature Conservation in Britain, Volume I* (Cambridge University Press, Cambridge, 1977).

Ratcliffe D, *A Nature Conservation Review– Site Accounts, Volume II* (Cambridge University Press, Cambridge, 1977).

Ritchie J, *The Influence of Man on Animal Life in Scotland* (Cambridge University Press, Cambridge, 1920).

Rothschild M and Marren P, *Rothschild's Reserves: Time and Fragile Nature* (Balaban/ Harley Books, Colchester, 1997).

Rowallan Lord (compiled by Lorn Macintyre), *The Autobiography of Lord Rowallan* (Paul Harris, Edinburgh, 1976).

RSPB (G Waterston and R Dennis), *Ospreys and Speyside Wildlife* (RSPB, Sandy, 1973).

Samstag T, *For Love of Birds– The Story of the RSPB* (RSPB, Sandy, 1988).

Scarlett MH, *In the Glens Where I Was Young* (Siskin, Milton of Moy, 1988).

Scott B, *Enjoying Wildlife: A Guide to RSPB Reserves* (RSPB, Sandy, 1994).

Scottish Omnibus Annual–1949 (Travel Press and Publicity Co., Edinburgh, 1949).

Scottish Wild Land Group, *Cairngorms at the Crossroads* (SWLG, Edinburgh, 1987).

Scroggie S, *Cairngorms Scene and Unseen* (Scottish Mountaineering Trust, Edinburgh, 1989).

Shairp JC (ed), *Dorothy Wordsworth: Recollections of a Tour Made in Scotland AD 1803* (Edmonston and Douglas, Edinburgh, 1874).

Sheail J, *Nature Conservation in Britain– the Formative Years* (HMSO, London, 1998).

Sheail J, *Nature in Trust – The History of Nature Conservation in Britain* (Blackie and Son, London, 1976).

Sheail J, *Rural Conservation in Inter-War Britain* (Clarendon Press, Oxford, 1981).

Sheail J, *Seventy-five Years in Ecology: The British Ecological Society* (Blackwell Scientific Publications, Oxford, 1987).

Sheail J, *Natural Environment Research Council– A History* (NERC, Swindon, 1992).

Shepherd N, *In the Cairngorms* (The Moray Press, Edinburgh, 1934).

Shortland M (ed), *Science and Nature– Essays in the History of the Environmental Sciences* (British Society for the History of Science/The Alden Press, Oxford, 1993).

Sim G, *The Vertebrate Fauna of Dee* (D Wyllie, Aberdeen, 1903).

Simms E, *A Natural History of Britain and Ireland* (JM Dent, London, 1979).

Sinton T, *The Poetry of Badenoch– Collected and Edited* (Northern Counties Publ., Inverness, 1906).

Smiles S, *Life of a Scotch Naturalist: Thomas Edward* (John Murray, London, 1876).

Smith R, *The Royal Glens* (John Donald, Edinburgh, 1990).

Smout TC, *The Highlands and the Roots of Green Consciousness, 1750–1990.* Occasional Paper No.1 (SNH, Battleby, 1993).

Smout TC (ed), *Scotland Since Prehistory – Natural Change and Human Impact* (Scottish Cultural Press, Aberdeen, 1993).

Smout TC (ed), *Scottish Woodland History* (Scottish Cultural Press, Edinburgh, 1997).

Smout TC and Lambert RA (eds), *Rothiemurchus: Nature and People on a Highland Estate, 1500–2000* (Scottish Cultural Press, Edinburgh, 1999).

Smout TC, *Nature Contested– Environmental History in Scotland and Northern England since 1600* (Edinburgh University Press, Edinburgh, 2000).

Somers R, *Letters from the Highlands: the Famine of 1847* (Simpkin, Marshall and Co., Glasgow, 1848).

St. John C, *Short Sketches of the Wild Sports and Natural History of the Highlands* (Ashford Press Publ, Southampton, 1986). First published in 1893.

Stamp D, *Nature Conservation in Britain* (Collins, London, 1969).

Stephenson T, *Forbidden Land– The Struggle for Access to Mountain and Moorland* (Manchester University Press, Manchester, 1989).

Steven HM and Carlisle A, *The Native Pinewoods of Scotland* (Oliver and Boyd, Edinburgh, 1959; reprint edition by Castlepoint Press, Dalbeattie, 1996).

Stevenson S and Morrison-Low AD (eds), *Scottish Photography – A Bibliography: 1839–1989* (Salvia Books, Edinburgh, 1990).

Stott L, *Robert Louis Stevenson and the Highlands and Islands of Scotland* (Creag Darach Publ., Milton-of-Aberfoyle, 1992).

Tansley AG, *Our Heritage of Wild Nature – A Plea for Organised Nature Conservation* (Cambridge University Press, Cambridge, 1945).

Taylor H, *A Claim on the Countryside– A History of the British Outdoor Movement* (Keele University Press, Edinburgh, 1997).

Taylor J (the Water Poet), *Early Prose and Poetical Works* (Thomas Morrison, Glasgow, 1888).

Taylor W, *Scot Easy– Travels of a Roads Scholar* (Max Reinhardt, London, 1955).

Tegner H, *A Naturalist on Speyside* (Geoffrey Bles, London, 1971).

Thom V, *Birds in Scotland* (T and AD Poyser, Calton, 1986).

Thompson F, *Discovering Speyside* (John Donald, Edinburgh, 1990).

Thompson F (ed), *Victorian and Edwardian Highlands from Old Photographs* (Tantallon Books, Edinburgh, 1989).

Thornton Colonel T, *A Sporting Tour Through the Northern Parts of England, and Great Parts of the Highlands of Scotland . . .* (James Swan, London, 1804).

Thornton Colonel T, *A Sporting Tour Through Various Parts of France in the Year 1802* (Longman *et al*, London, 1806).

Thornton Colonel T, *A Sporting Tour Through the Northern Parts of England, and Great Parts of the Highlands of Scotland* (Edward Arnold, London, 1896; for the Sportsman's Library).

Turnock D, *The Historical Geography of Scotland since 1707 – Geographical Aspects of Modernisation* (Cambridge University Press, Cambridge, 1982).

Vallance HA, *The Highland Railway* (David and Charles, Dawlish, 1963).

Ware EH, *Wing to Wing– Bird Watching Adventures at Home and Abroad with the RAF* (Paternoster, London, 1946).

Waterston G, *Ospreys in Speyside* (RSPB, Edinburgh, 1971).

Waterston G, *Ospreys in Scotland* (RSPB, Edinburgh, 1966).

Watson A and Conroy JWH (eds), *The Cairngorms – Planning Ahead* (Kincardine and Deeside District Council, Stonehaven, 1994).

Watt AS and Duffey E (eds), *The Scientific Management of Animal and Plant Communities for Conservation* (Blackwell Scientific Publ.,Oxford, 1971).

Whittington G (ed), *Fragile Environments: The Use and Management of Tentsmuir NNR, Fife* (Scottish Cultural Press, Edinburgh, 1996).

Wirth H (ed), *Nature Reserves in Europe* (Jupiter Books, London, 1981).

Wordsworth W, *A Guide Through the District of The Lakes, In the North of England, With a Description of The Scenery, for the Use of Tourists and Residents* (Hudson and Nicholson, Kendal, fifth edition 1835).

Youngson AJ, *Beyond the Highland Line – Three Journals of Travel in Eighteenth Century Scotland* (Collins, London, 1974).

Chapters and Journal Articles

Aitchison J, 'Birds on Film– The Work of the Film and Video Unit of the Royal Society for the Protection of Birds', *Image Technology*, December 1988, pp.454–456.

Aitken R, 'Stravagers and Marauders', *The Scottish Mountaineering Club Journal*, Volume 30, No.166, 1975, pp.351–357.

Alexander H, 'The Canadian Lumber Camps in the Cairngorms', *Cairngorm Club Journal*, Volume X, No.55, July 1920, pp.1–11.

An 'Old Tramp'(John Hill Burton), 'Hints for the Vacation Ramble', *Blackwood's Edinburgh Magazine*, Volume CXXX, No.DCCXC, August 1881, pp.173–174.

Anderson P, 'Memoranda of an Excursion to the Grampians and Strathspey in July 1863', *Cairngorm Club Journal*, Volume 4, No.21, July 1903, pp.156–166.

Anon, 'The Inverness Scientific Society and Field Club', *Transactions of the Inverness Scientific Society and Field Club*, Volume 1, 1875–1880, pp.1–3, 373-374.

Anon, 'Obituary: The Late John Hill Burton', *Blackwood's Edinburgh Magazine*, Volume CXXX, No.DCCXI, September 1881, pp.401–404.

Anon, 'Obituary: CG Cash', *Scottish Geographical Magazine*, Volume 33, October 1917, pp.465–466.

Anon, 'Glenmore: A National Forest', *Cairngorm Club Journal*, Volume 11, No.62, September 1924, pp.82–86.

Anon, 'The Cairngorms as a National Park', *Cairngorm Club Journal*, Volume 12, No.69, January 1930, pp.6–8.

Anon, 'A Day's Run– To the Majestic Cairngorms', *SMT Magazine*, Volume 19, No.3, September 1937, no page numbers.

Anon, 'Photograph: Loch-an-Eilein, Rothiemurchus', *Take Note*, October 1947, p.9.

Anon, 'Planning for 1997', *Take Note*, May 1947, pp.4–5.

Anon, 'School for Climbing', *Take Note*, February 1948, p.4.

Anon, 'Scotland opens third Forest Park', *Take Note*, July 1948, p.4.

Anon, 'Lairig Ghru', Anonymous poem and letter written at Honeybarrel, Kildrummy in October 1870, *The Deeside Field*, Second Series, No.5, 1966, pp.28–29.

Anon, 'Cairngorm Area', *Cairngorm Club Journal*, Volume 17, No.93, 1968, pp.248–251.

Anon, 'The Cairngorms Nature Reserve', *Cairngorm Club Journal*, Volume 17, No. 89, 1954, pp.21–24.

Anon, 'The Cairngorms Nature Reserve Consultative Panel', *Cairngorm Club Journal*, Volume 17, No.89, 1954, p.49.

Anon, ' The Cairngorms Nature Reserve', *Cairngorm Club Journal*, Volume 17, No.93, 1968, p.278.

Anon, 'Scottish Skiing Comes of Age', *The Highlands and Islands Today*, Issue No.6, November–December 1982, p.3.

Anon, 'The Future of Reindeer in Scotland', *Nature*, Volume 179, No.4572, 15 June 1957, pp.1233–1234.

Anon, 'Our Directory of Recommended British Hotels', *SMT Magazine*, April 1934 and susequent issues.

Anton S, 'Battles for Cairngorm Rights of Way', *Cairngorm Club Journal*, Volume 20, No.102, 1991, pp.23–29.

Backhouse E, 'Midnight Wanderings in the Lairig', *The Scottish Mountaineering Club Journal*, Volume 12, No.71, June 1913, pp.286–290.

Backhouse J, 'A Few Days in Canlochen Glen and c.', *Phytologist*, Volume 3, 1849, pp.441–444.

Baker EA, 'The Cairngorms as a National Park', *The Scots Magazine*, New Series, Volume 10, No.1, October 1928, pp.1–6.

Balfour JM, 'Notes of a Botanical Excursion, with Pupils, to the Mountains of Braemar, Glenisla, and Clova, and to Benlawers, in August 1847', *Edinburgh New Philosophical Journal*, Volume XLV, April 1848–October 1848, pp.122-128.

Barton JS, 'Wind and Weather on Cairn Gorm Summit', *The Scottish Mountaineering Club Journal*, Volume 33, No.175, 1984, pp.52–56.

Bates GH, 'Track Making by Man and Domestic Animals', *Journal of Animal Biology*, Volume 19, No.1, May 1950, pp.21–28.

Bayfield NG, 'Some Effects of Walking and Skiing on Vegetation at Cairngorm', in AS Watt and E Duffey (eds), *The Scientific Management of Animal And Plant Communities for Conservation* (Blackwell Scientific Publ., Oxford, 1971) pp.469–485.

Bayfield NG, 'Use and Deterioration of Some Scottish Hill Paths', *Journal of Applied Ecology*, Volume 10, 1973, pp.635–644.

Bayfield NG, 'Burial of Vegetation By Erosion Debris near Ski Lifts on Cairngorm, Scotland', *Biological Conservation*, Volume 6, No.4, October 1974, pp.246–251.

Bayfield NG, 'Recovery of Four Montane Heath Communities on Cairngorm, Scotland from Disturbance by Trampling', *Biological Conservation*, Volume 15, No.3, April 1979, pp.165–179.

Bayfield NG, Urquhart UH, Cooper SM, 'Susceptibility of Four Species of Cladonia to Disturbance by Trampling in the Cairngorm Mountains, Scotland', *Journal of Applied Ecology*, Volume 18, 1981, pp.303–310.

Beattie AB, 'A Day on Braeriach', *The Scottish Mountaineering Club Journal*, Volume 16, No.94, October 1922, pp.174–181.

Black D, 'Duty to the Duchus', *Country Living*, No.121, January 1996, pp.66-69.

Bocking S, 'Conserving Nature and Building a Science: British Ecologists and the Origins of the Nature Conservancy', in M Shortland (ed), *Science and Nature– Essays in the History of the Environmental Sciences* (British Society for the History of Science/ Alden Press, Oxford, 1993) pp.89–114.

Bonyhandy T, 'Artists With Axes', *Environment and History*, Volume 1, No.2, June 1995, pp.221–239.

Boyd JM, 'Nature Conservation', *Proceedings of the Royal Society of Edinburgh*, Volume 84B, 1983, pp.295–336.

Bremner A, 'The Glaciation of the Cairngorms', *The Deeside Field*, No.4, 1929, pp.29–37.

Brown H, 'Cairngorm Panorama– Photographs', *The Countryman*, Volume 84, No.2, Summer 1979, pp.33–39.

Bryce J, 'The Preservation of Natural Scenery– An Address', *Cairngorm Club Journal*, Volume II, No.9, July 1897, pp.125–139.

Buchanan EP, 'Through Rothiemurchus to Rebhoan', *The Scottish Mountaineering Club Journal*, Volume 13, No.77, June 1915, pp.251–258.

Burden RF and Randerson PF, 'Quantitative Studies of the Effects of Human Trampling on Vegetation as an Aid to the Management of Semi-Natural Areas', *Journal of Applied Ecology*, Volume 9, 1972, pp.439–457.

Burges A, 'The Ecology of the Cairngorms, Part III: The Empetrum-Vaccinium Zone', *Journal of Ecology*, Volume 39, 1951, pp.271–284.

Butler RW, 'Evolution of Tourism in the Scottish Highlands', *Annals of Tourism Research*, Volume 12, 1985, pp.371–395.

Calvert D and Lambert RA, 'A Highland Hotel Venture: the Case of the Doune of Rothiemurchus Hotel, 1935–1942', *Northern Scotland*, Volume 17, 1997, pp.153–172.

Carpenter G and Evans W, 'A List of Spiders Collected in the Neighbourhood of Aviemore, Inverness-shire', *Annals of Scottish Natural History*, No.12, October 1894, pp.227–235.

Cash CG, 'The Loch-an-Eilein Ospreys', *Cairngorm Club Journal*, Volume IV, No.21, July 1903, pp.125–131.

Cash CG, 'History of the Loch An Eilein Ospreys', *Scottish Naturalist*, No.31, July 1914, pp.149–158.

Cassels CJH, 'The Return of the Osprey: Its Haunts and Habits,' *The Animal World*, Volume 8, No.86, February 1913, pp.32–33.

Chessell AD, 'The Great Estates in the Cairngorm and Grampian Mountains', *Cairngorm Club Journal*, Volume 19, No.98, 1980, pp.28–31.

Cheyne GD, 'Rights of Way', *The Scottish Mountaineering Club Journal*, Volume 24, No.139, May 1948, pp.14–20.

Clark WI, 'The Mountaineer as a Searcher after the Beautiful', *The Scottish Mountaineering Club Journal*, Volume V, No. 26, May 1898, pp.121–125.

Clark WI, 'Reminiscences of the Cairngorms', *The Scottish Mountaineering Club Journal*, Volume 16, No.93, April 1922, pp.109–116.

Clifford T and Forster AN, 'Beinn Eighe National Nature Reserve: Woodland Management Policy and Practice, 1944–1994', in TC Smout (ed), *Scottish Woodland History* (Scottish Cultural Press, Edinburgh, 1997) pp.190–206.

Collinge WE, 'Wild Birds and Legislation', *Journal of the Land Agents Society*, Volume 17, July 1918, pp.278–285.

Collinge WE, 'The Necessity of State Action for the Protection of Wild Birds', *The Smithsonian Report for 1919* (Government Printing Office, Washington, USA, 1921) pp.349–353.

Coward TA, 'Ethics of Egg-Collecting', *The Nineteenth Century and After*, Volume 100, July 1926, pp.101–109.

Crabtree JR, 'National Park Designation in Scotland', *Land Use Policy*, Volume 8, No.3, July 1991, pp.241–252.

Curry-Lindahl K, 'The Cairngorms National Nature Reserve (NNR), the Foremost British Conservation Area of International Significance', in JWH Conroy, A Watson, AR Gunson, *Caring for the High Mountains– the Conservation of the Cairngorms* (ITE/Centre for Scottish Studies, Aberdeen, 1990) pp.108–119.

Darby HC, 'British National Parks', *Advancement of Science*, Volume 20, No.83, November 1963, pp.307–318.

Darroch of Torridon D, 'Deer and Deer Forests', *The Scottish Mountaineering Club Journal*, Volume VI, No.35, May 1901, pp.139–145.

Dickinson G, 'National Parks– Scottish needs and Spanish experience', *Scottish Geographical Magazine*, Volume 107, No.2, 1991, pp.124–129.

Diver C, 'The Work of the Nature Conservancy', *Transactions of the Royal Institution of Chartered Surveyors*, Volume LXXXV, Part II, Session 1952/53, pp.1–11.

Dunbabin JPD, 'Book Review: John Sheail, Rural Conservation in Inter-War Britain (1981)', *The English Historical Review*, Volume XCIX, No.391, April 1984, pp.469–470.

Duncan JL, 'Visitors' Book at the Shelter Stone', *Cairngorm Club Journal*, Volume 12, No.69, January 1930, pp.117–121.

Duncan JL, 'The Shelter Stone Visitors' Book', *Cairngorm Club Journal*, Volume 11, No.64, July 1926, pp.212–213.

Dunlop BMS, 'The Woods of Strathspey in the Nineteenth and Twentieth Centuries', in TC Smout (ed) *Scottish Woodland History* (Scottish Cultural Press, Edinburgh, 1997) pp.176–189.

Dunn JKW, 'National Parks in Scotland', *The Scottish Mountaineering Club Journal*, Volume 24, No.141, April 1950, pp.216–221.

Durie AJ, 'Tourism and Commercial Photography in Victorian Scotland: the Rise and Fall of GW Wilson and Co.,1853–1908', *Northern Scotland*, Volume 12, 1992, pp.89–104.

Durie AJ, 'Tourism in Victorian Scotland: the Case of Abbotsford', *Scottish Economic and Social History*, Volume 12, 1992, pp.42–54.

Dutton GJF, 'Skis in Scottish Mountaineering', *The Scottish Mountaineering Club Journal*, Volume 26, No.148, May 1957, pp.121–125.

Dybeck MW and Green FHW, 'The Cairngorms Weather Survey, 1953', *Weather*, Volume 10, 1955, pp.41–48..

Eaton J, 'In a Pine Wood', *The Deeside Field*, No.7, 1935, pp.21–25.

Eggeling WJ, 'Nature Conservation in Scotland', *Transactions of the Royal Highland and Agricultural Society of Scotland*, Sixth Series, Volume 8, 1964, pp.1–27.

Elliot RG, Lloyd MG, Rowan-Robinson J, 'Land Use Policy for Skiing In Scotland', *Land Use Policy*, Volume 5, No.2, April 1988, pp.232–244.

Erskine of Marr R, 'The Claim for a National Park', *The Scots Magazine*, New Series, Volume 10, No.6, March 1929, pp.416–420.

Ewen WA, 'Fifty Years of the Cairngorm Club', *Cairngorm Club Journal*, Volume 15, No.80, July 1939, pp.1–14.

Firsoff VA, 'The Forests of the Cairngorms', *Take Note*, April 1954, pp.12–13.

Fladmark JM and Lawson P, 'Access Through Hostelling– The Role and policies of the SYHA', in JM Fladmark (ed) *Heritage– Conservation, Interpretation and Enterprise* (Donhead, London, 1993) pp.161–174.

Forsyth W (lecture), 'Place Names of Abernethy', *Transactions of the Inverness Scientific Society and Field Club*, Volume IV, 1885–1895, pp.372–379.

Fraser CN, 'Scotland and Skiing', *The Scots Magazine*, New Series, Volume 26, No.5, February 1937, pp.344–349.

Frere RB, 'A Cairngorm Odyssey', *The Scottish Mountaineering Club Journal*, Volume 25, No.144, April 1953, pp.124–131.

Getz D, 'Tourism and Population Change: Long-term Impacts of Tourism in Badenoch and Strathspey District of the Scottish Highlands', *Scottish Geographical Magazine*, Volume 102, No.2, September 1986, pp.113–126.

Getz D, 'Resident's Attitudes Towards Tourism– A Longitudinal Study in Spey Valley, Scotland', *Tourism Management*, Volume 15, Part 4, 1994, pp.247–258.

Gibb AW, 'Cairngorms and Other Local Gemstones', *The Deeside Field*, No.2, 1925, pp.11–14.

Gilbert H, 'Scotland's Photographer', *Scotland's Magazine*, March 1947, pp.26–30.

Graeme A, 'Hills of Home– The Spiritual Claim for a National Park', *The Scots Magazine*, New Series, Volume 10, No.2, November 1928, pp.89–96.

Grant JM, 'Aerial Shadows seen from the Cairngorm Mountains', *Edinburgh New Philosophical Journal*, Volume 10, October 1830–April 1831, pp.165–166.

Grant O (lecture), 'Highland Ornithology', *Transactions of the Inverness Scientific Society and Field Club*, Volume III, 1883–1888 (Courier Office, Inverness, 1888) pp.310–311.

Green FHW, 'Climatological Work in the Nature Conservancy', *Weather*, Volume 10, 1955, pp.233–236.

Gregory JW, 'The Claim for a National Park', *The Scots Magazine*, New Series, Volume 10, No.3, December 1928, pp.173–177.

Gunn NM, ' "Gentlemen– the Tourist!" the New Highland Toast', *The Scots Magazine*, New Series, Volume 26, No.6, March 1937, pp.410–415.

Haldane J, 'Admiring the High Mountains: The Aesthetics of Environment', *Environmental Values*, Volume 3, No.2, Summer 1994, pp.97–106.

Harrison B, 'Animals and the State in Nineteenth-century England', *English Historical Review*, Volume LXXXVIII, No. CCCXLIX, October 1973, pp.786-820.

Hetherington A, 'The Cairngorms Nature Reserve', *The Scottish Mountaineering Club Journal*, Volume 25, No. 146, May 1955, pp.387–389.

Hinxman LW, 'The River Spey', *Scottish Geographical Magazine*, Volume XVII, 1901, pp.185–193.

Horn DB, 'The Origins of Mountaineering in Scotland', *The Scottish Mountaineering Club Journal*, Volume 28, No.157, May 1966, pp.157–173.

Humble BH, 'The Glenmore Story', *Climber and Rambler*, August 1975, pp.380–383.

Kardell L, 'Recreation Forests– A New Silviculture Concept?', *Ambio*, Volume 14, No.3, 1985, pp.139–147.

Kemp M, 'The Art of Seeing Nature: Points of View in the Perception of Landscape in Britain, c.1750–1850', in L Mondada, F Panese and O Soderstrom (eds), *De la beaute a l'ordre du monde: paysage et crise de la lisibilite* (Universite de Lausanne, Lausanne, 1992) pp.47–72.

King RB, 'Vegetation Destruction in the Sub-Alpine and Alpine Zones of the Cairngorm Mountains', *Scottish Geographical Magazine*, Volume 87, No.2, September 1971, pp.103–115.

Laidlaw D, 'Douglas Laidlaw's Strathspey', *The Scots Magazine*, New Series, Volume 141, No.3, September 1994, pp.254–260.

Lambert RA, 'Leisure and Recreation', in A Cooke, I Donnachie, A MacSween, CA Whatley (eds) *Modern Scottish History, 1707 to the Present: Volume II, The Modernisation of Scotland, 1850 to the Present* (Tuckwell Press/The Open University/University of Dundee, East Linton, 1998) Chapter 25, pp.257–276.

Lambert RA, 'Proposals to extend the range of the Crested Tit in Scotland,1945–1955', *Scottish Birds*, Volume 19, Part 5, December 1998, pp.304–305.

Lambert RA, 'Preserving a Remnant of the Old Natural Forest: the Joint Venture of the NTS and RSFS in the mid-1930s,' *Scottish Forestry*, Volume 51, No.1, Spring 1997, pp.31–33.

Lambert RA, 'Strathspey and Reel: Photography and the Cairngorms', *Inferno: St Andrews Journal of Art History*, Volume III, 1996, pp.68–81.

Lance A, Thaxton R, Watson A, 'Recent Changes in Footpath Width in the Cairngorms', *Scottish Geographical Magazine*, Volume 107, No.2, 1991, pp.106–109.

Lankester ER, 'Nature Reserves', *Nature*, Volume XCIII, No.2315, 12 March 1914, pp.33–35.

Lawrence M, 'Aviemore Amid the Pines', *SMT Magazine*, Volume 16, No.4, April 1936, pp.40–43.

Lawson GM, 'The Cairngorms– An Appreciation', *The Scottish Mountaineering Club Journal*, Volume 15, No.89, April 1920, pp.233–240.

Levitt I, 'The Creation of the Highlands and Islands Development Board, 1935–1965', *Northern Scotland*, Volume 19, 1999, pp.85–105.

Lippe R, 'The Cairngorm Club', *Cairngorm Club Journal*, Volume 1, No.1, July 1893, pp.7–14.

Litsios T, 'More than a Pretty Picture: Photography as a Tool in Wilderness Conservation', in V Martin and M Inglis (eds), *Wilderness, The Way Ahead* (Findhorn Press, Forres, 1984) pp.206–212.

Lumsden J, 'Deerstalking Experiences of an Urban Sportsman', *The Deeside Field*, No.3, 1927, pp.5–9.

Lythe SGE, 'Thomas Garnett: a Doctor on Tour in the Highlands', in G Cruickshank (ed), *A Sense of Place– Studies in Scottish Local History* (Scotland's Cultural Heritage Unit/University of Edinburgh, 1988) pp.100–108.

McConnochie AI, 'The Cairngorms In Winter', *The Scottish Mountaineering Club Journal*, No.1, January 1890, pp.12–19.

McConnochie AI, 'The National Nature of the Cairngorms', *The Scots Magazine*, New Series, Volume 10, No.3, December 1928, pp.178–183, with map of 'The Cairngorm Area'.

McVean DN, 'The Ecology of Scots Pine in the Scottish Highlands', *Journal of Ecology*, Volume 51, No.3, November 1963, pp.671–686.

Macartney WN, 'The Central Highlands and the Coasts of Lorne', *SMT Magazine*, Volume 12, No.6, June 1934, pp.106–115.

Macdonald JM (in an interview), 'Why I Support the Cairngorm National Park Scheme', *The Scots Magazine*, New Series, Volume 10, No.4. January 1929, pp.251–252.

Maclagan D, 'The Battle O' Glen Tilt', *Cairngorm Club Journal*, Volume 3, No.15, July 1900, pp.185–189.

Maclaren M, 'The Freedom of the Countryside– Scotland and the Motor Age', *SMT Magazine*, Volume 13, No.6, December 1934, pp.54–56.

Maclay J, 'The Cairngorms from Deeside', *The Scottish Mountaineering Club Journal*, Volume 8, No.46, January 1905, pp.192–196.

MacLean I, 'Mountain Men', in B Kay (ed), *Odyssey – Voices from Scotland's Recent Past* (BBC Scotland/Polygon, Edinburgh, 1980).

Macmillan HP, 'Rights of Way', *The Scottish Mountaineering Club Journal*, Volume 14, No.84, October 1917, pp.288–291.

Macpherson JI (in an interview), 'The Scheme Appeals to Me', *The Scots Magazine*, New Series, Volume 10, No.4, January 1929, pp.252–253.

Manley G, 'Meteorological Observations on Royal Deeside', *Weather*, Volume 23, 1978, pp.457–459.

Metcalfe G, 'The Ecology of the Cairngorms, Part II: The Mountain Callunetum', *Journal of Ecology*, Volume 38, 1950, pp.46–74.

Moir DG, 'Scottish Youth Hostels', *Cairngorm Club Journal*, Volume 13, No.74, July 1933, pp.132–138.

Munro J, 'The Golden Groves of Abernethy: the Cutting and Extraction of Timber before the Union', in G Cruickshank (ed), *A Sense of Place – Studies in Scottish Local History* (Scotland's Cultural Heritage Unit/University of Edinburgh, 1988) pp.152–162.

Murdoch ML, 'In the Heart of the Cairngorms– Through Glen Einich with a Camera', *SMT Magazine*, Volume 17, No.2, August 1936, pp.45–48.

Nenadic S, 'Land, the landed and relationships with England: literature and perception 1760–1830', in SJ Connolly, RA Houston, RJ Morris (eds), *Conflict, Identity and Economic Development: Ireland and Scotland, 1600–1939* (Carnegie, Preston, 1996) pp.148–160.

Osborne JG, 'National Parks in Scotland – Another View', *The Scottish Mountaineering Club Journal*, Volume 24, No.142, April 1951, pp.312–315.

Orr W, 'The Economic Impact of Deer Forests in the Scottish Highlands', *Scottish Economic and Social History*, Volume 2, 1982, pp.44–59.

Parker JA, 'Review: New Ordnance Survey Map of the Cairngorms', *The Scottish Mountaineering Club Journal*, Volume 16, No.94, October 1922, pp.202–203.

Patey T, 'Cairngorm Commentary', *The Scottish Mountaineering Club Journal*, Volume 27, No.153, May 1962, pp.207–220.

Pears NV, 'Man in the Cairngorms: A Population–Resource Balance Problem', *Scottish Geographical Magazine*, Volume 84, 1968, pp.45–55.

Perry AH, 'Climatic Influences on the Development of the Scottish Skiing Industry', *Scottish Geographical Magazine*, Volume 87, No.3, December 1971, pp.196–201.

Perry R, 'A Cairngorm Nature Reserve – The Urgent Need for Preservation', *The Scots Magazine*, New Series, Volume LX, No.2, November 1953, p.134.

Perry R, 'On Cairngorm Peaks', *Birds Of Britain*, No. IV, no date, pp.32–35.

Photographic Special Supplement, 'Behold the Cairngorms', *The Scots Magazine*, New Series, Volume 10, No.2, November 1928, no page numbers.

Robertson EB, 'Mountains and Art', *The Scottish Mountaineering Club Journal*, Volume XIII, No.77, June 1915, pp.259–267.

Robinson DW, 'Ghosts' High Noon on the Cairngorms', *The Scottish Mountaineering Club Journal*, Volume 19, No.112, November 1931, pp.261 265.

Russell AW, 'Some Memories of Braeriach', *The Scottish Mountaineering Club Journal*, Volume 18, No.106, November 1928, pp.214–219.

Salisbury EJ, 'A Proposed Biological Flora of Britain', *Journal of Ecology*, Volume 16, 1928, pp.161–162.

Sang G, 'The Menace to Rights-of-Way', *The Scottish Mountaineering Club Journal*, Volume 16, No.91, April 1921, pp.18–22.

Scot J, 'Letters of a Self-Thinking Scotsman to his Father', No.IV Legacy and Litter, *The Scots Magazine*, New Series, Volume 10, No.1, October 1928, pp.38–40.

Scott W, 'Article XI– Colonel Thornton's Sporting Tour', *The Edinburgh Review (or Critical Journal)*, Volume V, October–January 1804/05, pp.398-405.

Sheail J, 'The Concept of National Parks in Great Britain 1900–1950', *Transactions of the Institute of British Geographers*, No.66, November 1975, pp.41–56.

Sheail J, 'Nature Reserves, National Parks and Post-War Reconstruction in Britain', *Environmental Conservation*, Volume 11, No.1, Spring 1984, pp.29-34.

Sheail J, 'From Aspiration to Implementation– The Establishment of the First National Nature Reserves in Britain', *Landscape Research*, Volume 21, No.1, 1996, pp.37–54.

Simpson E, 'Aberdour: the Evolution of a Seaside Resort', in G Cruickshank (ed), *A Sense of Place– Studies in Scottish Local History* (Scotland's Cultural Heritage Unit, Edinburgh, 1988) pp.177–187.

Simpson R, 'Cairngorm Crossing,' *The Scottish Mountaineering Club Journal*, Volume 33, No.175, 1984, pp.39–42.

Smart R, 'Famous Throughout the World: Valentine and Sons Ltd. Dundee', in A Fenton, H Cheape, R Marshall (eds), *Review of Scottish Culture 4* (John Donald, Edinburgh, 1988) pp.75–87.

Smith JP, 'Access to Mountains', *Blackwood's Edinburgh Magazine*, Volume CL, No. DCCCCX, August 1891, pp.259–272.

Smith R, 'The Playground of the Future', in M Magnusson and G White (eds), *The Nature of Scotland– Landscape, Wildlife and People* (Canongate/Scottish Post Office Board, Edinburgh, 1991) pp.196–210.

Smith WA, 'The Cairngorms In Summer', *The Scottish Mountaineering Club Journal*, No.3, September 1890, pp.106–114.

Smith WA, 'A Visit to the Cairngorms in 1875', *The Scottish Mountaineering Club Journal*, Volume 14, No.83, June 1917, pp.224–234.

Smithard W, 'First Impressions of the Cairngorms', *Cairngorm Club Journal*, Volume 4, No.21, July 1903, pp.143–148.

Smout TC, 'Tours in the Scottish Highlands from the Eighteenth to the Twentieth Centuries', *Northern Scotland*, Volume 5, 1983, pp.99–121.

Smout TC, 'The Highlands and the Roots of Green Consciousness, 1750–1990', *Proceedings of the British Academy*, Volume 76, 1991, pp.237–264.

Smout TC, 'Scottish Native Woodlands in Historical Perspective', in D Mollison (ed) *Sharing the Land* (John Muir Trust, Musselburgh, 1994) pp.1-6.

Snyder AP, 'Wilderness Management– A Growing Challenge', *Journal of Forestry*, Volume 64, July 1966, pp.441–446.

Spaven FDN, 'Obituary: FHW Green', *Scottish Geographical Magazine*, Volume 99, No.2, September 1983, p.120.

Stewart C, 'A National Park for Scotland', *Nineteenth Century and After*, Volume LV, No.327, May 1904, pp.822–826.

Tomkins JP, 'Thirty Years Afield For Birds', *The BKSTS Journal*, September 1981, pp.585–587.

Walker G, 'Some Memorable Naturalists of the North-East', *The Deeside Field*, No.5, 1931, pp.2–4.

Waterston G, 'Operation Osprey, 1961', *Bird Notes*, Volume 30, No.1, Winter 1963, p.13.

Waterston G, 'Operation Osprey, 1964', *Bird Notes*, Volume 31, No.4, July-August 1964, pp.126–129.

Watson A, 'Cairngorm Langlauf', *The Scottish Mountaineering Club Journal*, Volume 27, 1960–1963, pp.348–352.

Watson A and Rae R, 'Dotterel Numbers, Habitat and Breeding Success in Scotland', *Scottish Birds*, Volume 14, No.4, Winter 1987, pp.191–198.

Watson A, 'Human Induced Increases of Carrion Crows and Gulls on Cairngorm Plateaux', *Scottish Birds*, Volume 18, No.4, Winter 1996, pp.205–213.

Watson A, 'Dotterel *Charadius morinellus* Numbers in Relation to Human Impact in Scotland', *Biological Conservation*, Volume 43, 1988, pp.245–256.

Watson A, 'Habitat Use by Snow Buntings in Scotland from Spring to Autumn', *Scottish Birds*, Volume 19, No.2, Winter 1997, pp.105–113.

Watson A, 'Bird and Mammal Numbers in Relation to Human Impact at Ski Lifts on Scottish Hills', *Journal of Applied Ecology*, Volume 16, 1979, pp.753–764.

Watson A , 'Increase of People on Cairn Gorm Plateau following Easier Access', *Scottish Geographical Magazine*, Volume 207, No.2, 1991, pp.99-105.

Watson A and Allan E, 'Papers relating to Game Poaching on Deeside 1766-1832', *Northern Scotland*, Volume 7, No.1, 1986, pp.39–45.

Watson A and Allan E, 'Depopulation by Clearances and Non-enforced Emigration in the North-East Highlands', *Northern Scotland*, Volume 10, 1990, pp.31–46.

Watson A, 'Internationally Important Environmental Features of the Cairngorms, Research, and Main Research Needs', *Botanical Journal of Scotland*, Volume 48, Part 1, 1996, pp.1–12.

Watt AS, 'The Ecology of the Cairngorms, Part I: The Environment and Altitudinal Zonation of the Vegetation', *Journal of Ecology*, Volume 36, 1948, pp.283–304.

Webb WM, 'The Nature Reserve Movement in Britain', *Journal of Ecology*, Volume 1, 1913, p.46.

Weir DN, 'Mortality of Hawks and Owls in Speyside', *Bird Study*, Volume 18, No.3, September 1971, pp.147–154.

Weir T, 'The Central Highlands', in JB Foreman (general ed), *Scotland's Splendour* (Collins, Glasgow, 1961) pp.175–206.

Weir T, 'A Cairngorm Nature Reserve– Why Not Rothiemurchus?', *The Scots Magazine*, New Series, Volume LX, No.2, November 1953, p.135.

Welsh H, 'Beauty in High Places', *The Deeside Field*, Second Series, No.6, 1970, pp.73–77.

Newspaper Articles/Cuttings in Archives

Aberdeen Daily Journal, 25 August 1906; Report on formation of Aberdeen, Banff and Kincardine Land Defence Association.

Anon, 'Law Report', *London Times*, 29 June 1801, No.5145, p.3.

Anon ('S'), 'The Osprey', *The Scotsman*, 12 June 1879, p.3.

Anon, 'A Braemar Right of Way Dispute', *Edinburgh Evening Dispatch*, 14 August 1891.

Anon, 'Photograph: Skiers on Cairngorm– Youth', *The Scotsman*, 14 March 1963, p.1. 'The Haunting Melodies of Speyside', p.2.

Anon, 'Upper Deeside Area Seen as Winter Sports Centre', *The Scotsman*, 3 March 1967.

Colin B, 'Focus of the Nation', *The Scotsman*, 28 July 1995, p.15.

Glasgow Herald, Friday 9 July 1954, p.8 'Britain's Newest and Largest Nature Reserve'.

Glasgow Herald, Friday 9 July 1954, p.6, editorial 'Cairngorms Nature Reserve'.

Glasgow Herald, Friday 9 July 1954, p.6 'Work of the Nature Conservancy'.

Jolly W, 'Loch-an-Eilein and its Ospreys', *The Scotsman*, 9 June 1879, p.5.

Kean J, 'Skiing the Slippery Slopes of Success', *The Scotsman*, 24 August 1996, p.6.

The Scotsman, February–June 1936; Hotel Adverts.

The Scotsman, 30 November 1946, p.6; Photograph.

The Scotsman, 23 March 1996; Obituary of WH Murray.

The Times, 18 December 1912, p.7, leader article.

The Times, 18 December 1912, p.9, editorial.

The Times, 9 July 1954, p.8 'Cairngorms Nature Reserve– New Status Today'.

Robertson A, 'Never Never Land', *Sunday Times*, Ecosse, Section 12, 21 September 1997, pp.1–2.

Theses

Blamey E, 'The Consequences of Skiing on Scottish Mountain Vegetation and a Review of Current Monitoring and Management Techniques', Unpublished B.Sc dissertation, Departments of Environmental Biology and Geography, University of St. Andrews, 1994.

Hebbletwaite R, 'Land Use Conflicts in the Cairngorms– A Review', Unpublished B.Sc dissertation, Department of Geography, University of St. Andrews, 1991.

Ruddock C, 'Visitors and Visitor Management in Glen More Forest Park', Unpublished dissertation for the degree of MA(Hons), Department of Geography, University of St. Andrews, Thesis No.334, January 1980.

Index

www.ingramcontent.com/pod-product-compliance
Lightning Source LLC
Chambersburg PA
CBHW021120270326
41929CB00009B/973